CHILDREN OF THE WHALES

Stor

Volume

15

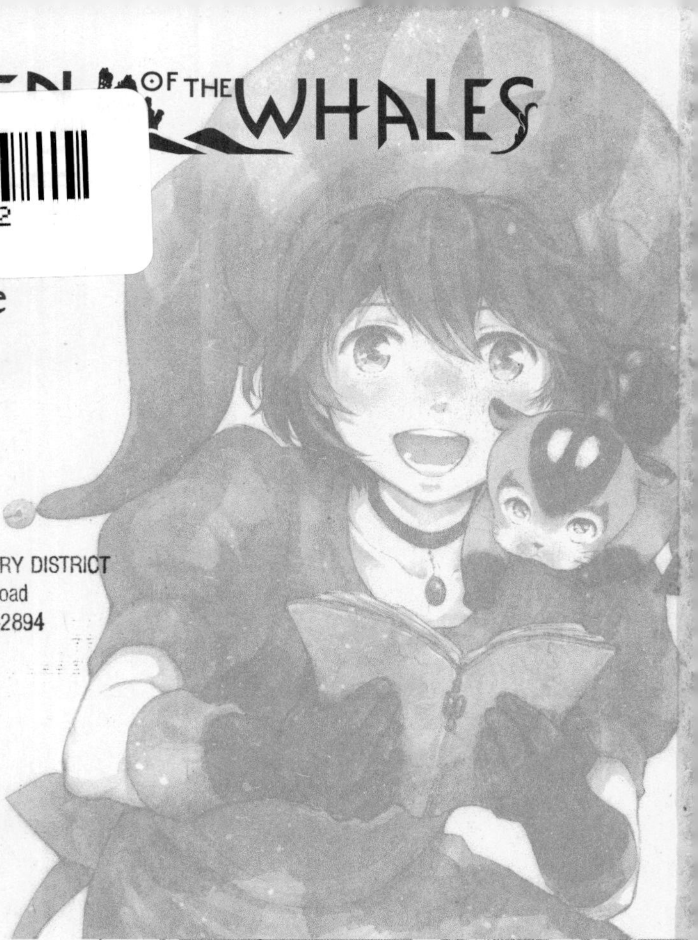

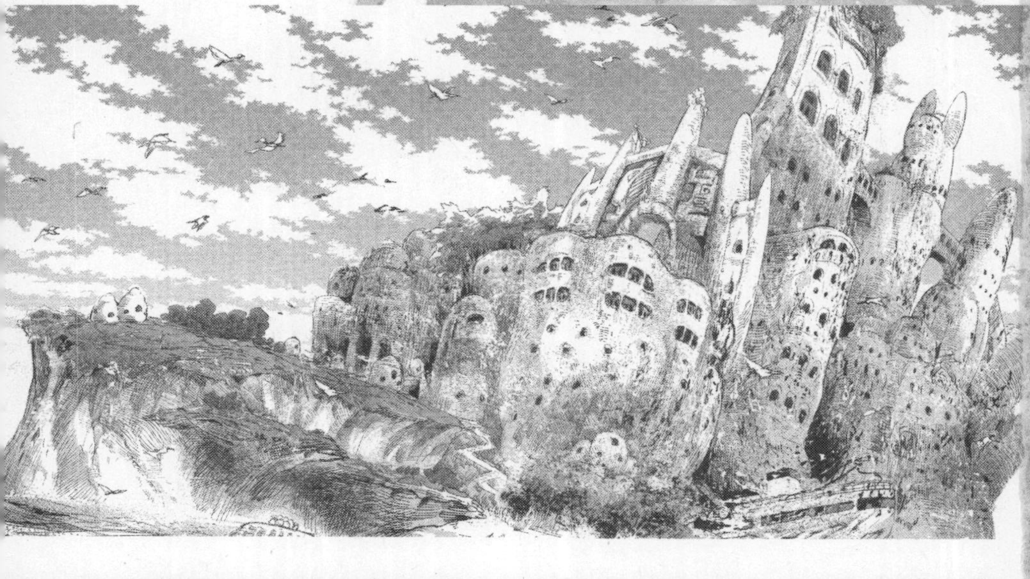

Table of Contents

 ## A Record of the Mud Whale and the Sea of Sand

Year 93 of the Sand Exile.

The Mud Whale drifts endlessly through the Sea of Sand, home to about 500 people who know nothing of the outside world.

Suou and Chakuro seem to be at odds about rescuing Lykos and Ouni, who were captured by Orca on Amonlogia. But in reality they are of the same mind.

Chakuro and a small team board Karcharías, Orca's battleship, with plans to convince him to give up on the idea of attacking the Mud Whale. With Itiã's help, they free Lykos on the way to find Orca.

But Orca finds them first and leads them into the depths of Karcharías, where he tells them the story of Kataklysmós and his plans to attack Fálaina for the future of humanity. What will Chakuro and the others do?

"The Mud Whale was our entire world."

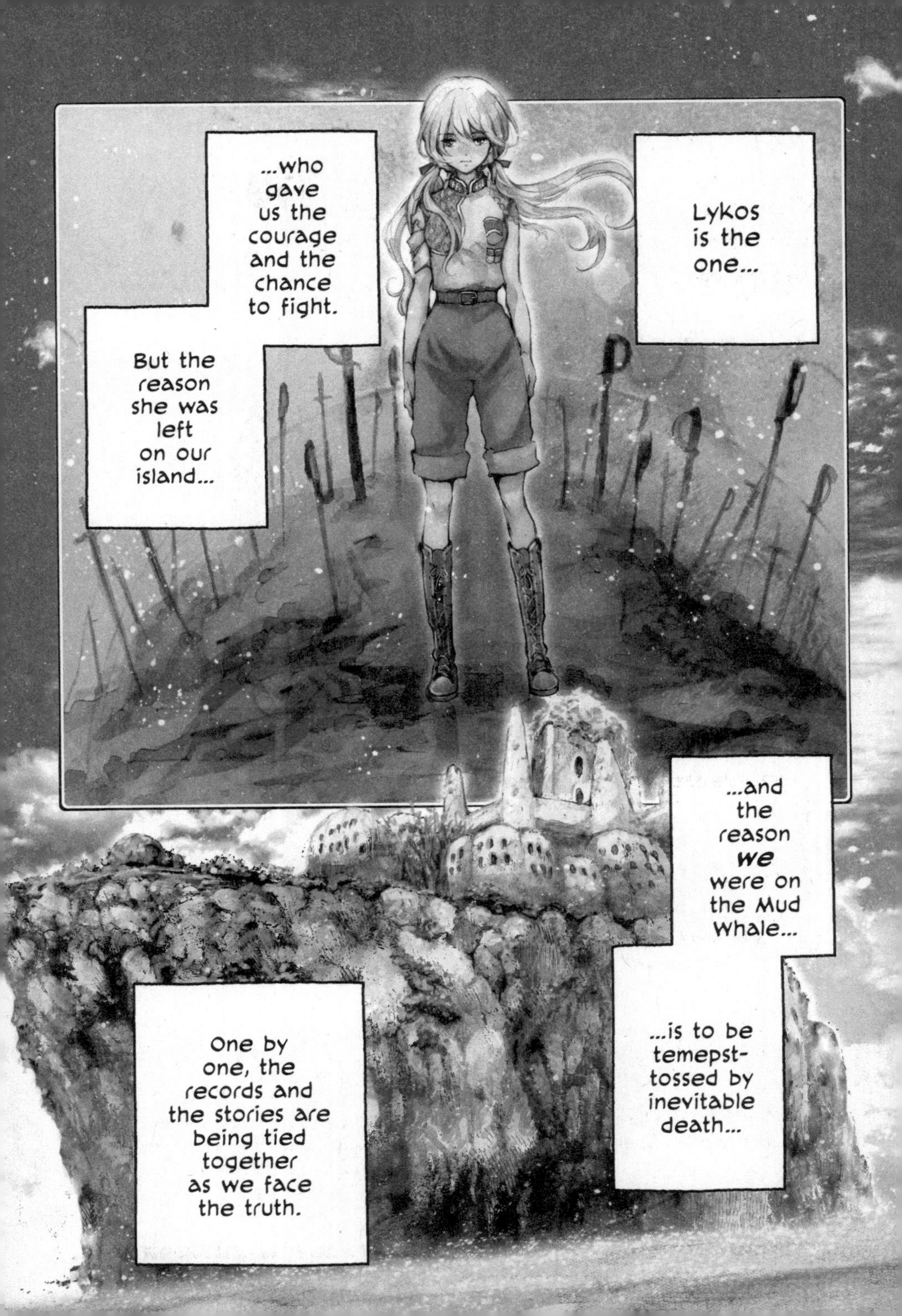
Lykos is the one...
...who gave us the courage and the chance to fight.
But the reason she was left on our island...
...and the reason *we* were on the Mud Whale...
...is to be temepst-tossed by inevitable death...
One by one, the records and the stories are being tied together as we face the truth.

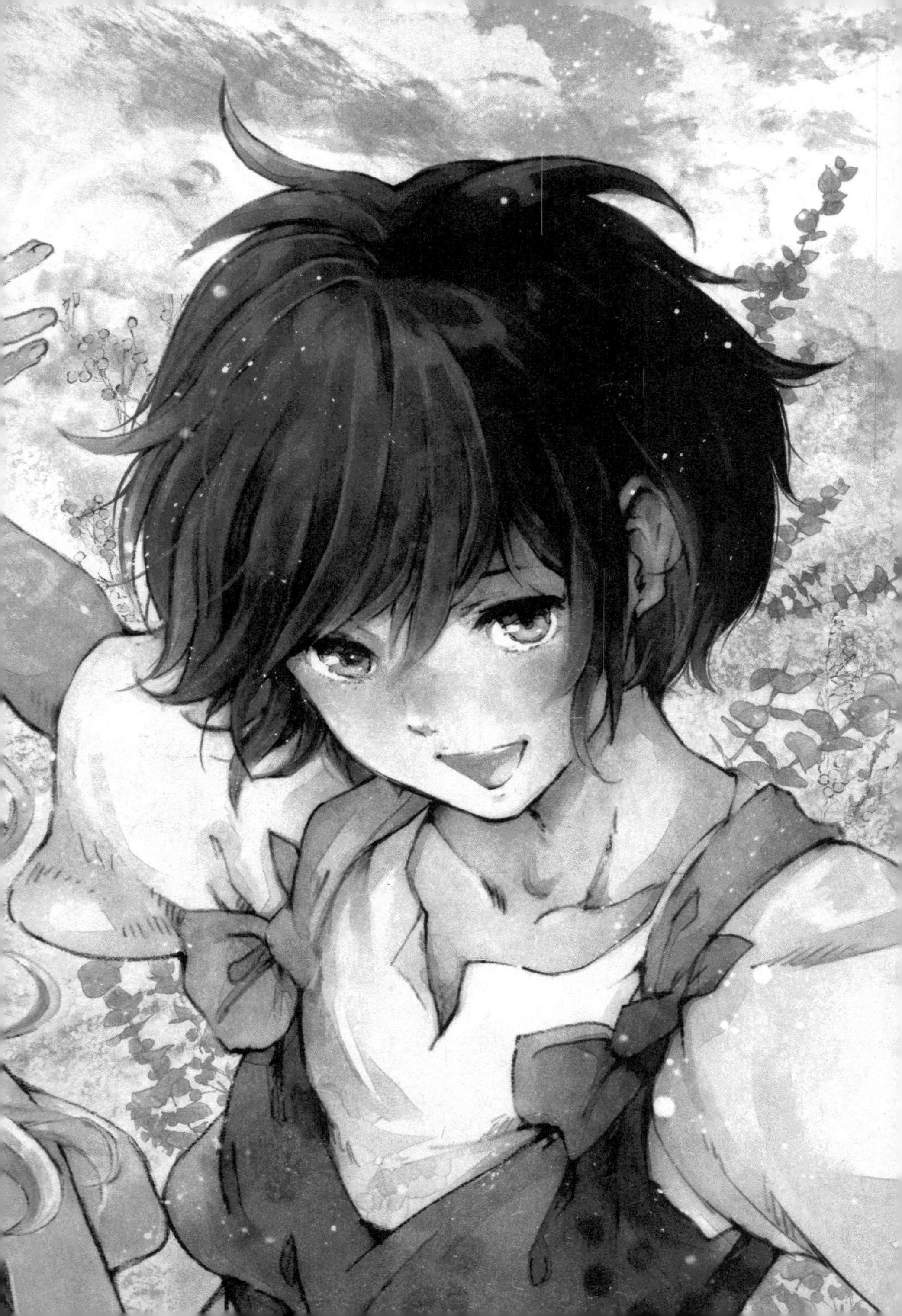

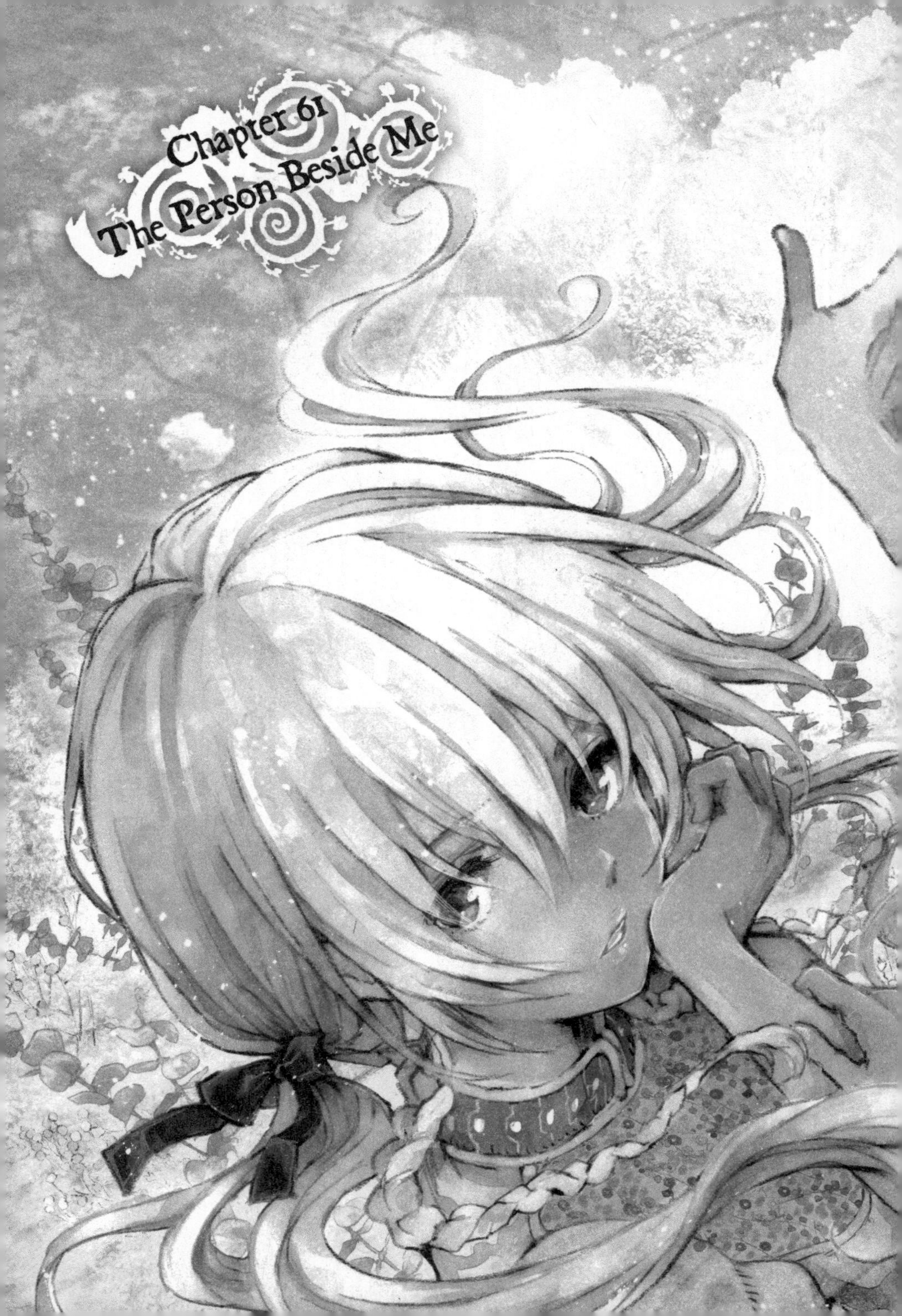
Chapter 61
The Person Beside Me

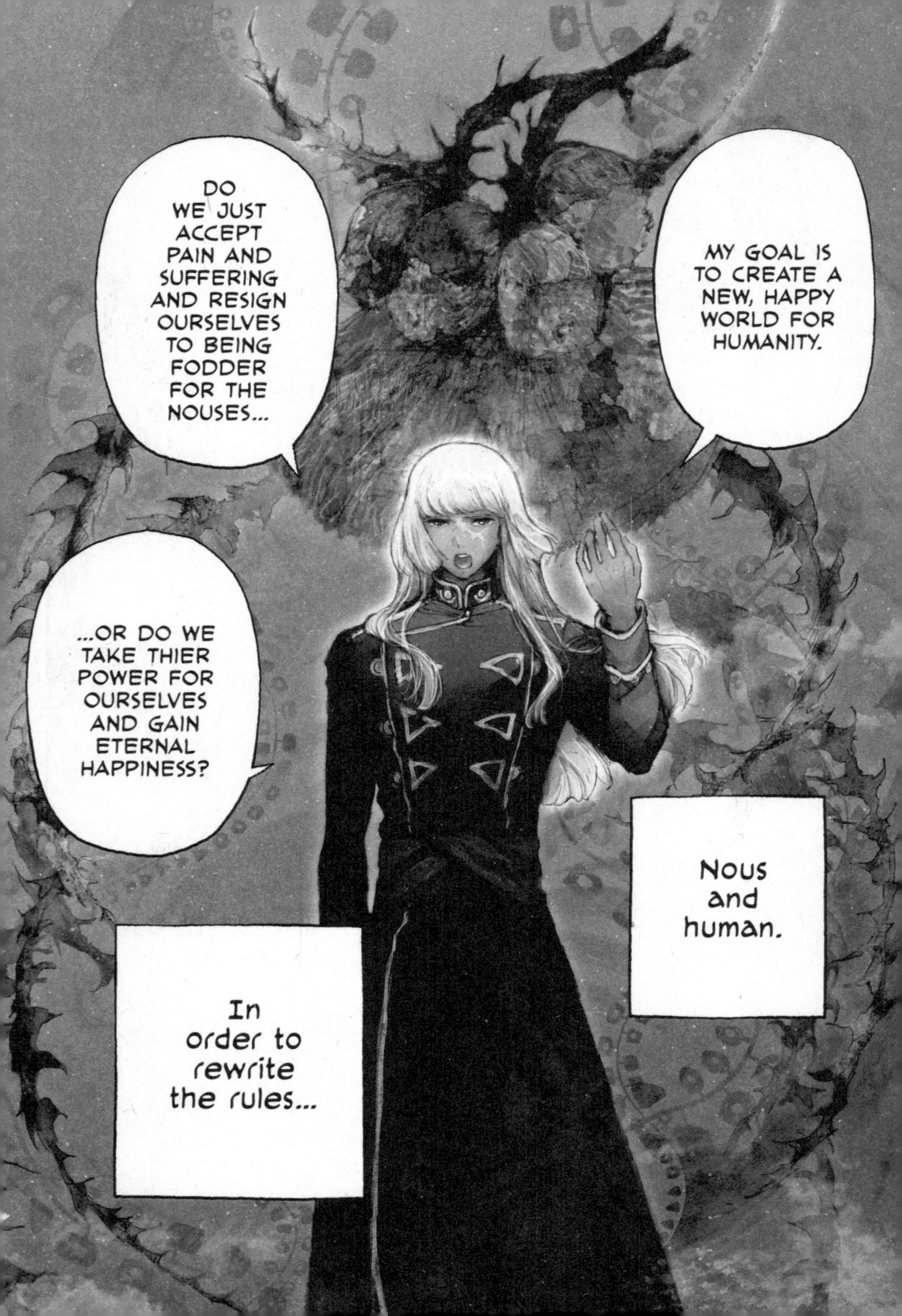
MY GOAL IS TO CREATE A NEW, HAPPY WORLD FOR HUMANITY.
DO WE JUST ACCEPT PAIN AND SUFFERING AND RESIGN OURSELVES TO BEING FODDER FOR THE NOUSES...
...OR DO WE TAKE THIER POWER FOR OURSELVES AND GAIN ETERNAL HAPPINESS?
Nous and human.
In order to rewrite the rules...

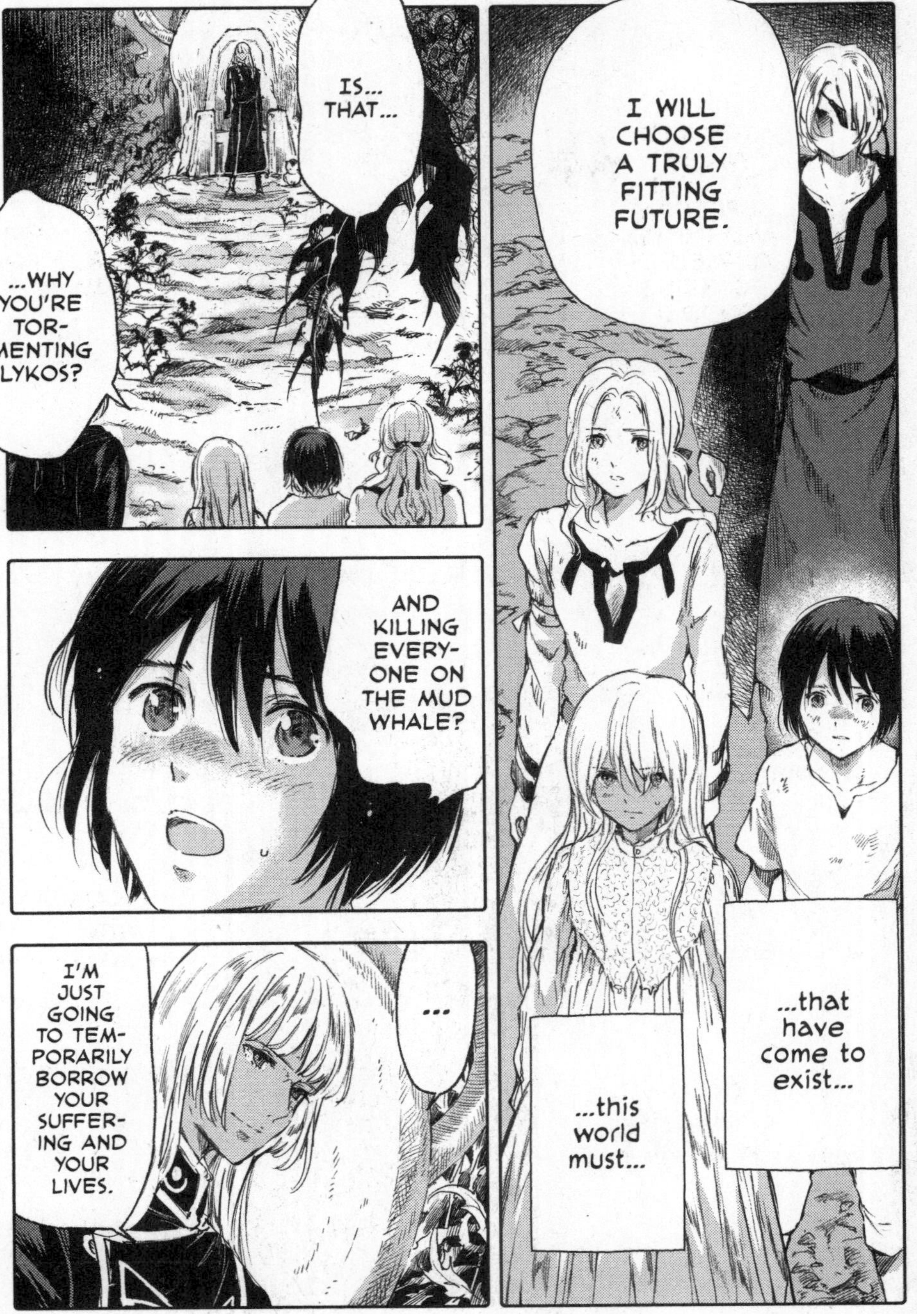
I WILL CHOOSE A TRULY FITTING FUTURE.
...that have come to exist...
...this world must...
IS... THAT...
...WHY YOU'RE TOR-MENTING LYKOS?
.....
AND KILLING EVERY-ONE ON THE MUD WHALE?
...
I'M JUST GOING TO TEM-PORARILY BORROW YOUR SUFFER-ING AND YOUR LIVES.

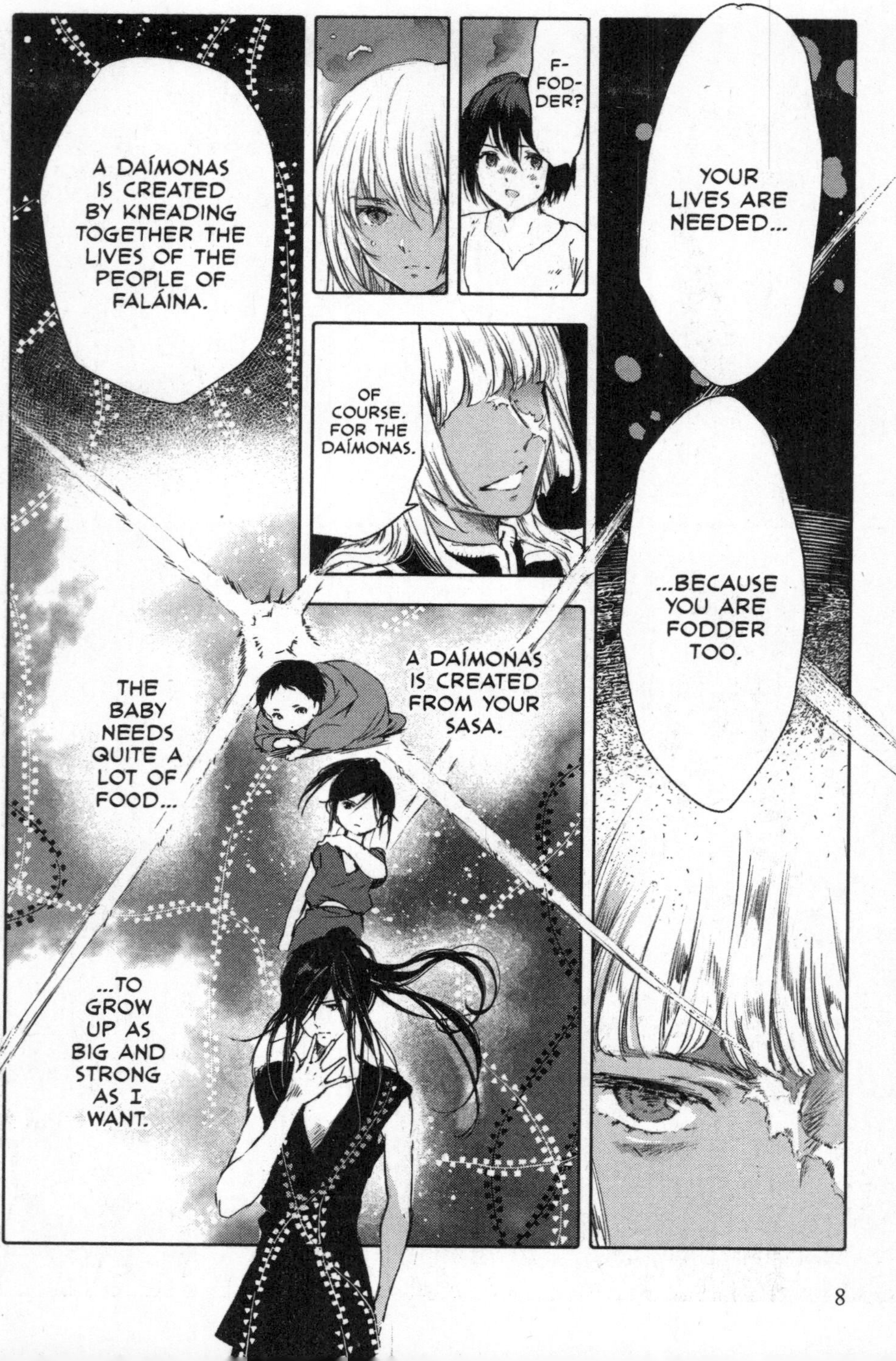
YOUR LIVES ARE NEEDED...
...BECAUSE YOU ARE FODDER TOO.
F-FODDER?
OF COURSE. FOR THE DAÍMONAS.
A DAÍMONAS IS CREATED BY KNEADING TOGETHER THE LIVES OF THE PEOPLE OF FALÁINA.
A DAÍMONAS IS CREATED FROM YOUR SASA.
THE BABY NEEDS QUITE A LOT OF FOOD...
...TO GROW UP AS BIG AND STRONG AS I WANT.

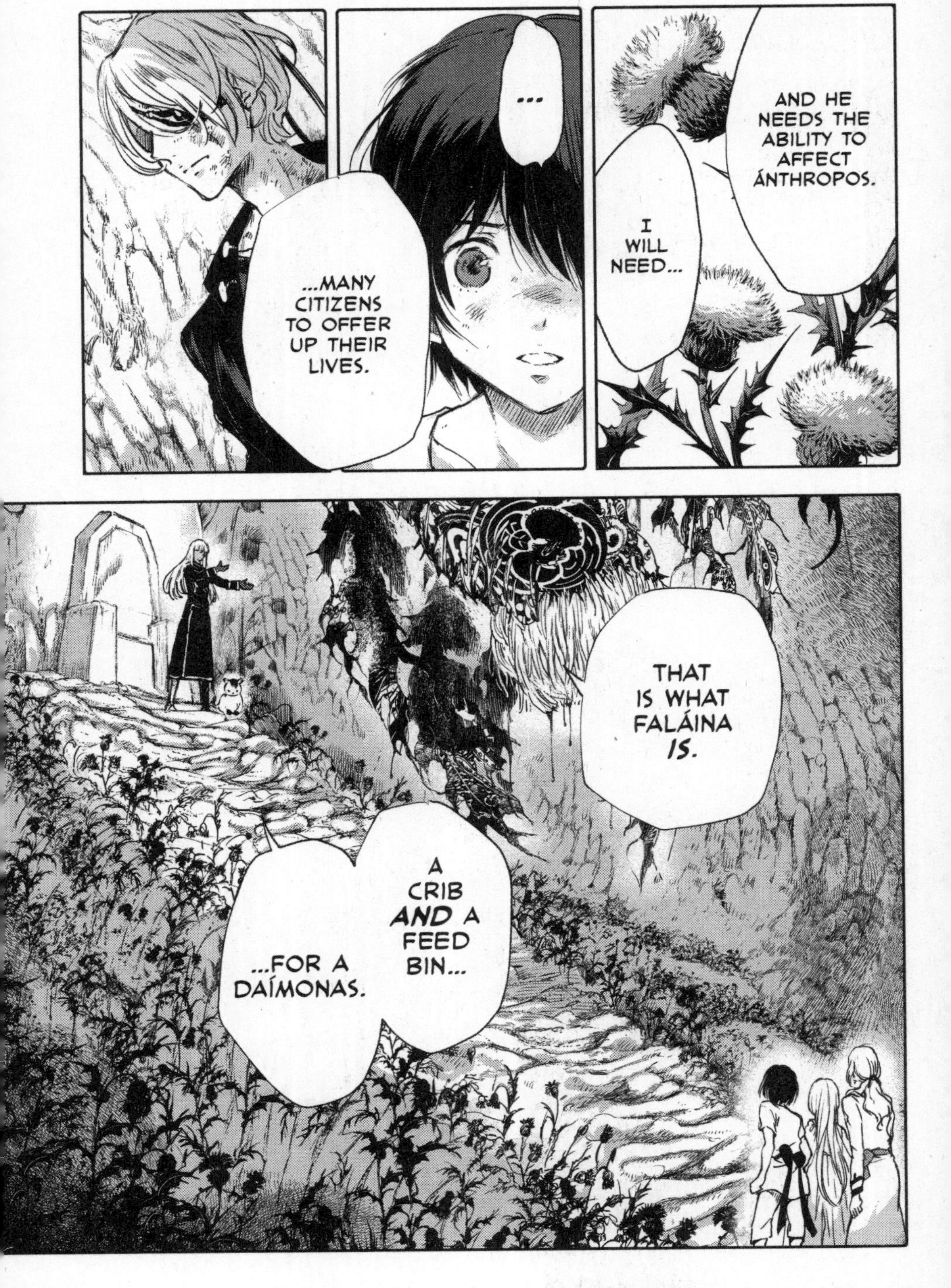
AND HE NEEDS THE ABILITY TO AFFECT ÁNTHROPOS.
I WILL NEED...
...
...MANY CITIZENS TO OFFER UP THEIR LIVES.
THAT IS WHAT FALÁINA *IS*.
A CRIB ***AND*** A FEED BIN...
...FOR A DAÍMONAS.

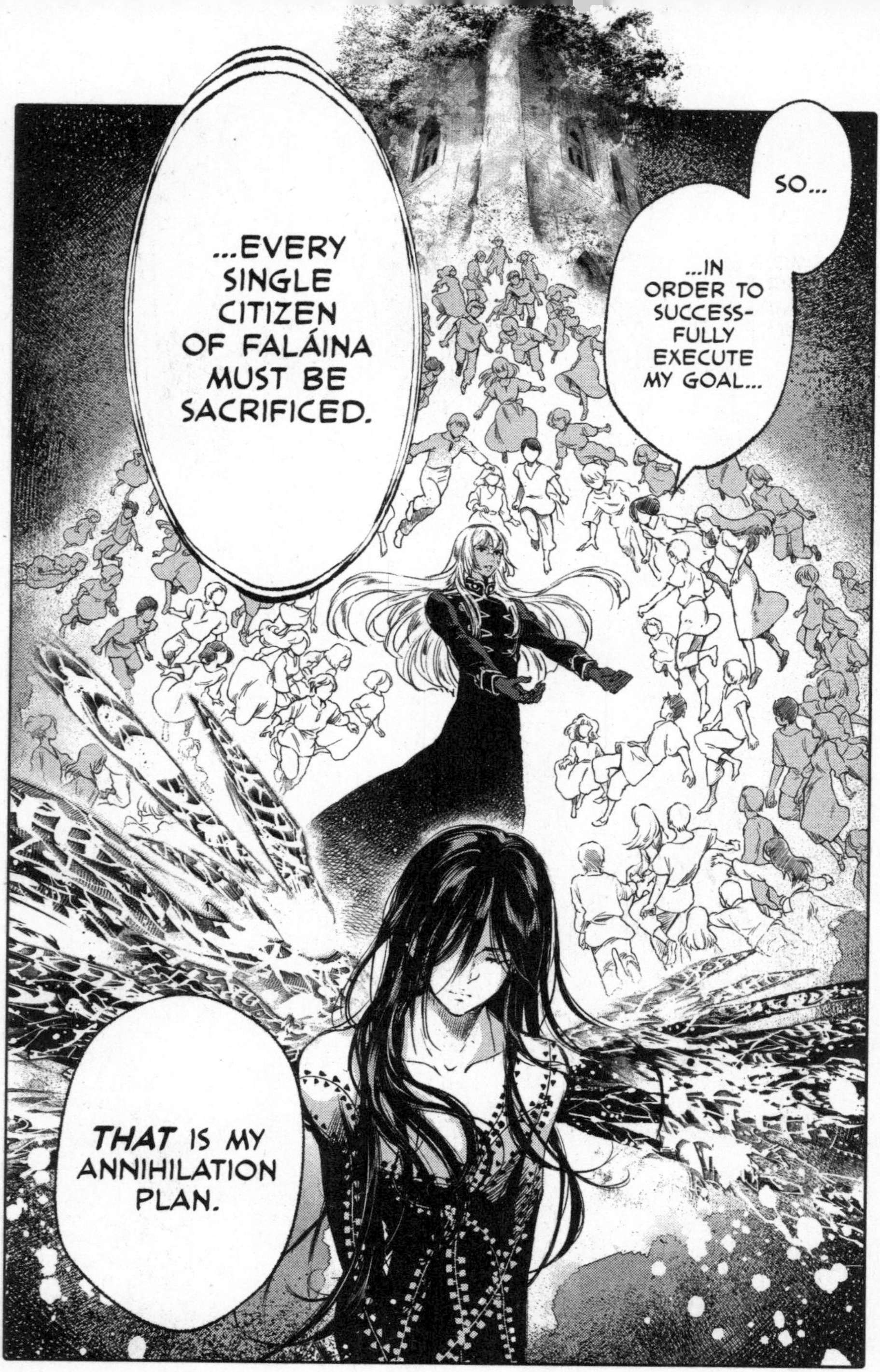
SO...
...IN ORDER TO SUCCESS-FULLY EXECUTE MY GOAL...
...EVERY SINGLE CITIZEN OF FALÁINA MUST BE SACRIFICED.
THAT IS MY ANNIHILATION PLAN.

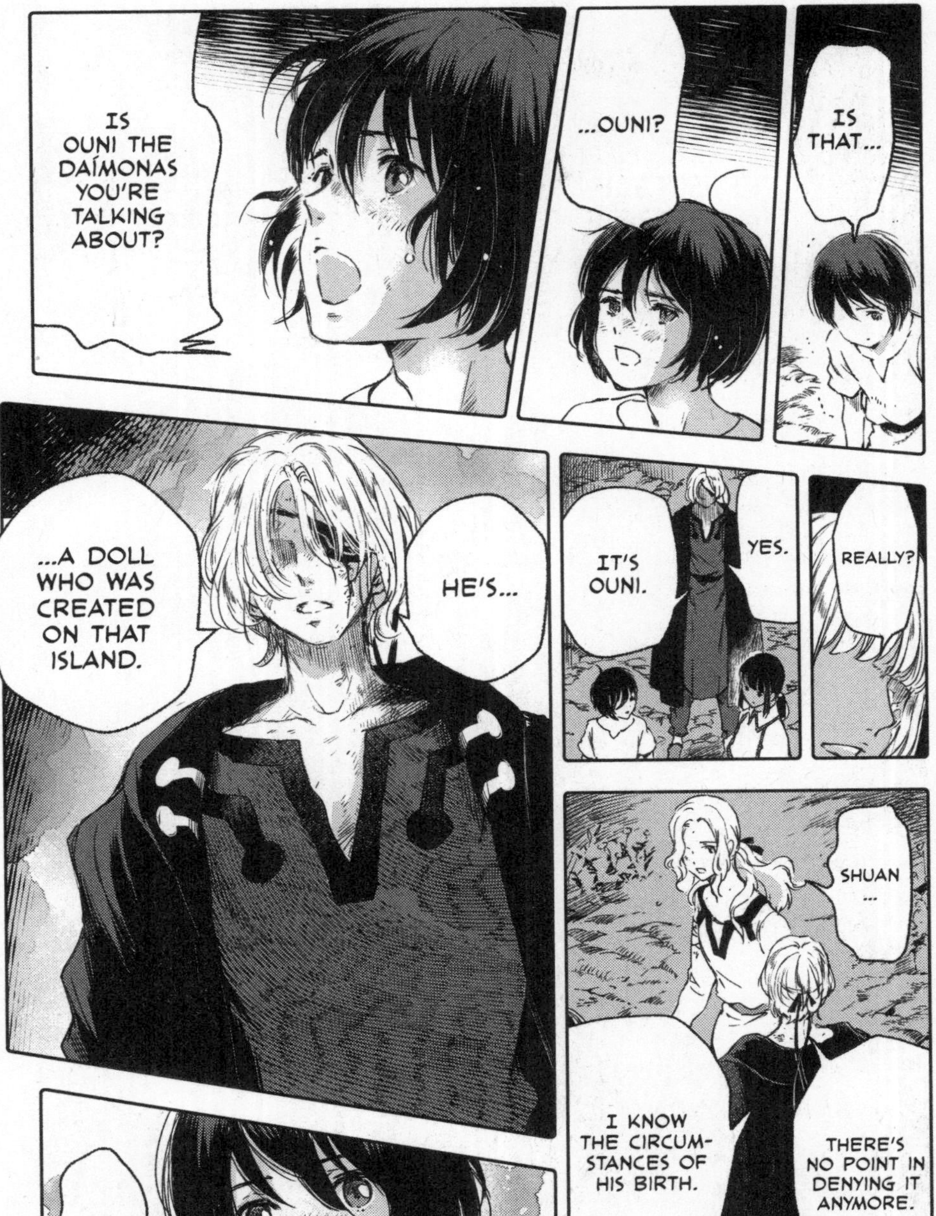
IS THAT...
...OUNI?
IS OUNI THE DAÍMONAS YOU'RE TALKING ABOUT?
REALLY?
YES.
IT'S OUNI.
SHUAN ...
THERE'S NO POINT IN DENYING IT ANYMORE.
I KNOW THE CIRCUM-STANCES OF HIS BIRTH.
HE'S...
...A DOLL WHO WAS CREATED ON THAT ISLAND.
...

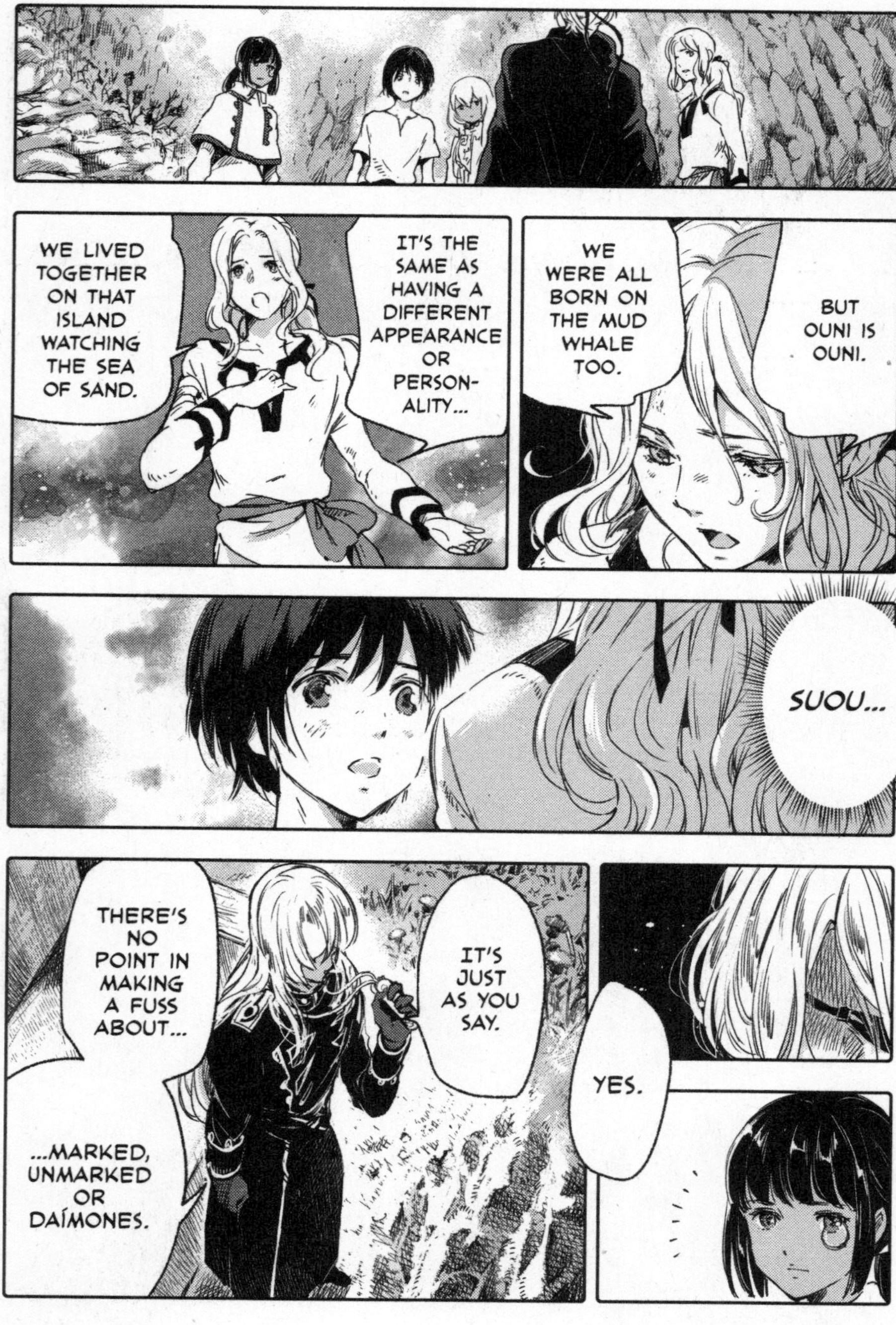
WE WERE ALL BORN ON THE MUD WHALE TOO.
BUT OUNI IS OUNI.
IT'S THE SAME AS HAVING A DIFFERENT APPEARANCE OR PERSON-ALITY...
WE LIVED TOGETHER ON THAT ISLAND WATCHING THE SEA OF SAND.
SUOU...
YES.
IT'S JUST AS YOU SAY.
THERE'S NO POINT IN MAKING A FUSS ABOUT...
...MARKED, UNMARKED OR DAÍMONES.

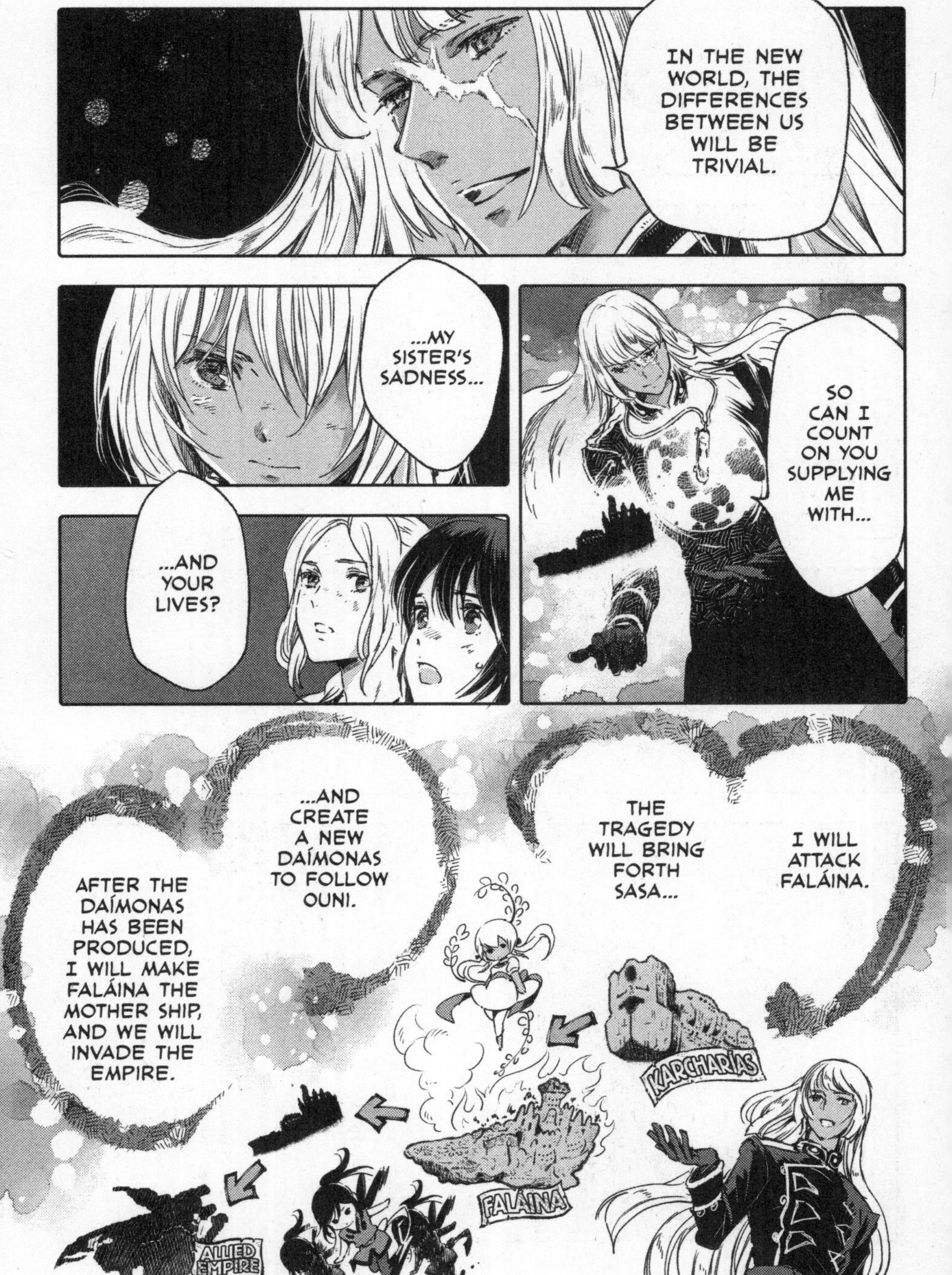
IN THE NEW WORLD, THE DIFFERENCES BETWEEN US WILL BE TRIVIAL.
SO CAN I COUNT ON YOU SUPPLYING ME WITH...
...MY SISTER'S SADNESS...
...AND YOUR LIVES?
I WILL ATTACK FALÁINA.
THE TRAGEDY WILL BRING FORTH SASA...
...AND CREATE A NEW DAÍMONAS TO FOLLOW OUNI.
AFTER THE DAÍMONAS HAS BEEN PRODUCED, I WILL MAKE FALÁINA THE MOTHER SHIP, AND WE WILL INVADE THE EMPIRE.
KARCHARÍAS
FALÁINA
ALLIED EMPIRE

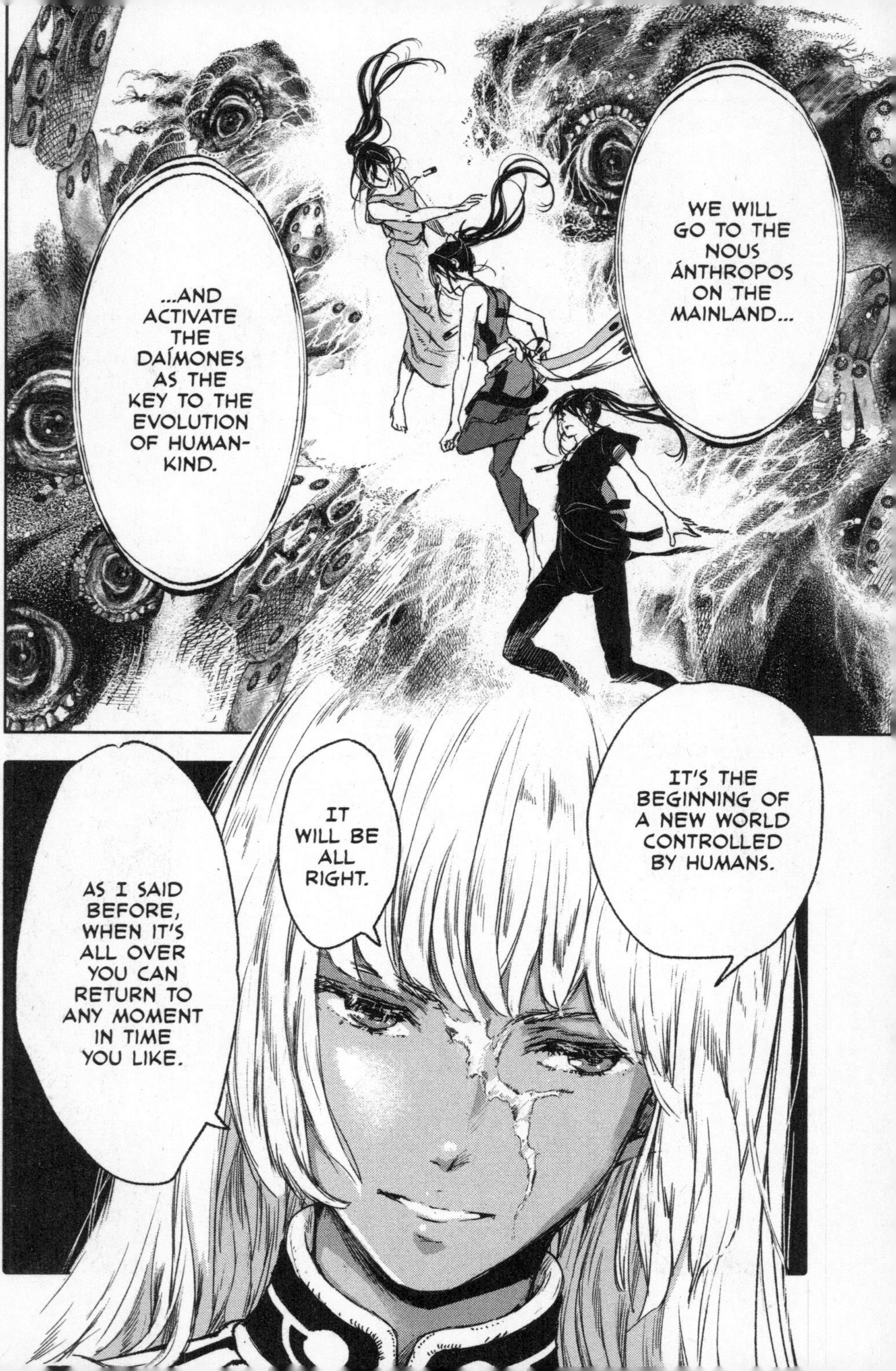
WE WILL GO TO THE NOUS ÁNTHROPOS ON THE MAINLAND...
...AND ACTIVATE THE DAÍMONES AS THE KEY TO THE EVOLUTION OF HUMAN-KIND.
IT'S THE BEGINNING OF A NEW WORLD CONTROLLED BY HUMANS.
IT WILL BE ALL RIGHT.
AS I SAID BEFORE, WHEN IT'S ALL OVER YOU CAN RETURN TO ANY MOMENT IN TIME YOU LIKE.

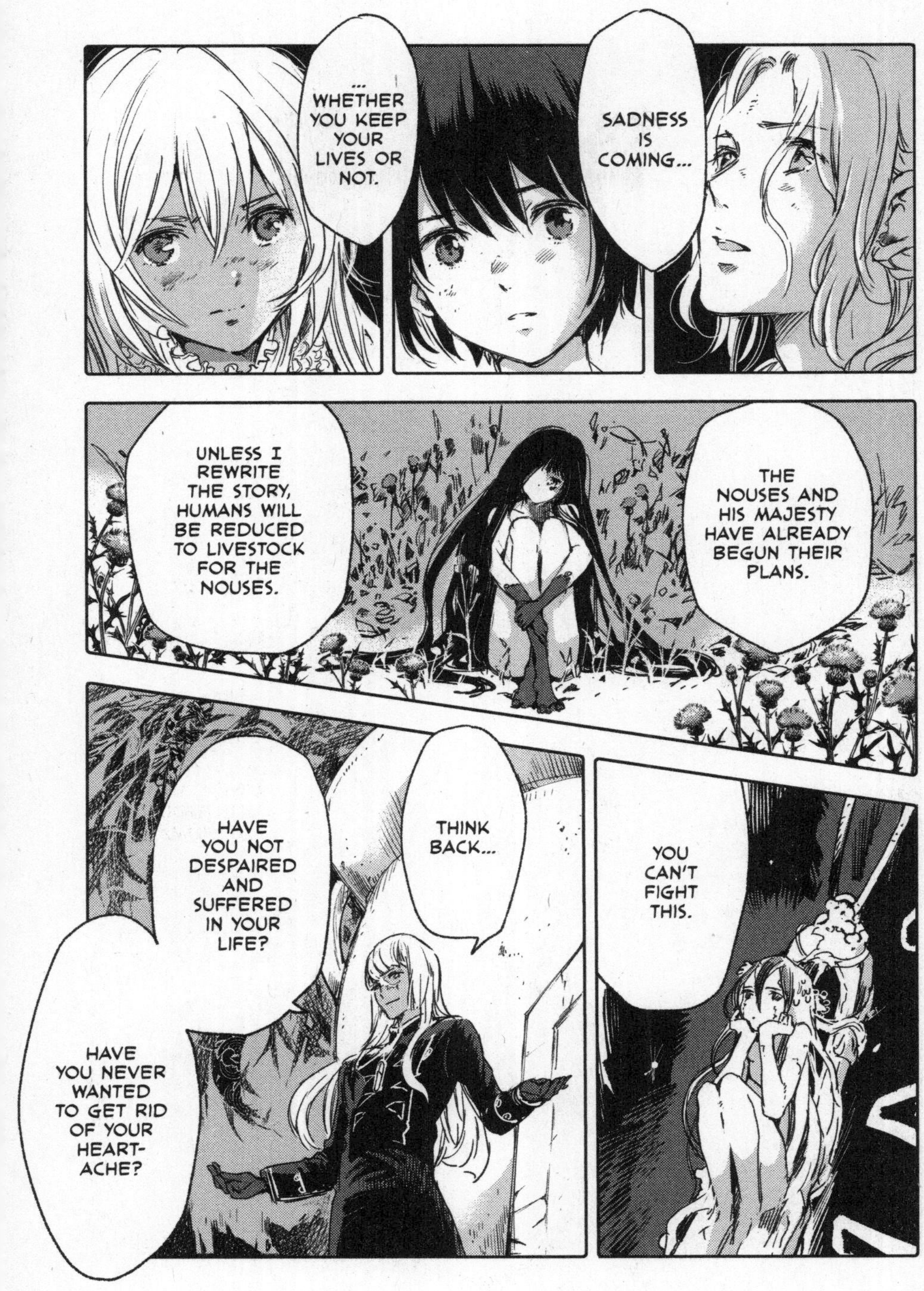
SADNESS IS COMING...
...WHETHER YOU KEEP YOUR LIVES OR NOT.
THE NOUSES AND HIS MAJESTY HAVE ALREADY BEGUN THEIR PLANS.
UNLESS I REWRITE THE STORY, HUMANS WILL BE REDUCED TO LIVESTOCK FOR THE NOUSES.
YOU CAN'T FIGHT THIS.
THINK BACK...
HAVE YOU NOT DESPAIRED AND SUFFERED IN YOUR LIFE?
HAVE YOU NEVER WANTED TO GET RID OF YOUR HEART-ACHE?

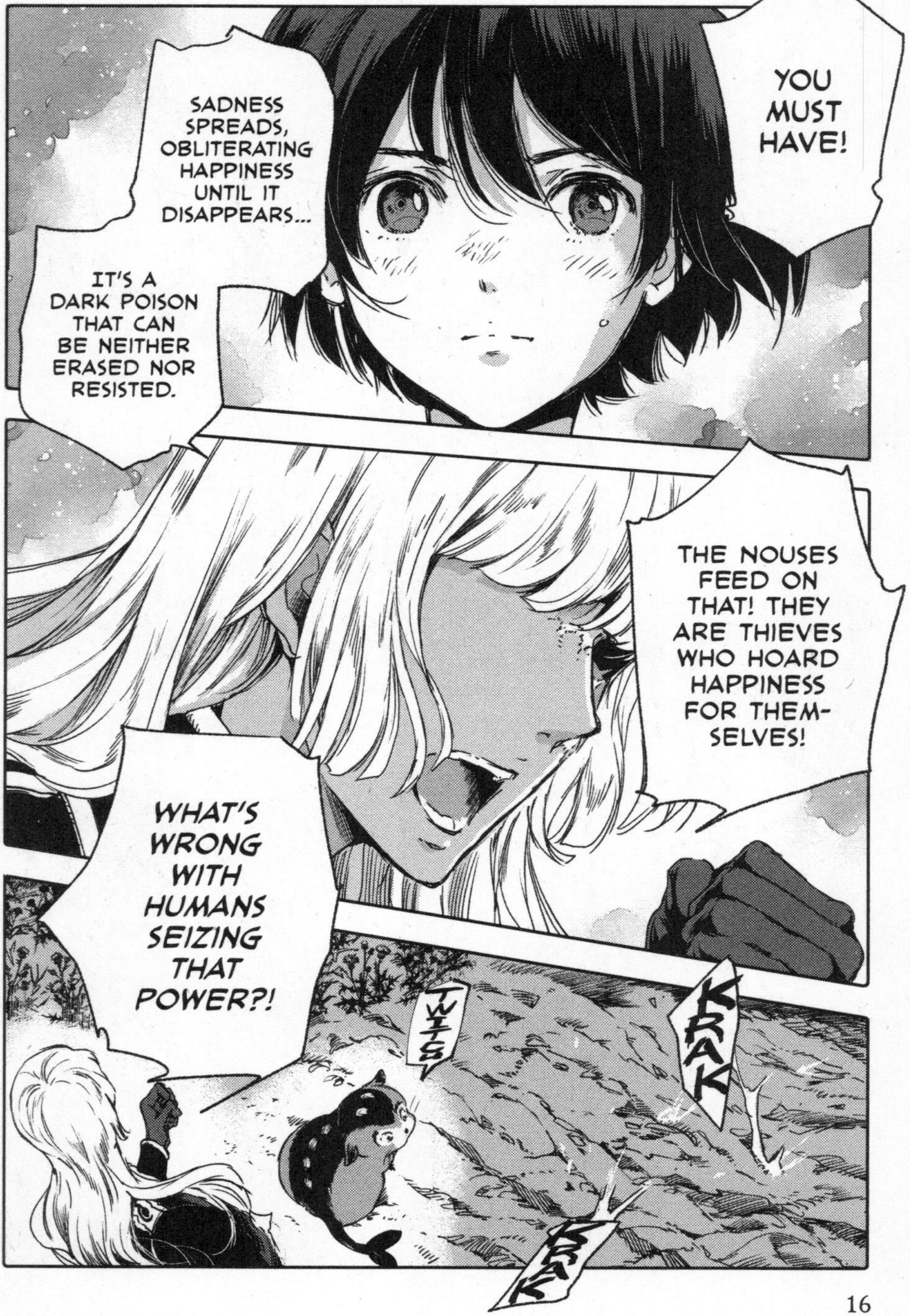
YOU MUST HAVE!
SADNESS SPREADS, OBLITERATING HAPPINESS UNTIL IT DISAPPEARS...
IT'S A DARK POISON THAT CAN BE NEITHER ERASED NOR RESISTED.
THE NOUSES FEED ON THAT! THEY ARE THIEVES WHO HOARD HAPPINESS FOR THEM-SELVES!
WHAT'S WRONG WITH HUMANS SEIZING THAT POWER?!
KRAK
TWITS
KRAK

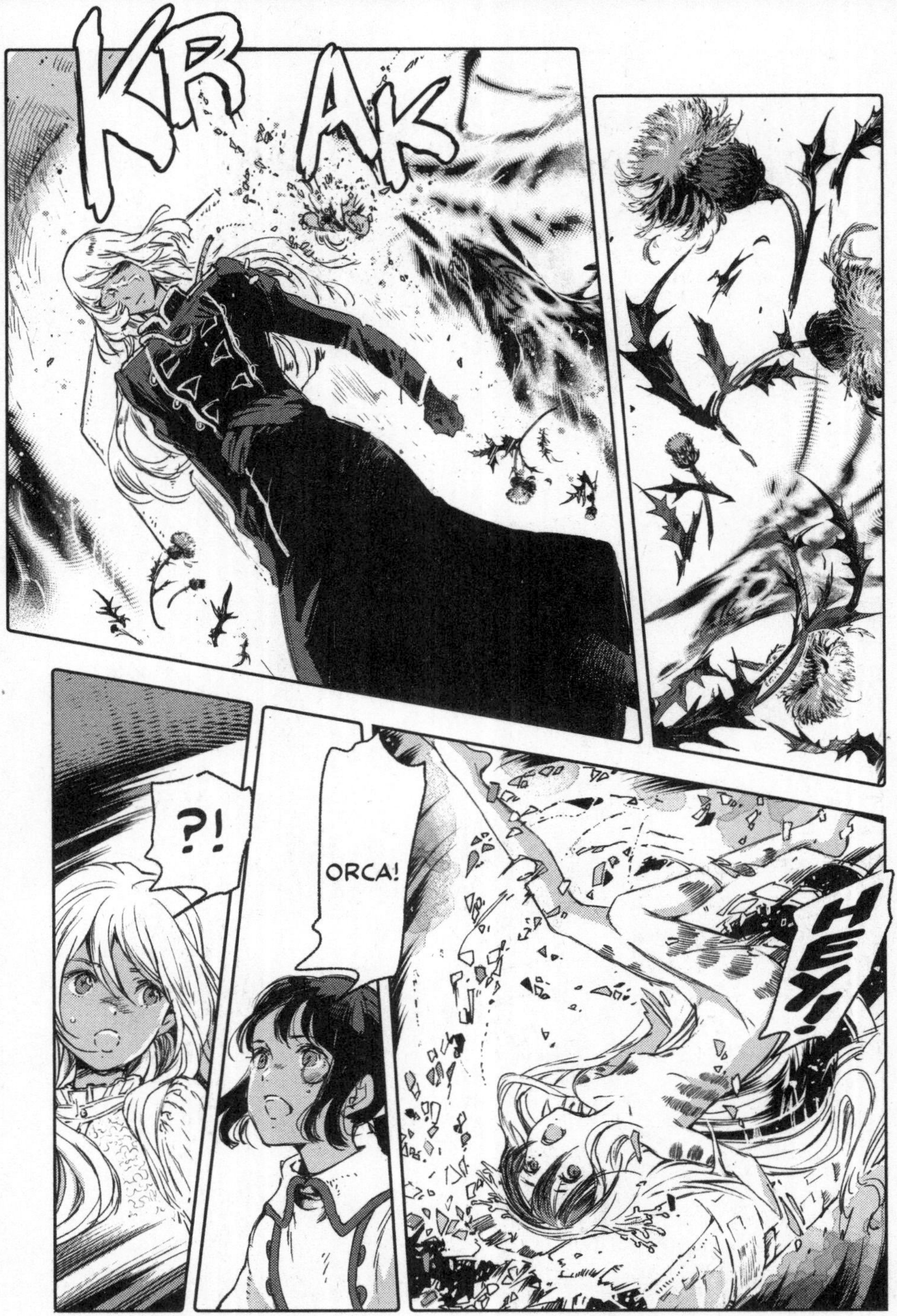
KRAK
HEY!
ORCA!
?!

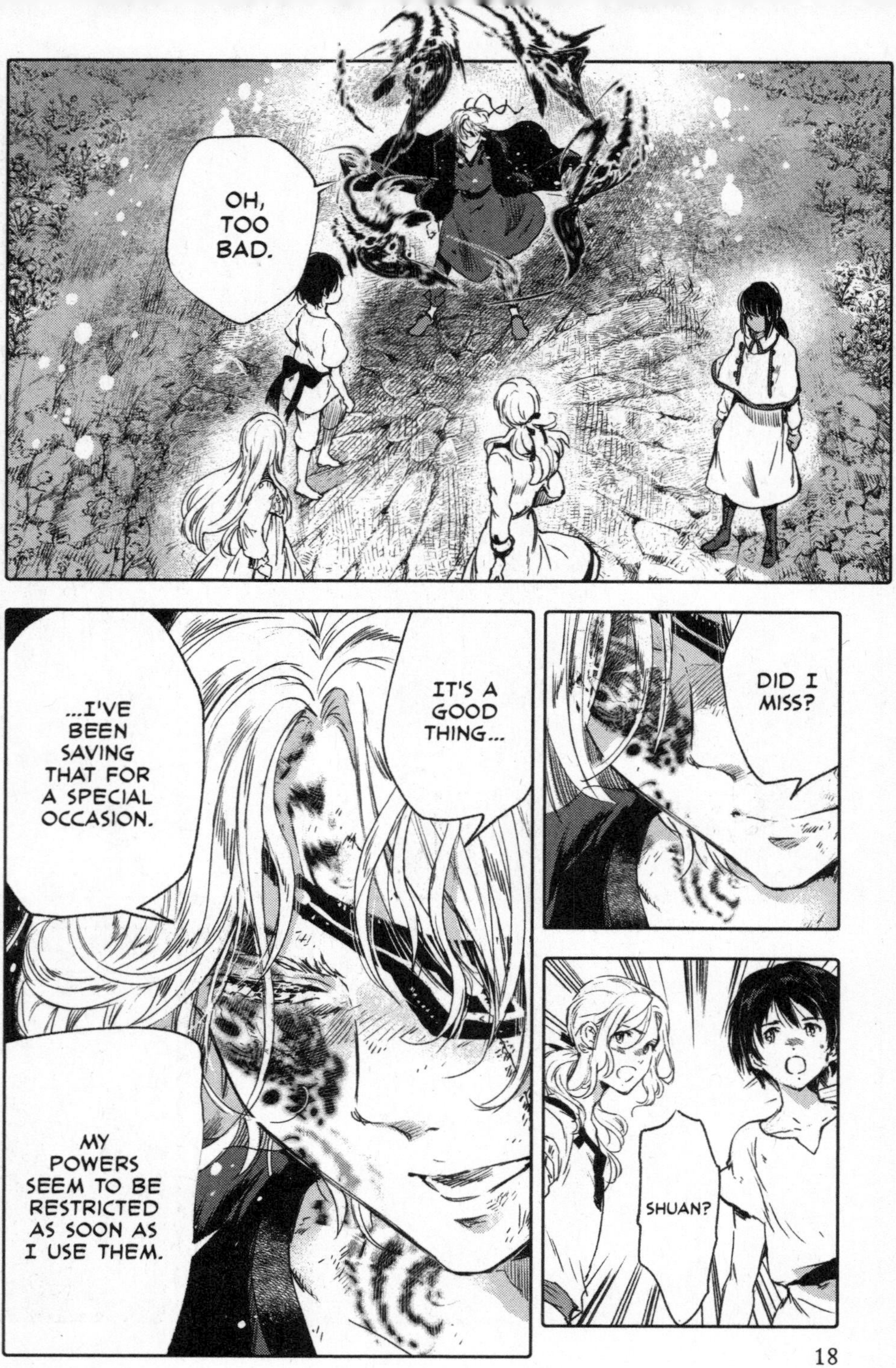
OH, TOO BAD.
DID I MISS?
SHUAN?
IT'S A GOOD THING...
...I'VE BEEN SAVING THAT FOR A SPECIAL OCCASION.
MY POWERS SEEM TO BE RESTRICTED AS SOON AS I USE THEM.

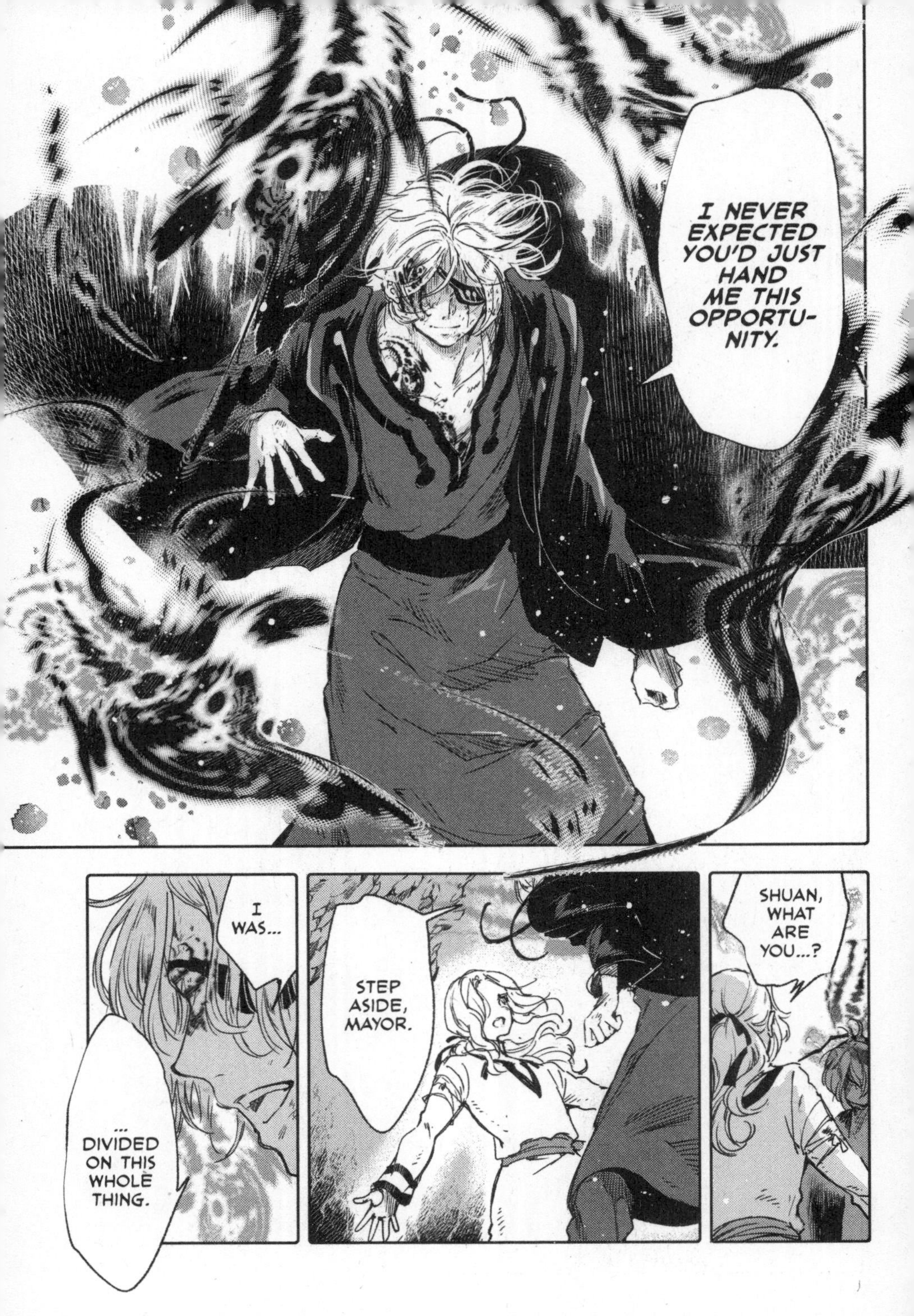
I NEVER EXPECTED YOU'D JUST HAND ME THIS OPPORTU-NITY.
SHUAN, WHAT ARE YOU...?
STEP ASIDE, MAYOR.
I WAS...
...DIVIDED ON THIS WHOLE THING.

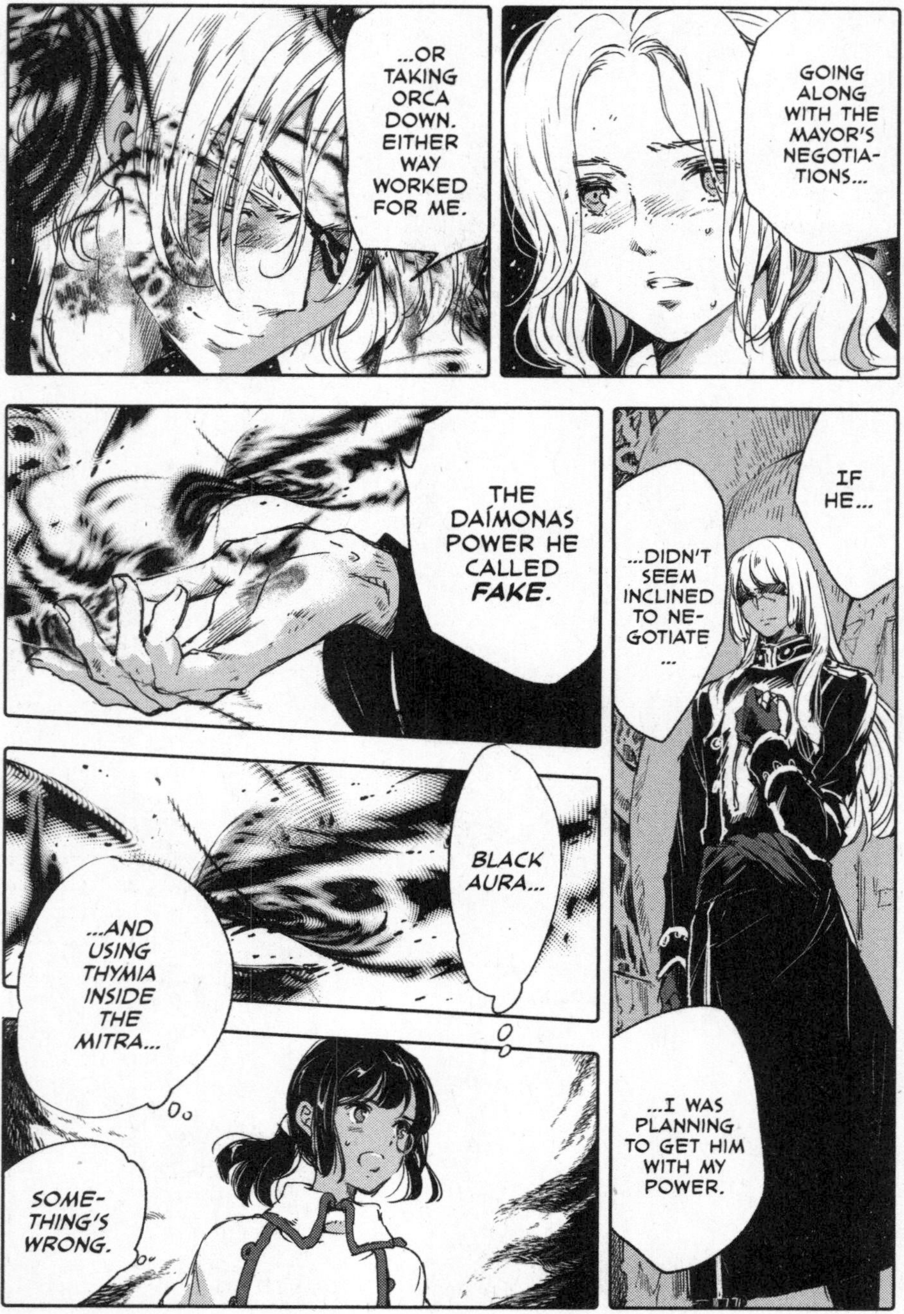
GOING ALONG WITH THE MAYOR'S NEGOTIATIONS...
...OR TAKING ORCA DOWN. EITHER WAY WORKED FOR ME.
IF HE...
...DIDN'T SEEM INCLINED TO NEGOTIATE...
...I WAS PLANNING TO GET HIM WITH MY POWER.
THE DAÍMONAS POWER HE CALLED *FAKE*.
BLACK AURA...
...AND USING THYMIA INSIDE THE MITRA...
SOMETHING'S WRONG.

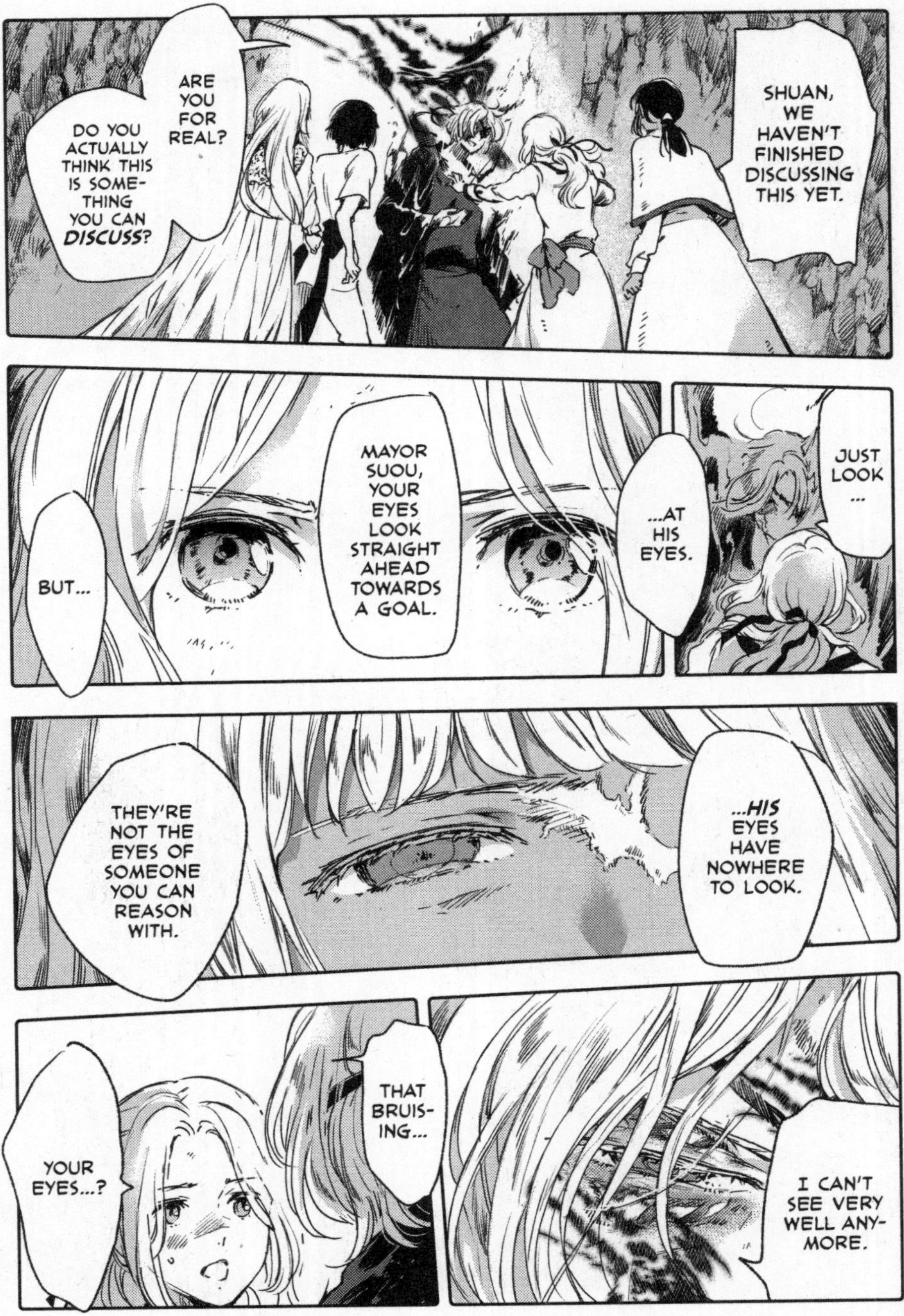
SHUAN, WE HAVEN'T FINISHED DISCUSSING THIS YET.
ARE YOU FOR REAL?
DO YOU ACTUALLY THINK THIS IS SOME-THING YOU CAN *DISCUSS*?
JUST LOOK...
...AT HIS EYES.
MAYOR SUOU, YOUR EYES LOOK STRAIGHT AHEAD TOWARDS A GOAL.
BUT...
...*HIS* EYES HAVE NOWHERE TO LOOK.
THEY'RE NOT THE EYES OF SOMEONE YOU CAN REASON WITH.
I CAN'T SEE VERY WELL ANY-MORE.
THAT BRUIS-ING...
YOUR EYES...?

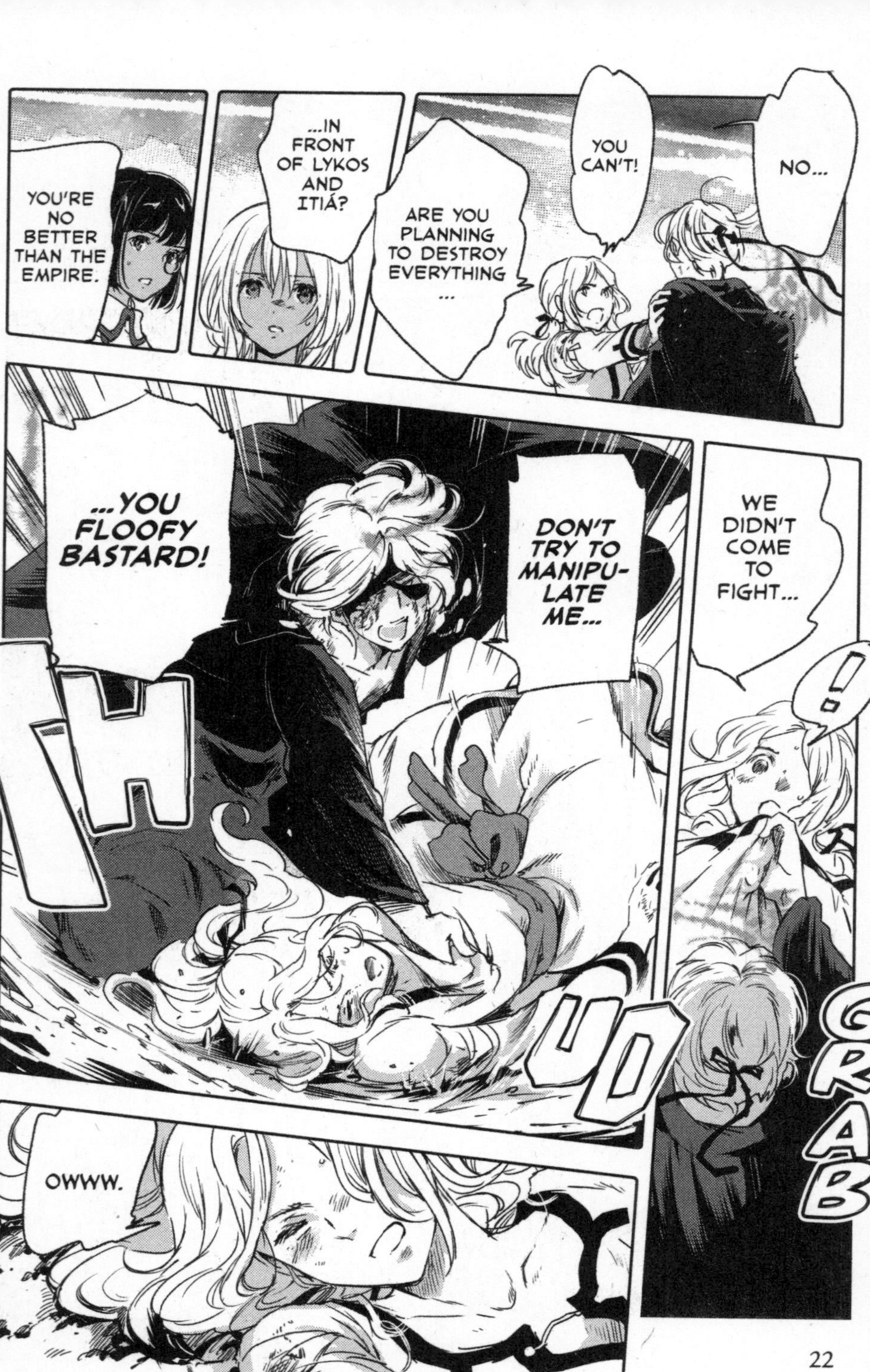
NO...
YOU CAN'T!
ARE YOU PLANNING TO DESTROY EVERYTHING ...
...IN FRONT OF LYKOS AND ITIÁ?
YOU'RE NO BETTER THAN THE EMPIRE.
WE DIDN'T COME TO FIGHT...
!
GRAB
DON'T TRY TO MANIPULATE ME...
...YOU FLOOFY BASTARD!
THUD
OWWW.

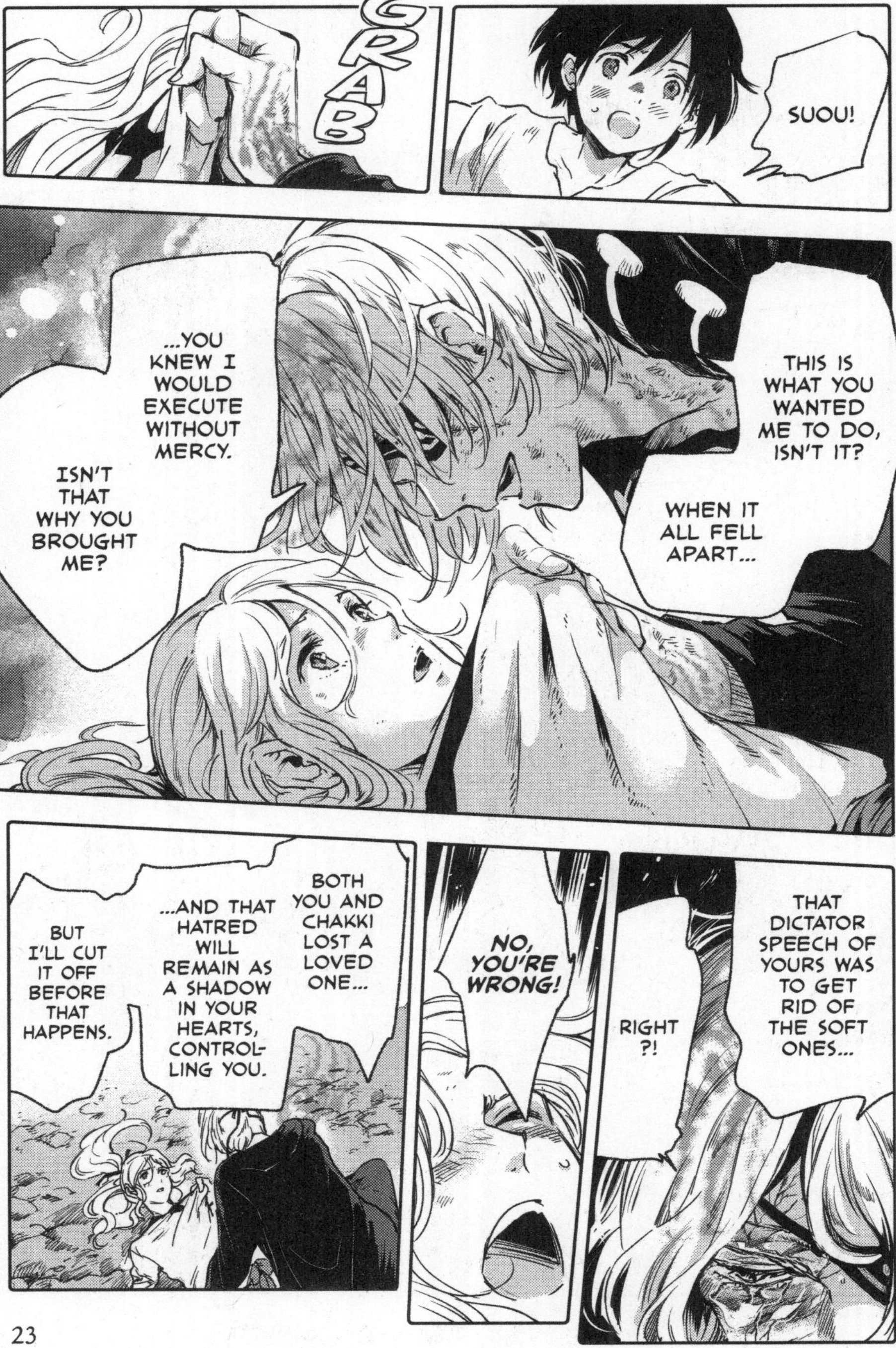
SUOU!
GRAB
THIS IS WHAT YOU WANTED ME TO DO, ISN'T IT?
WHEN IT ALL FELL APART...
...YOU KNEW I WOULD EXECUTE WITHOUT MERCY.
ISN'T THAT WHY YOU BROUGHT ME?
THAT DICTATOR SPEECH OF YOURS WAS TO GET RID OF THE SOFT ONES...
RIGHT?!
NO, YOU'RE WRONG!
BOTH YOU AND CHAKKI LOST A LOVED ONE...
...AND THAT HATRED WILL REMAIN AS A SHADOW IN YOUR HEARTS, CONTROL-LING YOU.
BUT I'LL CUT IT OFF BEFORE THAT HAPPENS.

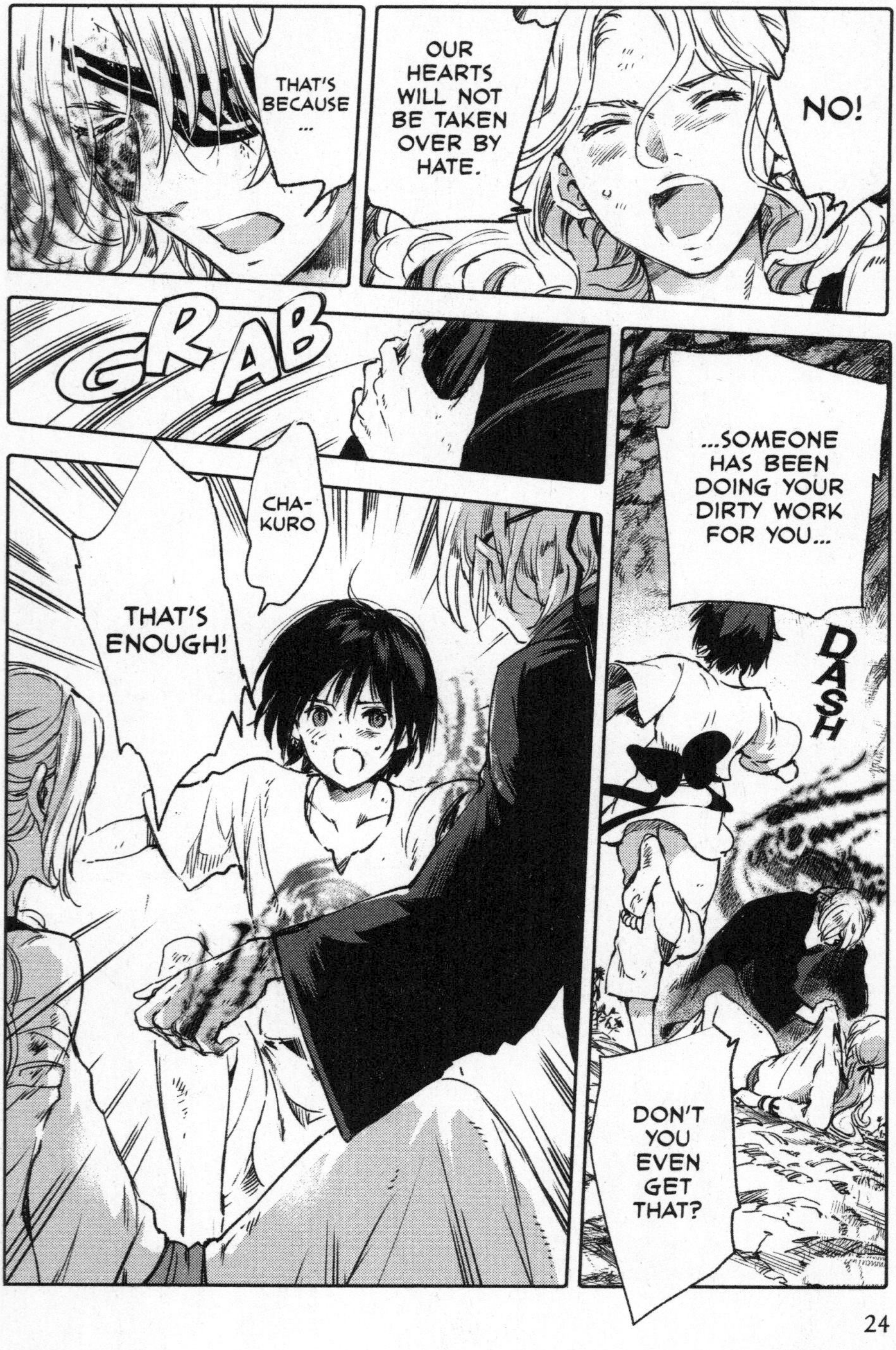
THAT'S BECAUSE …
OUR HEARTS WILL NOT BE TAKEN OVER BY HATE.
NO!
…SOMEONE HAS BEEN DOING YOUR DIRTY WORK FOR YOU…
DON'T YOU EVEN GET THAT?
DASH
GRAB
CHA-KURO
THAT'S ENOUGH!

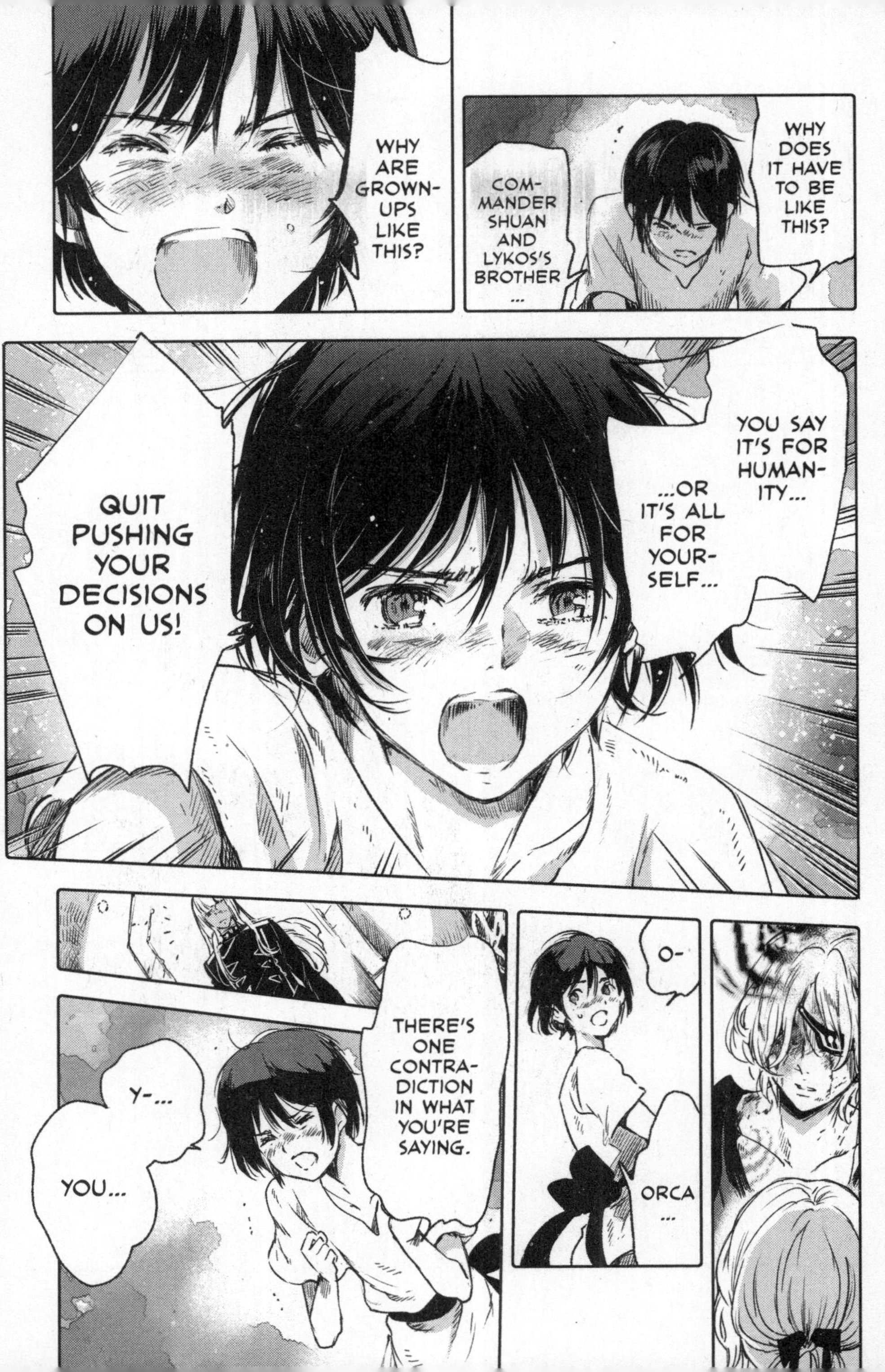
WHY DOES IT HAVE TO BE LIKE THIS?
COM-MANDER SHUAN AND LYKOS'S BROTHER ...
WHY ARE GROWN-UPS LIKE THIS?
YOU SAY IT'S FOR HUMAN-ITY...
...OR IT'S ALL FOR YOUR-SELF...
QUIT PUSHING YOUR DECISIONS ON US!
O-
ORCA ...
THERE'S ONE CONTRA-DICTION IN WHAT YOU'RE SAYING.
Y-...
YOU...

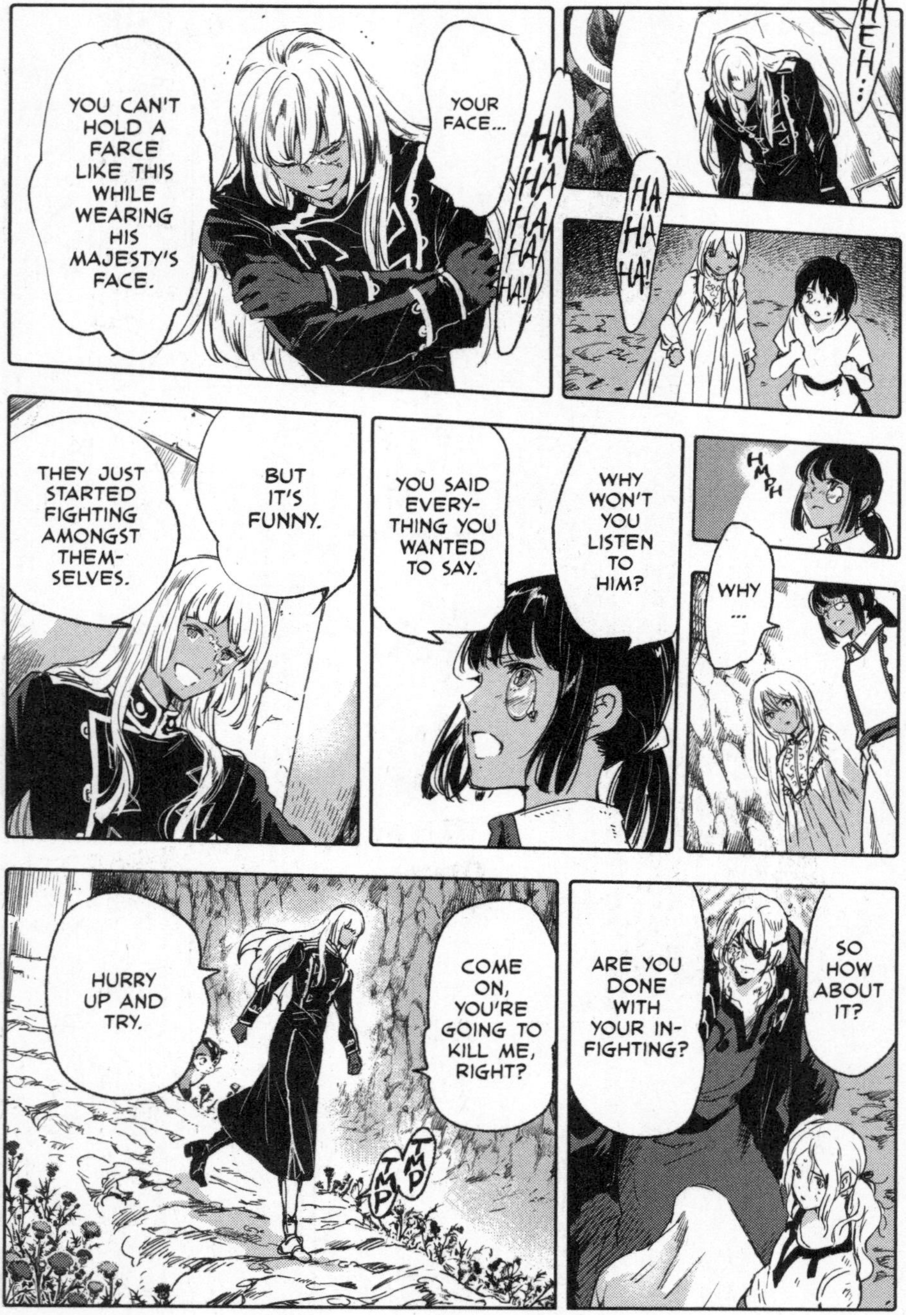
HEH...
HA HA HA!
YOUR FACE...
HA HA HA HA HA!
YOU CAN'T HOLD A FARCE LIKE THIS WHILE WEARING HIS MAJESTY'S FACE.
HMPH
WHY...
WHY WON'T YOU LISTEN TO HIM?
YOU SAID EVERYTHING YOU WANTED TO SAY.
BUT IT'S FUNNY.
THEY JUST STARTED FIGHTING AMONGST THEMSELVES.
SO HOW ABOUT IT?
ARE YOU DONE WITH YOUR IN-FIGHTING?
COME ON, YOU'RE GOING TO KILL ME, RIGHT?
TMP TMP
HURRY UP AND TRY.

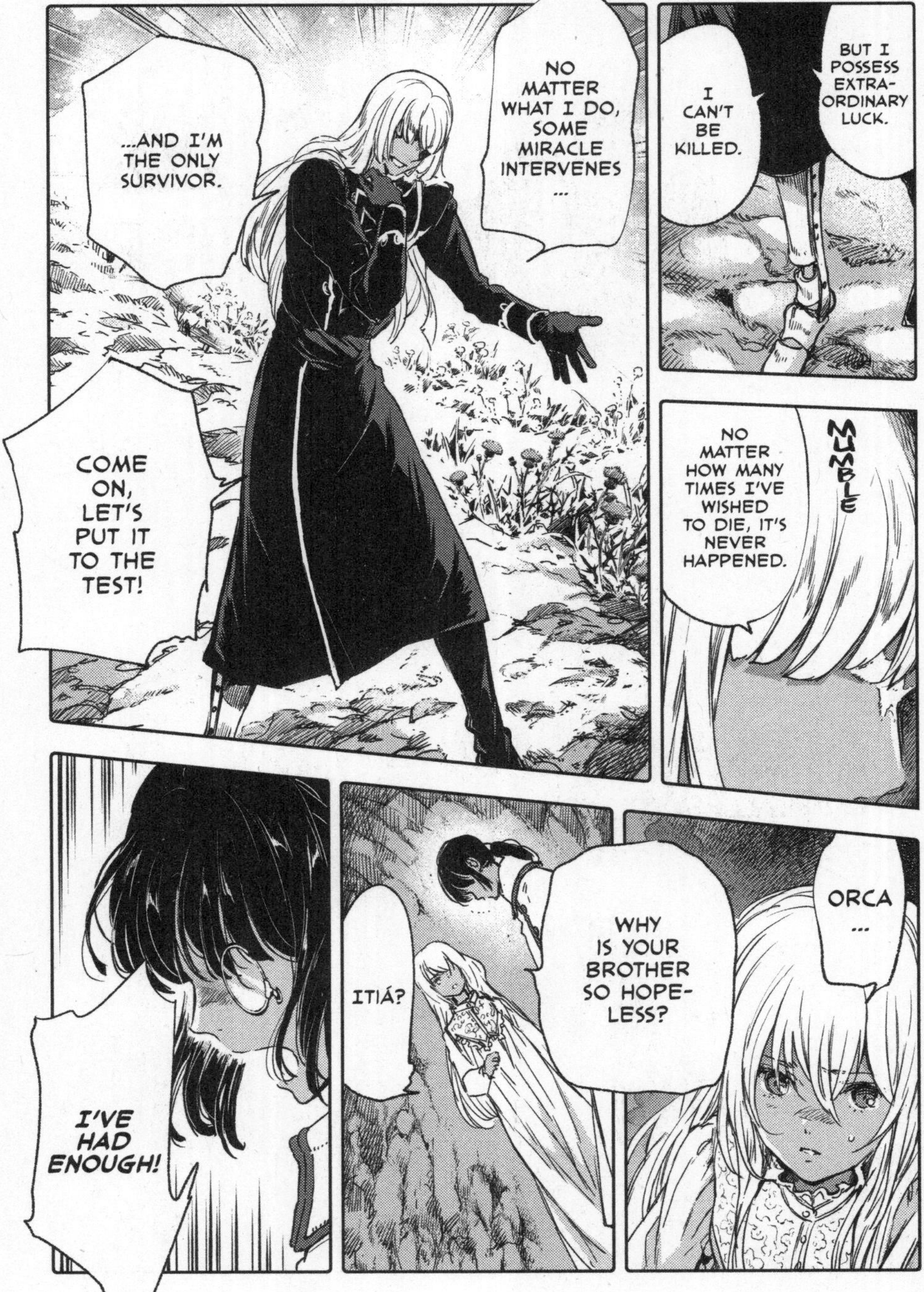
BUT I POSSESS EXTRA-ORDINARY LUCK.
I CAN'T BE KILLED.
MUMBLE
NO MATTER HOW MANY TIMES I'VE WISHED TO DIE, IT'S NEVER HAPPENED.
NO MATTER WHAT I DO, SOME MIRACLE INTERVENES ...
...AND I'M THE ONLY SURVIVOR.
COME ON, LET'S PUT IT TO THE TEST!
ORCA ...
WHY IS YOUR BROTHER SO HOPE-LESS?
ITIÁ?
I'VE HAD ENOUGH!

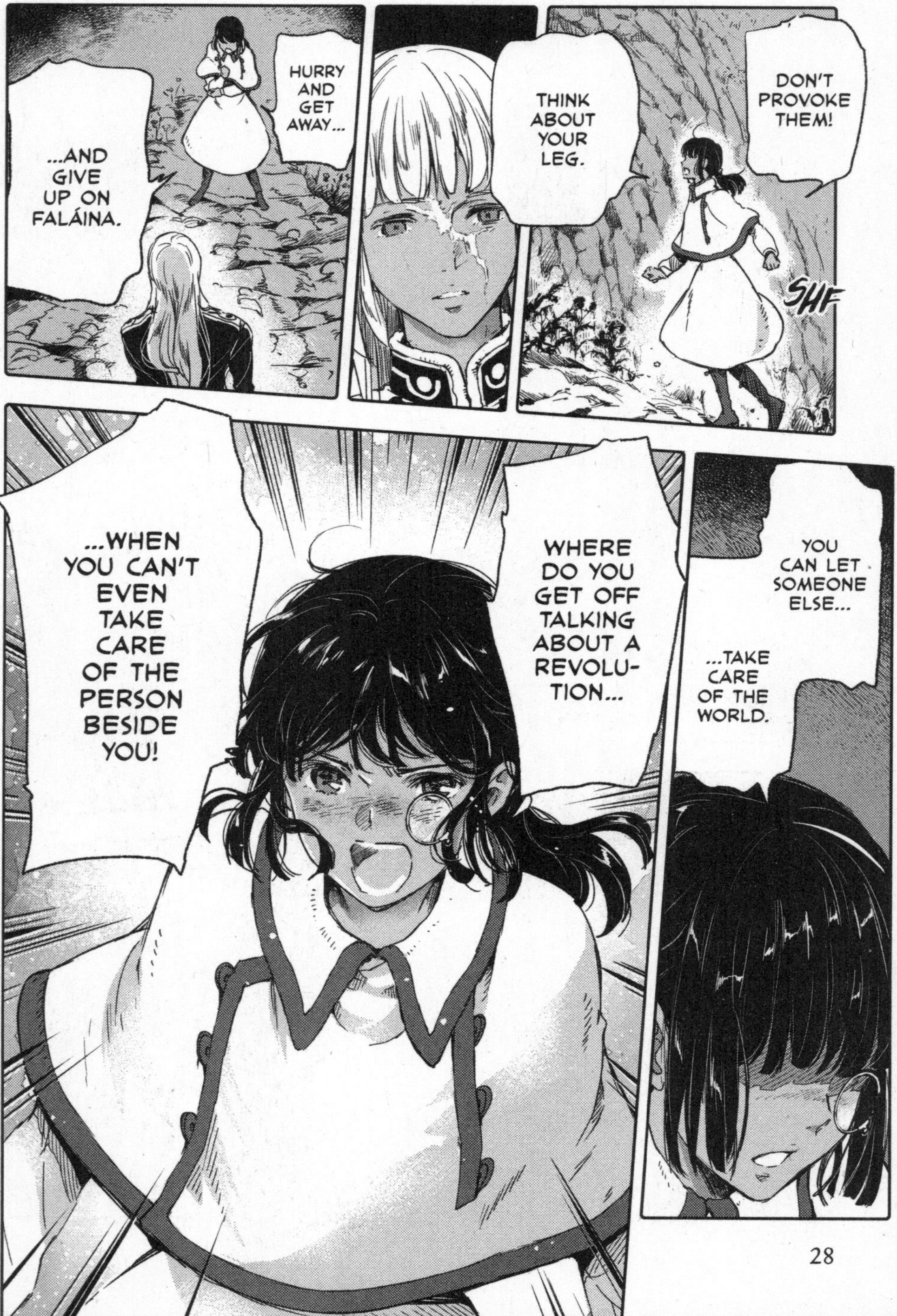
DON'T PROVOKE THEM!
SHF
THINK ABOUT YOUR LEG.
HURRY AND GET AWAY...
...AND GIVE UP ON FALÁINA.
YOU CAN LET SOMEONE ELSE...
...TAKE CARE OF THE WORLD.
WHERE DO YOU GET OFF TALKING ABOUT A REVOLUTION...
...WHEN YOU CAN'T EVEN TAKE CARE OF THE PERSON BESIDE YOU!

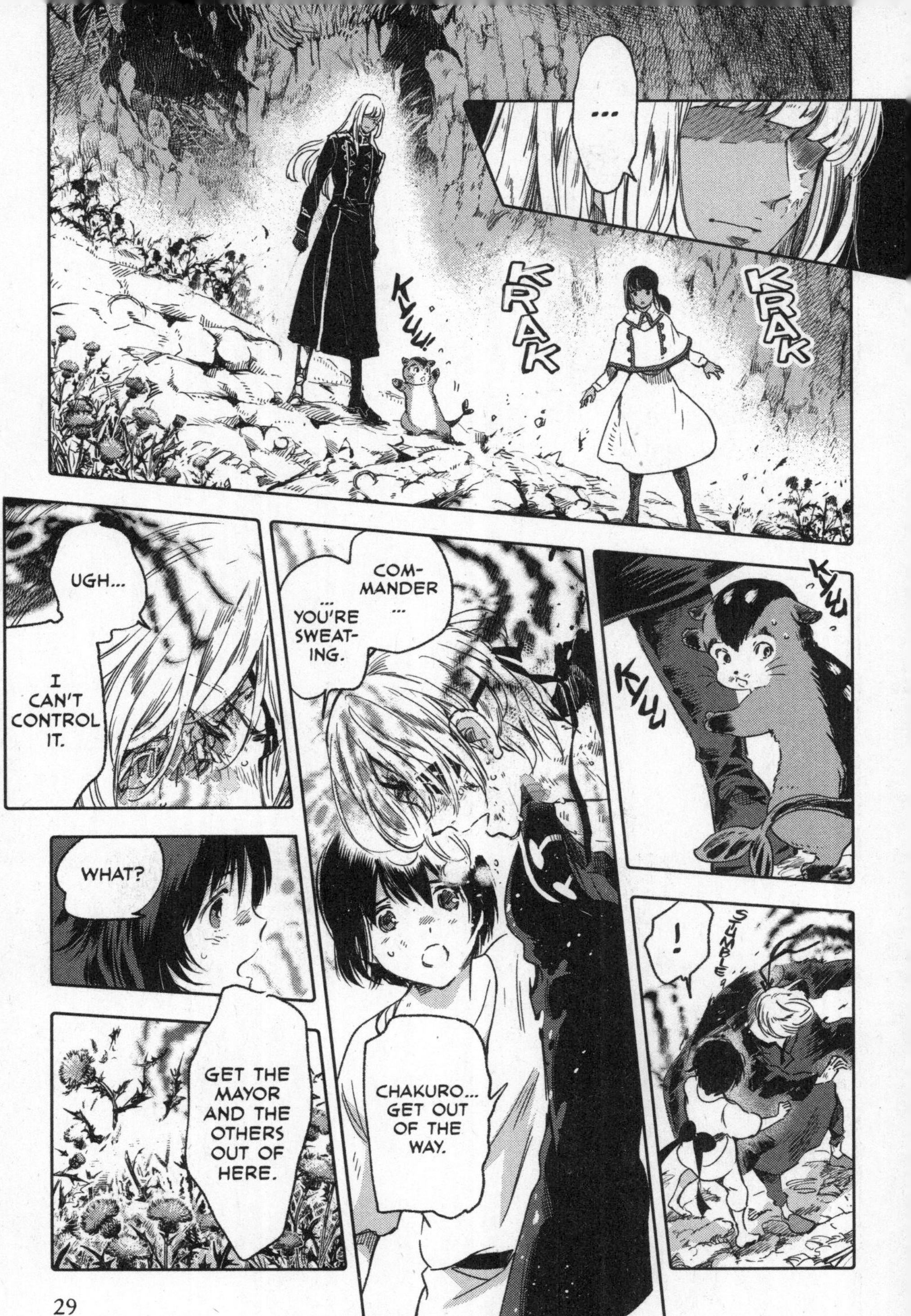
...
KRAK
KRAK
KYUU!
KYUU
KYUU
!
STUMBLE
COMMANDER... YOU'RE SWEATING.
CHAKURO... GET OUT OF THE WAY.
UGH...
I CAN'T CONTROL IT.
WHAT?
GET THE MAYOR AND THE OTHERS OUT OF HERE.

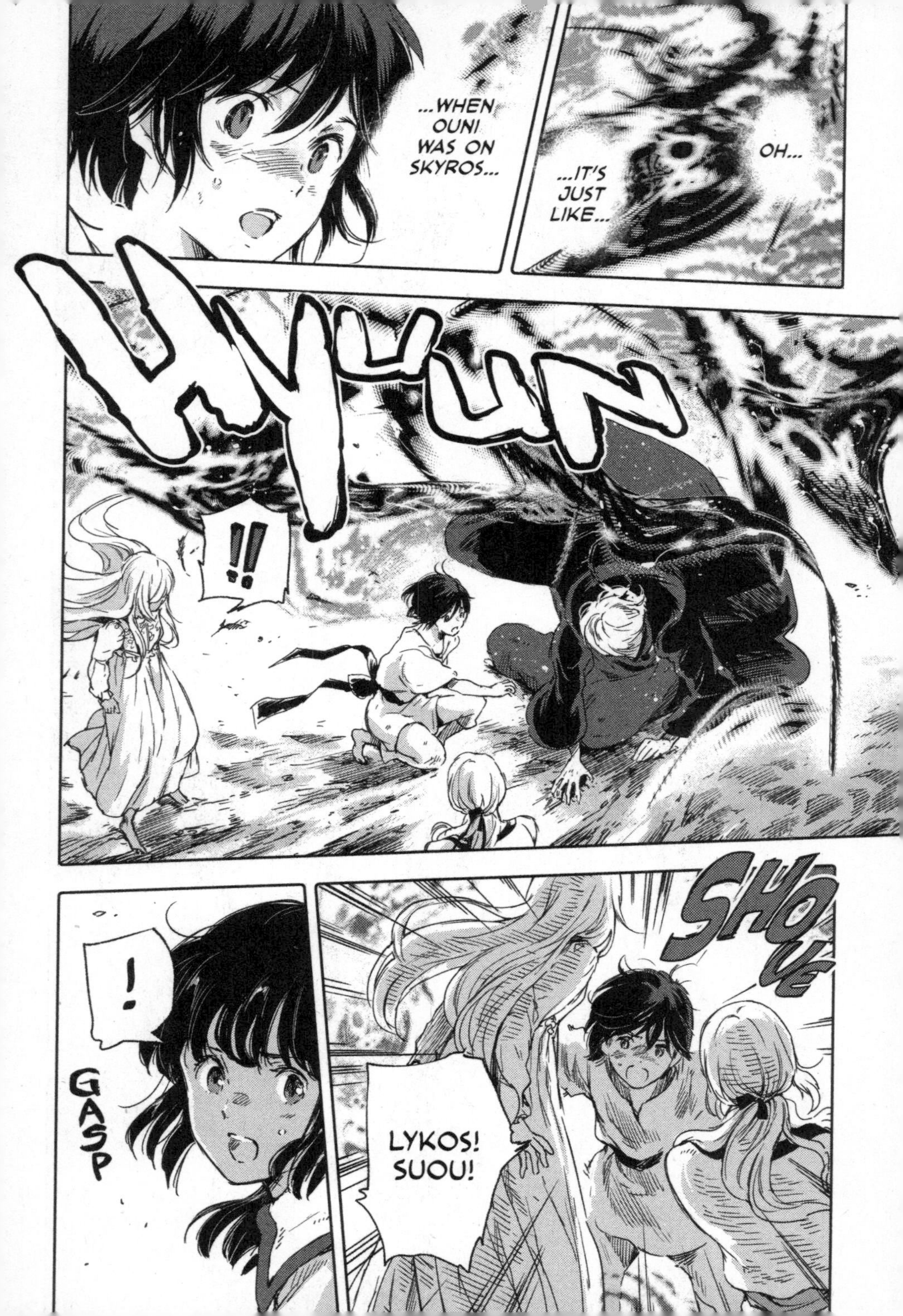
OH...
...IT'S JUST LIKE...
...WHEN OUNI WAS ON SKYROS...
HYUN
!!
SHOVE
LYKOS! SUOU!
!
GASP

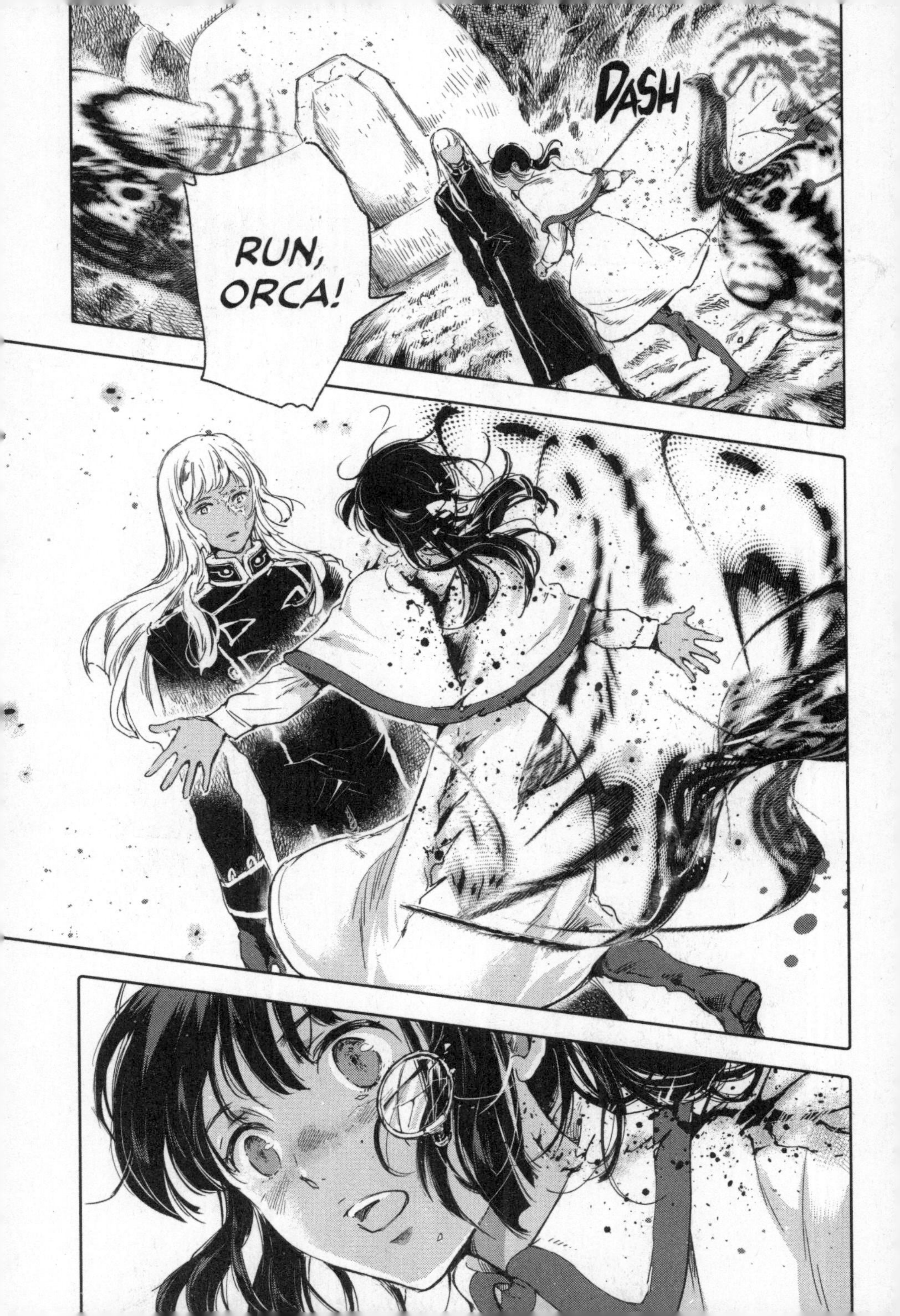
DASH
RUN, ORCA!

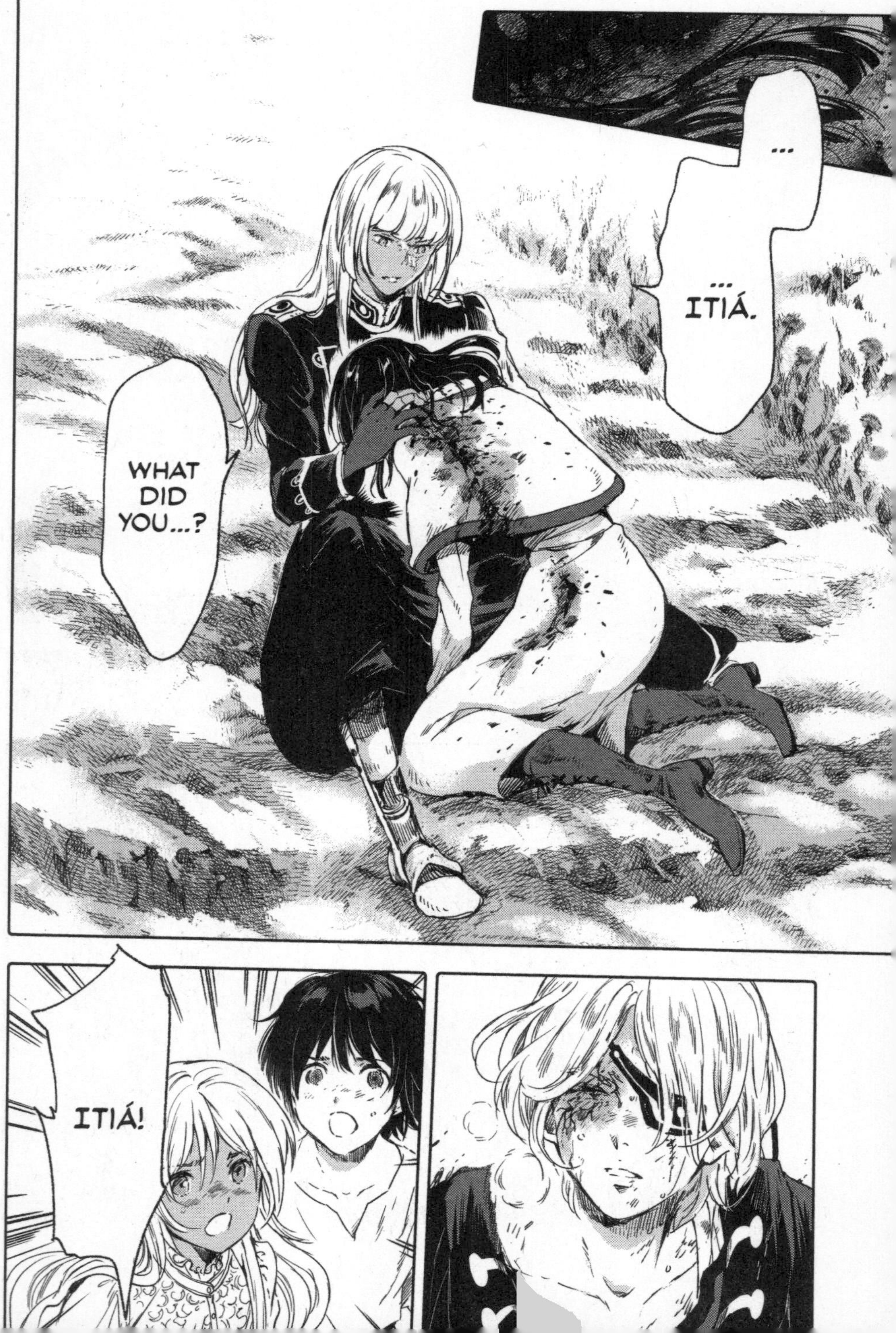
...
... ITIÁ.
WHAT DID YOU...?
ITIÁ!

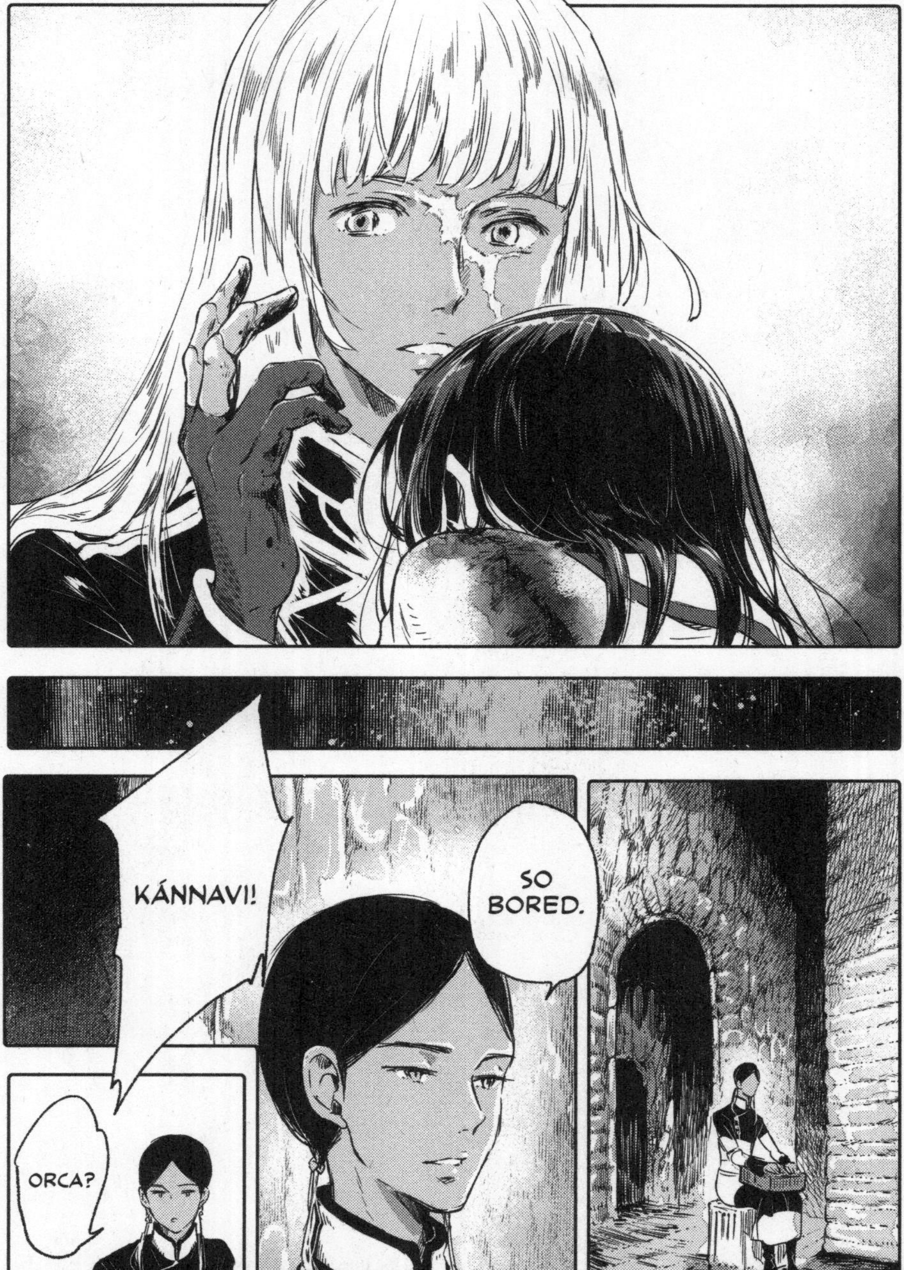
SO BORED.
KÁNNAVI!
ORCA?

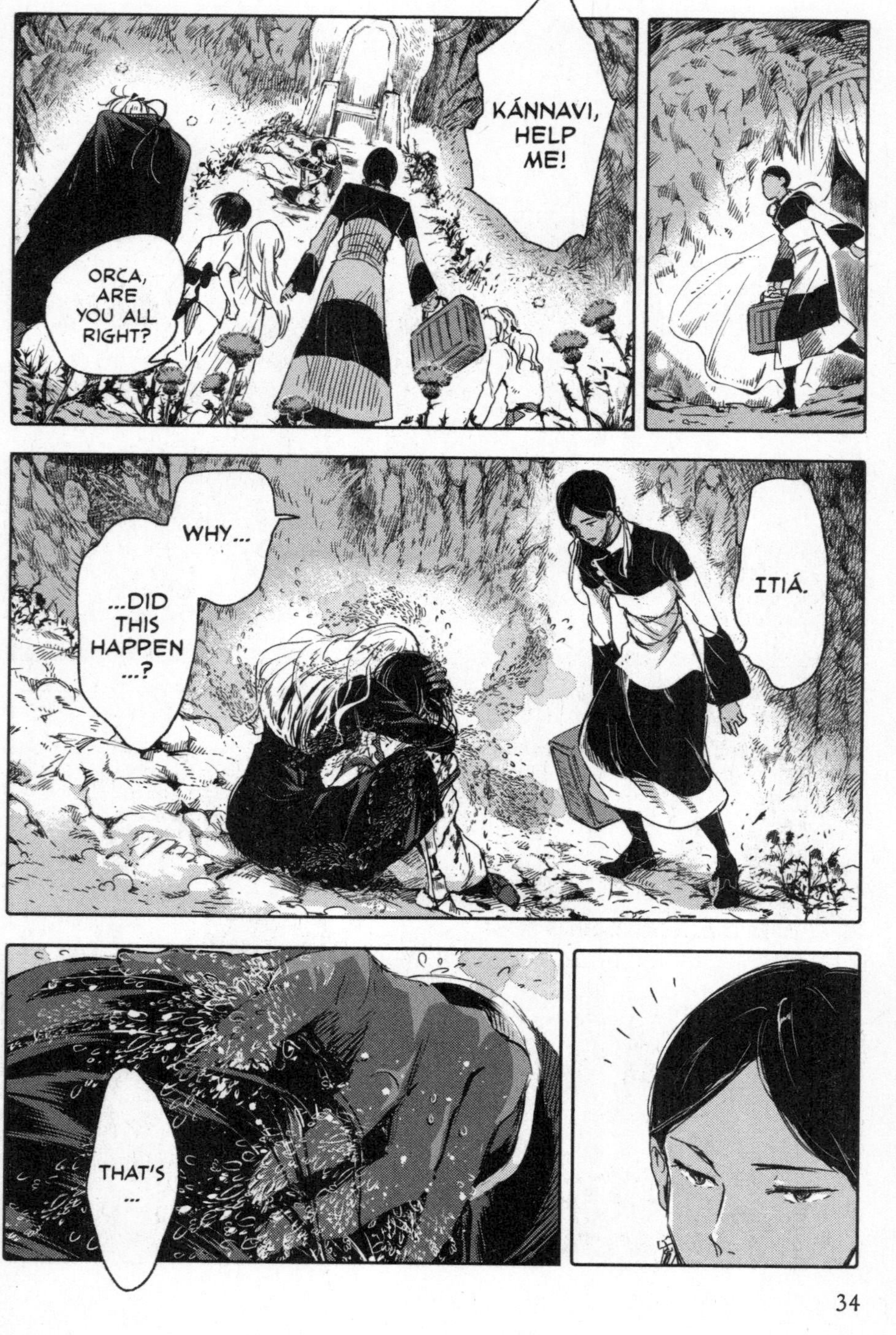
KÁNNAVI, HELP ME!
ORCA, ARE YOU ALL RIGHT?
ITIÁ.
WHY...
...DID THIS HAPPEN ...?
THAT'S ...

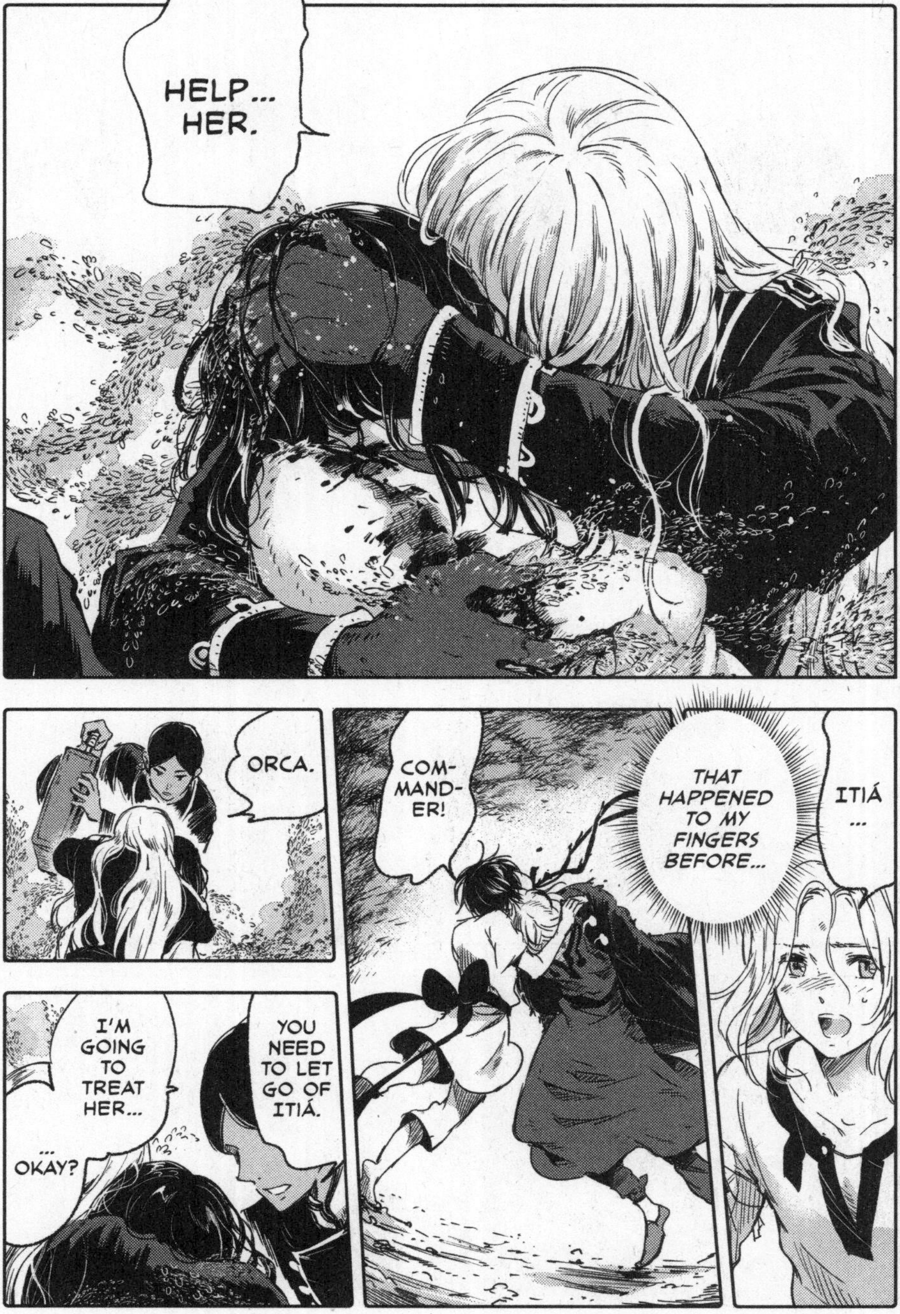
HELP... HER.
ITIÁ ...
THAT HAPPENED TO MY FINGERS BEFORE...
COM-MANDER!
ORCA.
YOU NEED TO LET GO OF ITIÁ.
I'M GOING TO TREAT HER...
... OKAY?

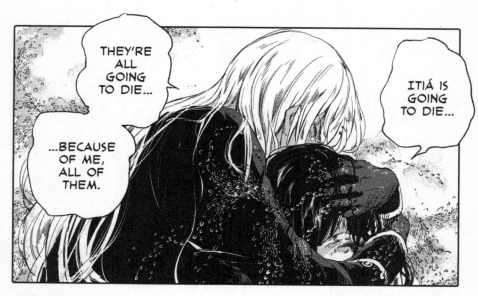

ITIÁ IS GOING TO DIE...
THEY'RE ALL GOING TO DIE...
...BECAUSE OF ME, ALL OF THEM.
CALM DOWN, ORCA...
STOP SQUEEZING HER.
I HAVE TO HURRY UP AND TURN IT BACK...
EVERY-ONE... EVERY-ONE...
I HAVE TO GET THEM BACK.
IT'S OKAY, LET ME SEE TO ITIÁ.
PLEASE, JUST LET GO OF HER SLOWLY.

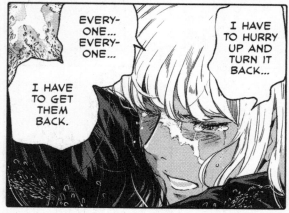

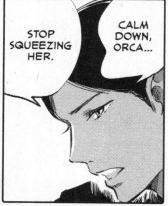

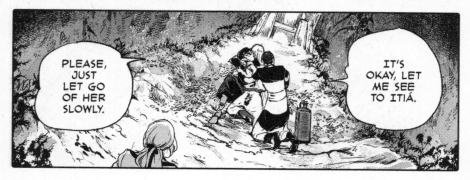

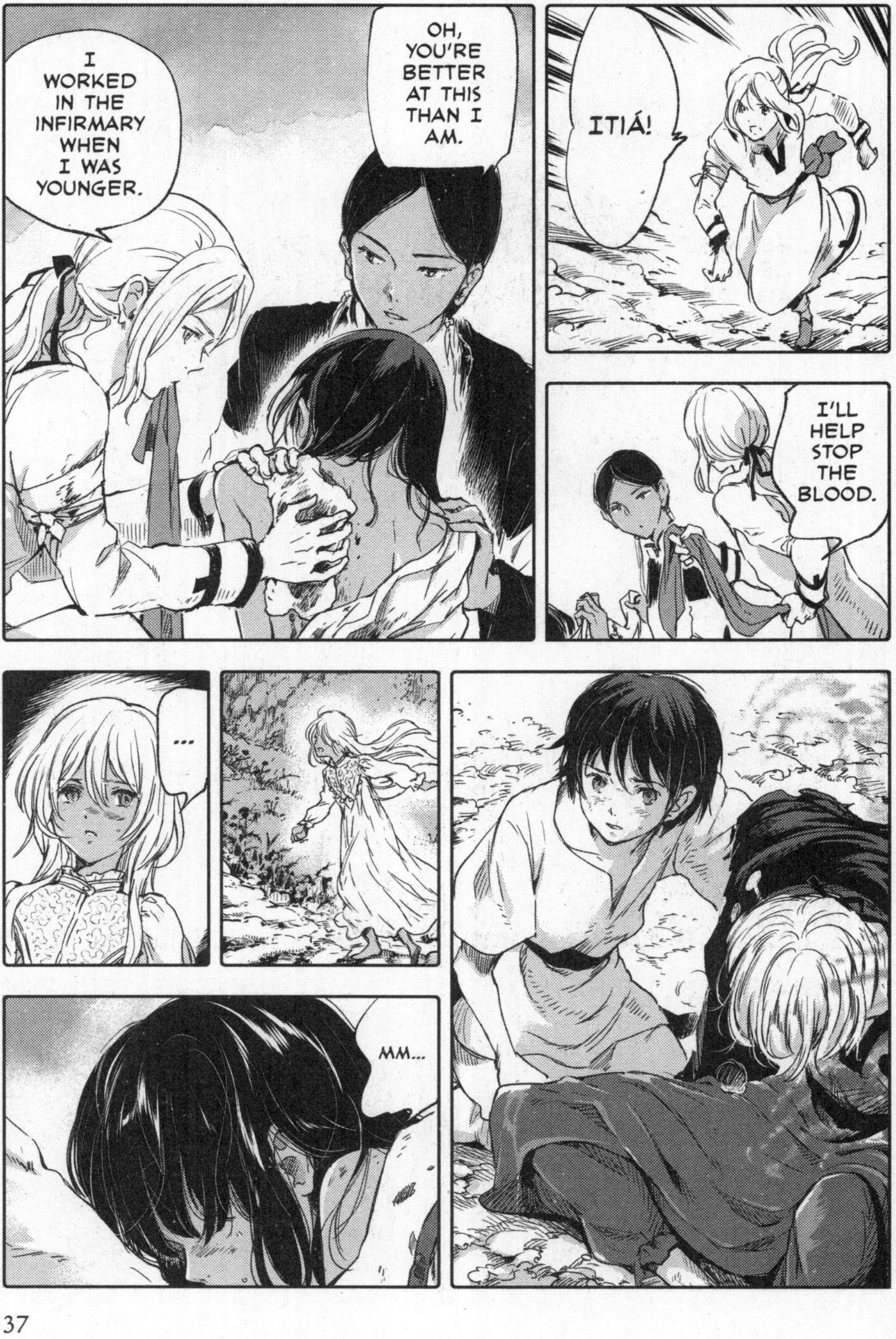
ITIÁ!
I'LL HELP STOP THE BLOOD.
OH, YOU'RE BETTER AT THIS THAN I AM.
I WORKED IN THE INFIRMARY WHEN I WAS YOUNGER.
...
MM...

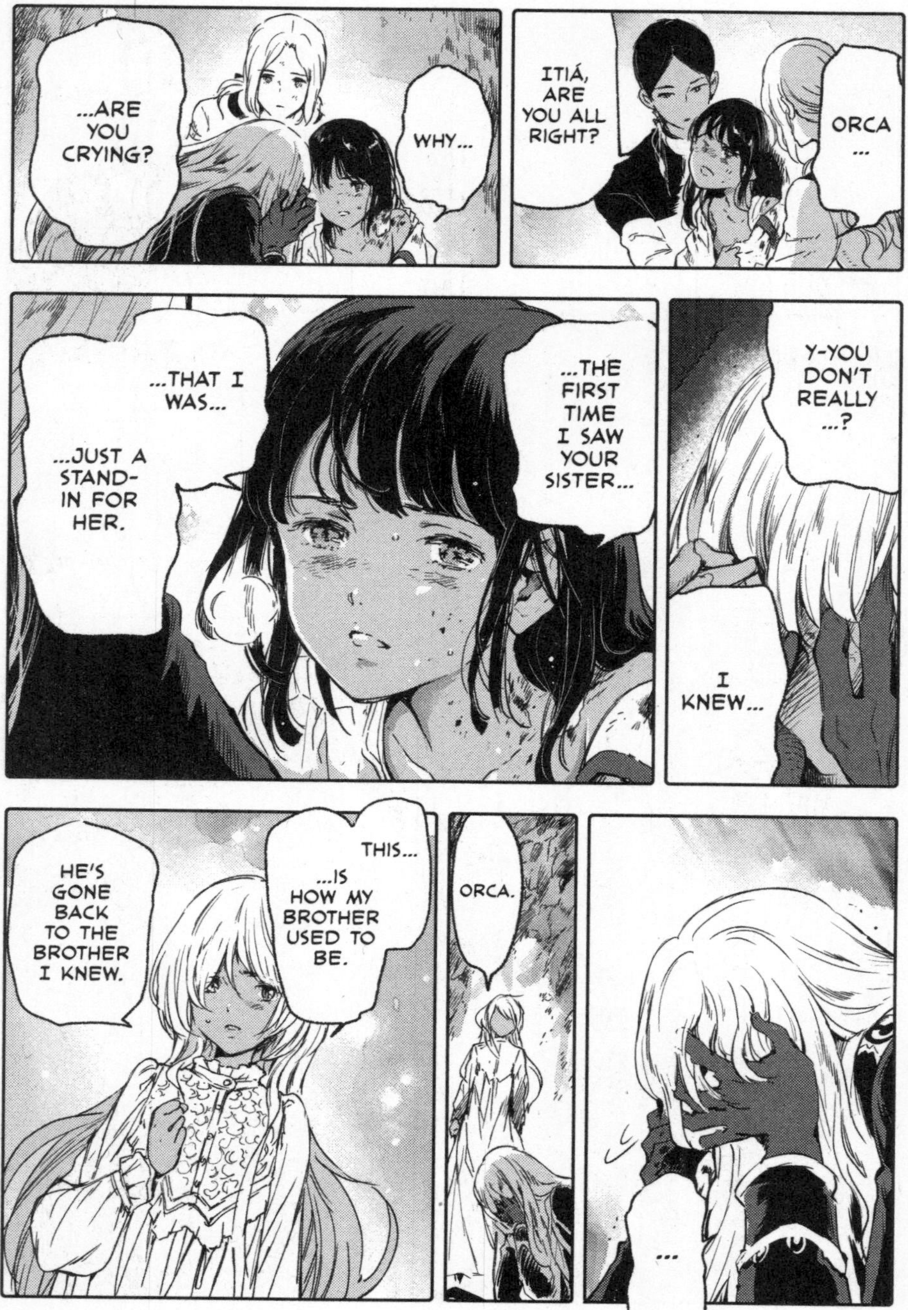
ORCA ...
ITIÁ, ARE YOU ALL RIGHT?
WHY...
...ARE YOU CRYING?
Y-YOU DON'T REALLY ...?
I KNEW...
...THE FIRST TIME I SAW YOUR SISTER...
...THAT I WAS...
...JUST A STAND-IN FOR HER.
...
ORCA.
THIS...
...IS HOW MY BROTHER USED TO BE.
HE'S GONE BACK TO THE BROTHER I KNEW.

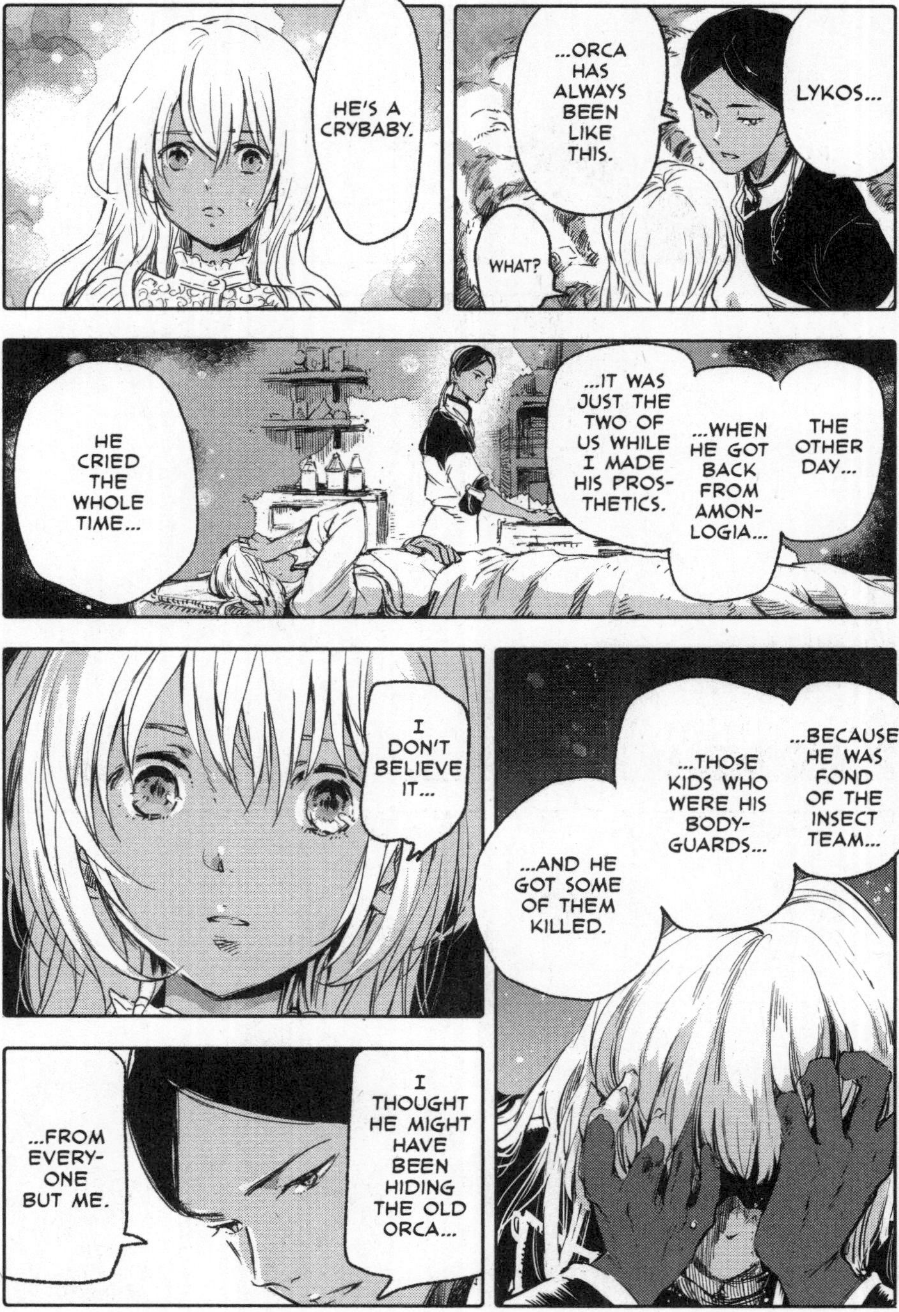
LYKOS...
...ORCA HAS ALWAYS BEEN LIKE THIS.
WHAT?
HE'S A CRYBABY.
THE OTHER DAY...
...WHEN HE GOT BACK FROM AMONLOGIA...
...IT WAS JUST THE TWO OF US WHILE I MADE HIS PROSTHETICS.
HE CRIED THE WHOLE TIME...
...BECAUSE HE WAS FOND OF THE INSECT TEAM...
...THOSE KIDS WHO WERE HIS BODYGUARDS...
...AND HE GOT SOME OF THEM KILLED.
I DON'T BELIEVE IT...
I THOUGHT HE MIGHT HAVE BEEN HIDING THE OLD ORCA...
...FROM EVERYONE BUT ME.

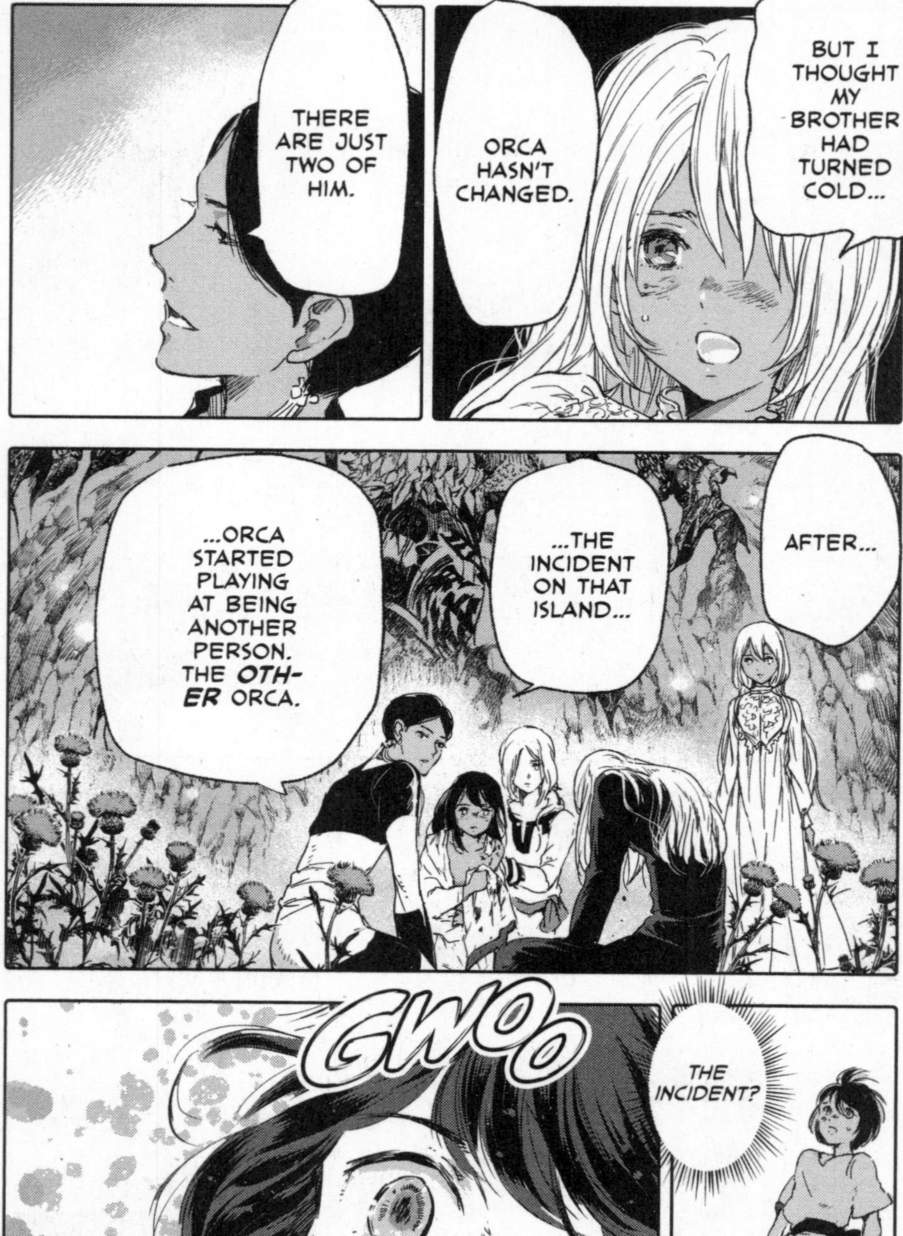
BUT I THOUGHT MY BROTHER HAD TURNED COLD...
ORCA HASN'T CHANGED.
THERE ARE JUST TWO OF HIM.
AFTER...
...THE INCIDENT ON THAT ISLAND...
...ORCA STARTED PLAYING AT BEING ANOTHER PERSON. THE *OTHER* ORCA.
THE INCIDENT?
GWOO

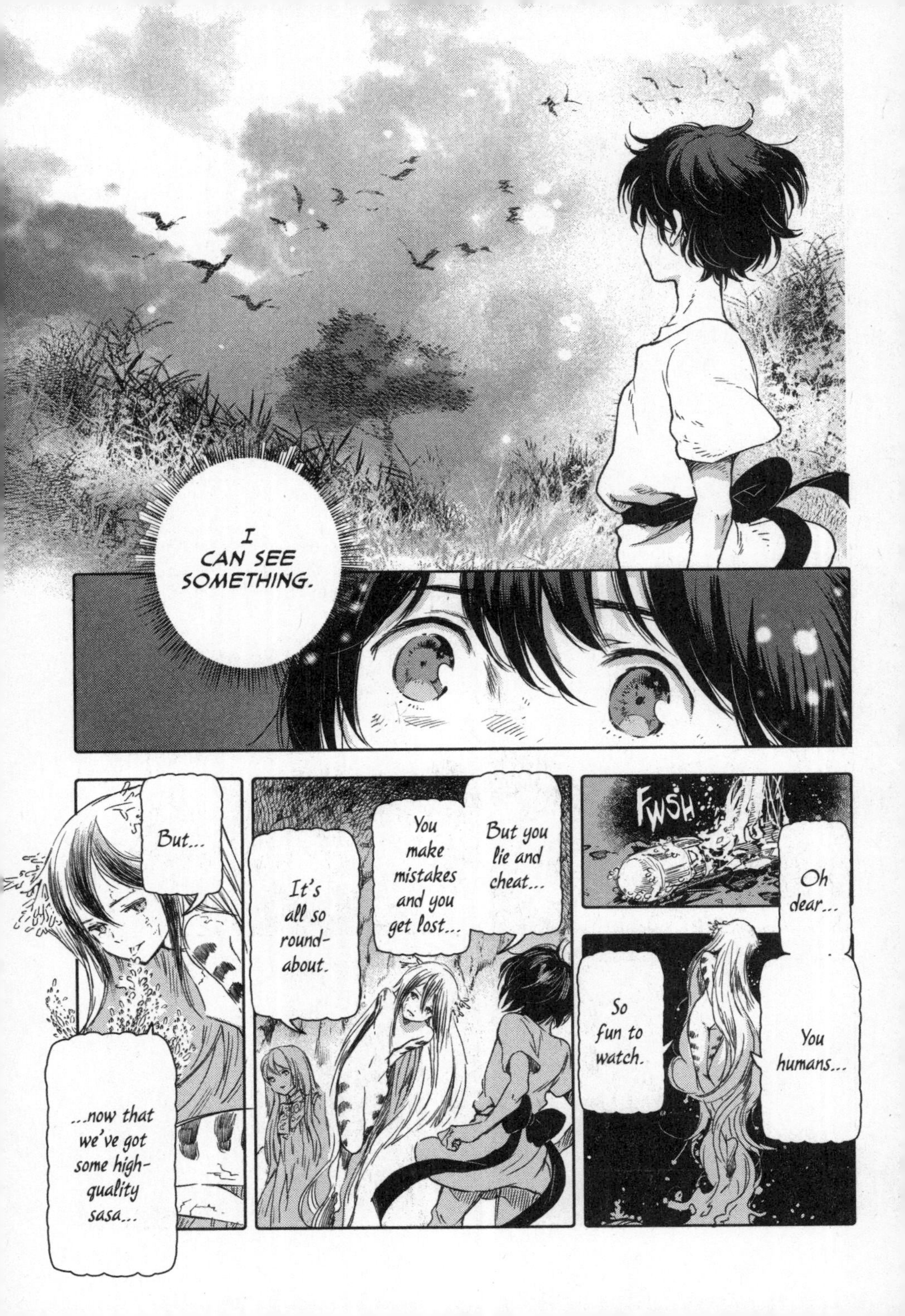
I CAN SEE SOMETHING.
FWSH
Oh dear...
You humans...
So fun to watch.
But you lie and cheat...
You make mistakes and you get lost...
It's all so roundabout.
But...
...now that we've got some high-quality sasa...

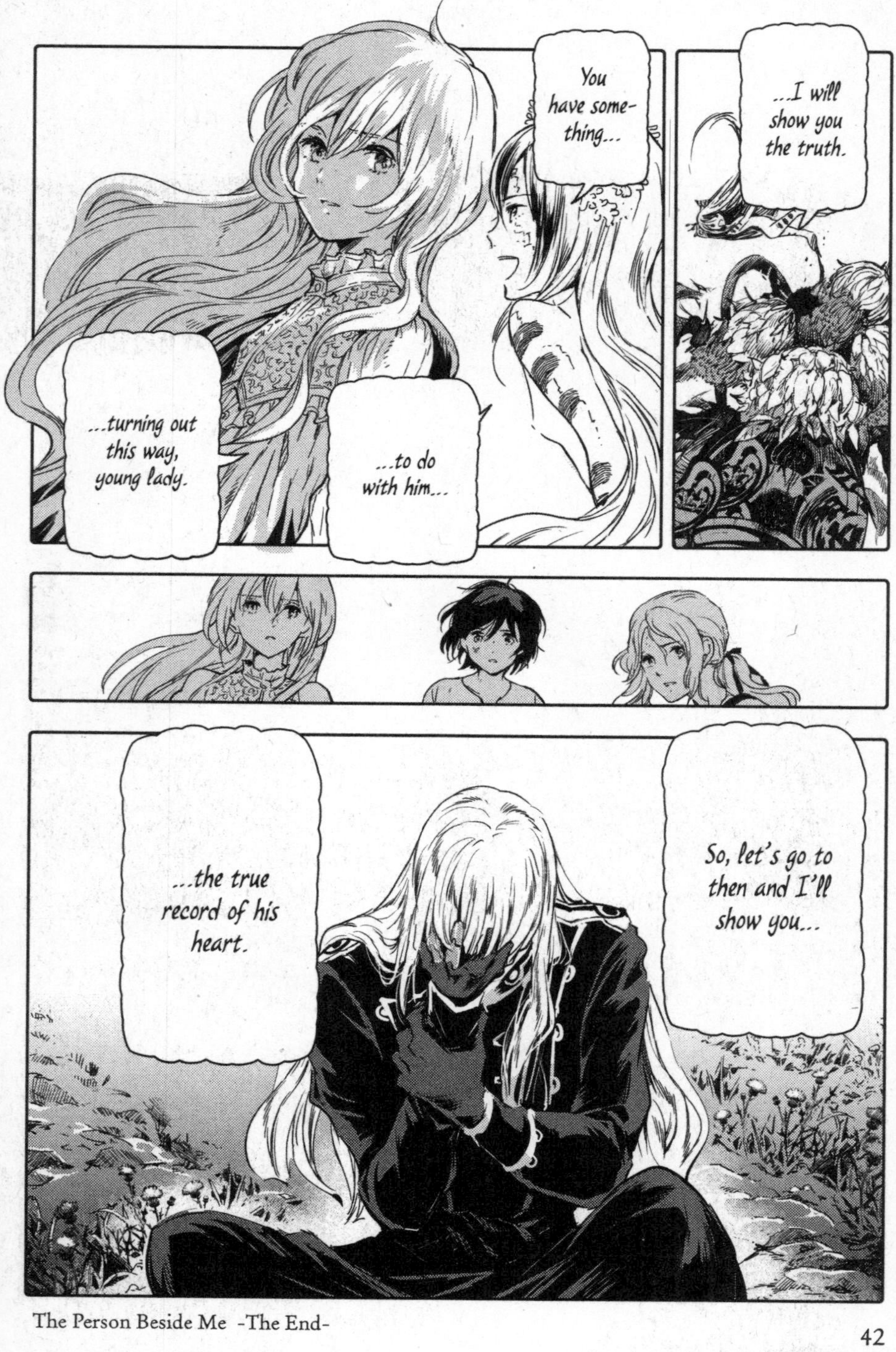
...I will show you the truth.
You have some-thing...
...to do with him...
...turning out this way, young lady.
So, let's go to then and I'll show you...
...the true record of his heart.

The Person Beside Me -The End-

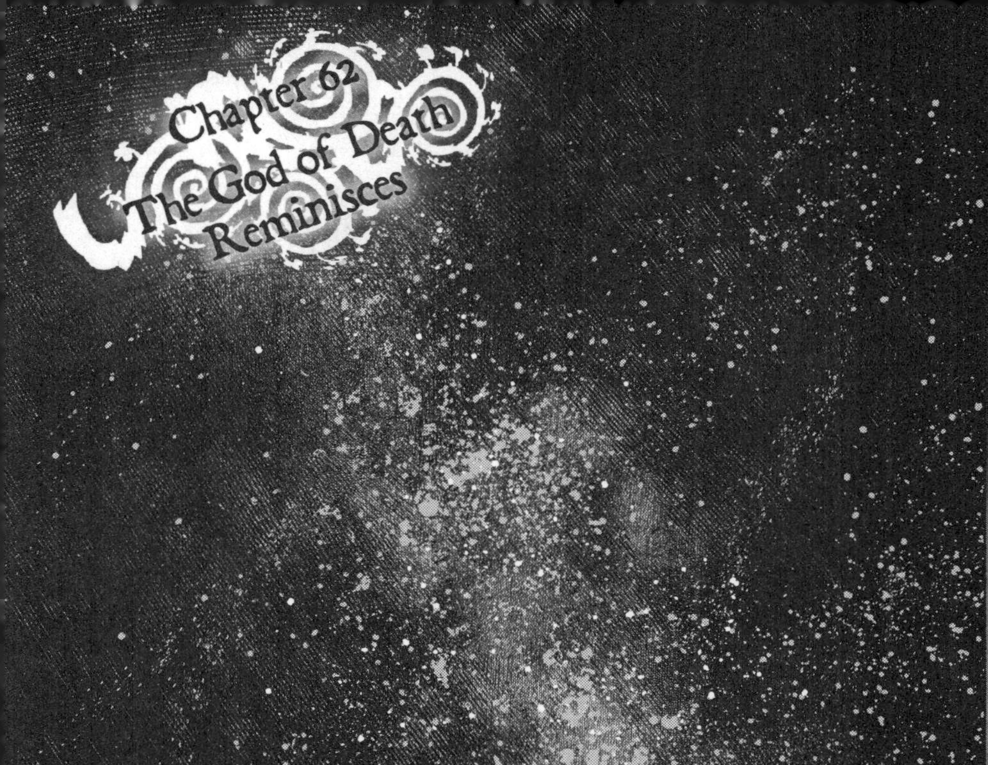
Chapter 62
The God of Death Reminisces
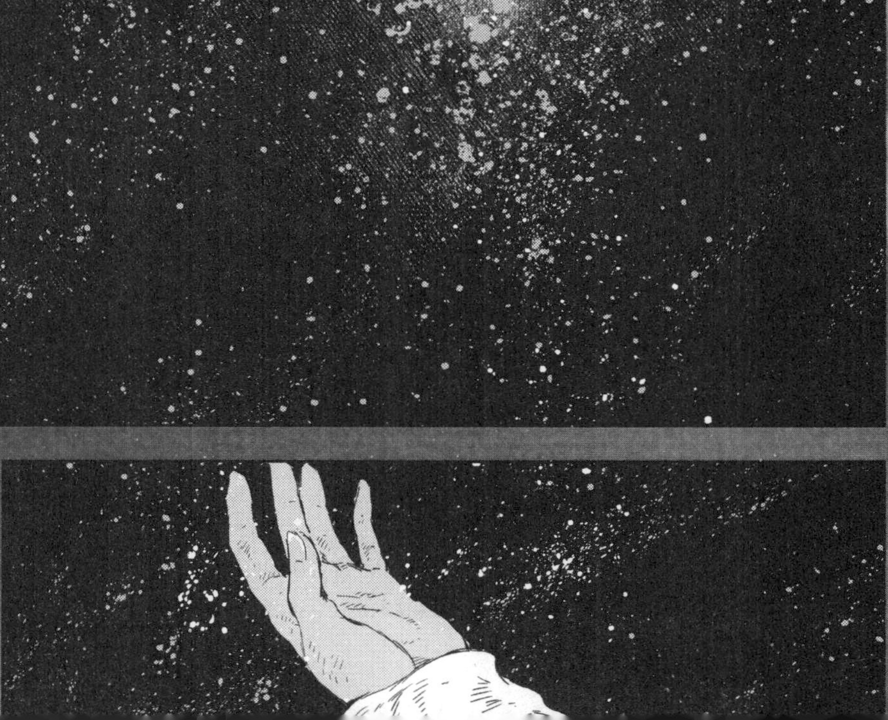

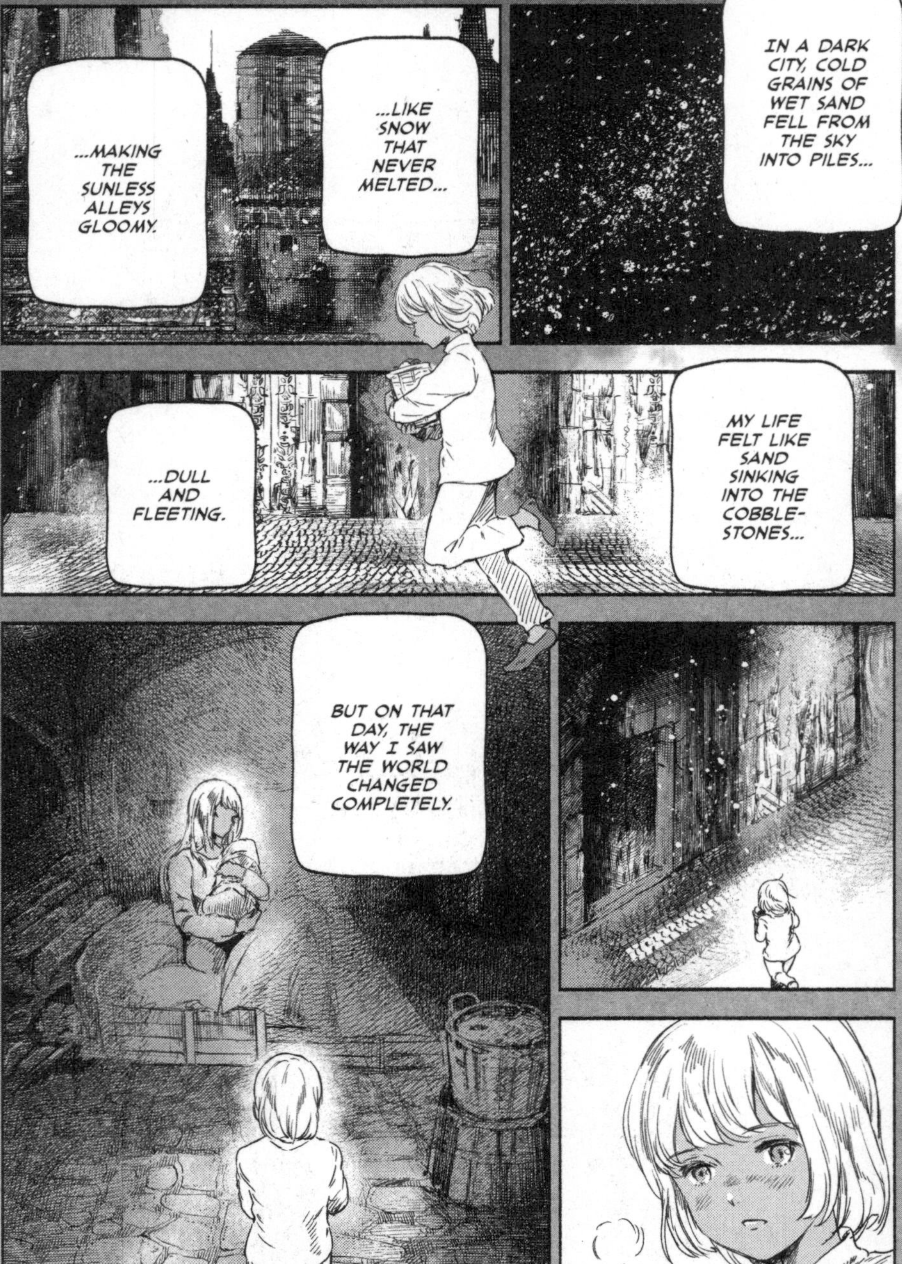
IN A DARK CITY, COLD GRAINS OF WET SAND FELL FROM THE SKY INTO PILES...
...LIKE SNOW THAT NEVER MELTED...
...MAKING THE SUNLESS ALLEYS GLOOMY.
MY LIFE FELT LIKE SAND SINKING INTO THE COBBLE-STONES...
...DULL AND FLEETING.
BUT ON THAT DAY, THE WAY I SAW THE WORLD CHANGED COMPLETELY.

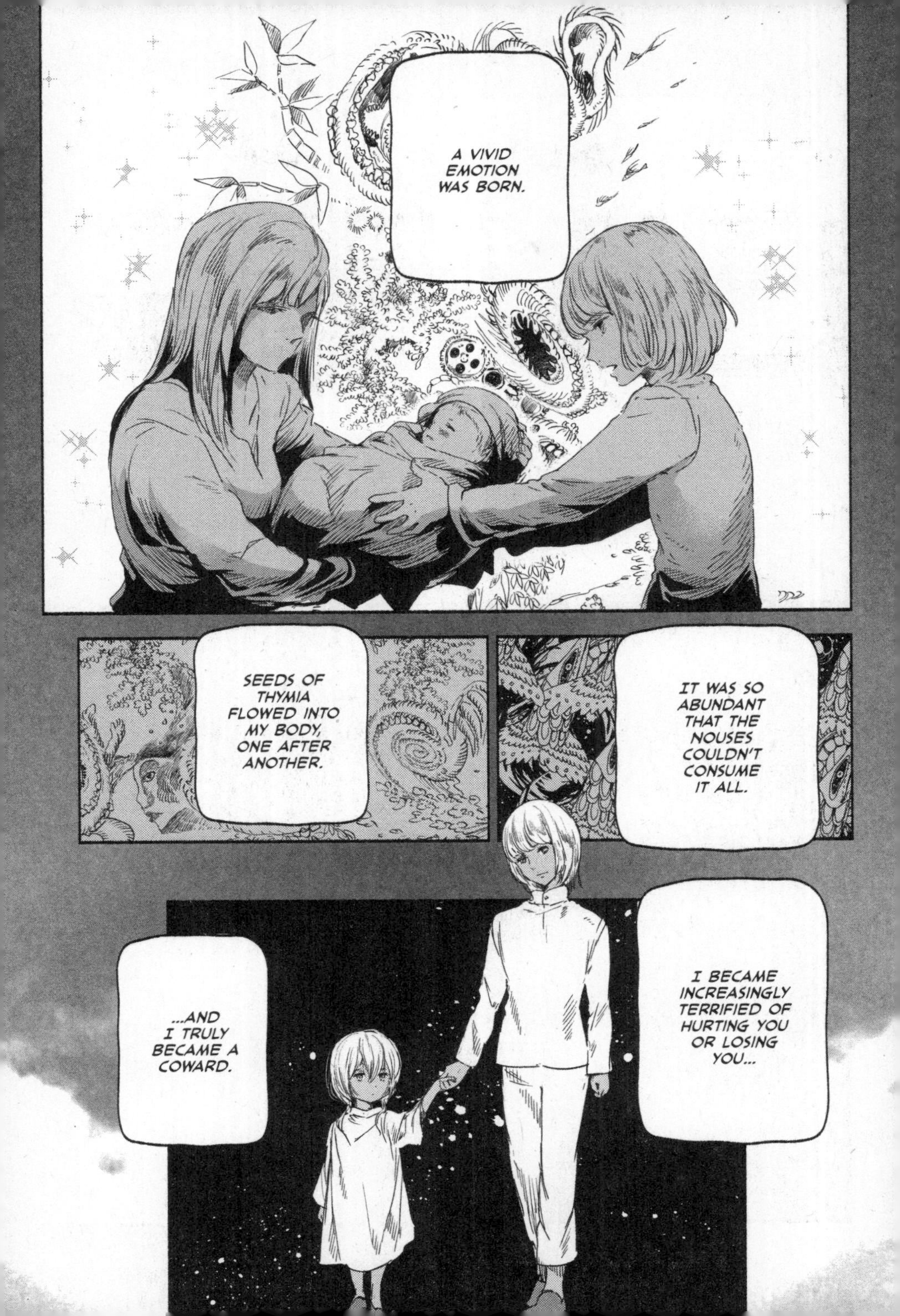
A VIVID EMOTION WAS BORN.
IT WAS SO ABUNDANT THAT THE NOUSES COULDN'T CONSUME IT ALL.
SEEDS OF THYMIA FLOWED INTO MY BODY, ONE AFTER ANOTHER.
I BECAME INCREASINGLY TERRIFIED OF HURTING YOU OR LOSING YOU...
...AND I TRULY BECAME A COWARD.

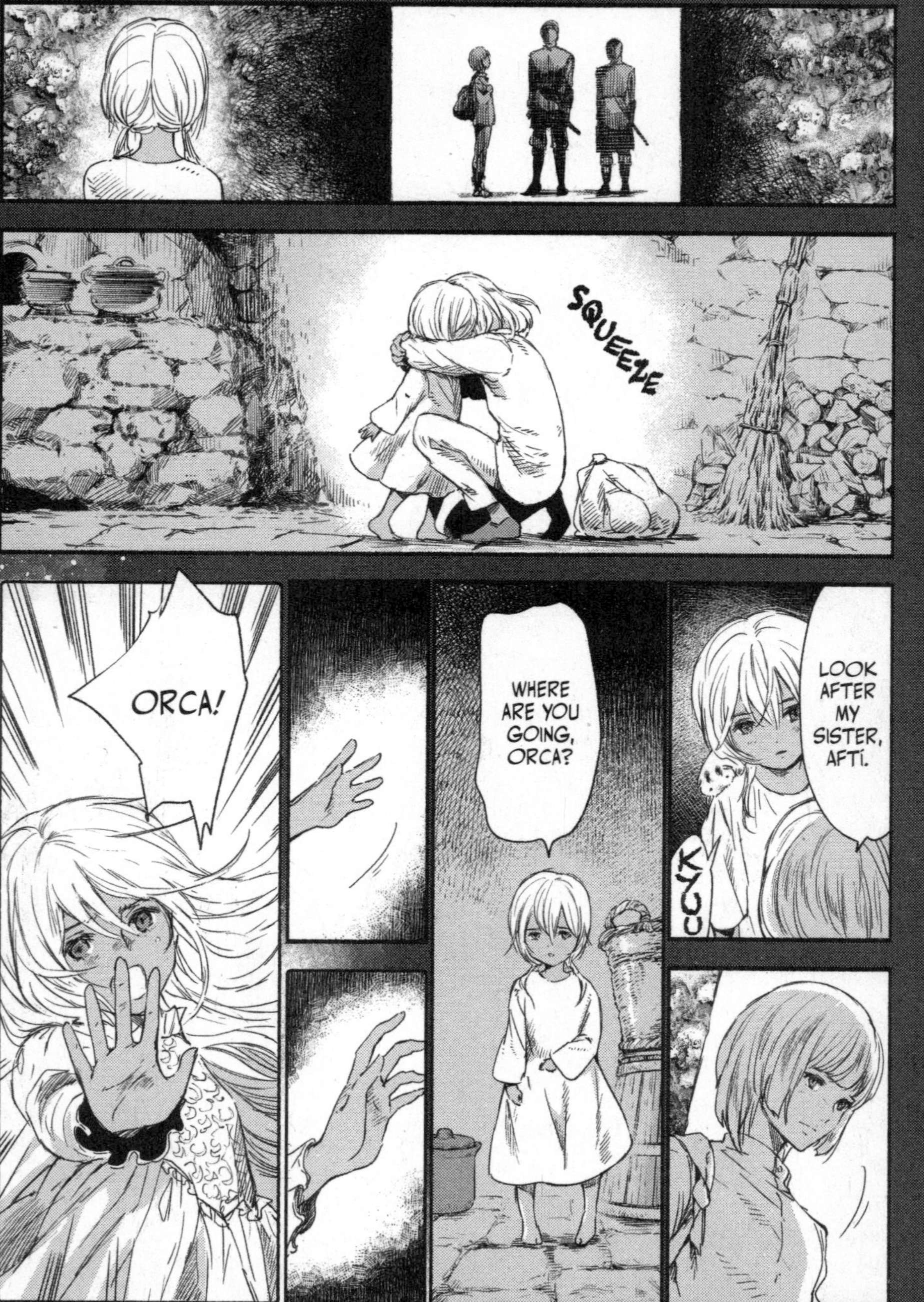
SQUEEZE
LOOK AFTER MY SISTER, AFTI.
WHERE ARE YOU GOING, ORCA?
ORCA!

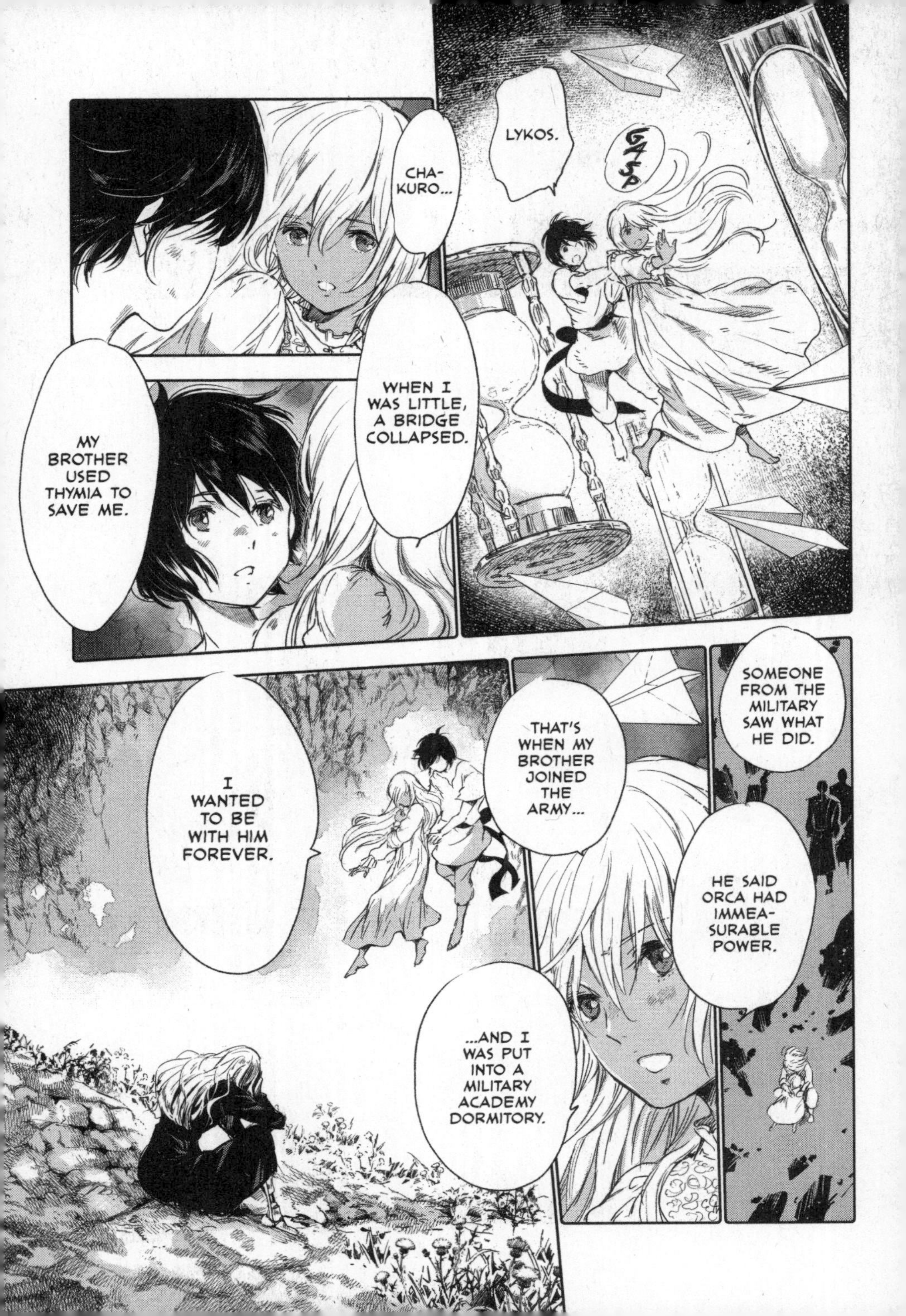
LYKOS.
GATSA
CHA-KURO...
WHEN I WAS LITTLE, A BRIDGE COLLAPSED.
MY BROTHER USED THYMIA TO SAVE ME.
SOMEONE FROM THE MILITARY SAW WHAT HE DID.
HE SAID ORCA HAD IMMEA-SURABLE POWER.
THAT'S WHEN MY BROTHER JOINED THE ARMY...
...AND I WAS PUT INTO A MILITARY ACADEMY DORMITORY.
I WANTED TO BE WITH HIM FOREVER.

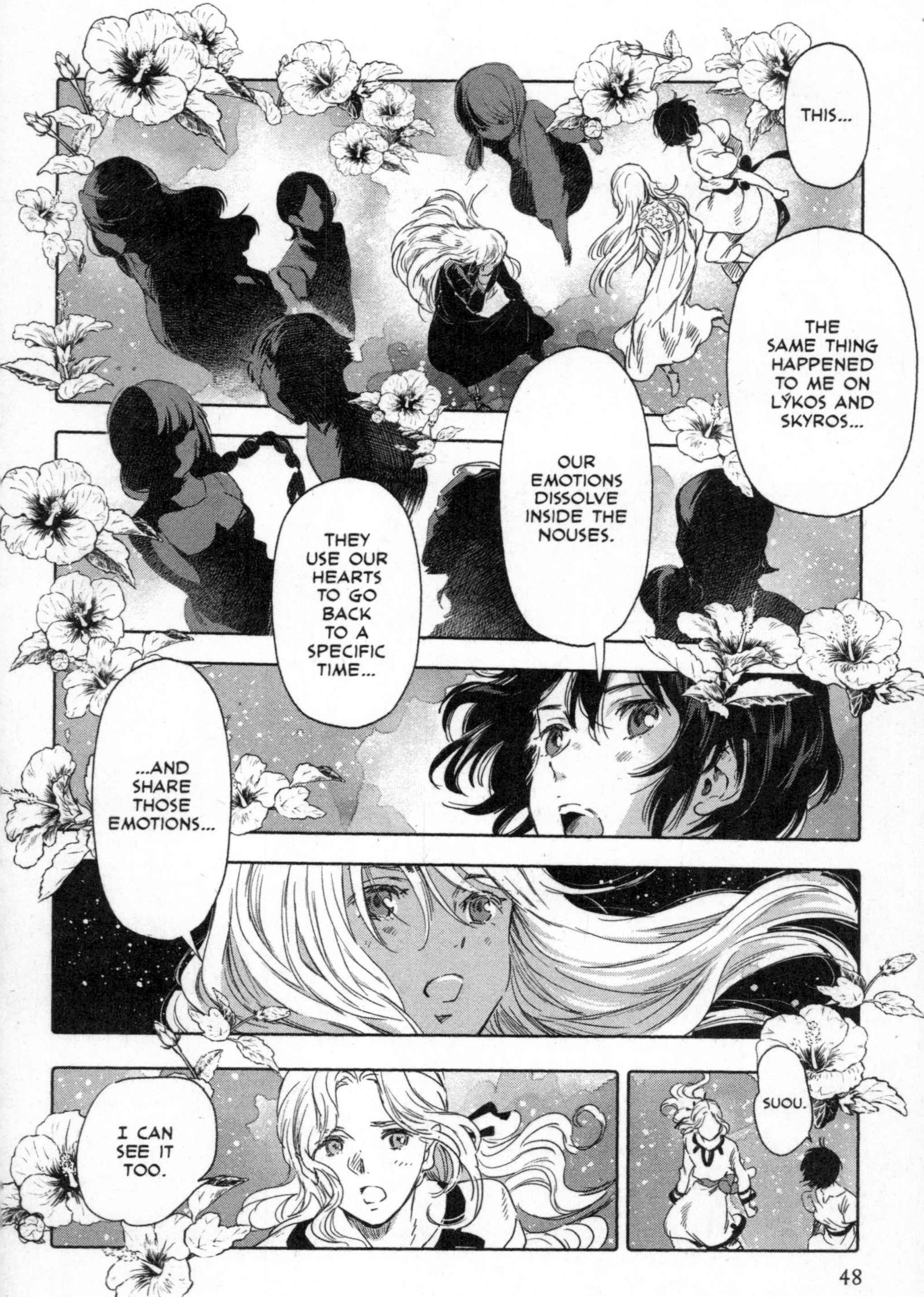
THIS...
THE SAME THING HAPPENED TO ME ON LÝKOS AND SKYROS...
OUR EMOTIONS DISSOLVE INSIDE THE NOUSES.
THEY USE OUR HEARTS TO GO BACK TO A SPECIFIC TIME...
...AND SHARE THOSE EMOTIONS...
SUOU.
I CAN SEE IT TOO.

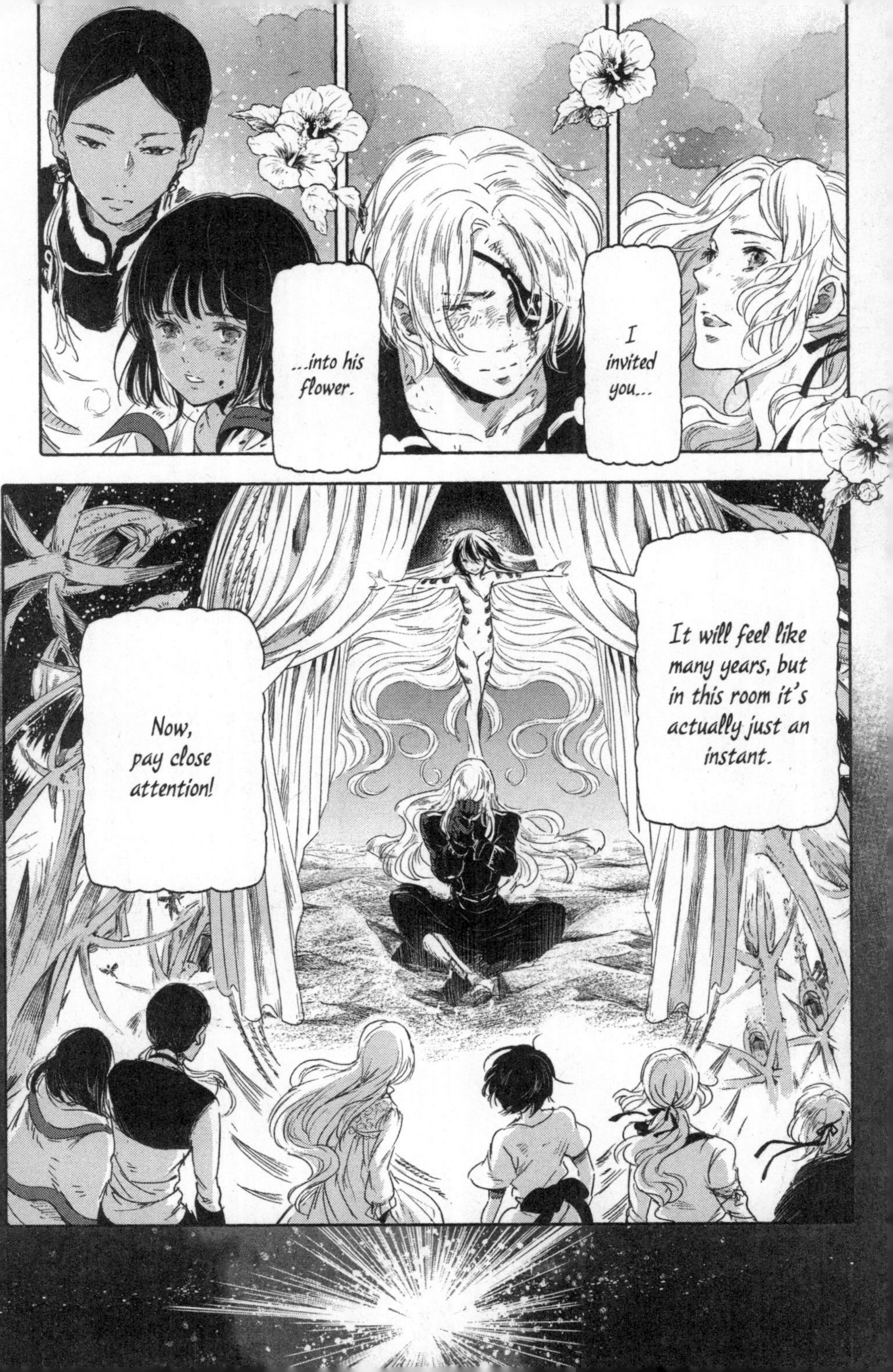
I invited you...
...into his flower.
It will feel like many years, but in this room it's actually just an instant.
Now, pay close attention!

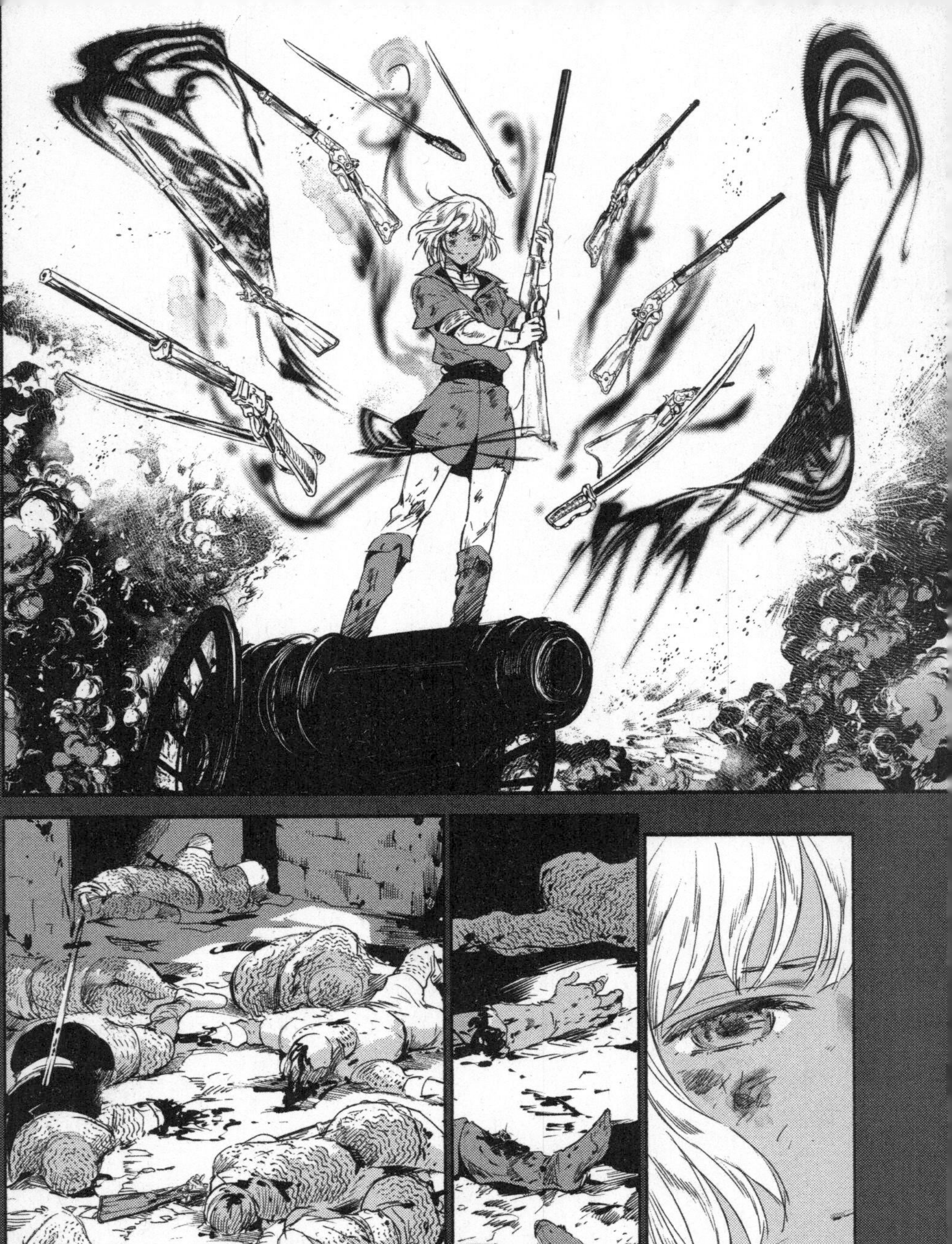

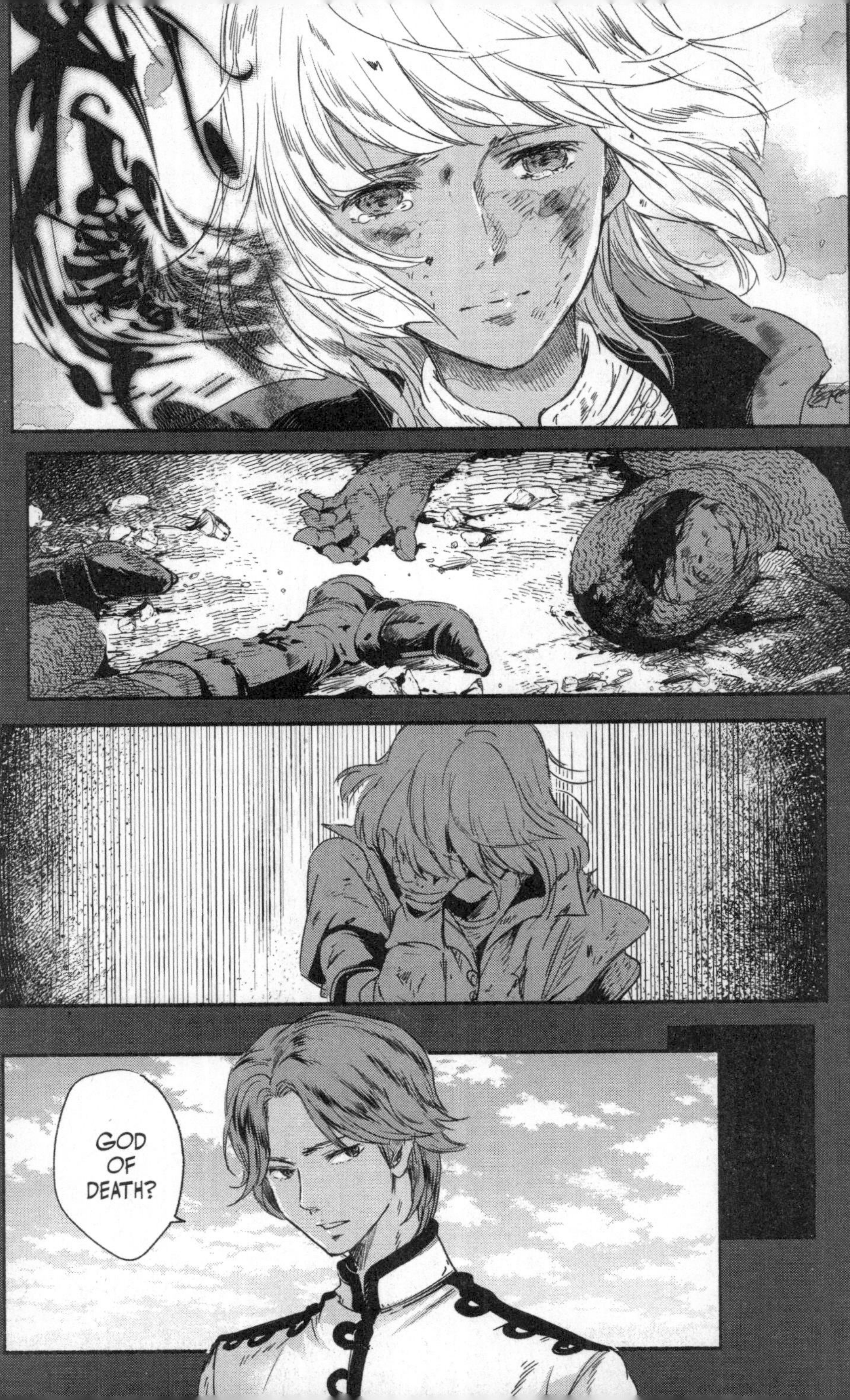
GOD OF DEATH?

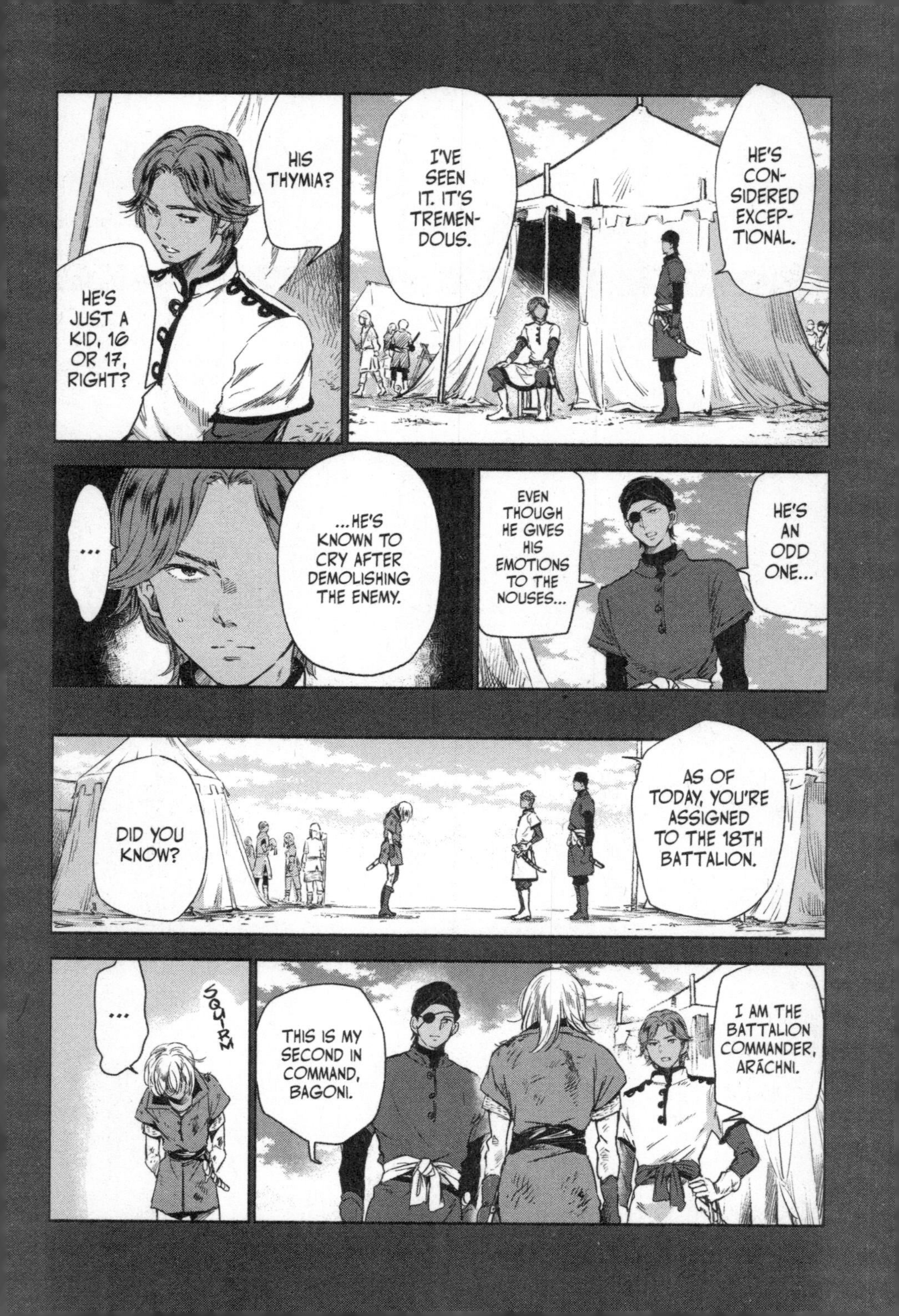

HE'S CONSIDERED EXCEPTIONAL.
I'VE SEEN IT. IT'S TREMENDOUS.
HIS THYMIA?
HE'S JUST A KID, 16 OR 17, RIGHT?
HE'S AN ODD ONE...
EVEN THOUGH HE GIVES HIS EMOTIONS TO THE NOUSES...
...HE'S KNOWN TO CRY AFTER DEMOLISHING THE ENEMY.
...
AS OF TODAY, YOU'RE ASSIGNED TO THE 18TH BATTALION.
DID YOU KNOW?
I AM THE BATTALION COMMANDER, ARĀCHNI.
THIS IS MY SECOND IN COMMAND, BAGONI.
SQUIRM
...

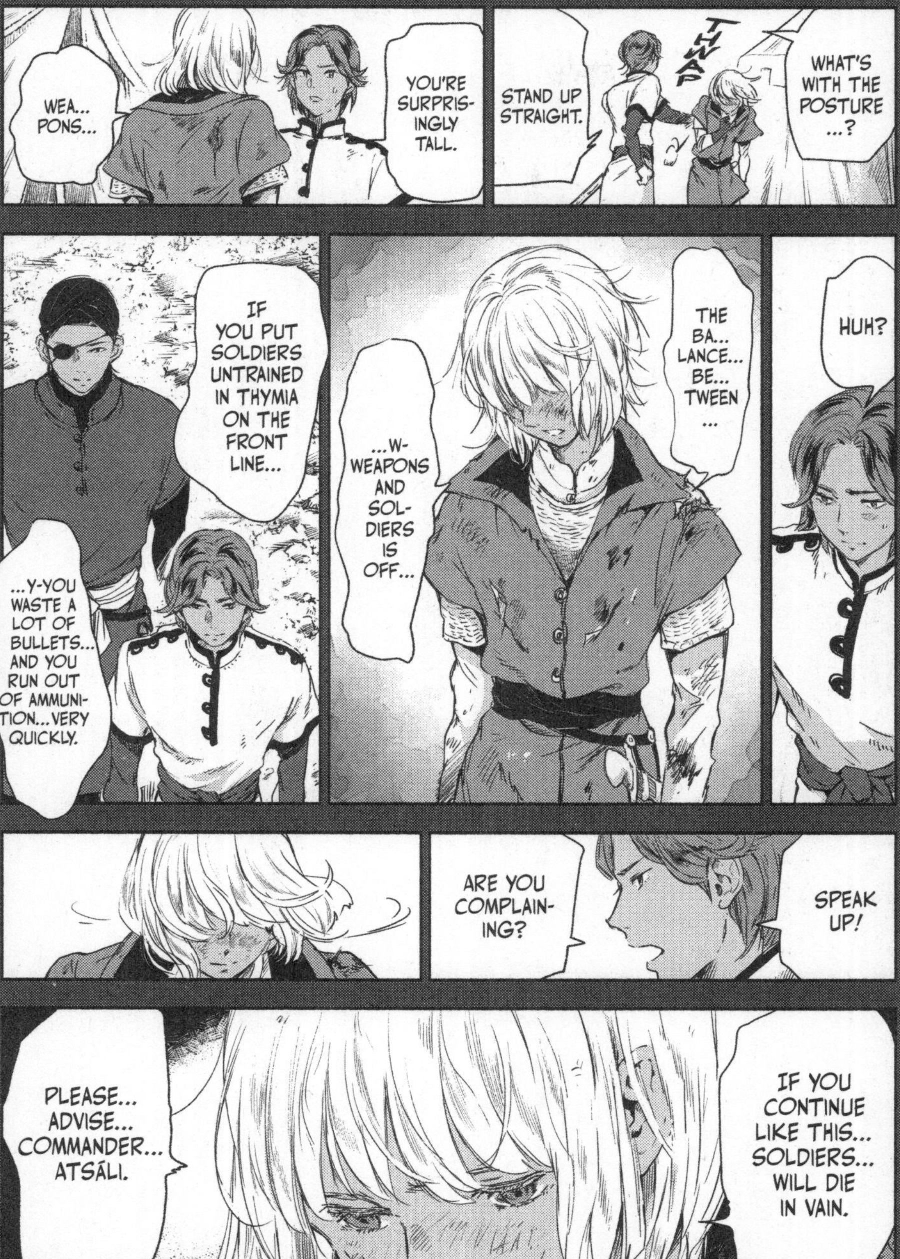
WHAT'S WITH THE POSTURE ...?
THWAP
STAND UP STRAIGHT.
YOU'RE SURPRIS-INGLY TALL.
WEA... PONS...
HUH?
THE BA... LANCE... BE... TWEEN ...
...W-WEAPONS AND SOL-DIERS IS OFF...
IF YOU PUT SOLDIERS UNTRAINED IN THYMIA ON THE FRONT LINE...
...Y-YOU WASTE A LOT OF BULLETS... AND YOU RUN OUT OF AMMUNI-TION...VERY QUICKLY.
SPEAK UP!
ARE YOU COMPLAIN-ING?
IF YOU CONTINUE LIKE THIS... SOLDIERS... WILL DIE IN VAIN.
PLEASE... ADVISE... COMMANDER... ATSÁLI.

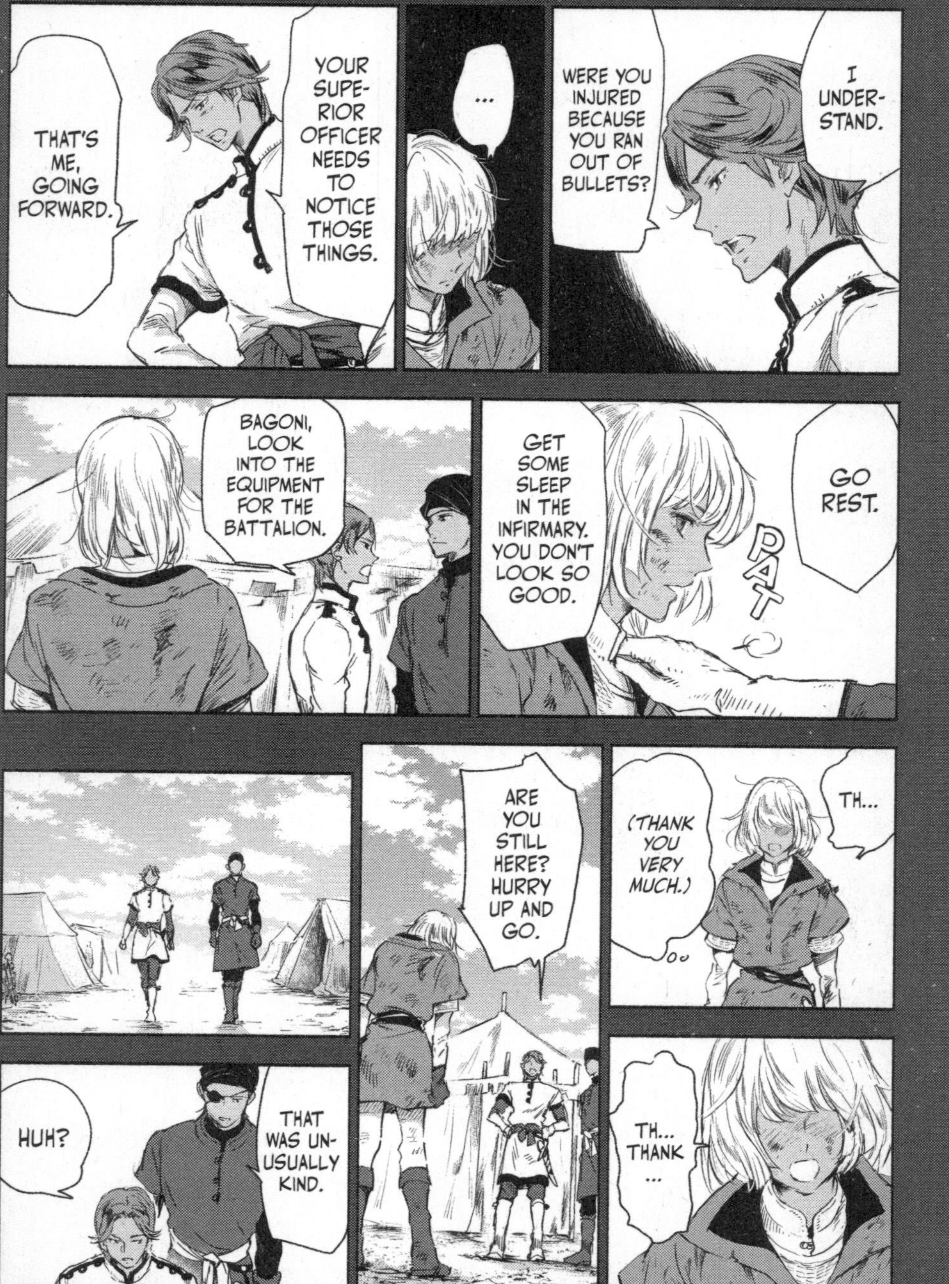
I UNDER-STAND.
WERE YOU INJURED BECAUSE YOU RAN OUT OF BULLETS?
...
YOUR SUPE-RIOR OFFICER NEEDS TO NOTICE THOSE THINGS.
THAT'S ME, GOING FORWARD.
GO REST.
PAT
GET SOME SLEEP IN THE INFIRMARY. YOU DON'T LOOK SO GOOD.
BAGONI, LOOK INTO THE EQUIPMENT FOR THE BATTALION.
TH...
(THANK YOU VERY MUCH.)
TH... THANK ...
ARE YOU STILL HERE? HURRY UP AND GO.
THAT WAS UN-USUALLY KIND.
HUH?

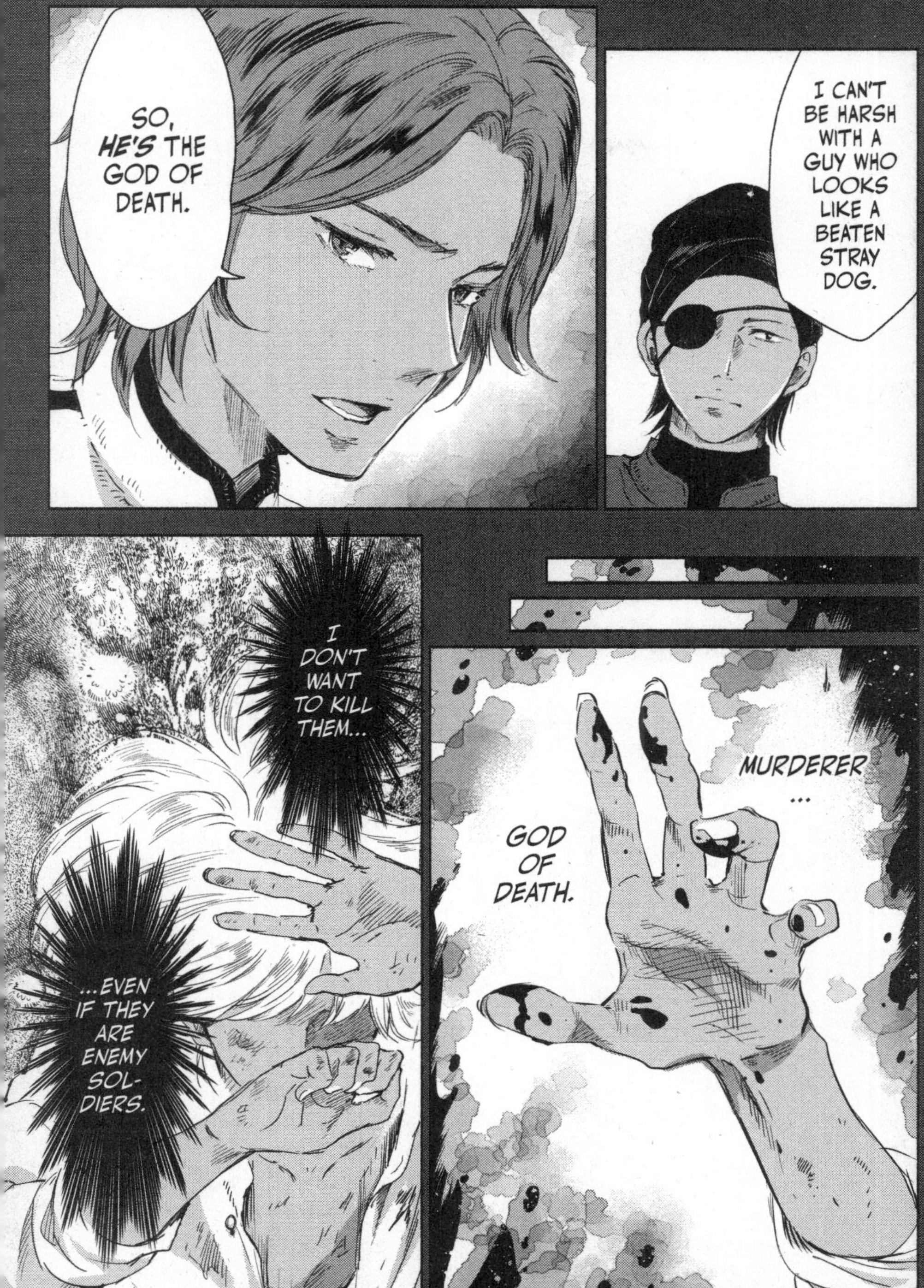
I CAN'T BE HARSH WITH A GUY WHO LOOKS LIKE A BEATEN STRAY DOG.
SO, HE'S THE GOD OF DEATH.
MURDERER ...
GOD OF DEATH.
I DON'T WANT TO KILL THEM...
...EVEN IF THEY ARE ENEMY SOL-DIERS.

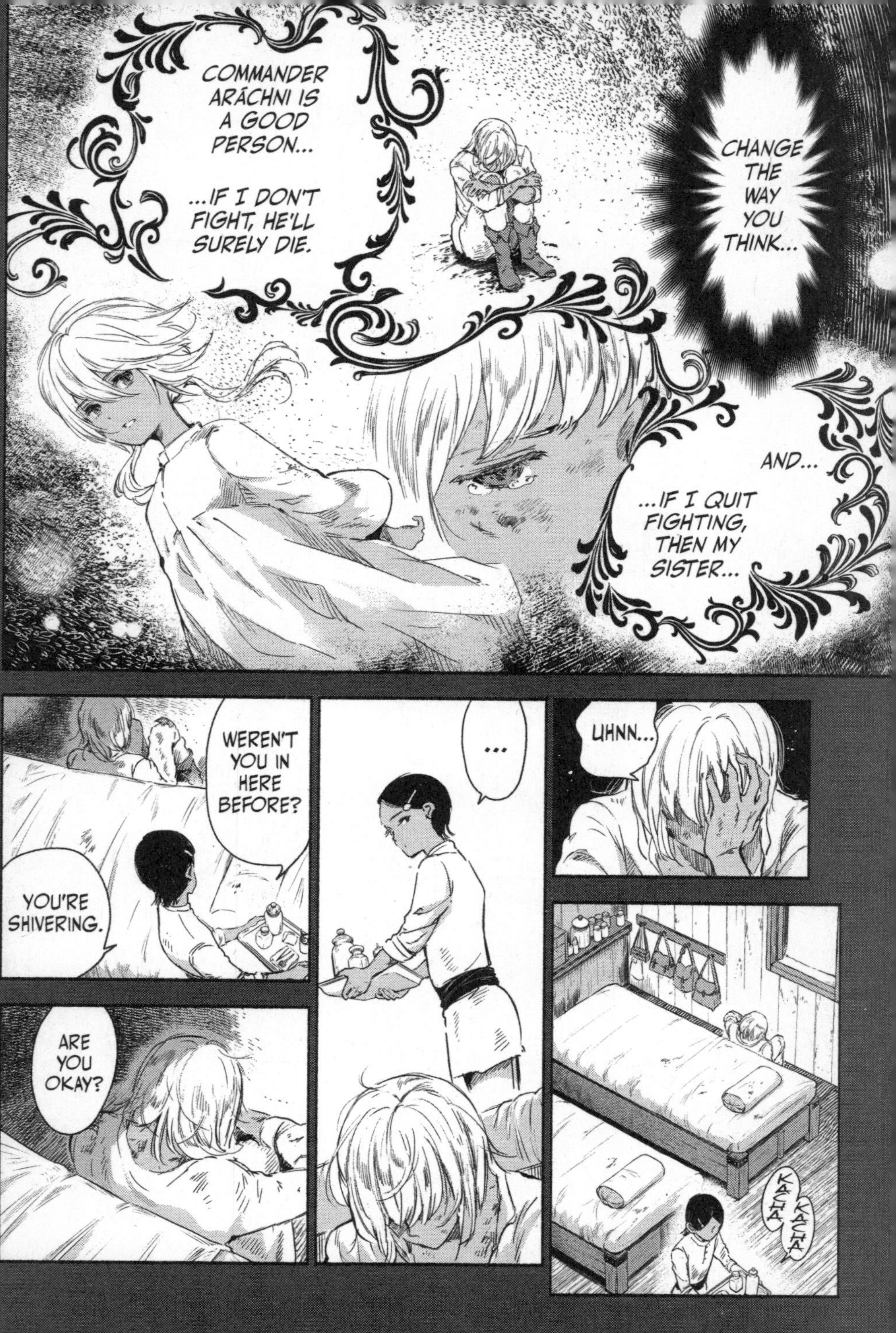
CHANGE THE WAY YOU THINK...
COMMANDER ARĀCHNI IS A GOOD PERSON...
...IF I DON'T FIGHT, HE'LL SURELY DIE.
AND...
...IF I QUIT FIGHTING, THEN MY SISTER...
UHNN...
KACHA KACHA
...
WEREN'T YOU IN HERE BEFORE?
YOU'RE SHIVERING.
ARE YOU OKAY?
...

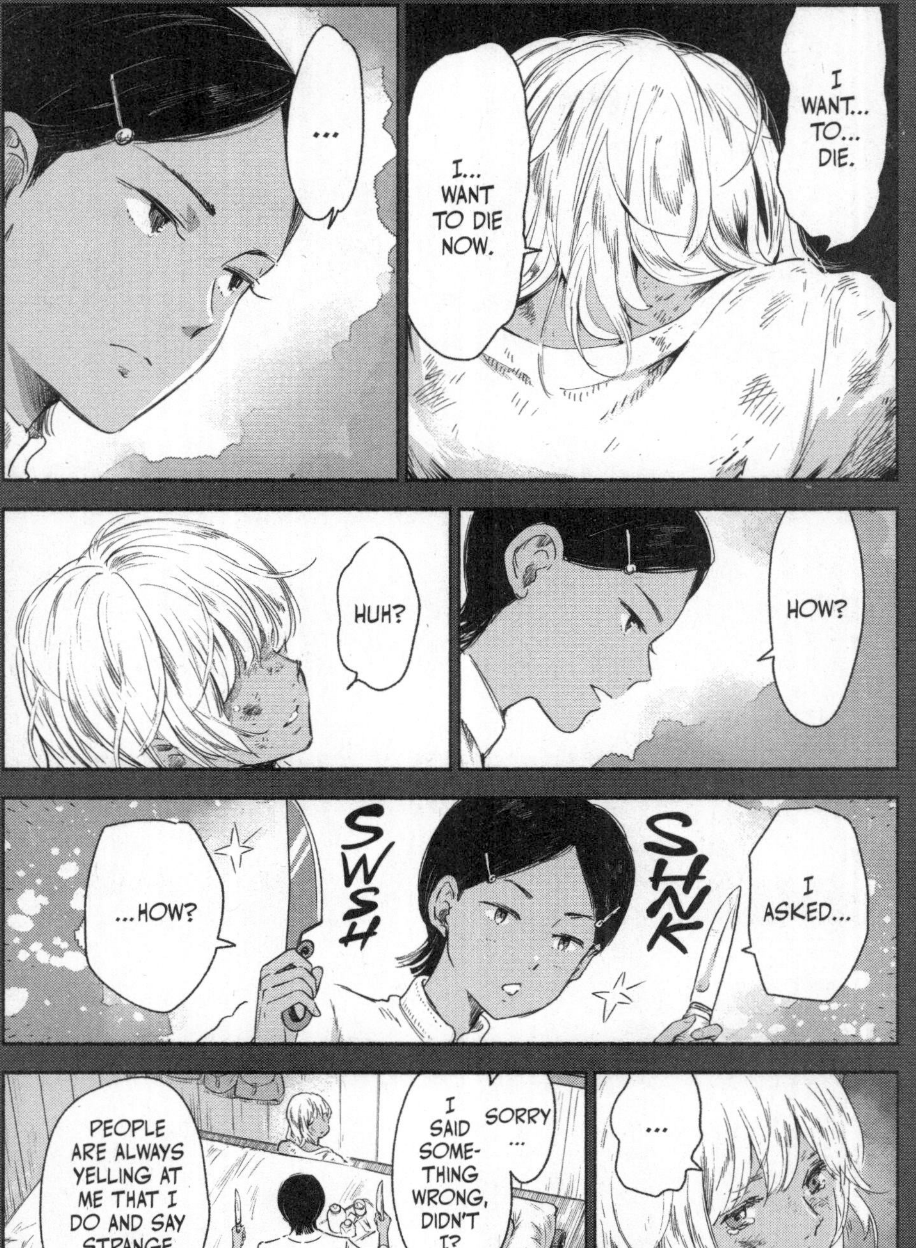
I WANT... TO... DIE.
I... WANT TO DIE NOW.
...
HOW?
HUH?
I ASKED...
SHNK
SWSH
...HOW?
...
SORRY...
I SAID SOME-THING WRONG, DIDN'T I?
PEOPLE ARE ALWAYS YELLING AT ME THAT I DO AND SAY STRANGE THINGS.

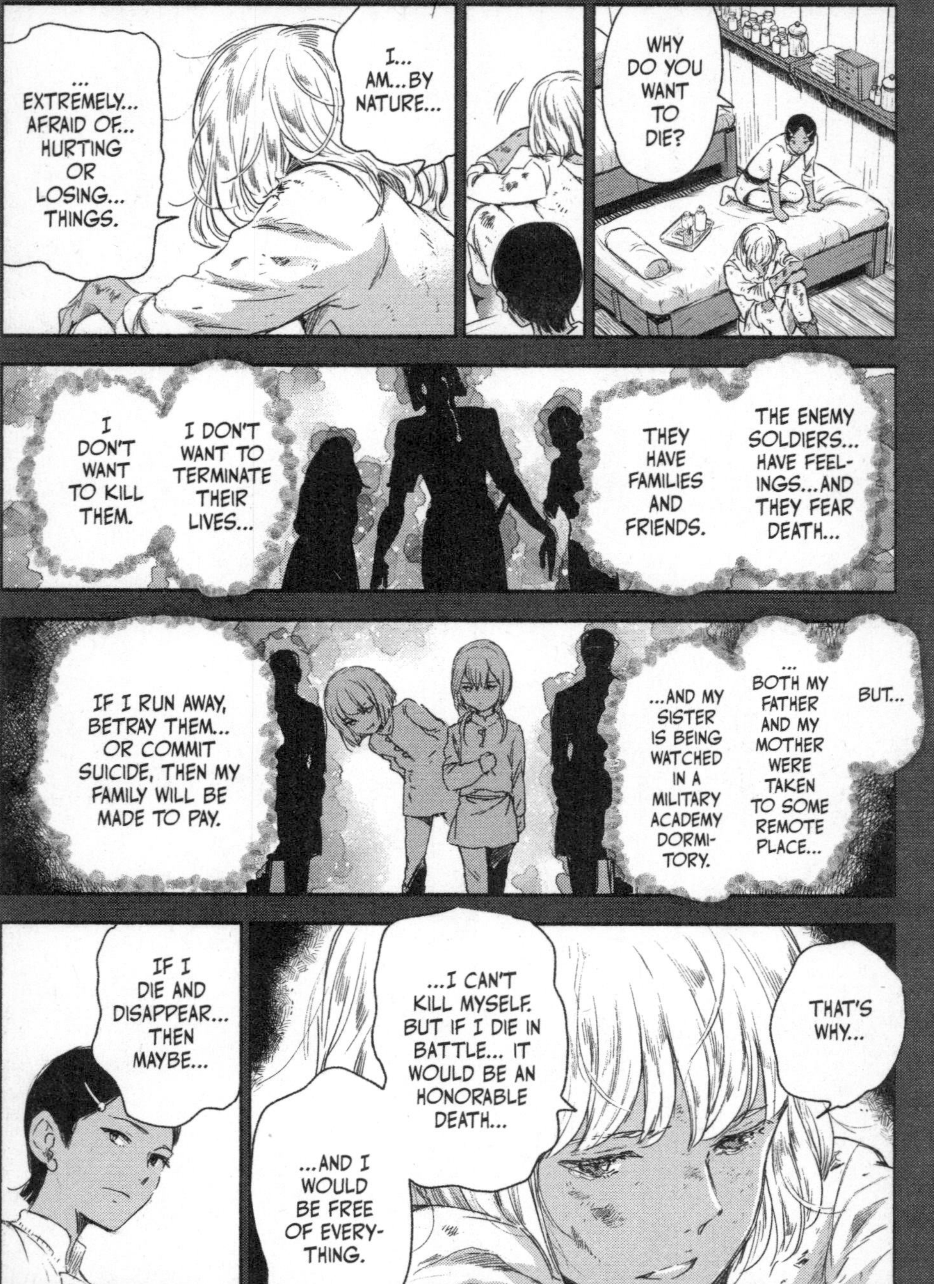
WHY DO YOU WANT TO DIE?
I... AM...BY NATURE...
... EXTREMELY... AFRAID OF... HURTING OR LOSING... THINGS.
THE ENEMY SOLDIERS... HAVE FEEL-INGS...AND THEY FEAR DEATH...
THEY HAVE FAMILIES AND FRIENDS.
I DON'T WANT TO TERMINATE THEIR LIVES...
I DON'T WANT TO KILL THEM.
BUT...
... BOTH MY FATHER AND MY MOTHER WERE TAKEN TO SOME REMOTE PLACE...
...AND MY SISTER IS BEING WATCHED IN A MILITARY ACADEMY DORMI-TORY.
IF I RUN AWAY, BETRAY THEM... OR COMMIT SUICIDE, THEN MY FAMILY WILL BE MADE TO PAY.
THAT'S WHY...
...I CAN'T KILL MYSELF. BUT IF I DIE IN BATTLE... IT WOULD BE AN HONORABLE DEATH...
...AND I WOULD BE FREE OF EVERY-THING.
IF I DIE AND DISAPPEAR... THEN MAYBE...

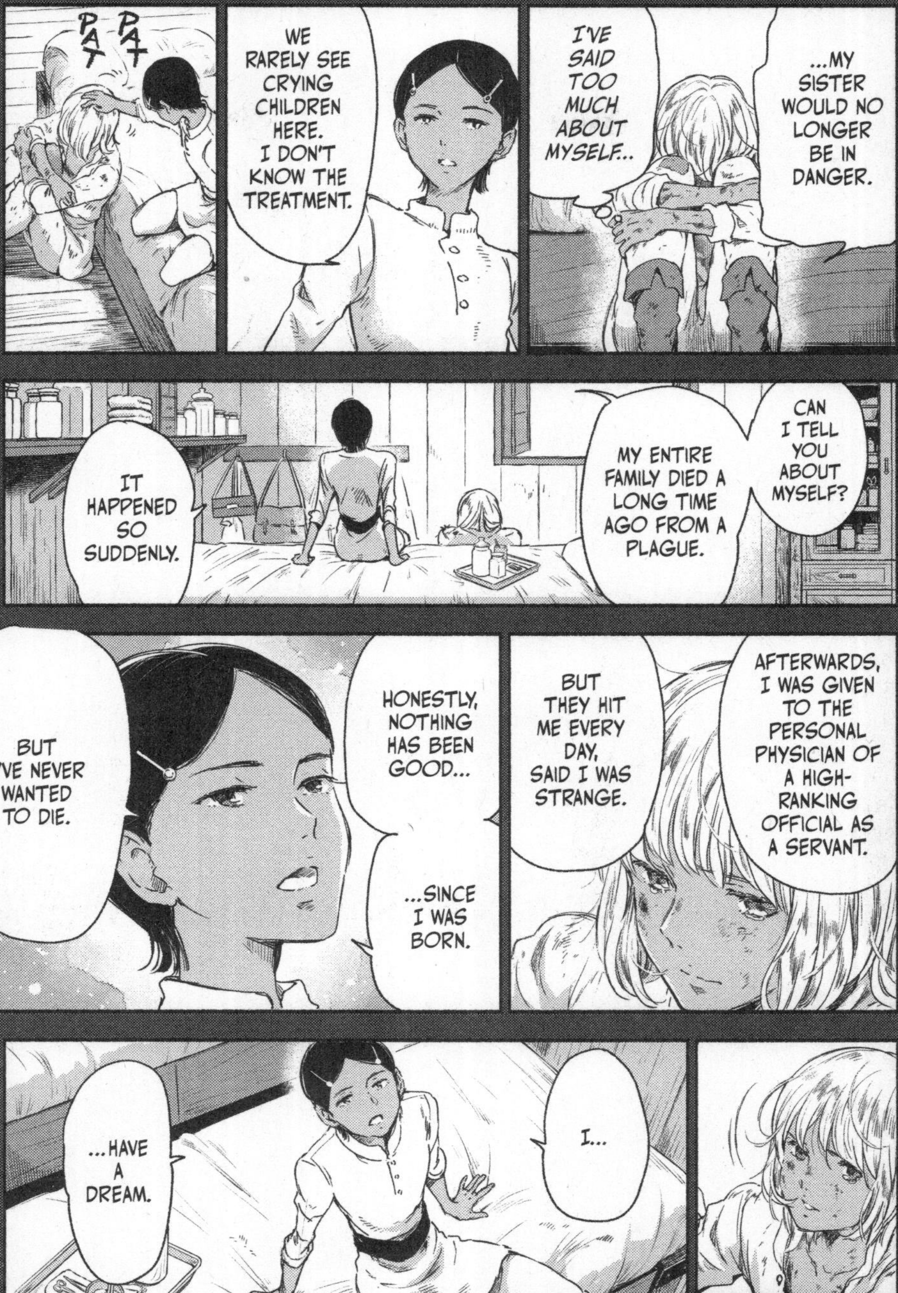
...MY SISTER WOULD NO LONGER BE IN DANGER.
I'VE SAID TOO MUCH ABOUT MYSELF...
WE RARELY SEE CRYING CHILDREN HERE. I DON'T KNOW THE TREATMENT.
PAT PAT
CAN I TELL YOU ABOUT MYSELF?
MY ENTIRE FAMILY DIED A LONG TIME AGO FROM A PLAGUE.
IT HAPPENED SO SUDDENLY.
AFTERWARDS, I WAS GIVEN TO THE PERSONAL PHYSICIAN OF A HIGH-RANKING OFFICIAL AS A SERVANT.
BUT THEY HIT ME EVERY DAY, SAID I WAS STRANGE.
HONESTLY, NOTHING HAS BEEN GOOD...
...SINCE I WAS BORN.
BUT I'VE NEVER WANTED TO DIE.
I...
...HAVE A DREAM.

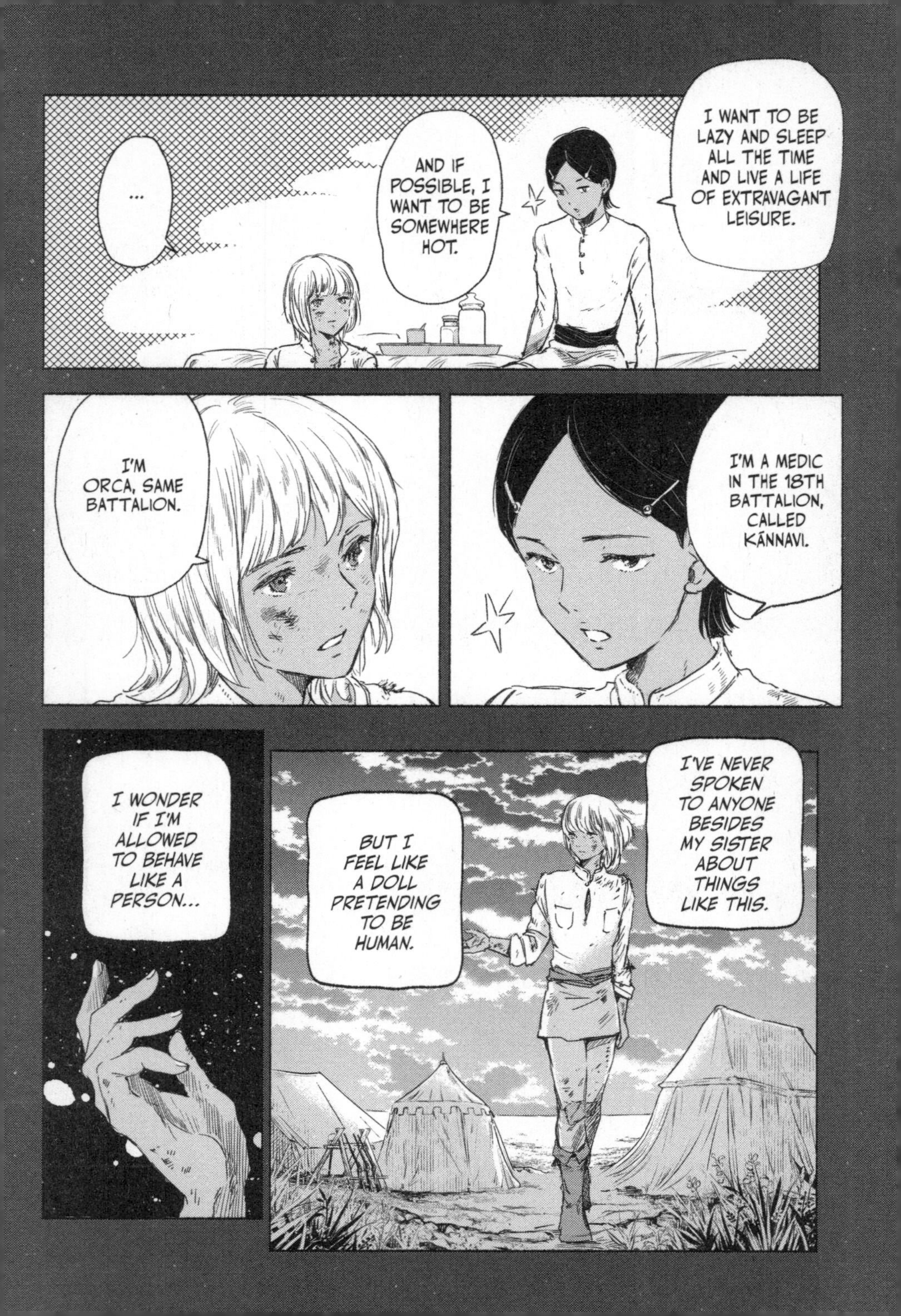
I WANT TO BE LAZY AND SLEEP ALL THE TIME AND LIVE A LIFE OF EXTRAVAGANT LEISURE.
AND IF POSSIBLE, I WANT TO BE SOMEWHERE HOT.
...
I'M A MEDIC IN THE 18TH BATTALION, CALLED KÄNNAVI.
I'M ORCA, SAME BATTALION.
I'VE NEVER SPOKEN TO ANYONE BESIDES MY SISTER ABOUT THINGS LIKE THIS.
BUT I FEEL LIKE A DOLL PRETENDING TO BE HUMAN.
I WONDER IF I'M ALLOWED TO BEHAVE LIKE A PERSON...

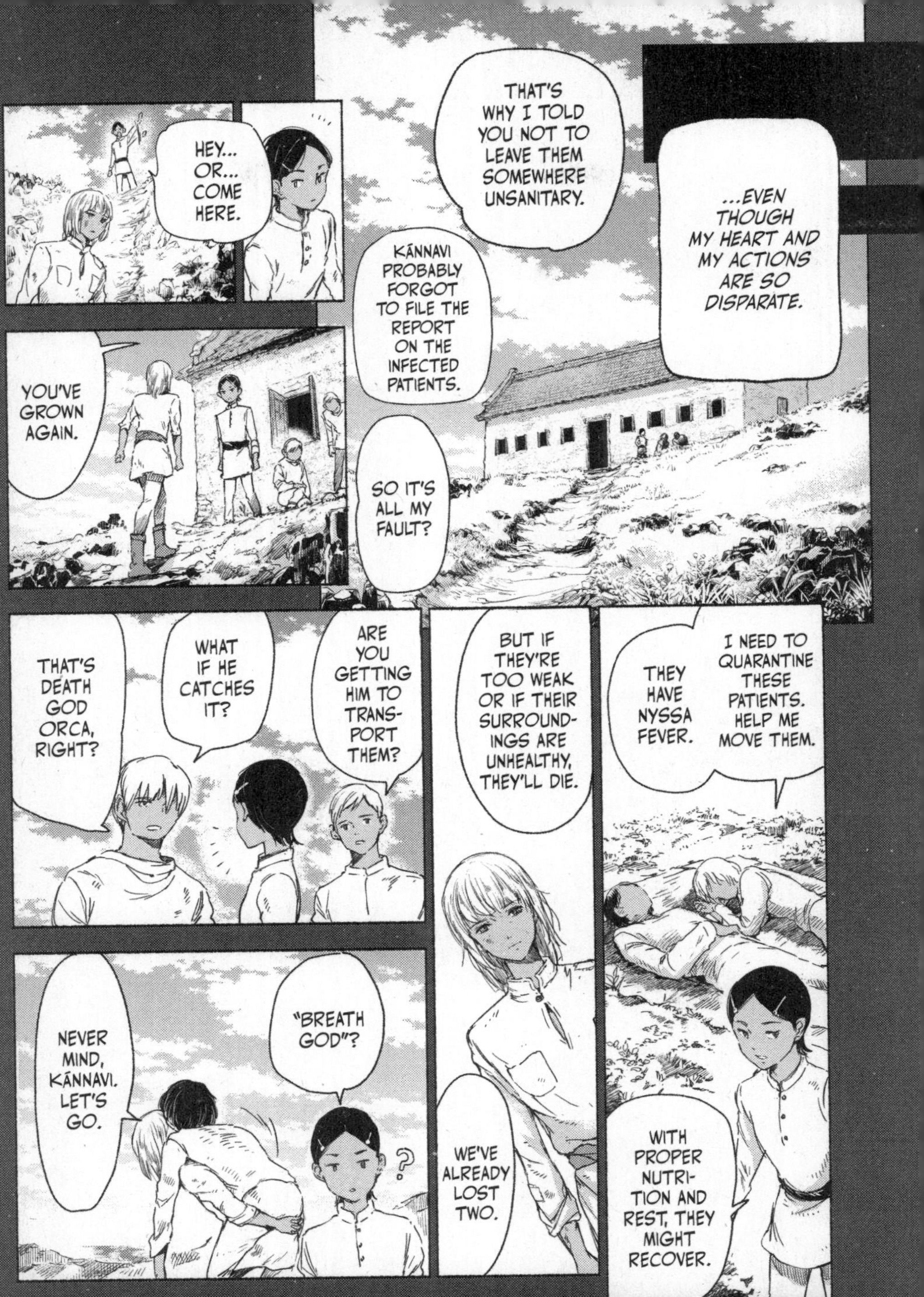
...EVEN THOUGH MY HEART AND MY ACTIONS ARE SO DISPARATE.
THAT'S WHY I TOLD YOU NOT TO LEAVE THEM SOMEWHERE UNSANITARY.
KĀNNAVI PROBABLY FORGOT TO FILE THE REPORT ON THE INFECTED PATIENTS.
SO IT'S ALL MY FAULT?
HEY... OR... COME HERE.
YOU'VE GROWN AGAIN.
I NEED TO QUARANTINE THESE PATIENTS. HELP ME MOVE THEM.
THEY HAVE NYSSA FEVER.
WITH PROPER NUTRITION AND REST, THEY MIGHT RECOVER.
BUT IF THEY'RE TOO WEAK OR IF THEIR SURROUNDINGS ARE UNHEALTHY, THEY'LL DIE.
WE'VE ALREADY LOST TWO.
ARE YOU GETTING HIM TO TRANSPORT THEM?
WHAT IF HE CATCHES IT?
THAT'S DEATH GOD ORCA, RIGHT?
"BREATH GOD"?
NEVER MIND, KĀNNAVI. LET'S GO.

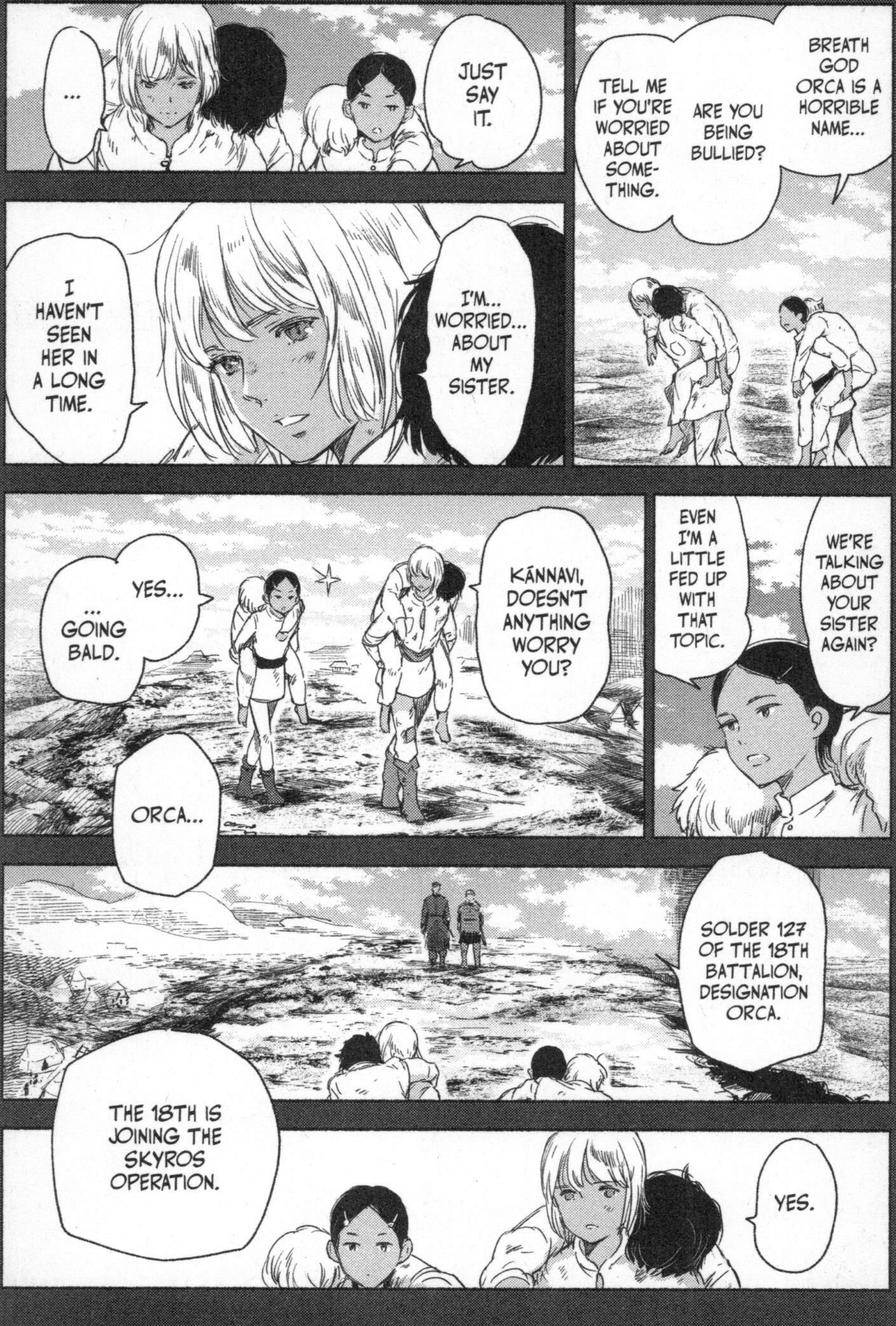
BREATH GOD ORCA IS A HORRIBLE NAME...
ARE YOU BEING BULLIED?
TELL ME IF YOU'RE WORRIED ABOUT SOME-THING.
JUST SAY IT.
...
I'M... WORRIED... ABOUT MY SISTER.
I HAVEN'T SEEN HER IN A LONG TIME.
WE'RE TALKING ABOUT YOUR SISTER AGAIN?
EVEN I'M A LITTLE FED UP WITH THAT TOPIC.
KÁNNAVI, DOESN'T ANYTHING WORRY YOU?
YES...
... GOING BALD.
ORCA...
SOLDER 127 OF THE 18TH BATTALION, DESIGNATION ORCA.
THE 18TH IS JOINING THE SKYROS OPERATION.
YES.

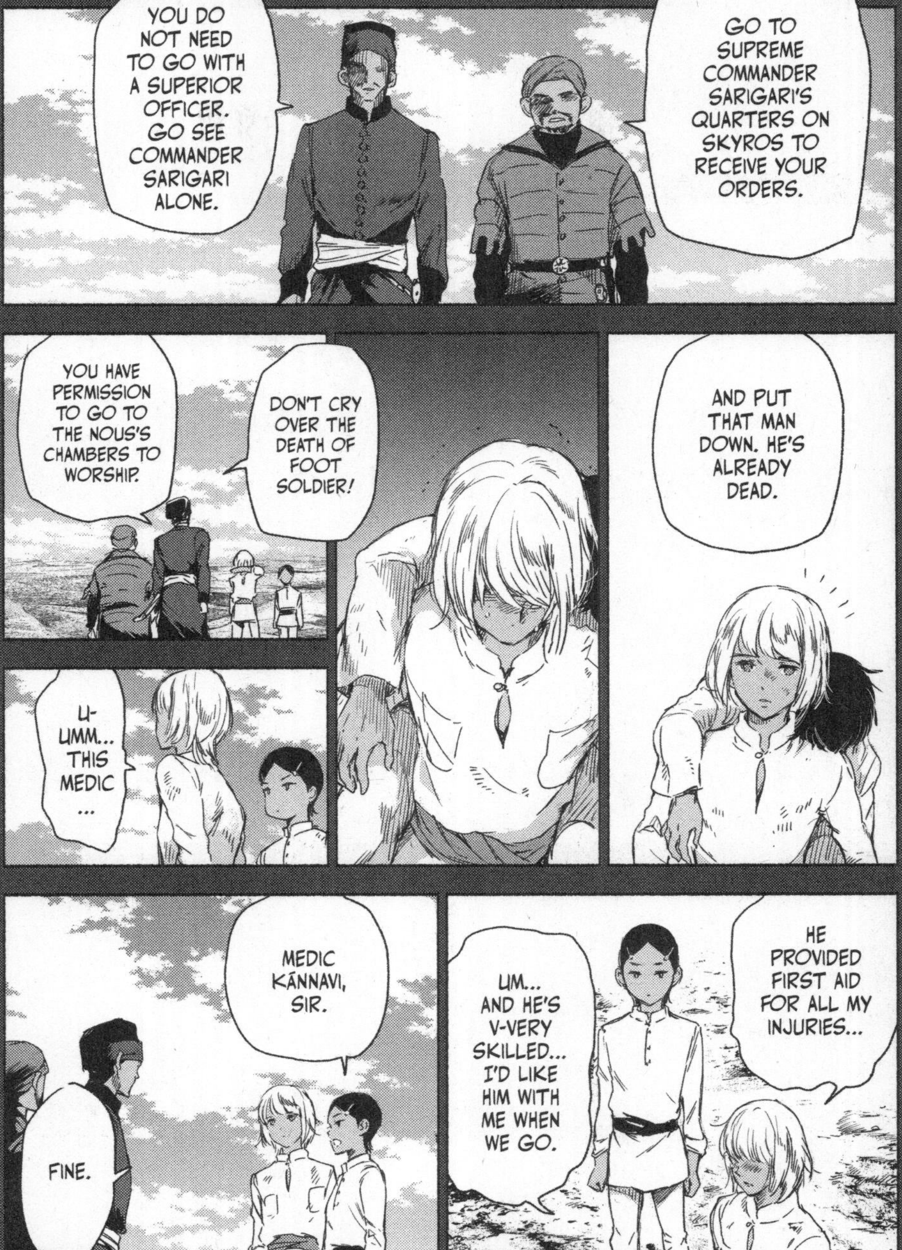
GO TO SUPREME COMMANDER SARIGARI'S QUARTERS ON SKYROS TO RECEIVE YOUR ORDERS.
YOU DO NOT NEED TO GO WITH A SUPERIOR OFFICER. GO SEE COMMANDER SARIGARI ALONE.
AND PUT THAT MAN DOWN. HE'S ALREADY DEAD.
DON'T CRY OVER THE DEATH OF FOOT SOLDIER!
YOU HAVE PERMISSION TO GO TO THE NOUS'S CHAMBERS TO WORSHIP.
U-UMM... THIS MEDIC...
HE PROVIDED FIRST AID FOR ALL MY INJURIES...
UM... AND HE'S V-VERY SKILLED... I'D LIKE HIM WITH ME WHEN WE GO.
MEDIC KÁNNAVI, SIR.
FINE.

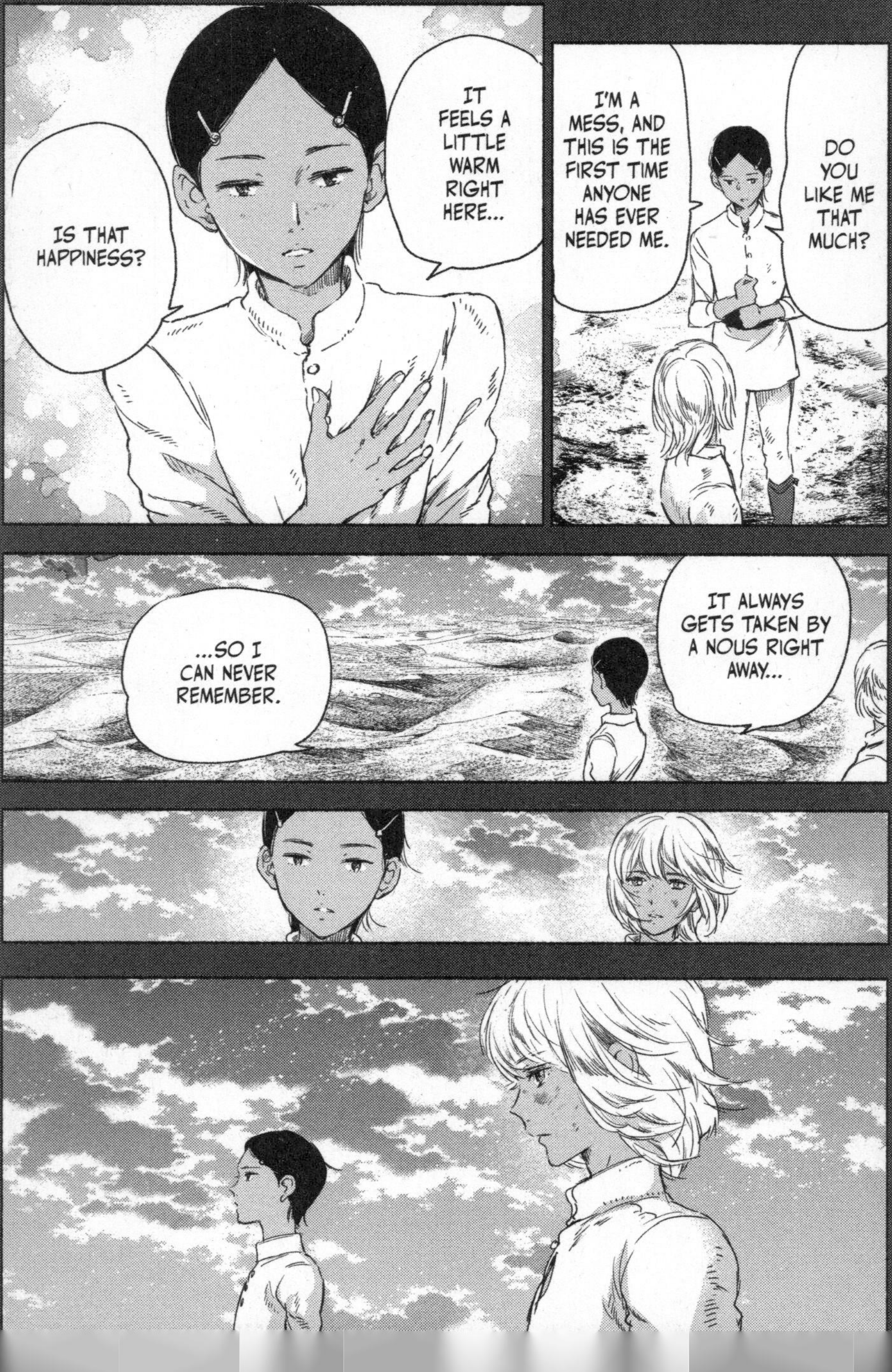
DO YOU LIKE ME THAT MUCH?
I'M A MESS, AND THIS IS THE FIRST TIME ANYONE HAS EVER NEEDED ME.
IT FEELS A LITTLE WARM RIGHT HERE...
IS THAT HAPPINESS?
IT ALWAYS GETS TAKEN BY A NOUS RIGHT AWAY...
...SO I CAN NEVER REMEMBER.

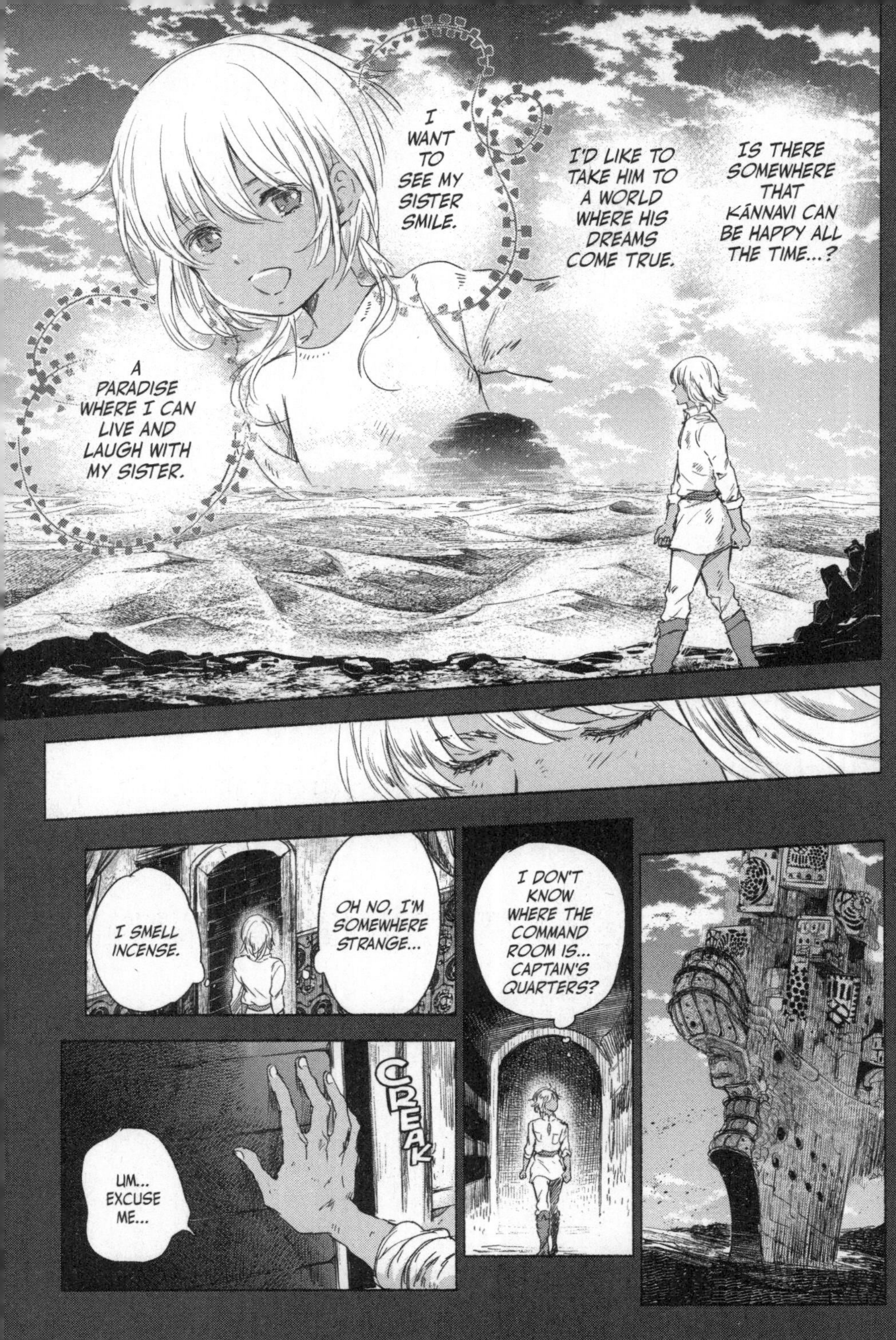
IS THERE SOMEWHERE THAT KĀNNAVI CAN BE HAPPY ALL THE TIME...?
I'D LIKE TO TAKE HIM TO A WORLD WHERE HIS DREAMS COME TRUE.
I WANT TO SEE MY SISTER SMILE.
A PARADISE WHERE I CAN LIVE AND LAUGH WITH MY SISTER.
I DON'T KNOW WHERE THE COMMAND ROOM IS... CAPTAIN'S QUARTERS?
OH NO, I'M SOMEWHERE STRANGE...
I SMELL INCENSE.
CREAK
UM... EXCUSE ME...

...

A BLUE...
SEA?

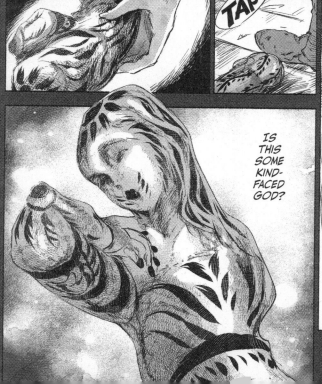

TAP

IS
THIS
SOME
KIND-
FACED
GOD?

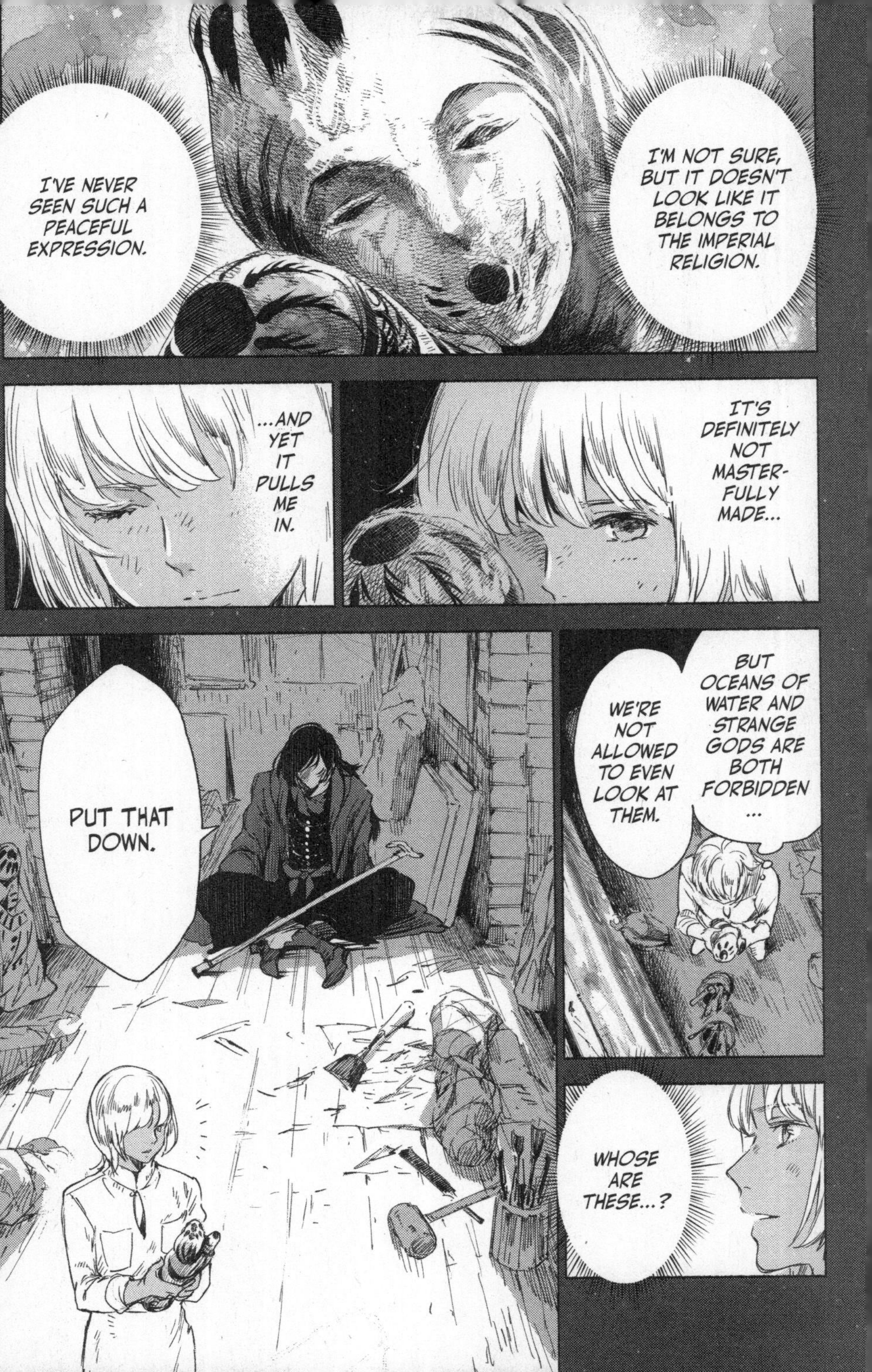
I'M NOT SURE, BUT IT DOESN'T LOOK LIKE IT BELONGS TO THE IMPERIAL RELIGION.
I'VE NEVER SEEN SUCH A PEACEFUL EXPRESSION.
IT'S DEFINITELY NOT MASTER-FULLY MADE...
...AND YET IT PULLS ME IN.
BUT OCEANS OF WATER AND STRANGE GODS ARE BOTH FORBIDDEN ...
WE'RE NOT ALLOWED TO EVEN LOOK AT THEM.
WHOSE ARE THESE...?
PUT THAT DOWN.

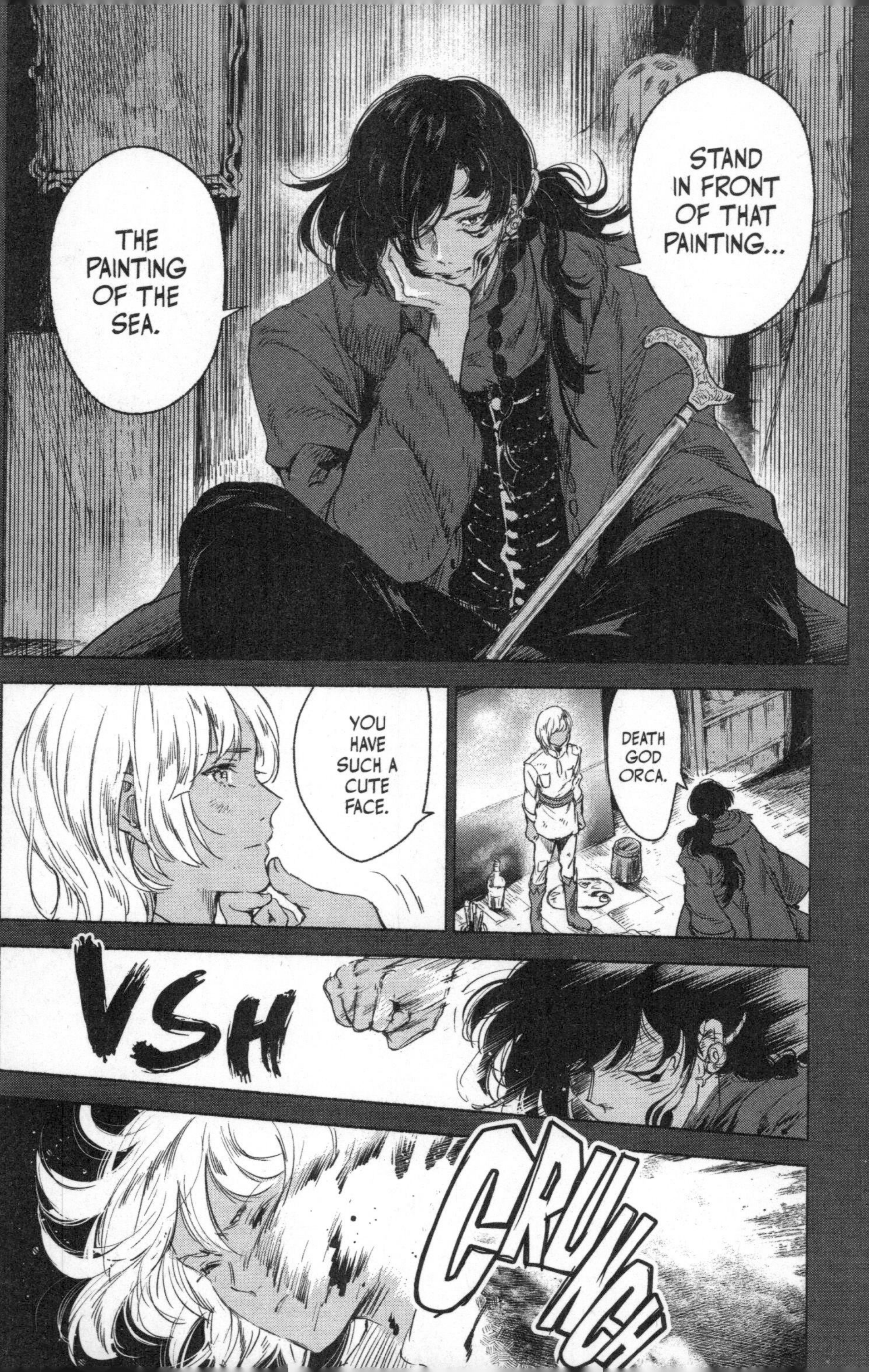
STAND IN FRONT OF THAT PAINTING...
THE PAINTING OF THE SEA.
DEATH GOD ORCA.
YOU HAVE SUCH A CUTE FACE.
VSH
CRUNCH

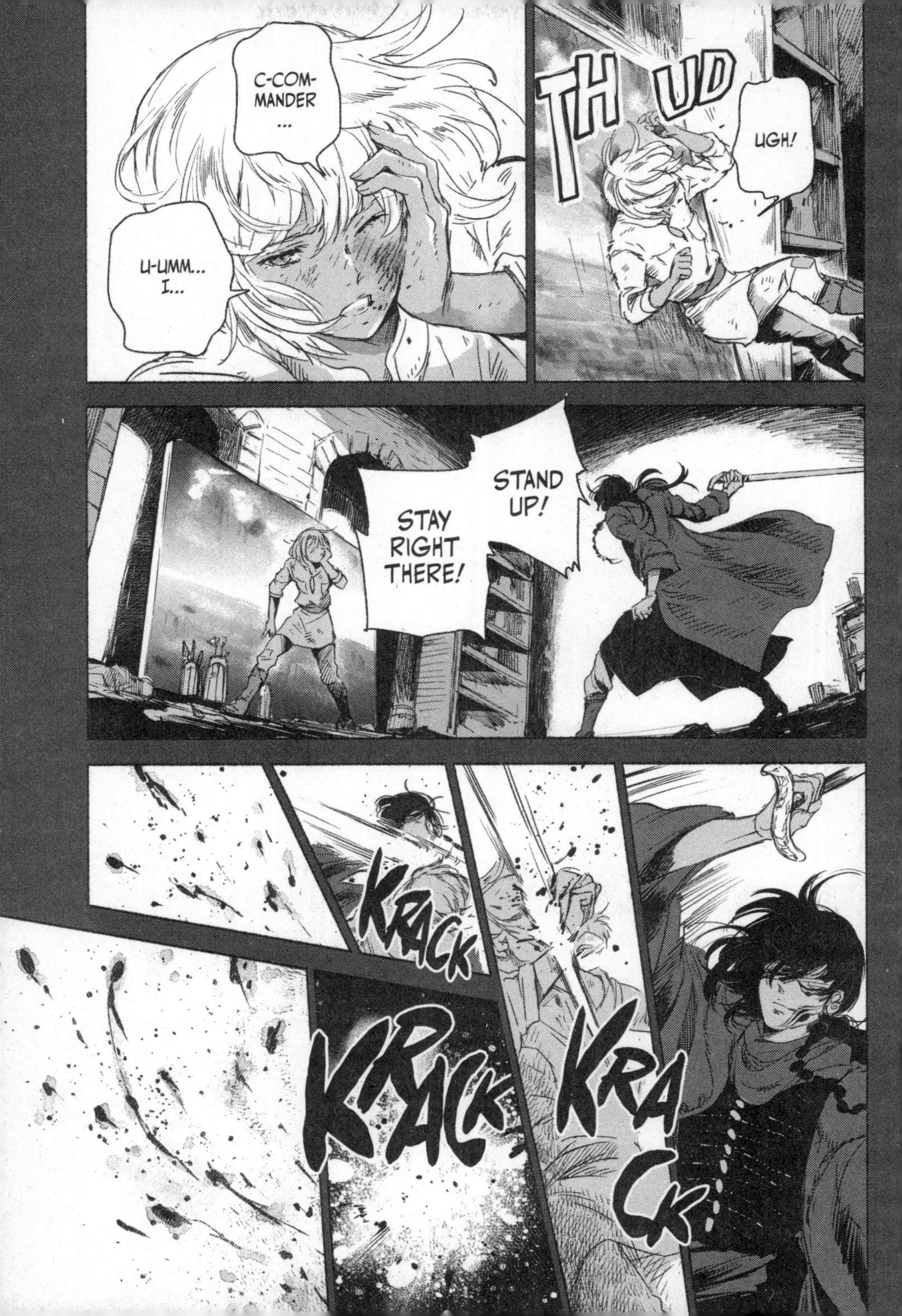
THUD
UGH!
C-COM-MANDER ...
U-UMM... I...
STAND UP!
STAY RIGHT THERE!
KRACK
KRACK
KRACK

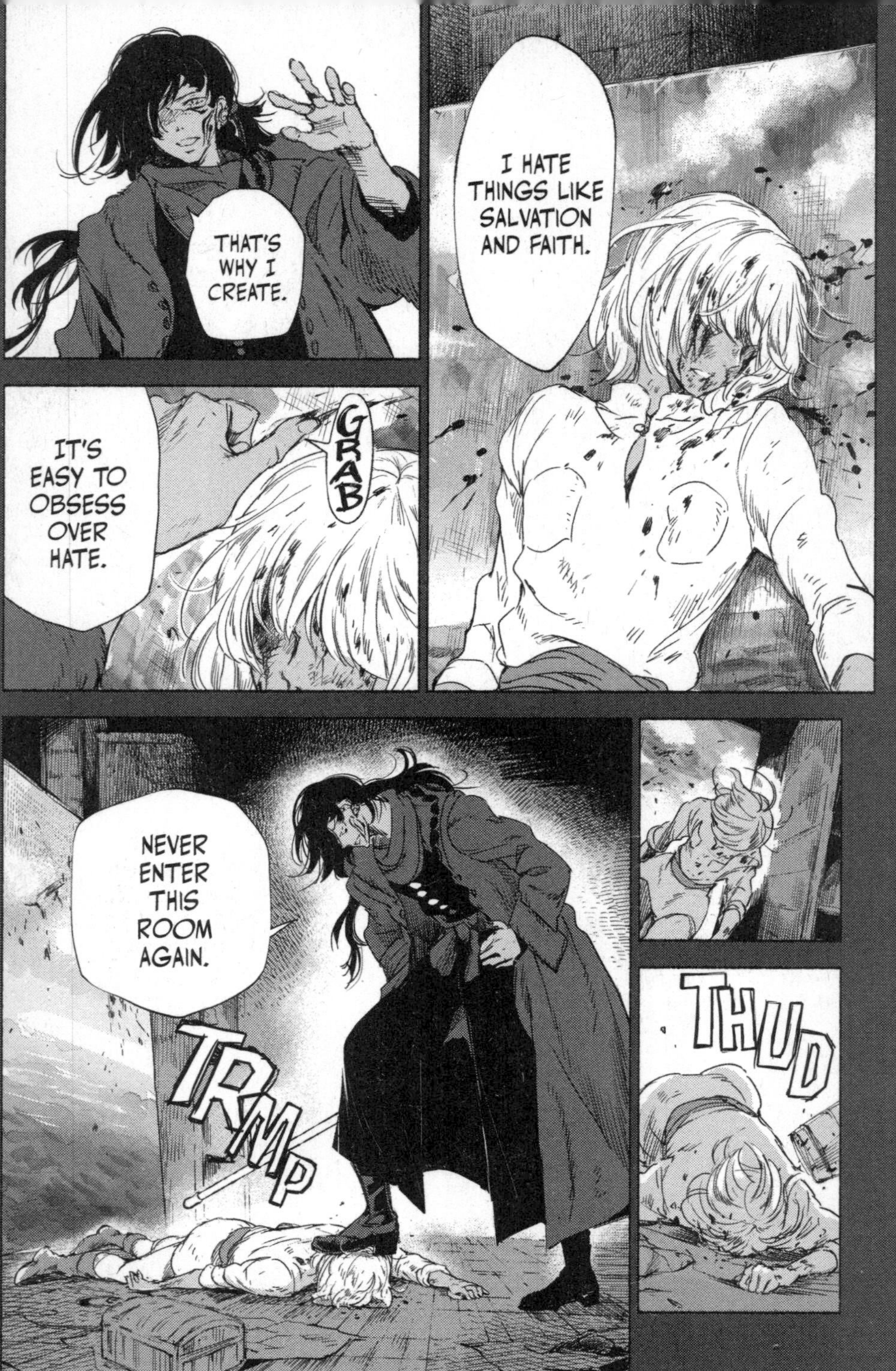
I HATE THINGS LIKE SALVATION AND FAITH.
THAT'S WHY I CREATE.
IT'S EASY TO OBSESS OVER HATE.
GRAB
THUD
NEVER ENTER THIS ROOM AGAIN.
TRMP

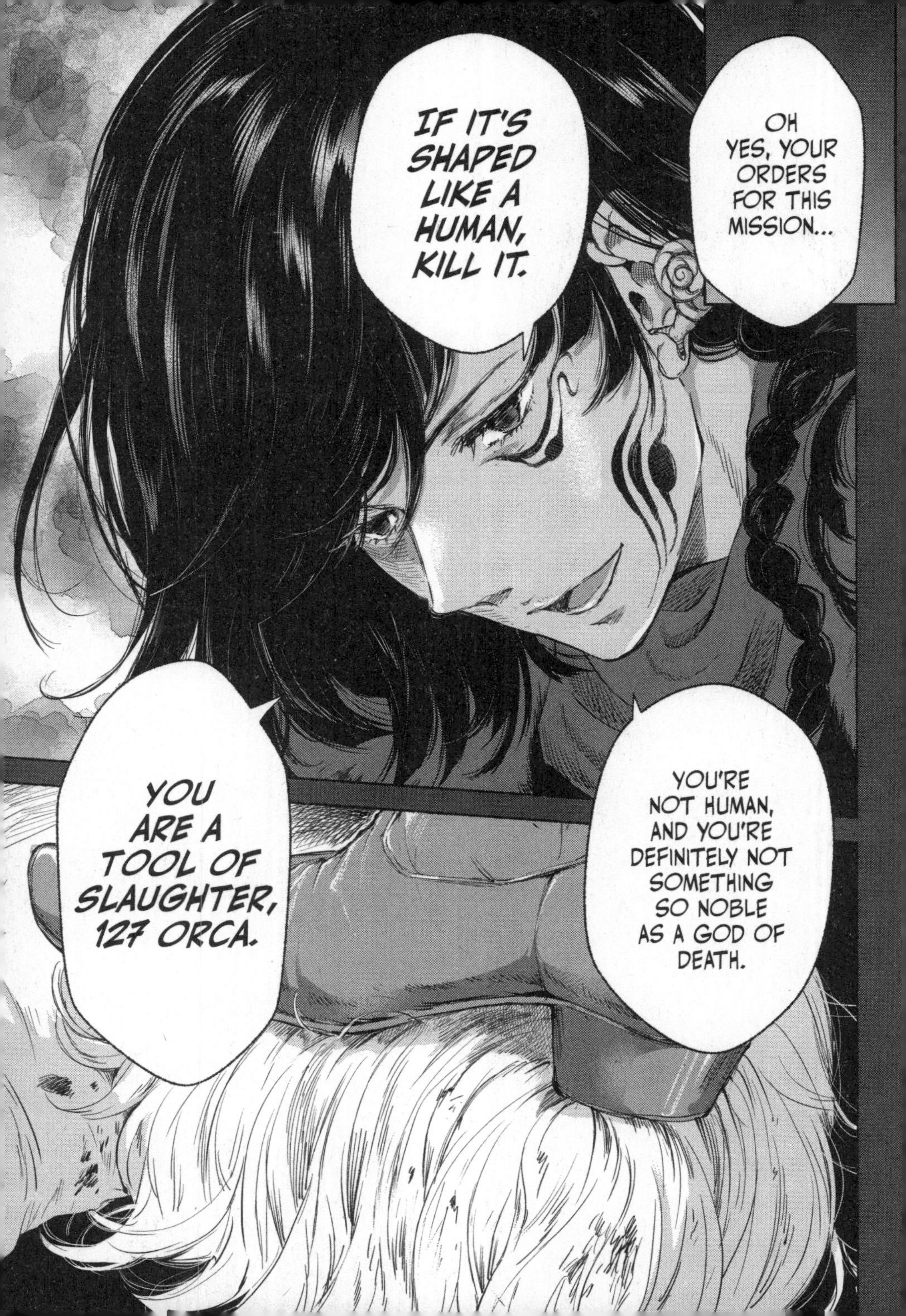
OH YES, YOUR ORDERS FOR THIS MISSION...
IF IT'S SHAPED LIKE A HUMAN, KILL IT.
YOU'RE NOT HUMAN, AND YOU'RE DEFINITELY NOT SOMETHING SO NOBLE AS A GOD OF DEATH.
YOU ARE A TOOL OF SLAUGHTER, 127 ORCA.

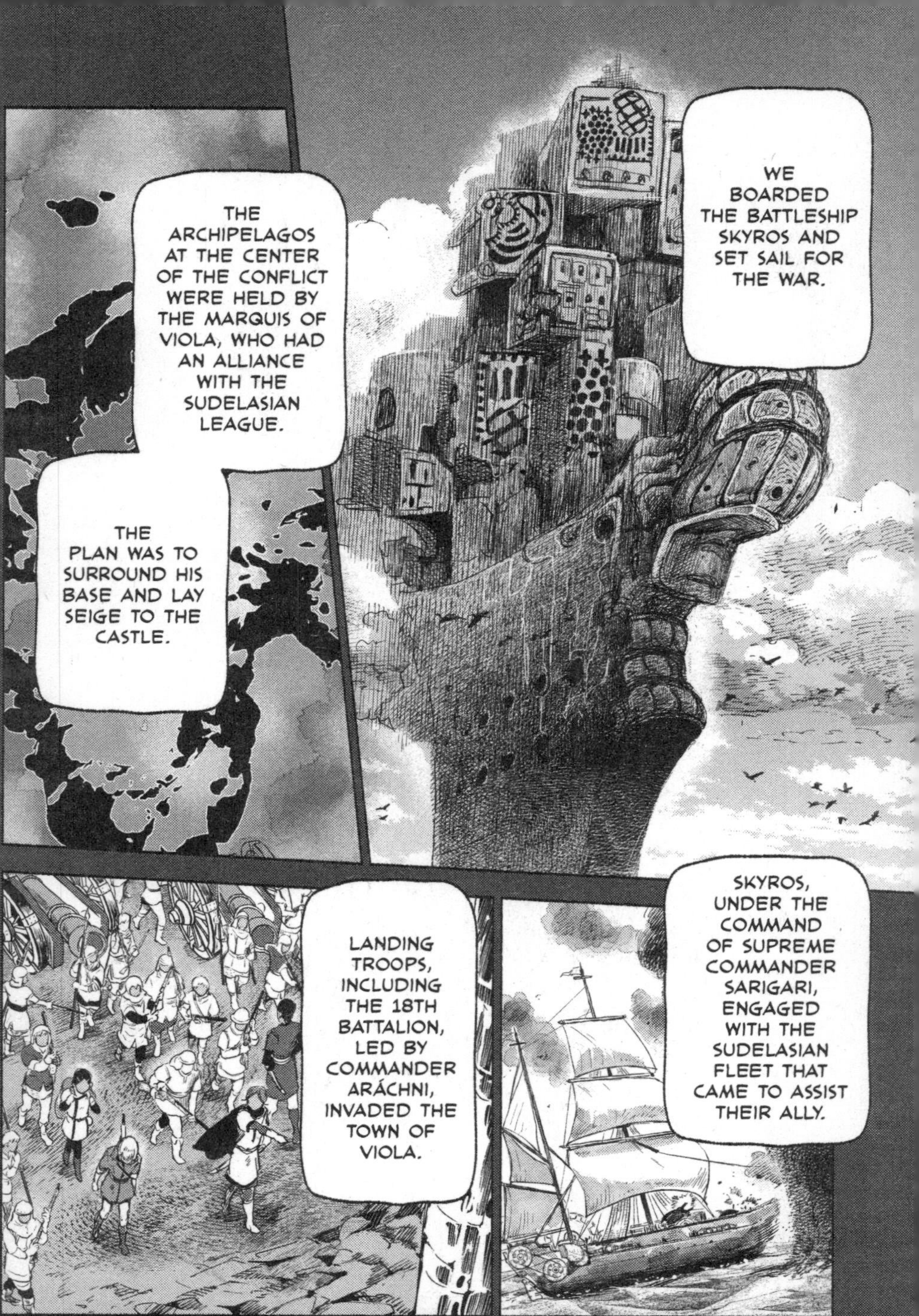
WE BOARDED THE BATTLESHIP SKYROS AND SET SAIL FOR THE WAR.
THE ARCHIPELAGOS AT THE CENTER OF THE CONFLICT WERE HELD BY THE MARQUIS OF VIOLA, WHO HAD AN ALLIANCE WITH THE SUDELASIAN LEAGUE.
THE PLAN WAS TO SURROUND HIS BASE AND LAY SEIGE TO THE CASTLE.
SKYROS, UNDER THE COMMAND OF SUPREME COMMANDER SARIGARI, ENGAGED WITH THE SUDELASIAN FLEET THAT CAME TO ASSIST THEIR ALLY.
LANDING TROOPS, INCLUDING THE 18TH BATTALION, LED BY COMMANDER ARÁCHNI, INVADED THE TOWN OF VIOLA.

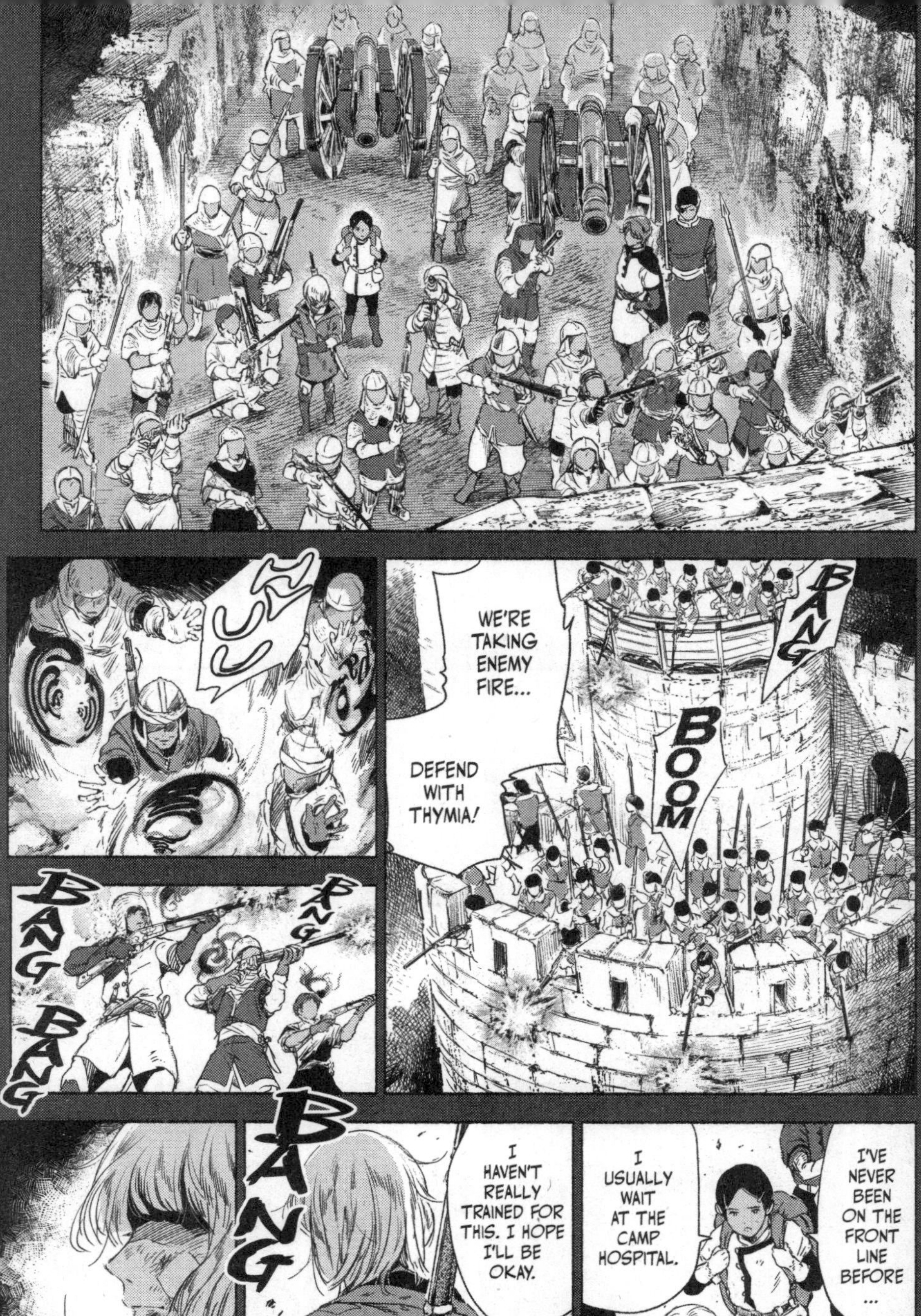
BANG
WE'RE TAKING ENEMY FIRE...
BOOM
DEFEND WITH THYMIA!
BANG
BANG BANG BANG
I'VE NEVER BEEN ON THE FRONT LINE BEFORE...
I USUALLY WAIT AT THE CAMP HOSPITAL.
I HAVEN'T REALLY TRAINED FOR THIS. I HOPE I'LL BE OKAY.
BANG

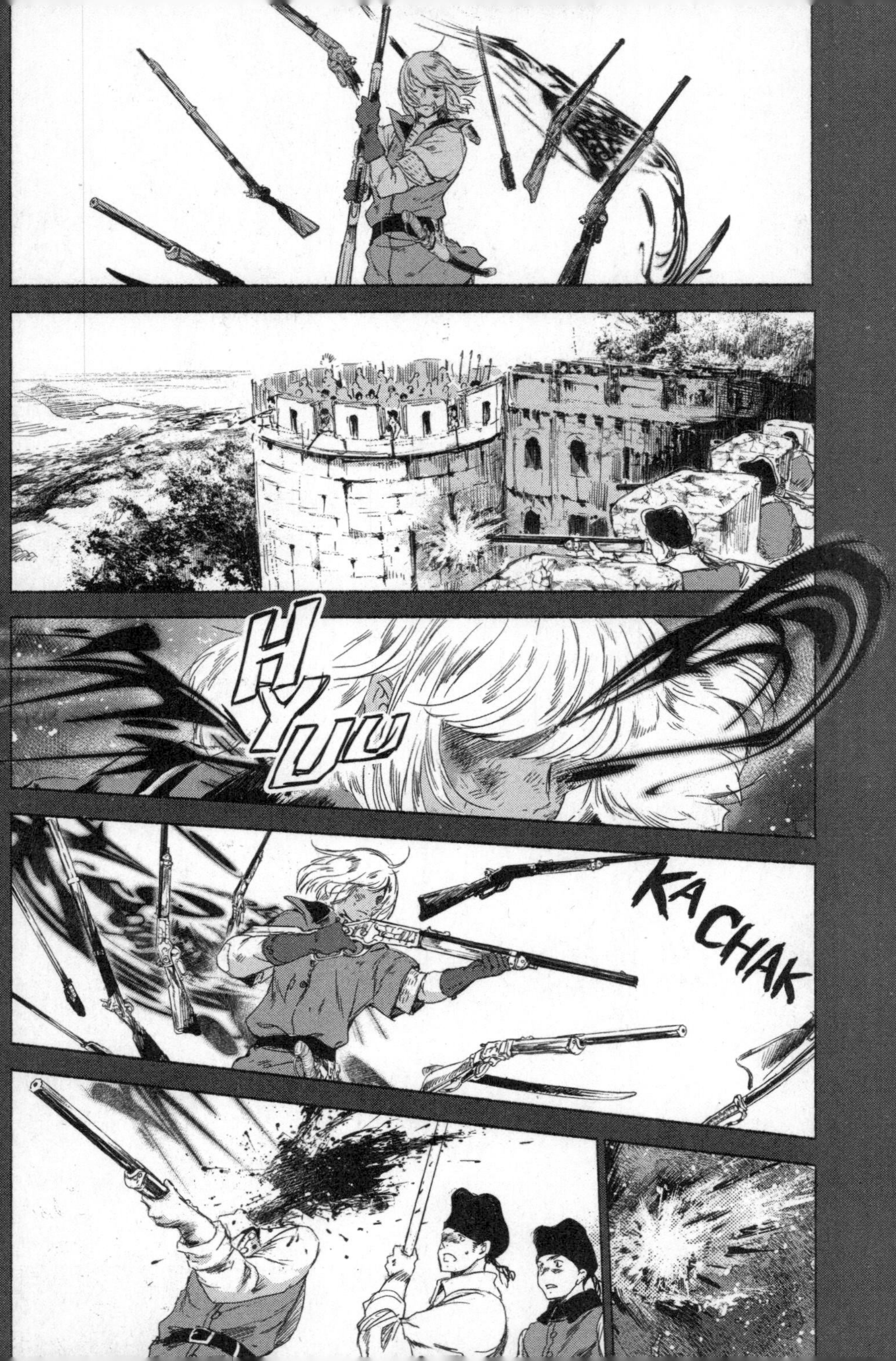
HYUU
KA CHAK

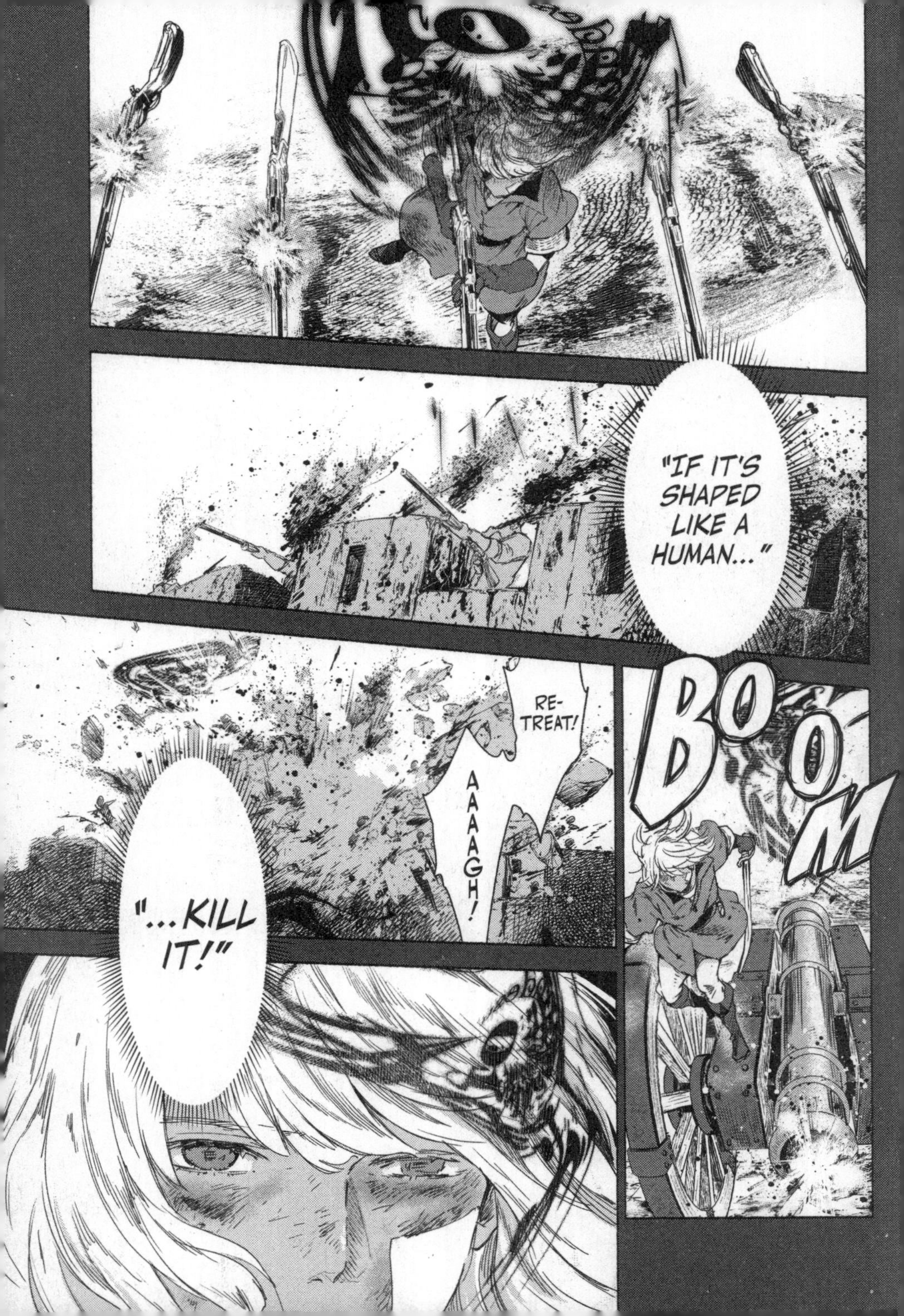
"IF IT'S SHAPED LIKE A HUMAN..."
BOOM
RE-TREAT!
AAAAGH!
"...KILL IT!"

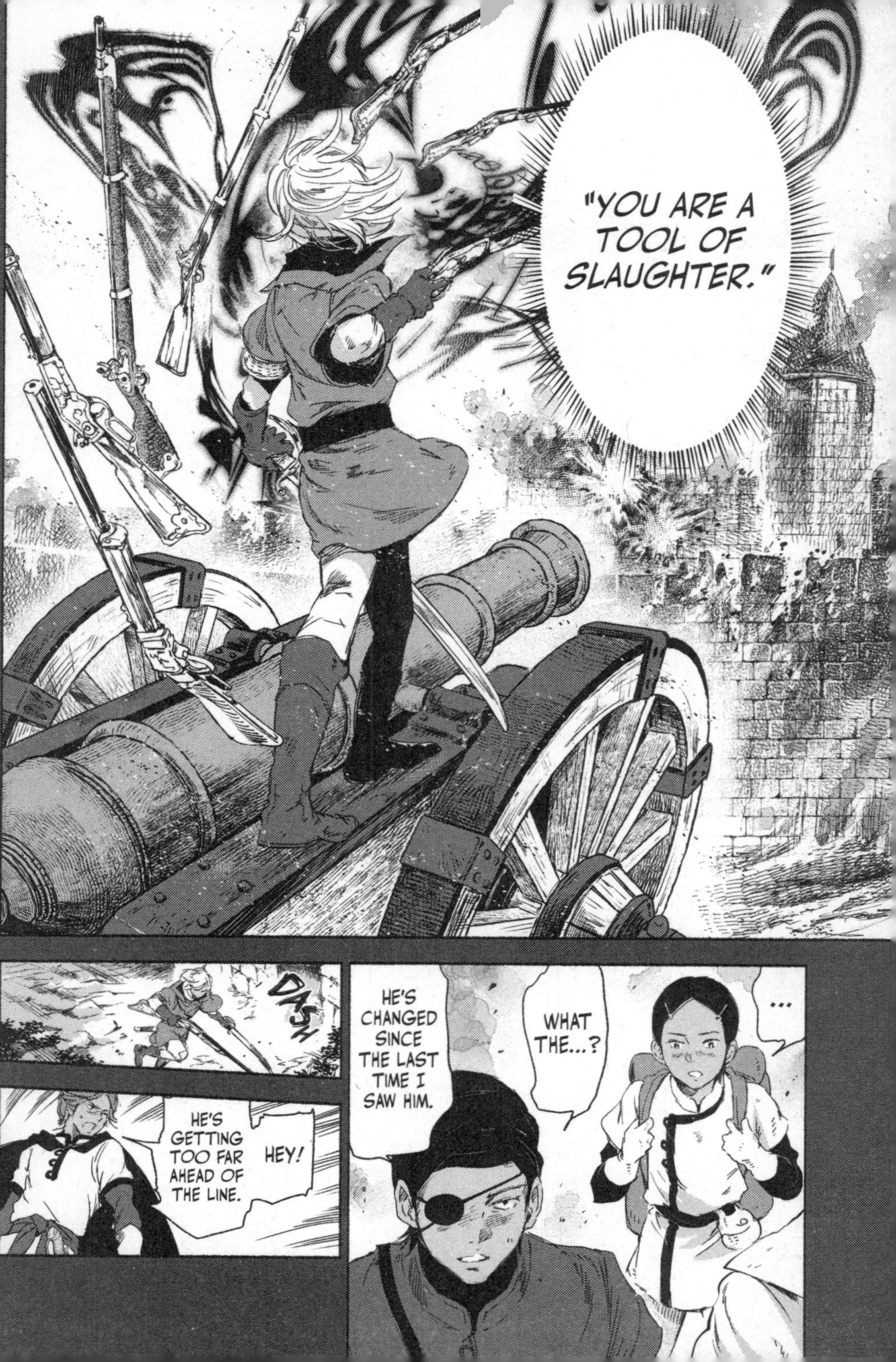
"YOU ARE A TOOL OF SLAUGHTER."
...
WHAT THE...?
HE'S CHANGED SINCE THE LAST TIME I SAW HIM.
DASH
HEY!
HE'S GETTING TOO FAR AHEAD OF THE LINE.

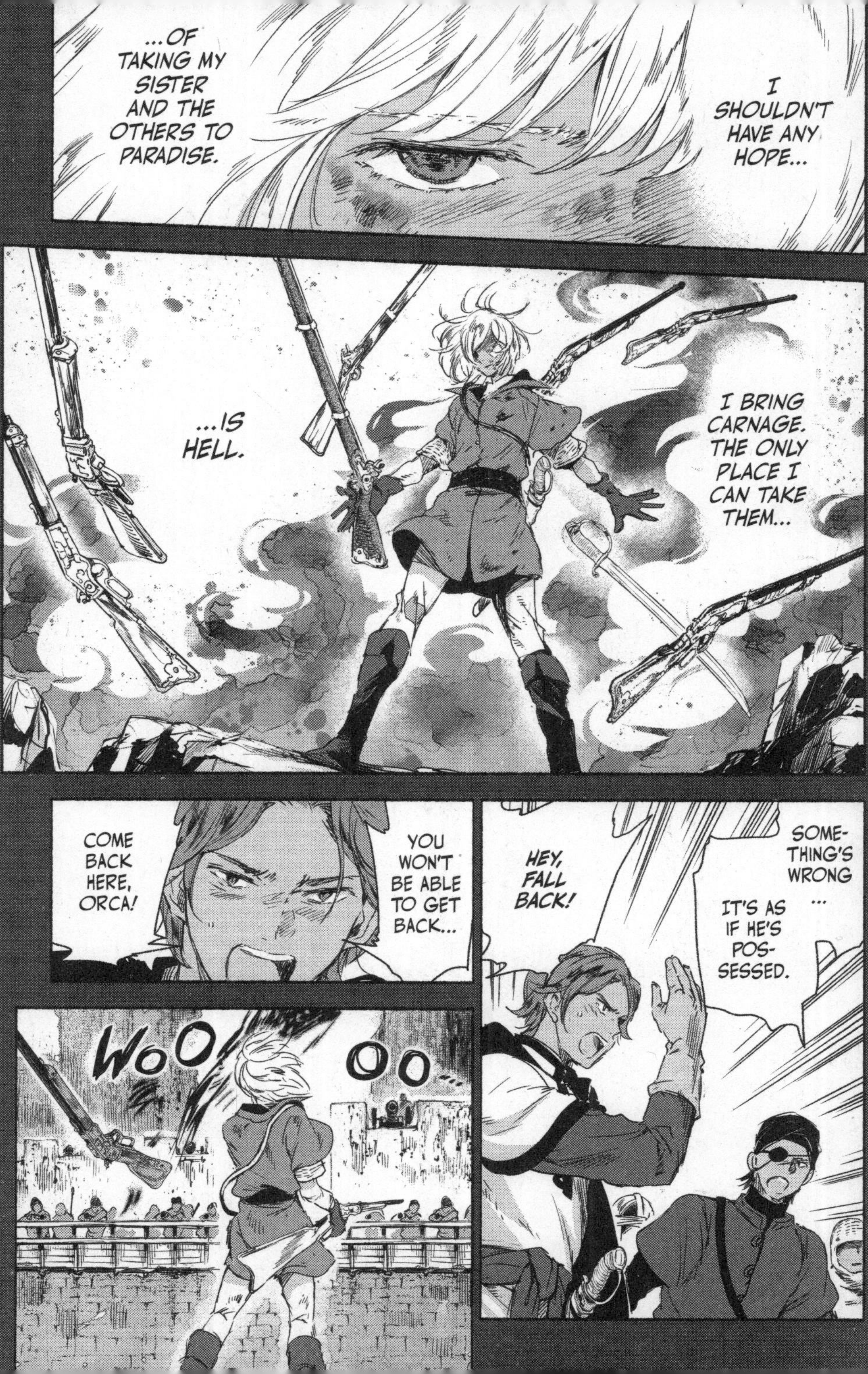
I SHOULDN'T HAVE ANY HOPE...
...OF TAKING MY SISTER AND THE OTHERS TO PARADISE.
I BRING CARNAGE. THE ONLY PLACE I CAN TAKE THEM...
...IS HELL.
SOME-THING'S WRONG ...
IT'S AS IF HE'S POS-SESSED.
HEY, FALL BACK!
YOU WON'T BE ABLE TO GET BACK...
COME BACK HERE, ORCA!
WOO OO

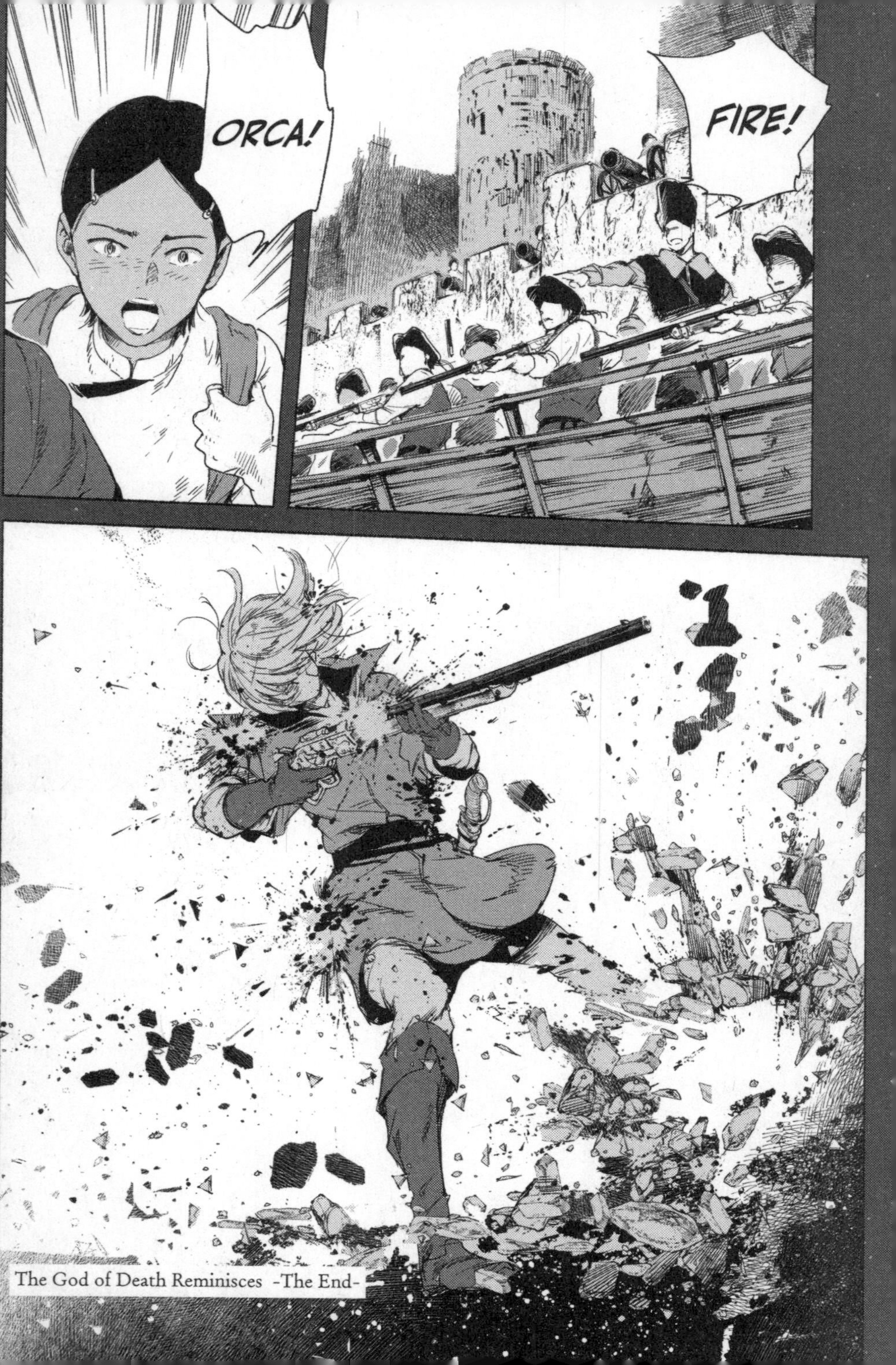
FIRE!
ORCA!
The God of Death Reminisces -The End-

Chapter 63
Kitrino

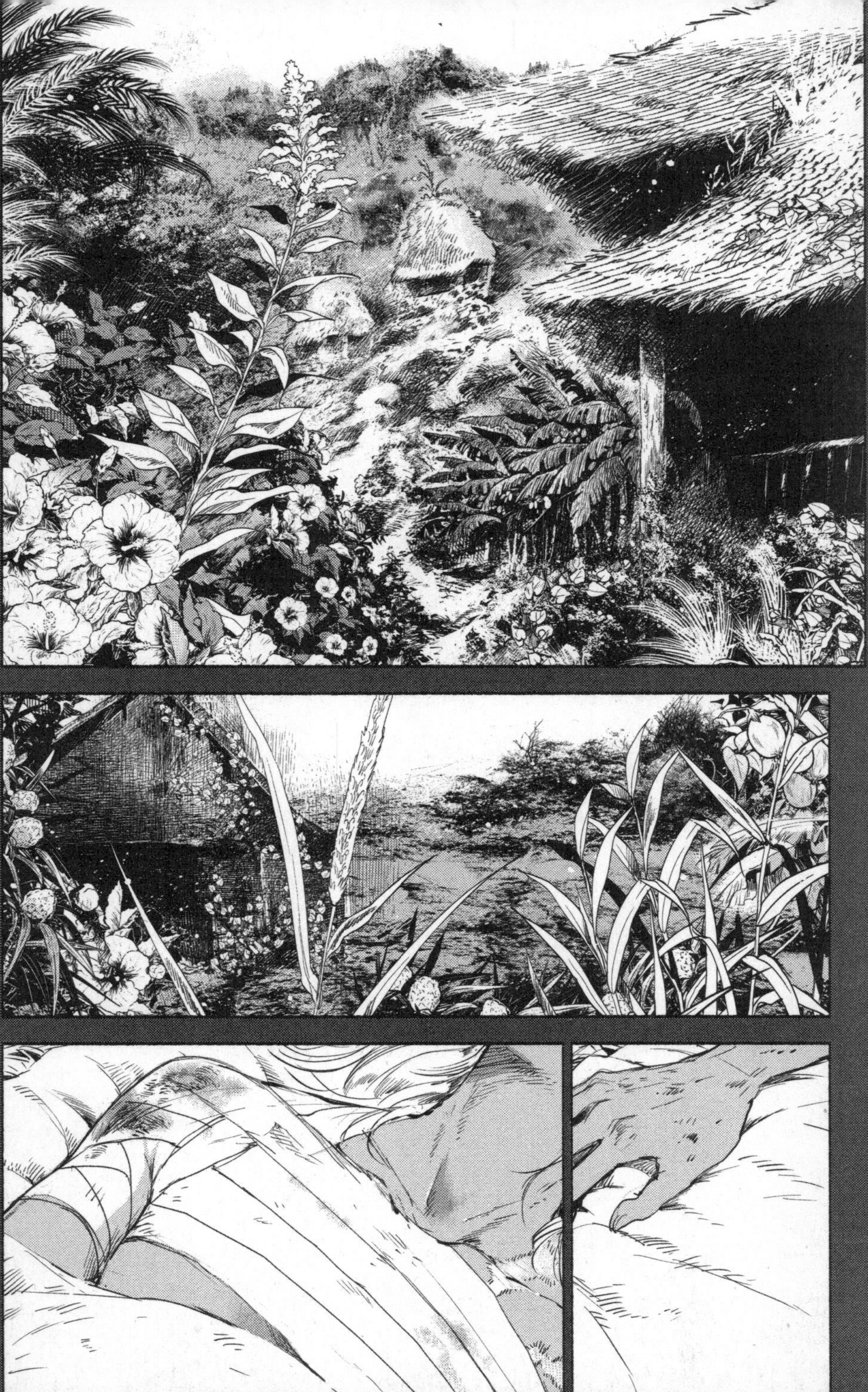

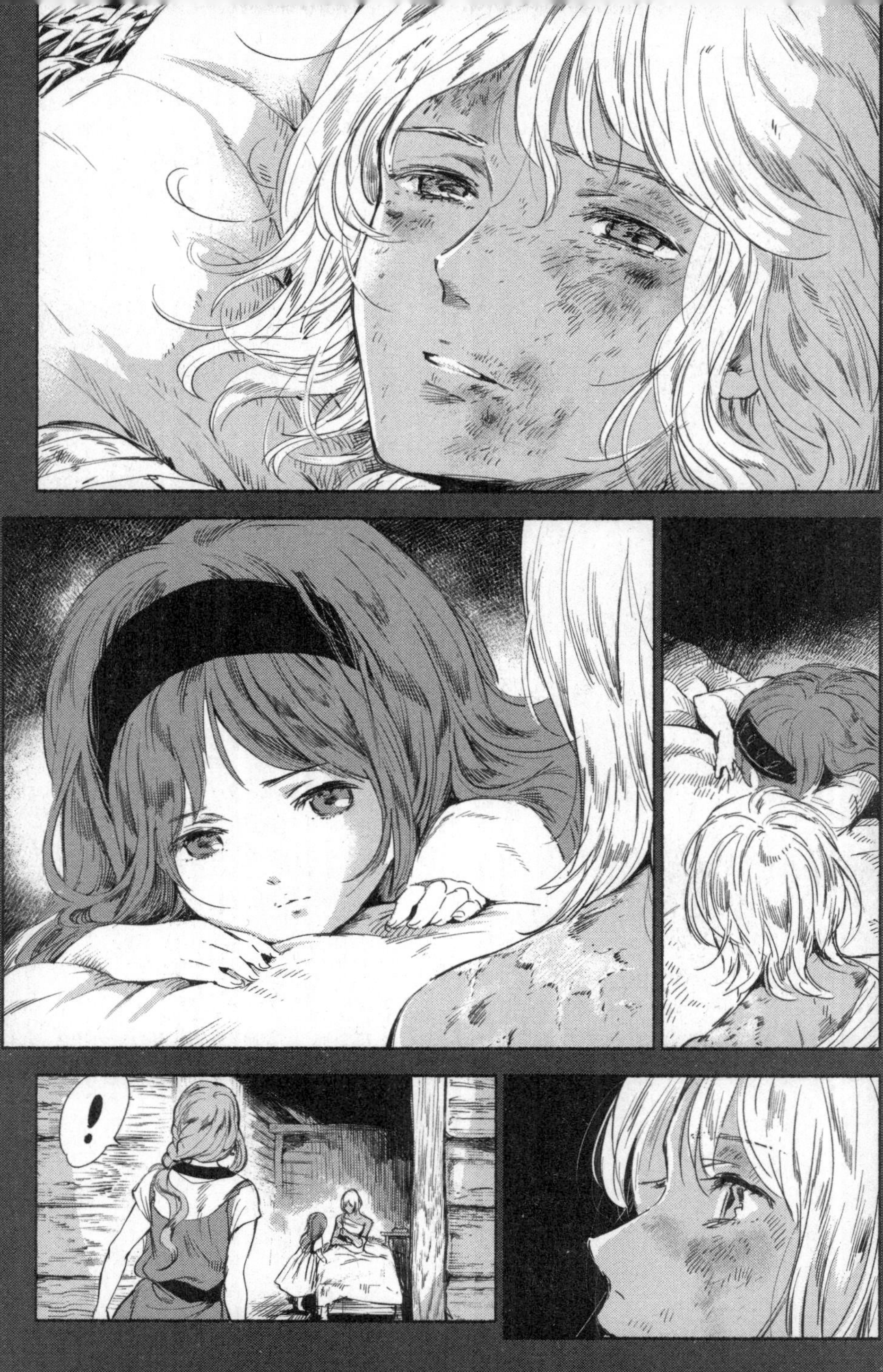
!

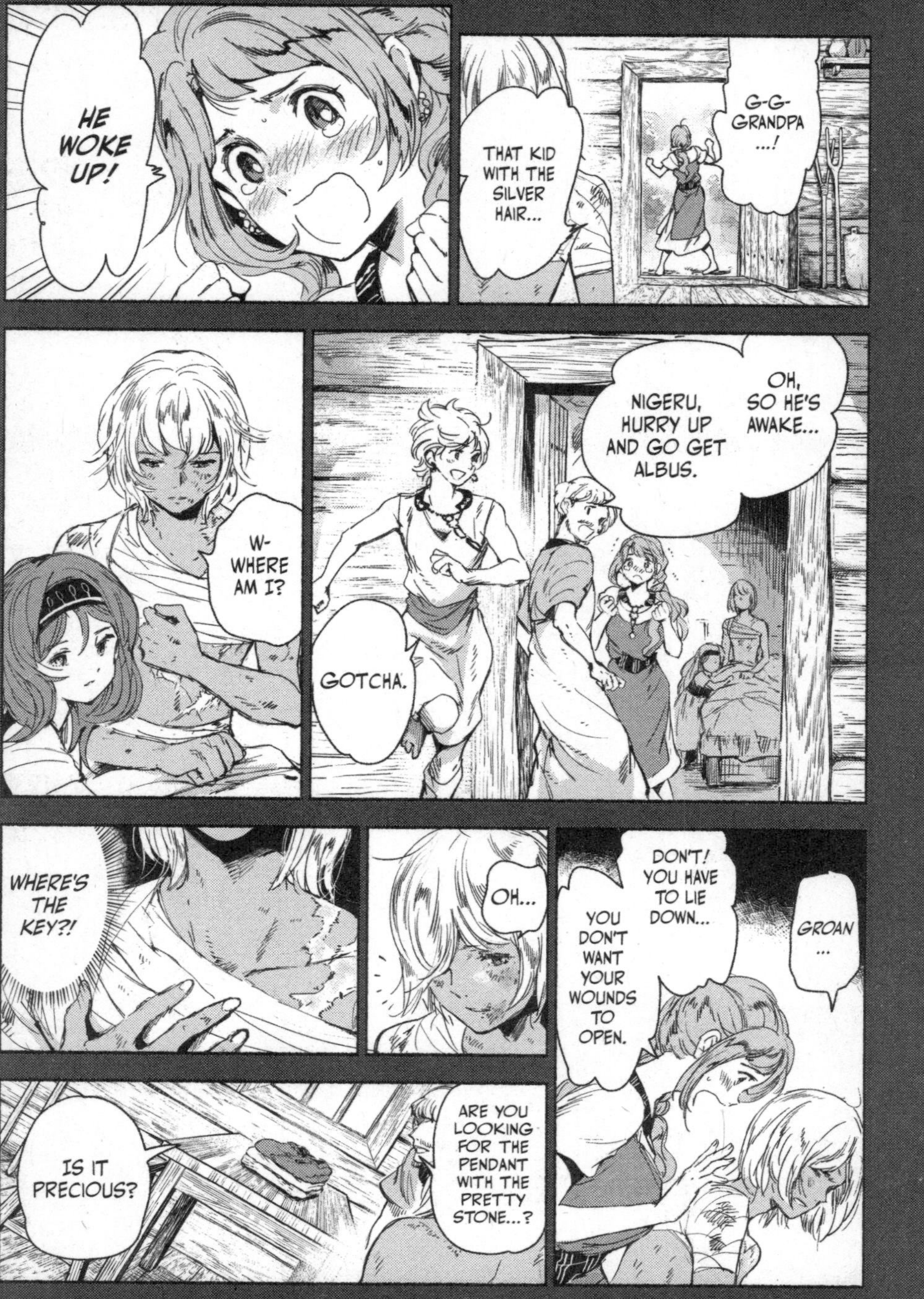
G-G-GRANDPA ...!
THAT KID WITH THE SILVER HAIR...
HE WOKE UP!
OH, SO HE'S AWAKE...
NIGERU, HURRY UP AND GO GET ALBUS.
GOTCHA.
W-WHERE AM I?
GROAN ...
DON'T! YOU HAVE TO LIE DOWN...
YOU DON'T WANT YOUR WOUNDS TO OPEN.
OH...
WHERE'S THE KEY?!
ARE YOU LOOKING FOR THE PENDANT WITH THE PRETTY STONE...?
IS IT PRECIOUS?

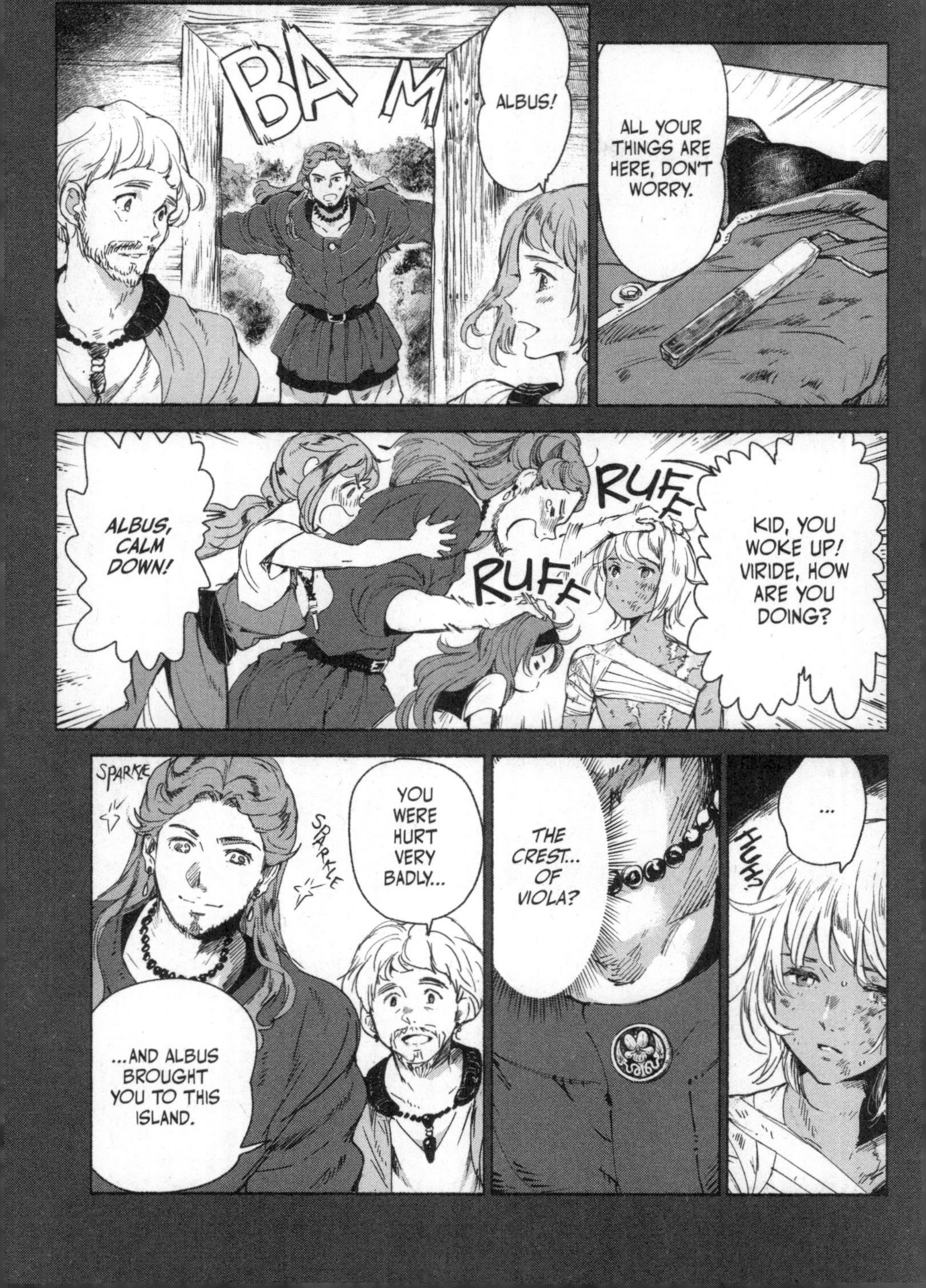
ALL YOUR THINGS ARE HERE, DON'T WORRY.
ALBUS!
BAM
KID, YOU WOKE UP! VIRIDE, HOW ARE YOU DOING?
RUFF
RUFF
ALBUS, CALM DOWN!
...
HUH?
THE CREST... OF VIOLA?
YOU WERE HURT VERY BADLY...
SPARKLE
SPARKLE
...AND ALBUS BROUGHT YOU TO THIS ISLAND.

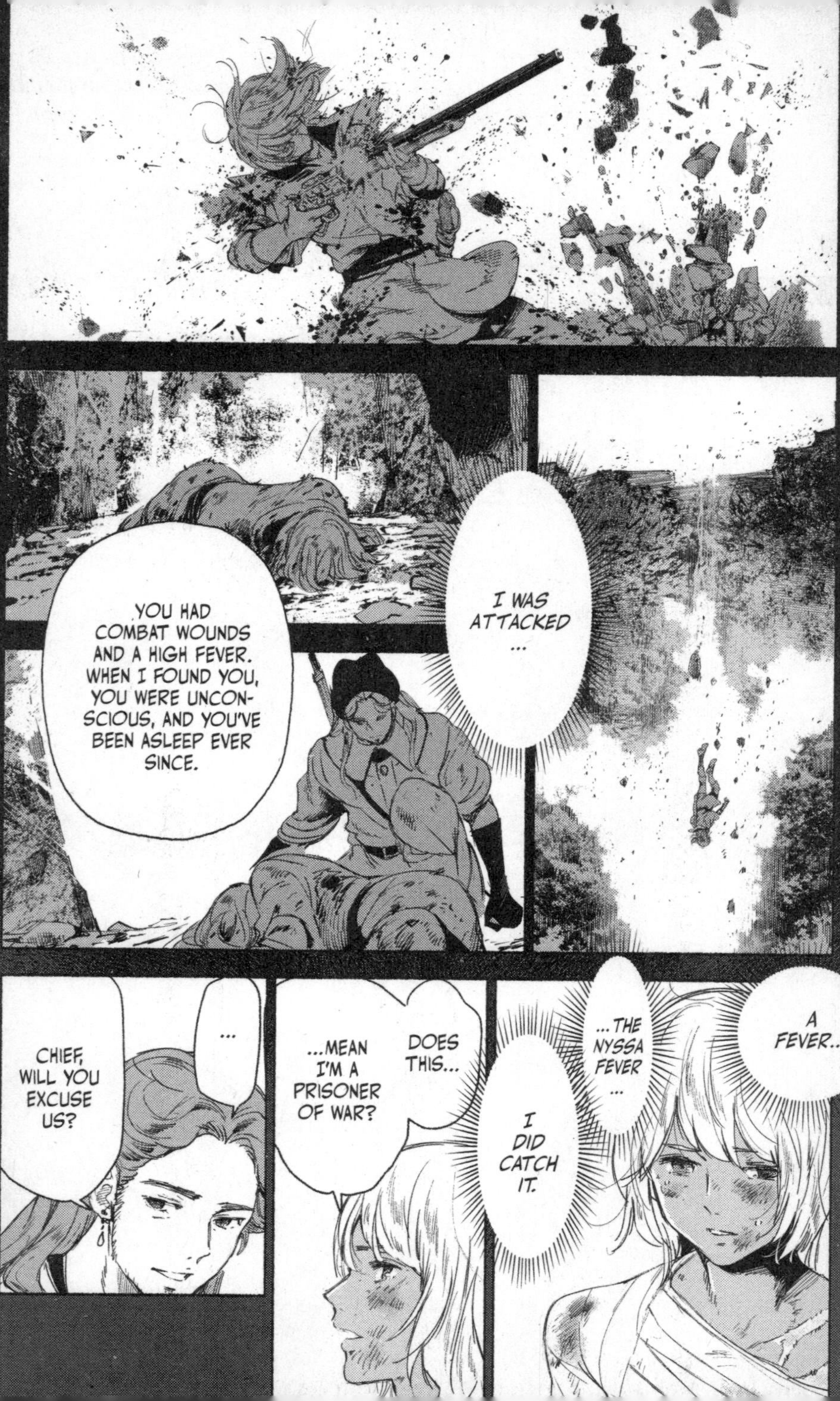
I WAS ATTACKED ...
YOU HAD COMBAT WOUNDS AND A HIGH FEVER. WHEN I FOUND YOU, YOU WERE UNCON-SCIOUS, AND YOU'VE BEEN ASLEEP EVER SINCE.
A FEVER...
...THE NYSSA FEVER ...
I DID CATCH IT.
DOES THIS...
...MEAN I'M A PRISONER OF WAR?
...
CHIEF, WILL YOU EXCUSE US?

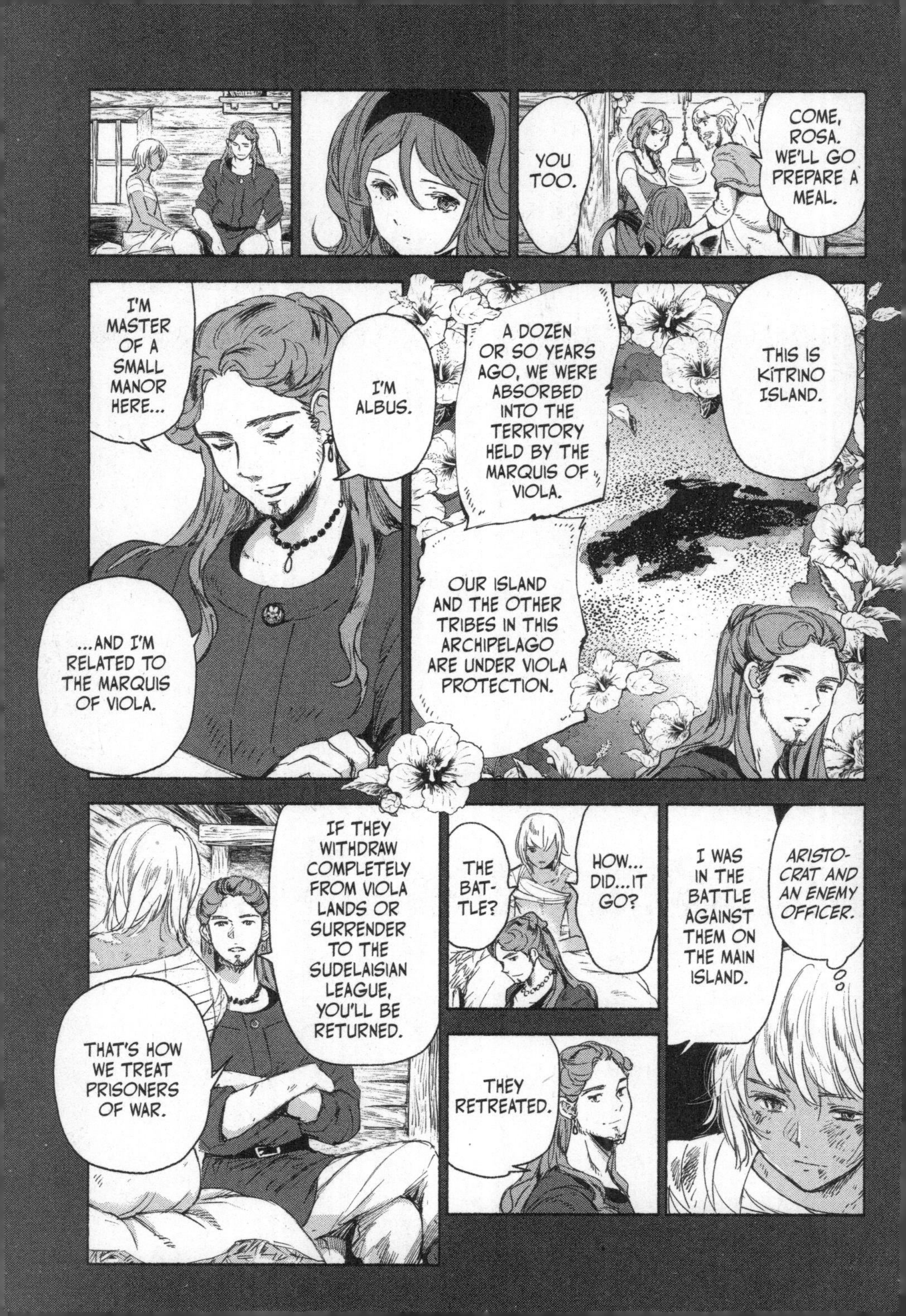
COME, ROSA. WE'LL GO PREPARE A MEAL.
YOU TOO.
THIS IS KÍTRINO ISLAND.
A DOZEN OR SO YEARS AGO, WE WERE ABSORBED INTO THE TERRITORY HELD BY THE MARQUIS OF VIOLA.
OUR ISLAND AND THE OTHER TRIBES IN THIS ARCHIPELAGO ARE UNDER VIOLA PROTECTION.
I'M ALBUS.
I'M MASTER OF A SMALL MANOR HERE...
...AND I'M RELATED TO THE MARQUIS OF VIOLA.
ARISTO-CRAT AND AN ENEMY OFFICER.
I WAS IN THE BATTLE AGAINST THEM ON THE MAIN ISLAND.
HOW... DID...IT GO?
THE BAT-TLE?
THEY RETREATED.
IF THEY WITHDRAW COMPLETELY FROM VIOLA LANDS OR SURRENDER TO THE SUDELAISIAN LEAGUE, YOU'LL BE RETURNED.
THAT'S HOW WE TREAT PRISONERS OF WAR.

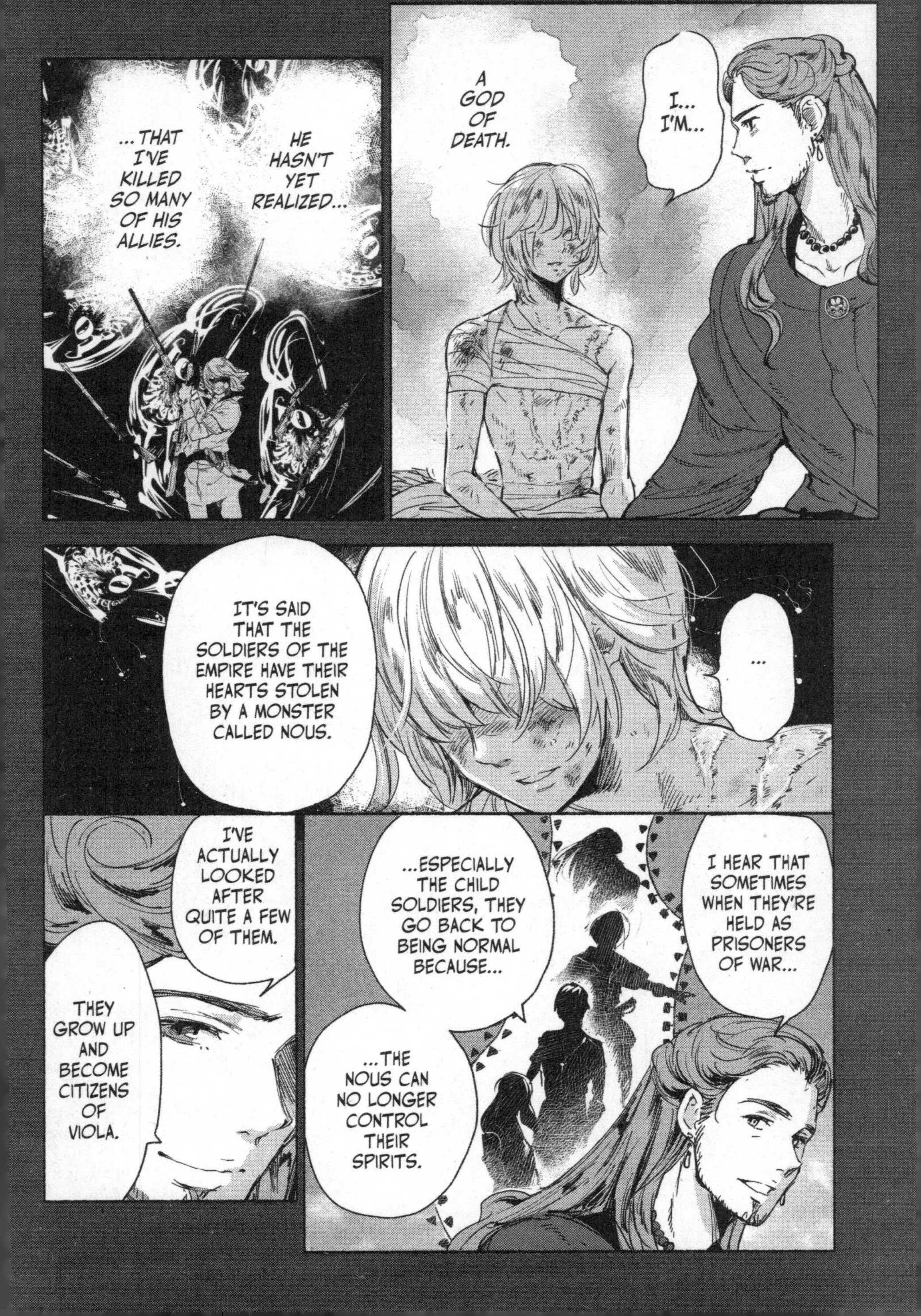
I... I'M...
A GOD OF DEATH.
HE HASN'T YET REALIZED...
...THAT I'VE KILLED SO MANY OF HIS ALLIES.
...
IT'S SAID THAT THE SOLDIERS OF THE EMPIRE HAVE THEIR HEARTS STOLEN BY A MONSTER CALLED NOUS.
I HEAR THAT SOMETIMES WHEN THEY'RE HELD AS PRISONERS OF WAR...
...ESPECIALLY THE CHILD SOLDIERS, THEY GO BACK TO BEING NORMAL BECAUSE...
...THE NOUS CAN NO LONGER CONTROL THEIR SPIRITS.
I'VE ACTUALLY LOOKED AFTER QUITE A FEW OF THEM.
THEY GROW UP AND BECOME CITIZENS OF VIOLA.

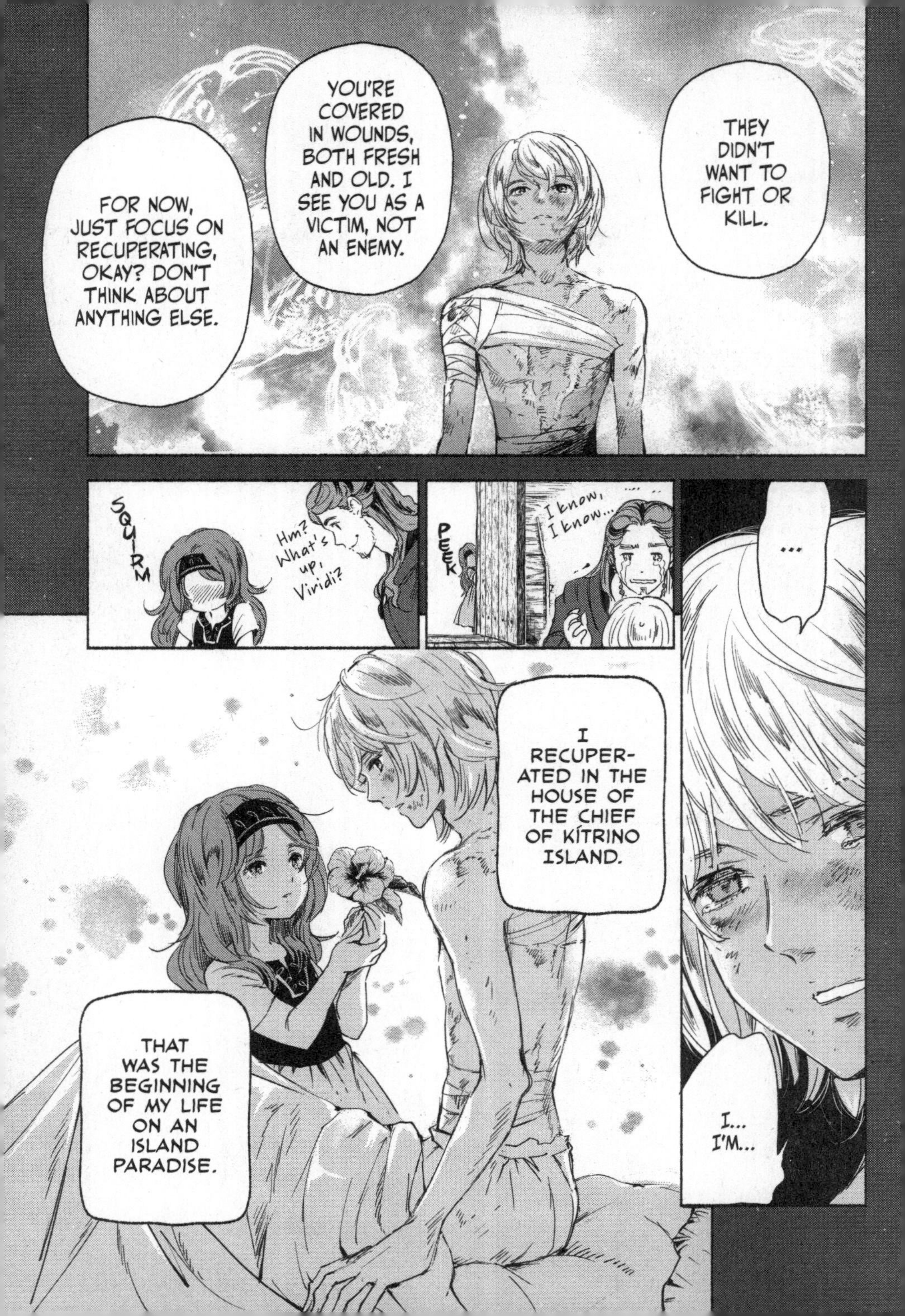
THEY DIDN'T WANT TO FIGHT OR KILL.
YOU'RE COVERED IN WOUNDS, BOTH FRESH AND OLD. I SEE YOU AS A VICTIM, NOT AN ENEMY.
FOR NOW, JUST FOCUS ON RECUPERATING, OKAY? DON'T THINK ABOUT ANYTHING ELSE.
...
I... I'M...
...
I know, I know...
PEEK
Hm? What's up, Viridi?
SQUIRM
I RECUPERATED IN THE HOUSE OF THE CHIEF OF KÍTRINO ISLAND.
THAT WAS THE BEGINNING OF MY LIFE ON AN ISLAND PARADISE.

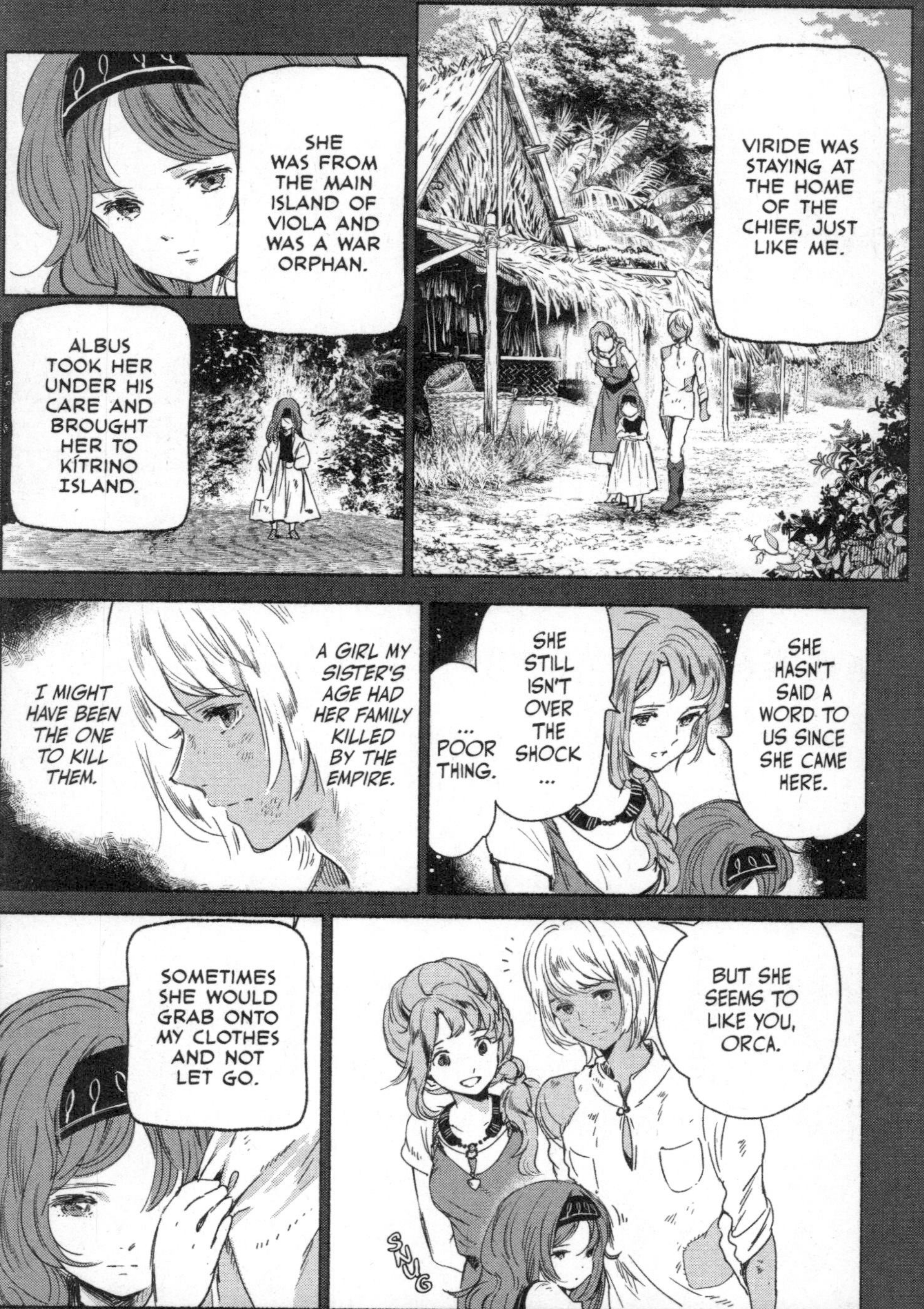
VIRIDE WAS STAYING AT THE HOME OF THE CHIEF, JUST LIKE ME.
SHE WAS FROM THE MAIN ISLAND OF VIOLA AND WAS A WAR ORPHAN.
ALBUS TOOK HER UNDER HIS CARE AND BROUGHT HER TO KÍTRINO ISLAND.
SHE HASN'T SAID A WORD TO US SINCE SHE CAME HERE.
SHE STILL ISN'T OVER THE SHOCK ...
... POOR THING.
A GIRL MY SISTER'S AGE HAD HER FAMILY KILLED BY THE EMPIRE.
I MIGHT HAVE BEEN THE ONE TO KILL THEM.
BUT SHE SEEMS TO LIKE YOU, ORCA.
SNUG
SOMETIMES SHE WOULD GRAB ONTO MY CLOTHES AND NOT LET GO.

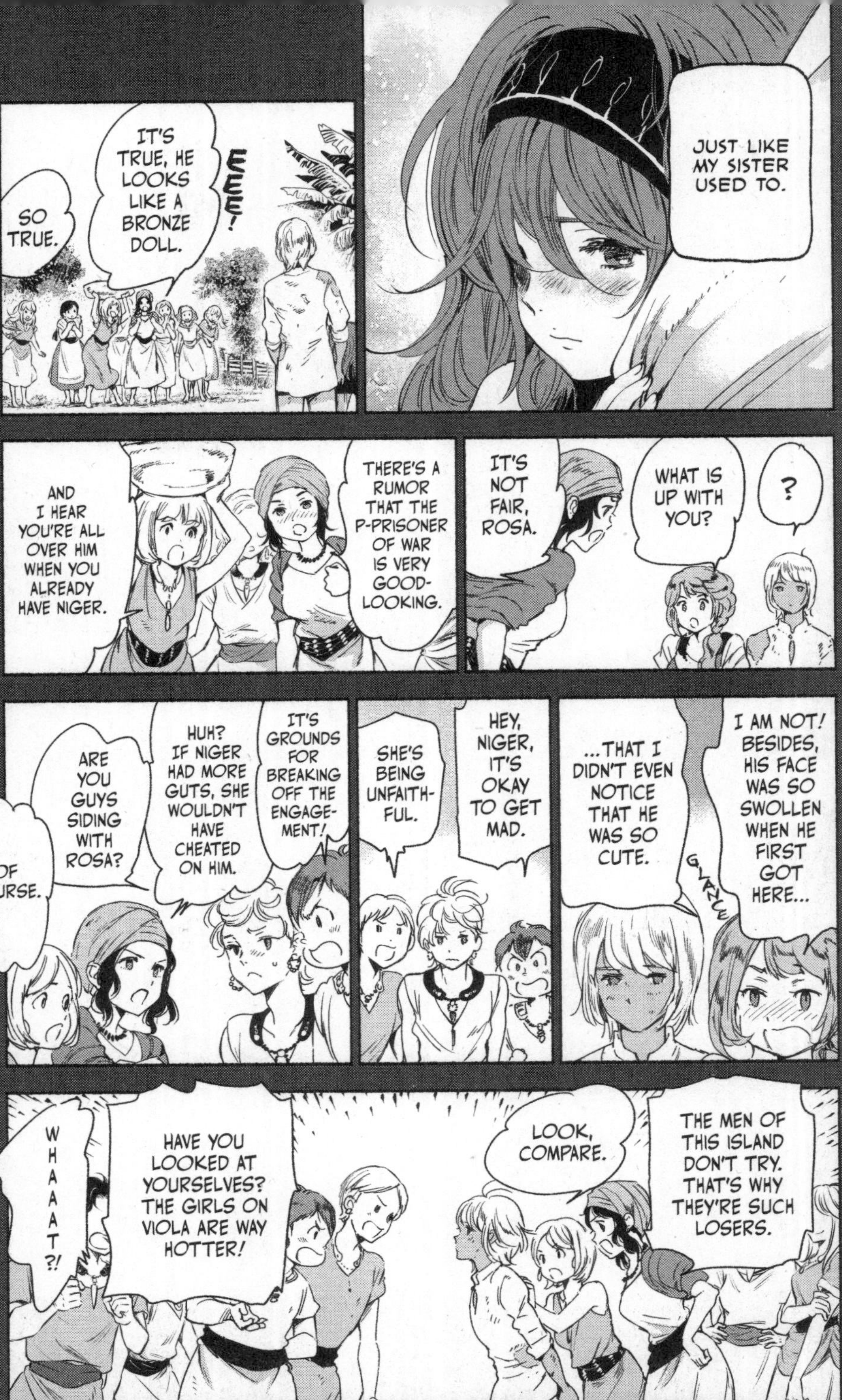
JUST LIKE MY SISTER USED TO.
EEE!
IT'S TRUE, HE LOOKS LIKE A BRONZE DOLL.
SO TRUE.
?
WHAT IS UP WITH YOU?
IT'S NOT FAIR, ROSA.
THERE'S A RUMOR THAT THE P-PRISONER OF WAR IS VERY GOOD-LOOKING.
AND I HEAR YOU'RE ALL OVER HIM WHEN YOU ALREADY HAVE NIGER.
I AM NOT! BESIDES, HIS FACE WAS SO SWOLLEN WHEN HE FIRST GOT HERE...
GLANCE
...THAT I DIDN'T EVEN NOTICE THAT HE WAS SO CUTE.
HEY, NIGER, IT'S OKAY TO GET MAD.
SHE'S BEING UNFAITHFUL.
IT'S GROUNDS FOR BREAKING OFF THE ENGAGEMENT!
HUH? IF NIGER HAD MORE GUTS, SHE WOULDN'T HAVE CHEATED ON HIM.
ARE YOU GUYS SIDING WITH ROSA?
OF COURSE.
THE MEN OF THIS ISLAND DON'T TRY. THAT'S WHY THEY'RE SUCH LOSERS.
LOOK, COMPARE.
HAVE YOU LOOKED AT YOURSELVES? THE GIRLS ON VIOLA ARE WAY HOTTER!
WHAAAAT?!

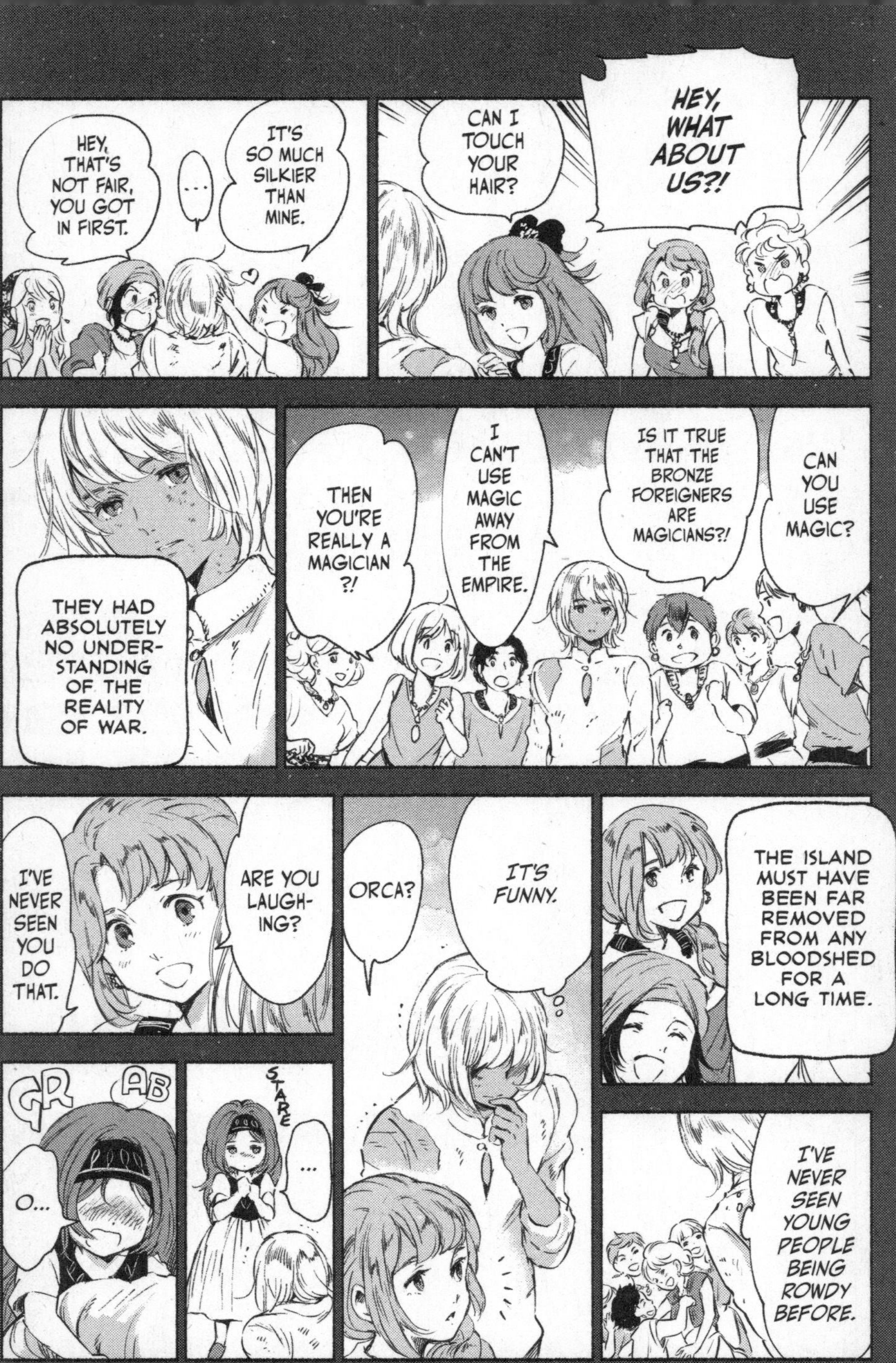
HEY, WHAT ABOUT US?!
CAN I TOUCH YOUR HAIR?
IT'S SO MUCH SILKIER THAN MINE.
...
HEY, THAT'S NOT FAIR, YOU GOT IN FIRST.
CAN YOU USE MAGIC?
IS IT TRUE THAT THE BRONZE FOREIGNERS ARE MAGICIANS?!
I CAN'T USE MAGIC AWAY FROM THE EMPIRE.
THEN YOU'RE REALLY A MAGICIAN?!
THEY HAD ABSOLUTELY NO UNDER-STANDING OF THE REALITY OF WAR.
THE ISLAND MUST HAVE BEEN FAR REMOVED FROM ANY BLOODSHED FOR A LONG TIME.
I'VE NEVER SEEN YOUNG PEOPLE BEING ROWDY BEFORE.
IT'S FUNNY.
ORCA?
ARE YOU LAUGH-ING?
I'VE NEVER SEEN YOU DO THAT.
STARE
...
GRAB
O...

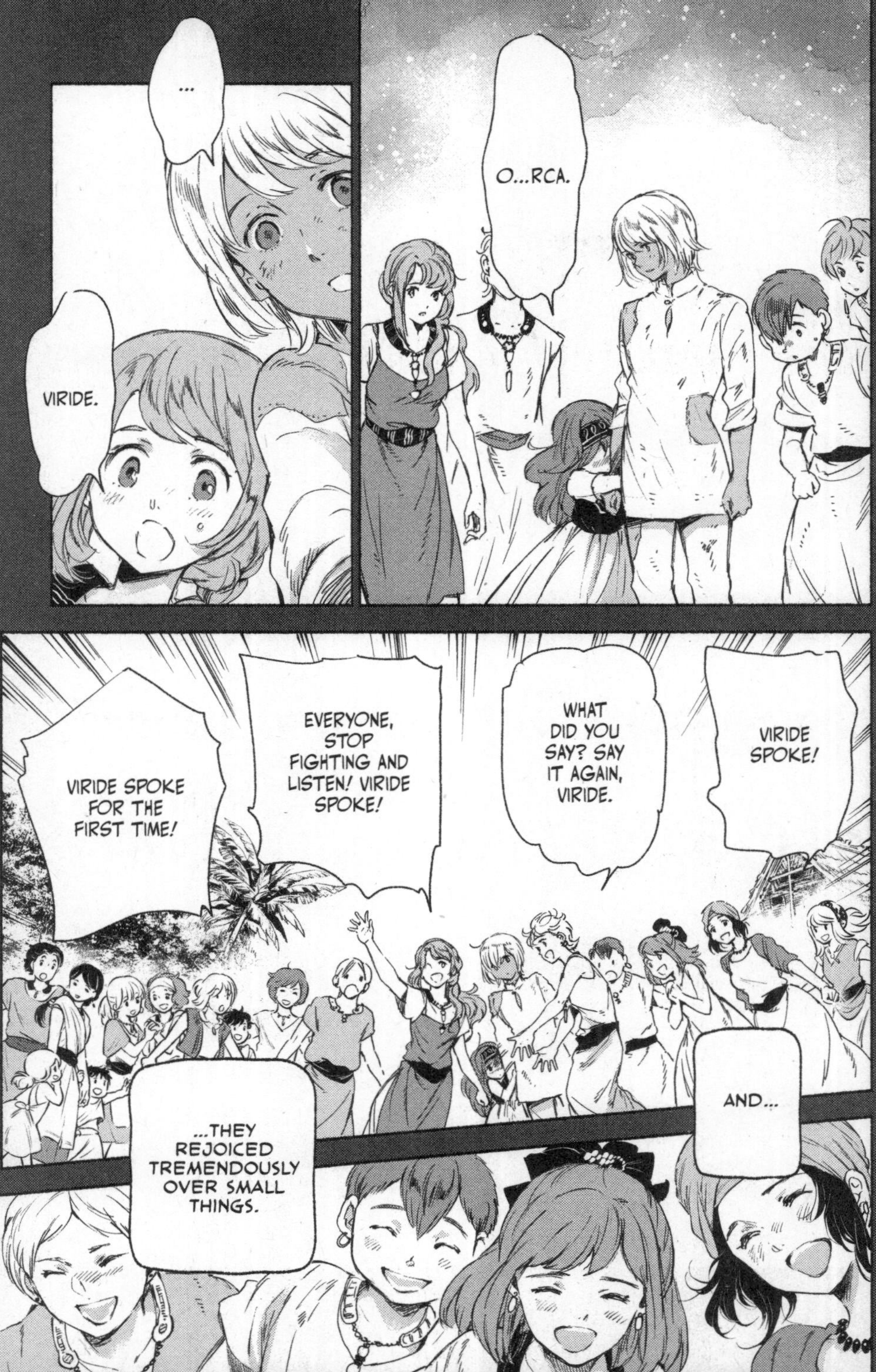
O...RCA.
...
VIRIDE.
VIRIDE SPOKE!
WHAT DID YOU SAY? SAY IT AGAIN, VIRIDE.
EVERYONE, STOP FIGHTING AND LISTEN! VIRIDE SPOKE!
VIRIDE SPOKE FOR THE FIRST TIME!
AND...
...THEY REJOICED TREMENDOUSLY OVER SMALL THINGS.

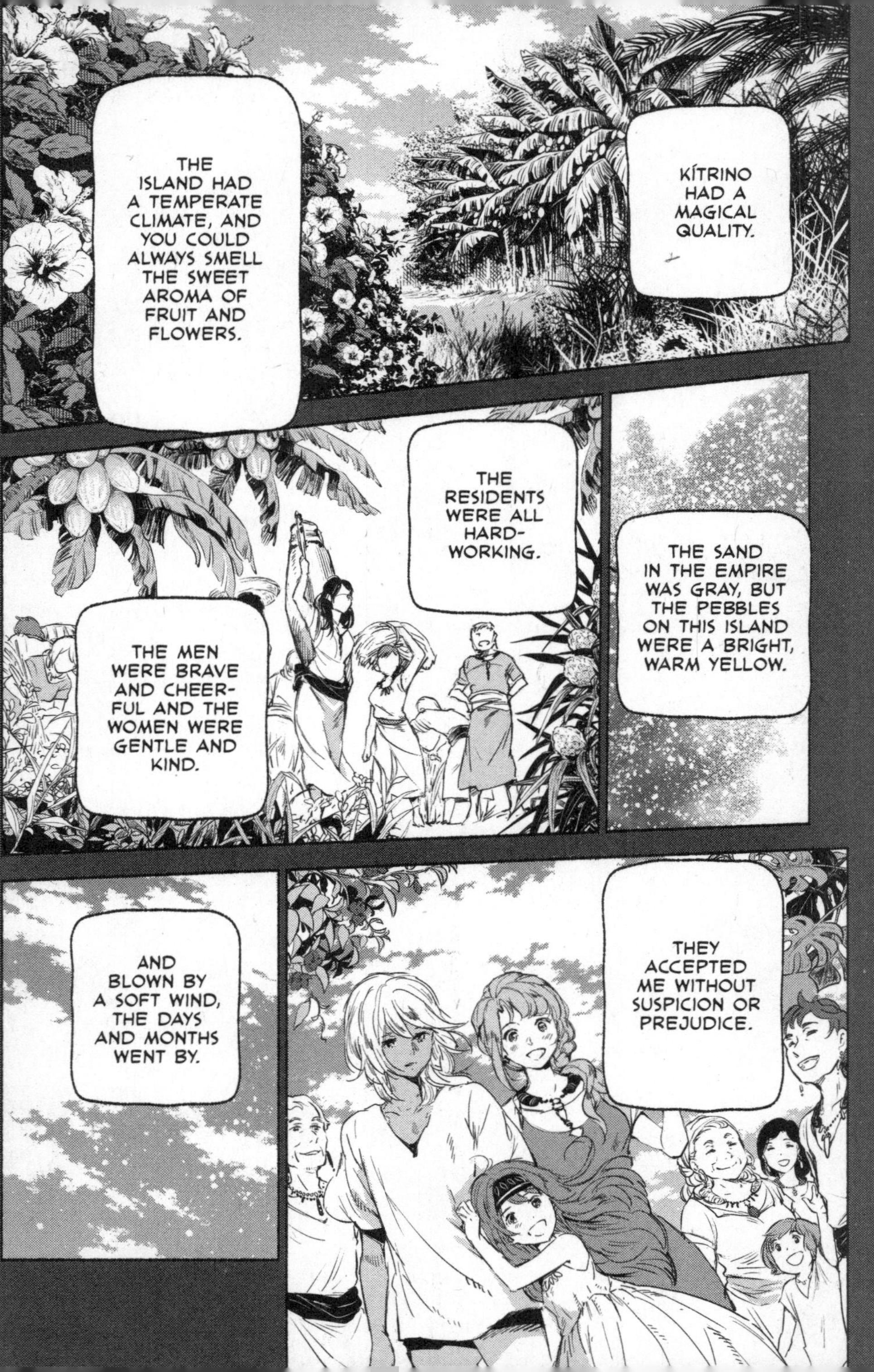
KÍTRINO HAD A MAGICAL QUALITY.
THE ISLAND HAD A TEMPERATE CLIMATE, AND YOU COULD ALWAYS SMELL THE SWEET AROMA OF FRUIT AND FLOWERS.
THE SAND IN THE EMPIRE WAS GRAY, BUT THE PEBBLES ON THIS ISLAND WERE A BRIGHT, WARM YELLOW.
THE RESIDENTS WERE ALL HARD-WORKING.
THE MEN WERE BRAVE AND CHEERFUL AND THE WOMEN WERE GENTLE AND KIND.
THEY ACCEPTED ME WITHOUT SUSPICION OR PREJUDICE.
AND BLOWN BY A SOFT WIND, THE DAYS AND MONTHS WENT BY.

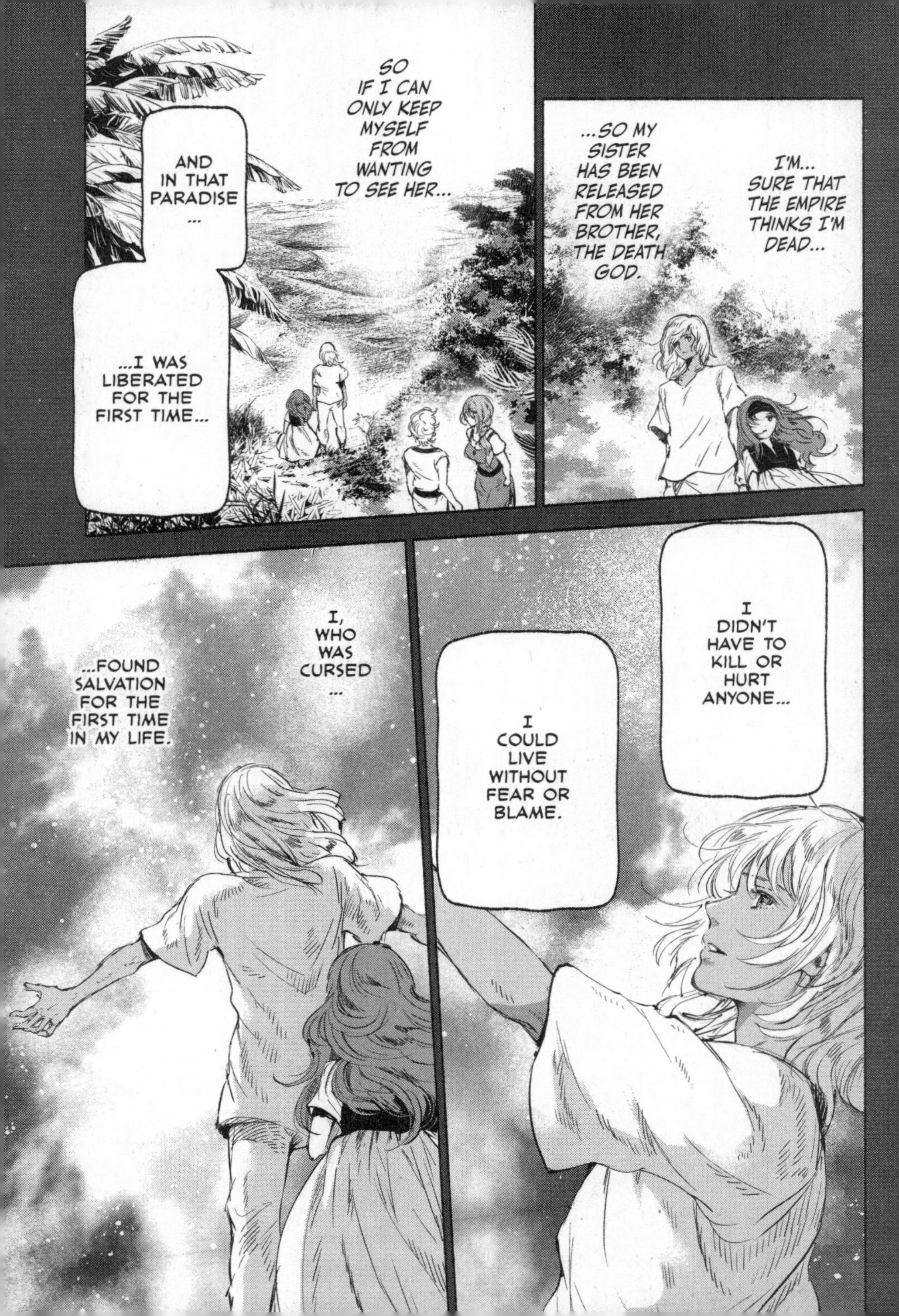
I'M... SURE THAT THE EMPIRE THINKS I'M DEAD...
...SO MY SISTER HAS BEEN RELEASED FROM HER BROTHER, THE DEATH GOD.
SO IF I CAN ONLY KEEP MYSELF FROM WANTING TO SEE HER...
AND IN THAT PARADISE...
...I WAS LIBERATED FOR THE FIRST TIME...
I DIDN'T HAVE TO KILL OR HURT ANYONE...
I COULD LIVE WITHOUT FEAR OR BLAME.
I, WHO WAS CURSED...
...FOUND SALVATION FOR THE FIRST TIME IN MY LIFE.

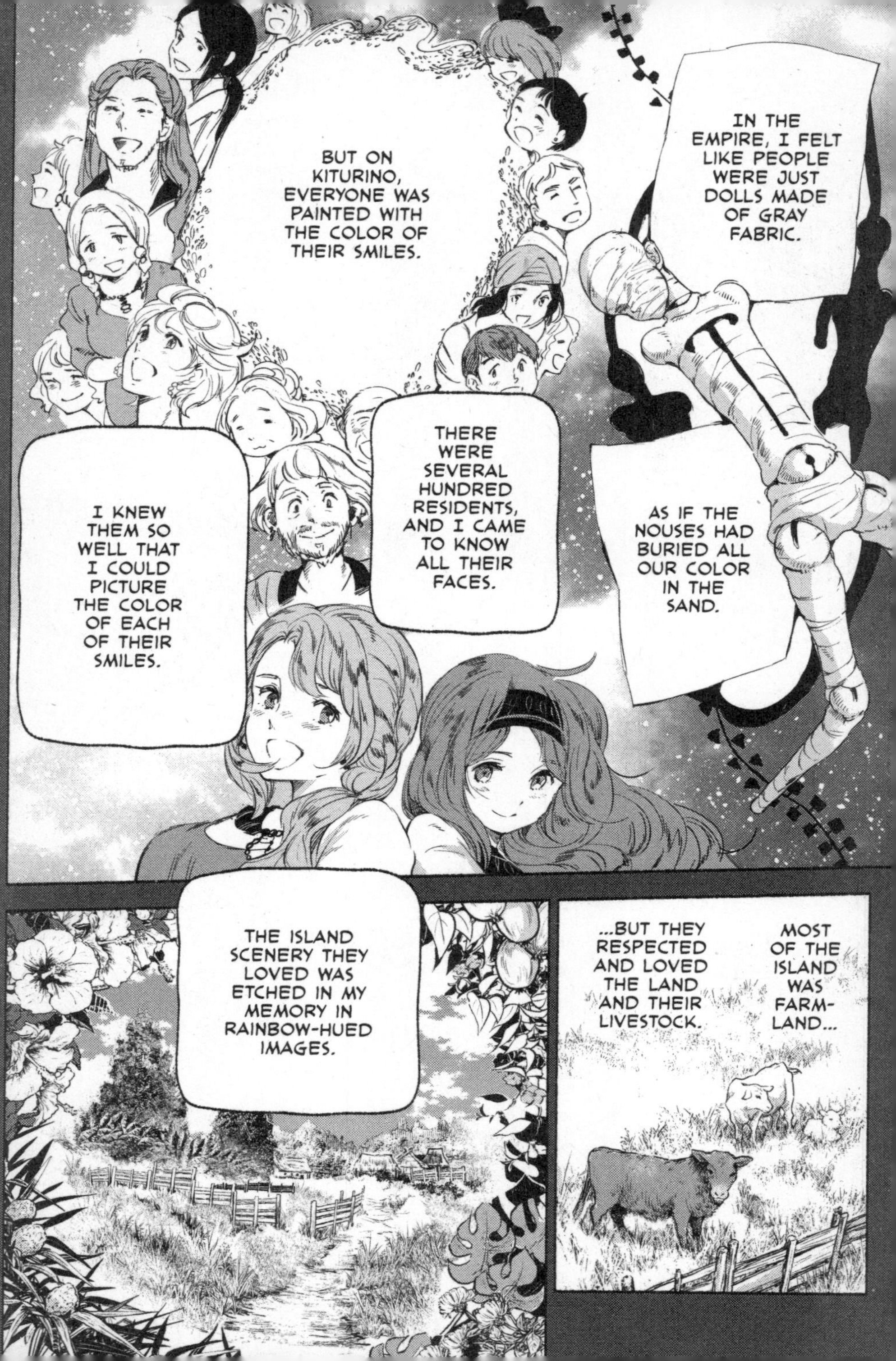
IN THE EMPIRE, I FELT LIKE PEOPLE WERE JUST DOLLS MADE OF GRAY FABRIC.
AS IF THE NOUSES HAD BURIED ALL OUR COLOR IN THE SAND.
BUT ON KITURINO, EVERYONE WAS PAINTED WITH THE COLOR OF THEIR SMILES.
THERE WERE SEVERAL HUNDRED RESIDENTS, AND I CAME TO KNOW ALL THEIR FACES.
I KNEW THEM SO WELL THAT I COULD PICTURE THE COLOR OF EACH OF THEIR SMILES.
MOST OF THE ISLAND WAS FARM-LAND...
...BUT THEY RESPECTED AND LOVED THE LAND AND THEIR LIVESTOCK.
THE ISLAND SCENERY THEY LOVED WAS ETCHED IN MY MEMORY IN RAINBOW-HUED IMAGES.

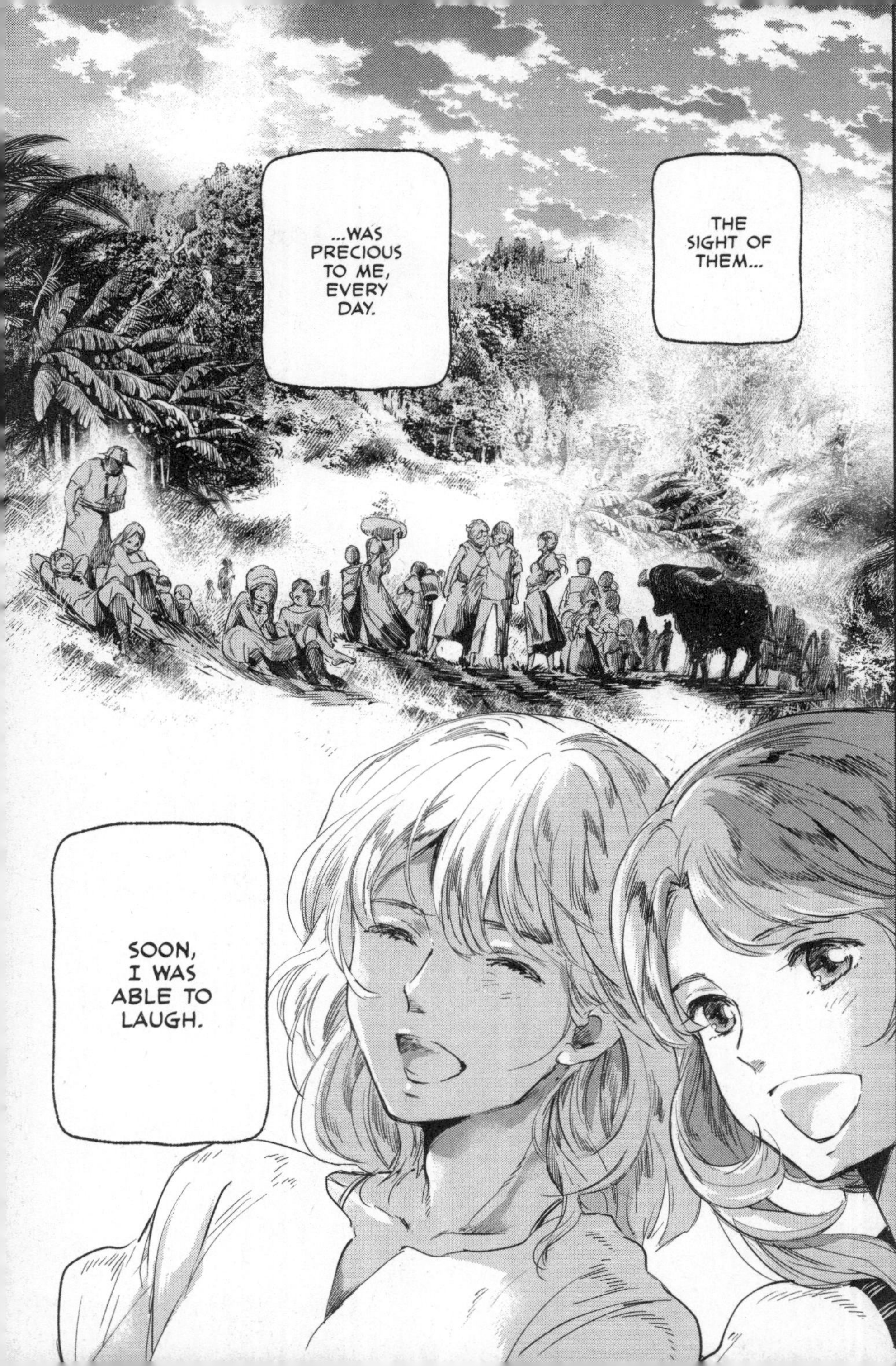
THE SIGHT OF THEM...
...WAS PRECIOUS TO ME, EVERY DAY.
SOON, I WAS ABLE TO LAUGH.

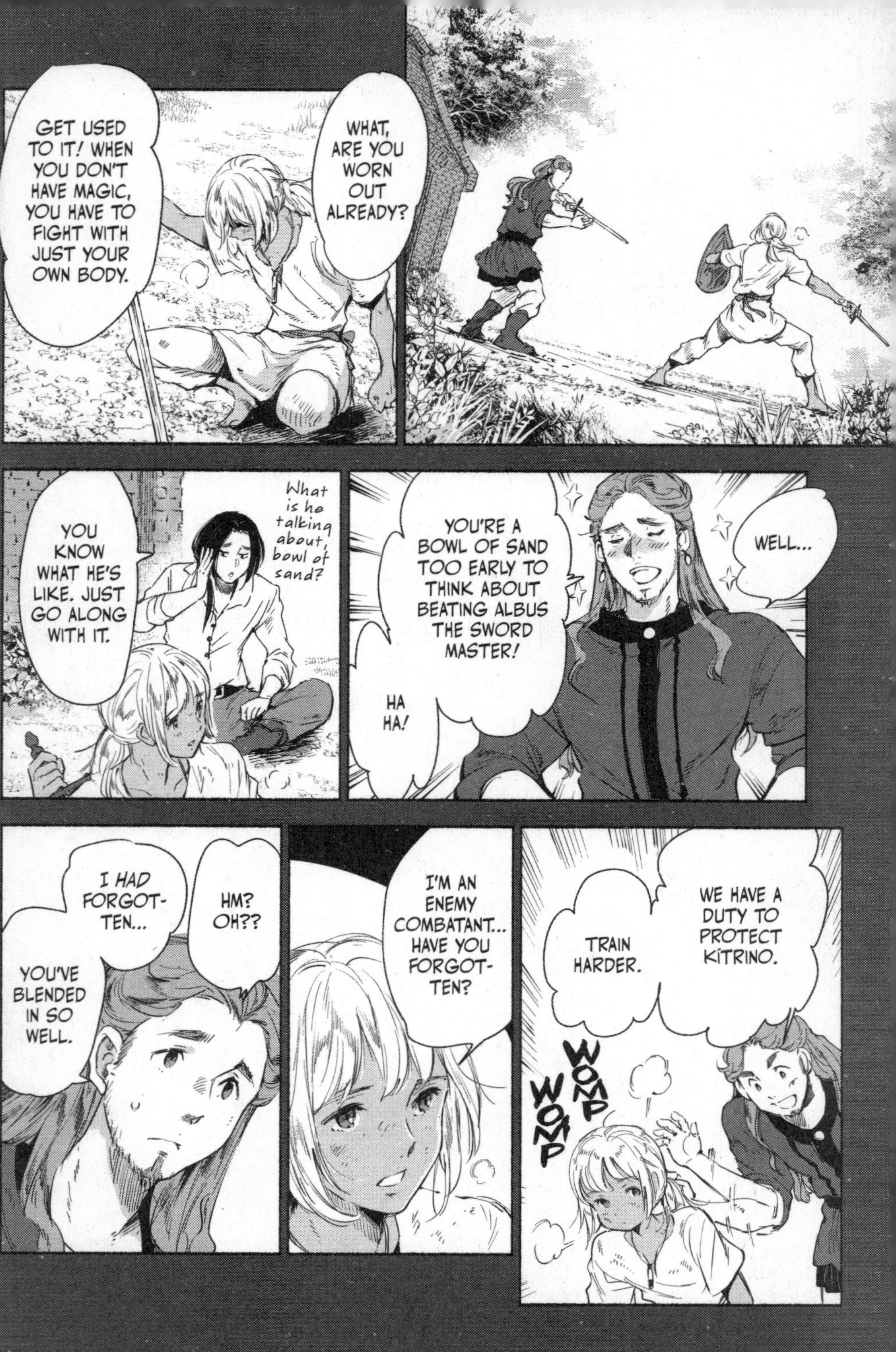
WHAT, ARE YOU WORN OUT ALREADY?
GET USED TO IT! WHEN YOU DON'T HAVE MAGIC, YOU HAVE TO FIGHT WITH JUST YOUR OWN BODY.
WELL...
YOU'RE A BOWL OF SAND TOO EARLY TO THINK ABOUT BEATING ALBUS THE SWORD MASTER!
HA HA!
What is he talking about, bowl of sand?
YOU KNOW WHAT HE'S LIKE. JUST GO ALONG WITH IT.
WE HAVE A DUTY TO PROTECT KITRINO.
TRAIN HARDER.
WOMP WOMP
I'M AN ENEMY COMBATANT... HAVE YOU FORGOT-TEN?
HM? OH??
I HAD FORGOT-TEN...
YOU'VE BLENDED IN SO WELL.

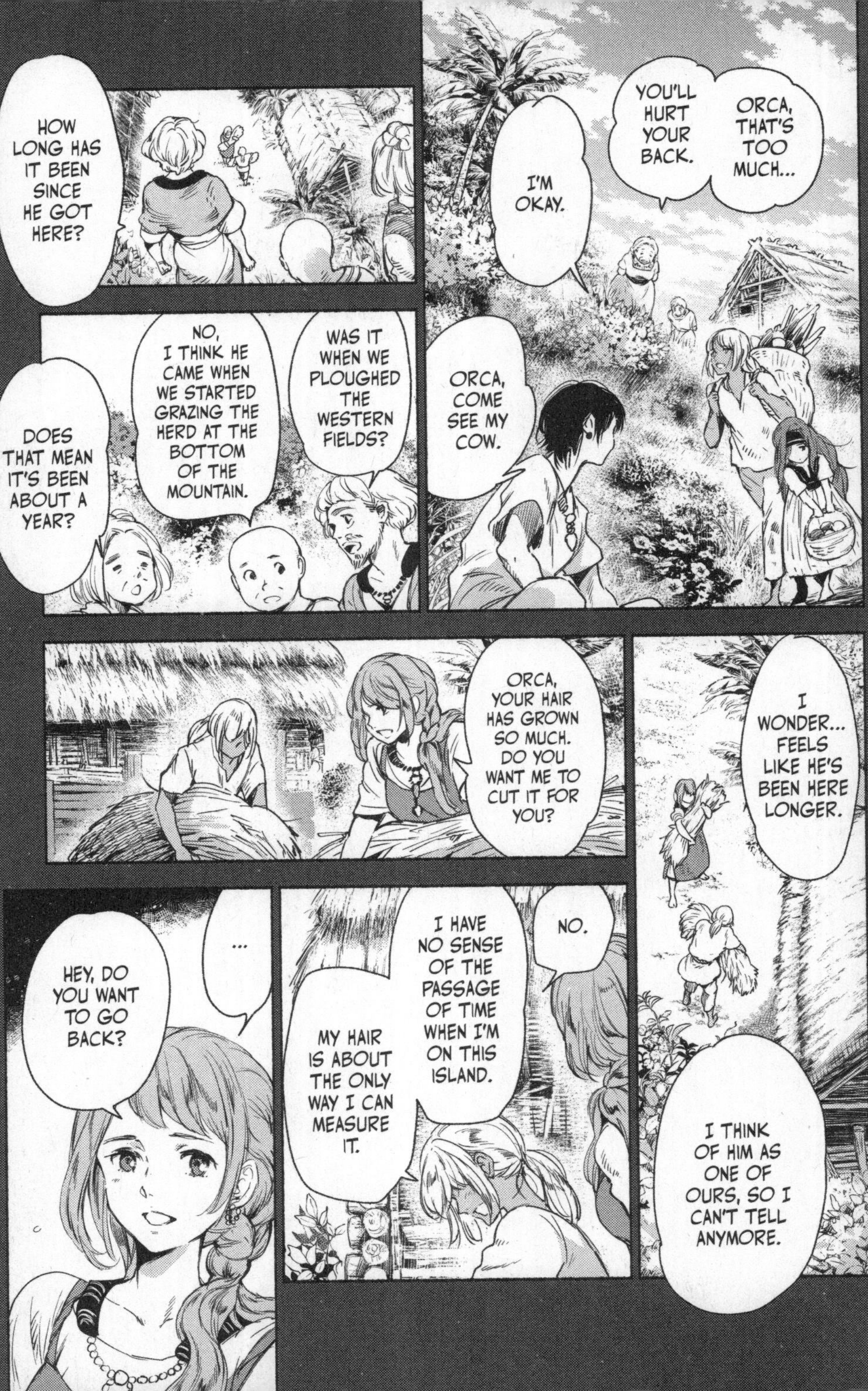
ORCA, THAT'S TOO MUCH...
YOU'LL HURT YOUR BACK.
I'M OKAY.
ORCA, COME SEE MY COW.
HOW LONG HAS IT BEEN SINCE HE GOT HERE?
WAS IT WHEN WE PLOUGHED THE WESTERN FIELDS?
NO, I THINK HE CAME WHEN WE STARTED GRAZING THE HERD AT THE BOTTOM OF THE MOUNTAIN.
DOES THAT MEAN IT'S BEEN ABOUT A YEAR?
I WONDER... FEELS LIKE HE'S BEEN HERE LONGER.
I THINK OF HIM AS ONE OF OURS, SO I CAN'T TELL ANYMORE.
ORCA, YOUR HAIR HAS GROWN SO MUCH. DO YOU WANT ME TO CUT IT FOR YOU?
NO.
I HAVE NO SENSE OF THE PASSAGE OF TIME WHEN I'M ON THIS ISLAND.
MY HAIR IS ABOUT THE ONLY WAY I CAN MEASURE IT.
...
HEY, DO YOU WANT TO GO BACK?

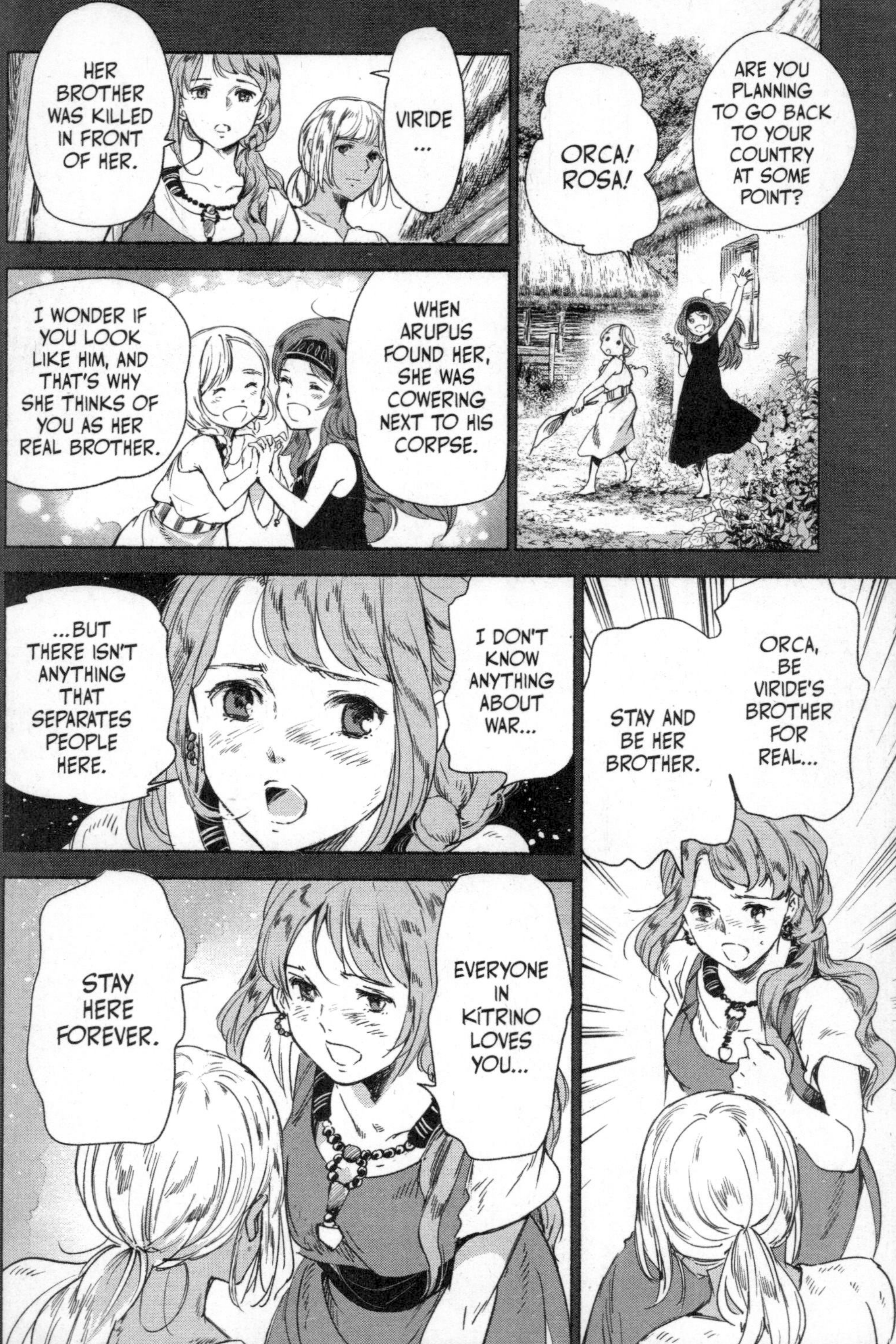
ARE YOU PLANNING TO GO BACK TO YOUR COUNTRY AT SOME POINT?
ORCA! ROSA!
VIRIDE ...
HER BROTHER WAS KILLED IN FRONT OF HER.
WHEN ARUPUS FOUND HER, SHE WAS COWERING NEXT TO HIS CORPSE.
I WONDER IF YOU LOOK LIKE HIM, AND THAT'S WHY SHE THINKS OF YOU AS HER REAL BROTHER.
ORCA, BE VIRIDE'S BROTHER FOR REAL...
STAY AND BE HER BROTHER.
I DON'T KNOW ANYTHING ABOUT WAR...
...BUT THERE ISN'T ANYTHING THAT SEPARATES PEOPLE HERE.
EVERYONE IN KÍTRINO LOVES YOU...
STAY HERE FOREVER.

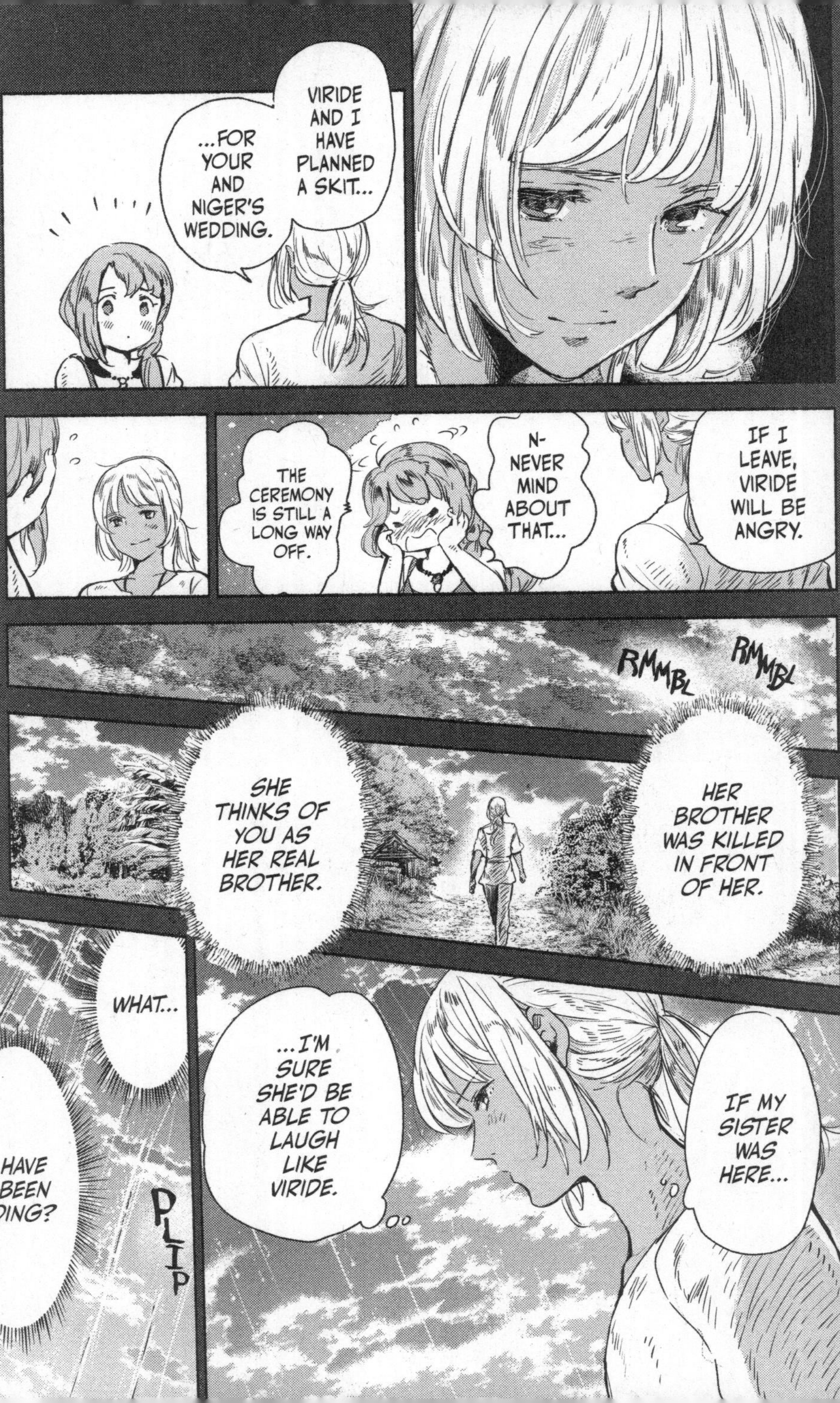
VIRIDE AND I HAVE PLANNED A SKIT...
...FOR YOUR AND NIGER'S WEDDING.
IF I LEAVE, VIRIDE WILL BE ANGRY.
N- NEVER MIND ABOUT THAT...
THE CEREMONY IS STILL A LONG WAY OFF.
RMMBL
RMMBL
HER BROTHER WAS KILLED IN FRONT OF HER.
SHE THINKS OF YOU AS HER REAL BROTHER.
IF MY SISTER WAS HERE...
...I'M SURE SHE'D BE ABLE TO LAUGH LIKE VIRIDE.
WHAT...
...HAVE I BEEN DOING?
PLIP

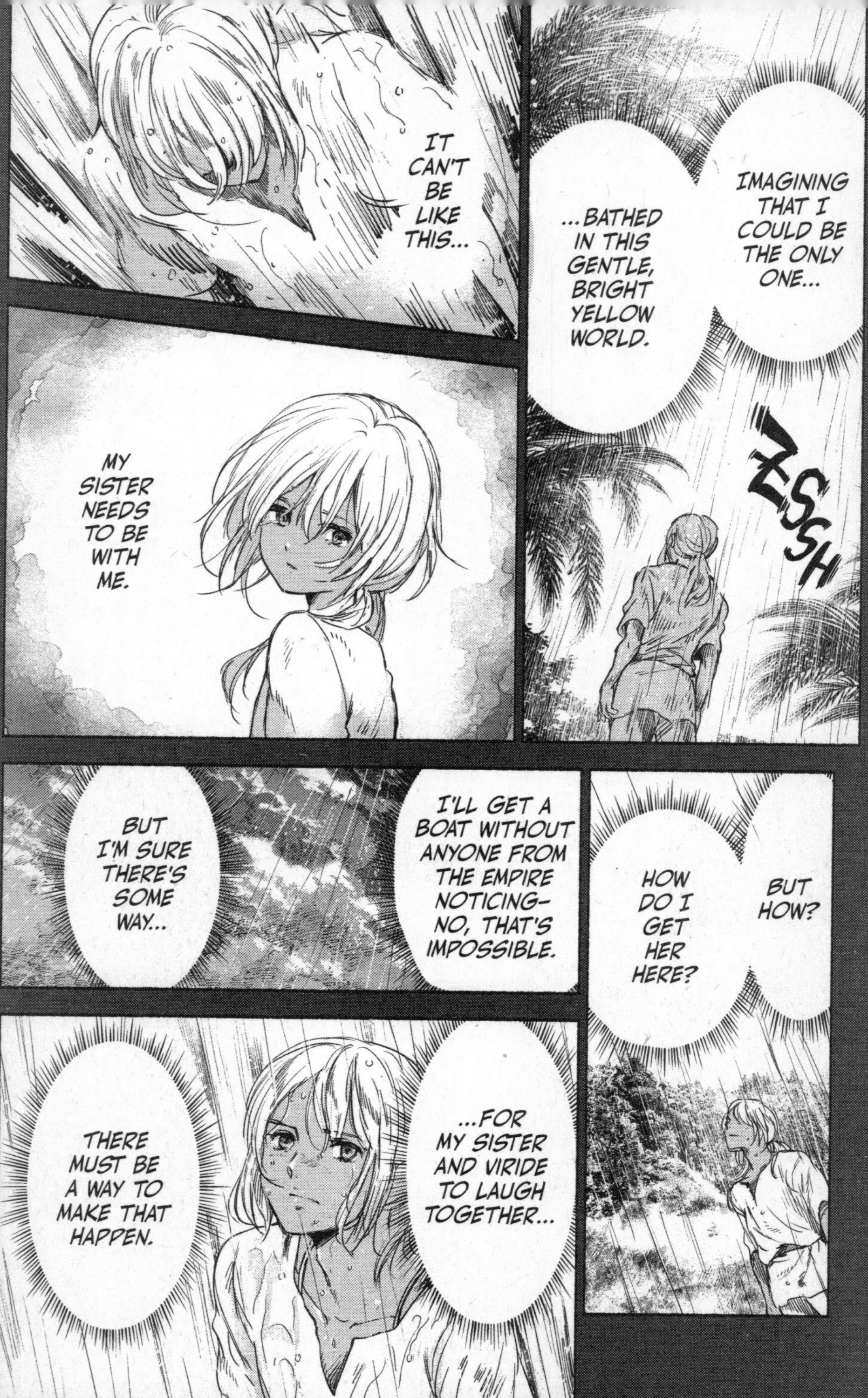
IMAGINING THAT I COULD BE THE ONLY ONE...
...BATHED IN THIS GENTLE, BRIGHT YELLOW WORLD.
ZSSH
IT CAN'T BE LIKE THIS...
MY SISTER NEEDS TO BE WITH ME.
BUT HOW?
HOW DO I GET HER HERE?
I'LL GET A BOAT WITHOUT ANYONE FROM THE EMPIRE NOTICING— NO, THAT'S IMPOSSIBLE.
BUT I'M SURE THERE'S SOME WAY...
...FOR MY SISTER AND VIRIDE TO LAUGH TOGETHER...
THERE MUST BE A WAY TO MAKE THAT HAPPEN.

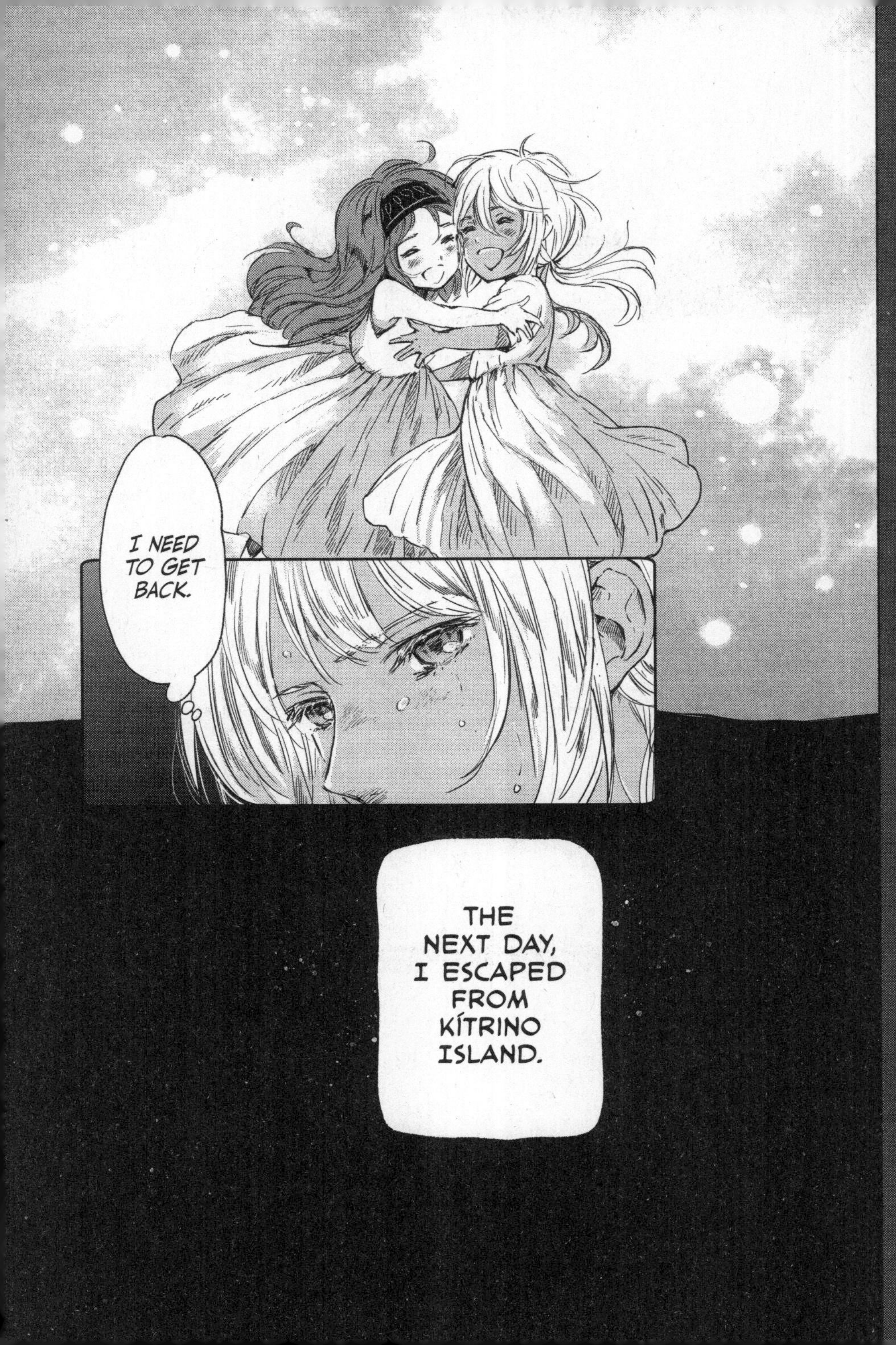
I NEED TO GET BACK.
THE NEXT DAY, I ESCAPED FROM KÍTRINO ISLAND.

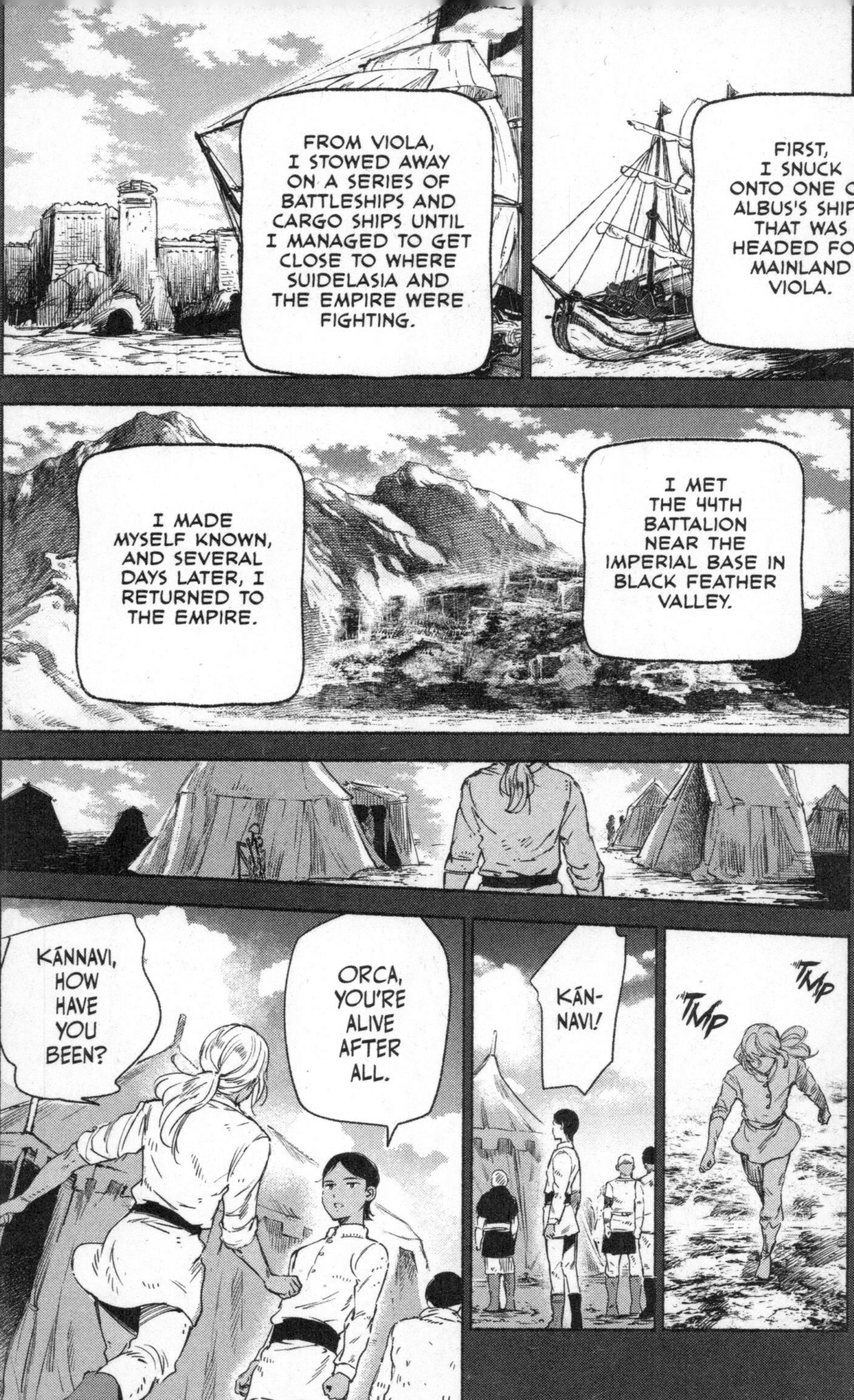
FIRST, I SNUCK ONTO ONE OF ALBUS'S SHIPS THAT WAS HEADED FOR MAINLAND VIOLA.
FROM VIOLA, I STOWED AWAY ON A SERIES OF BATTLESHIPS AND CARGO SHIPS UNTIL I MANAGED TO GET CLOSE TO WHERE SUIDELASIA AND THE EMPIRE WERE FIGHTING.
I MET THE 44TH BATTALION NEAR THE IMPERIAL BASE IN BLACK FEATHER VALLEY.
I MADE MYSELF KNOWN, AND SEVERAL DAYS LATER, I RETURNED TO THE EMPIRE.
TMP
TMP
KĀN-NAVI!
ORCA, YOU'RE ALIVE AFTER ALL.
KĀNNAVI, HOW HAVE YOU BEEN?

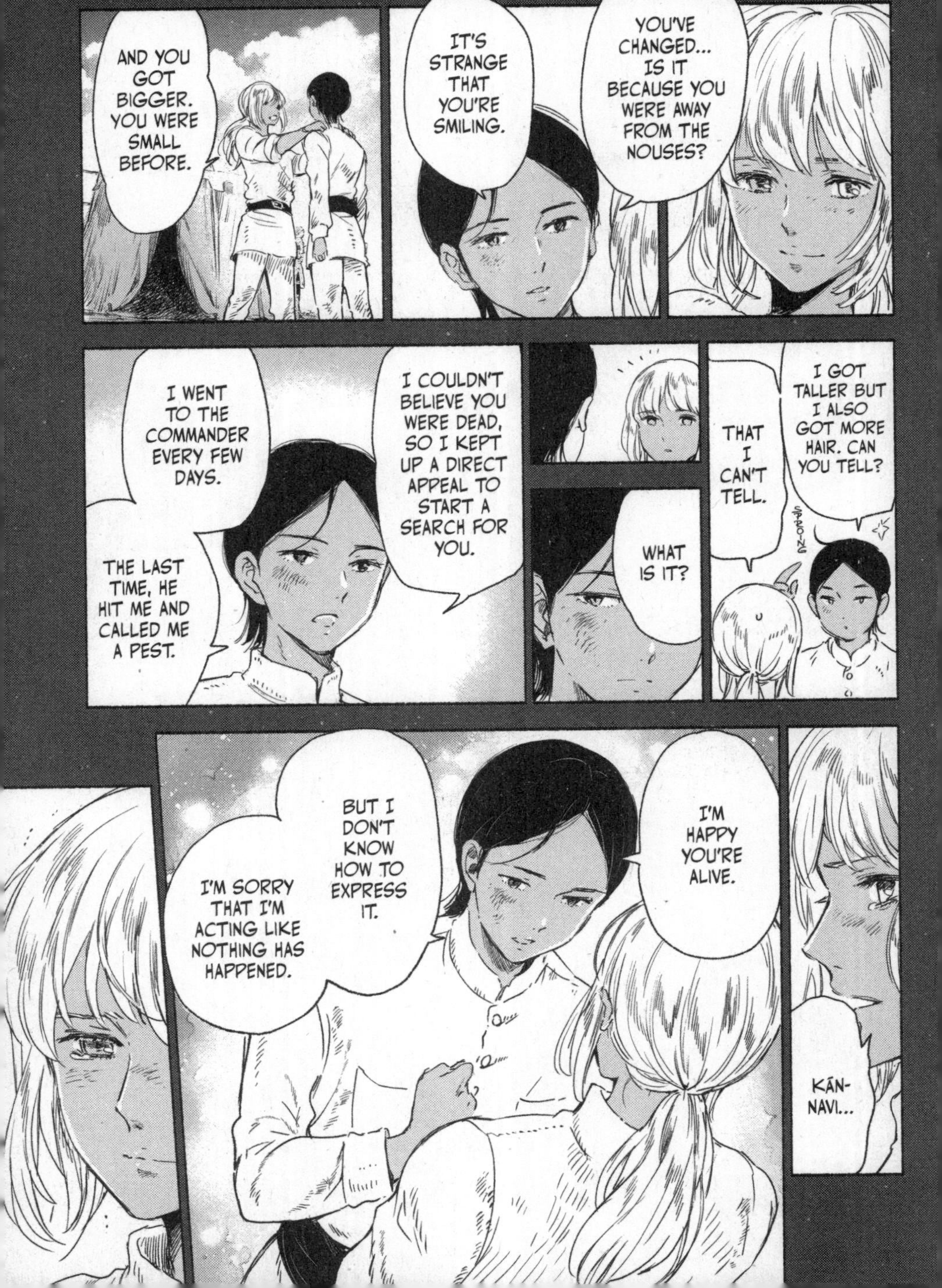
YOU'VE CHANGED... IS IT BECAUSE YOU WERE AWAY FROM THE NOUSES?
IT'S STRANGE THAT YOU'RE SMILING.
AND YOU GOT BIGGER. YOU WERE SMALL BEFORE.
I GOT TALLER BUT I ALSO GOT MORE HAIR. CAN YOU TELL?
THAT I CAN'T TELL.
SPROING
WHAT IS IT?
I COULDN'T BELIEVE YOU WERE DEAD, SO I KEPT UP A DIRECT APPEAL TO START A SEARCH FOR YOU.
I WENT TO THE COMMANDER EVERY FEW DAYS.
THE LAST TIME, HE HIT ME AND CALLED ME A PEST.
KĀN-NAVI...
I'M HAPPY YOU'RE ALIVE.
BUT I DON'T KNOW HOW TO EXPRESS IT.
I'M SORRY THAT I'M ACTING LIKE NOTHING HAS HAPPENED.
...

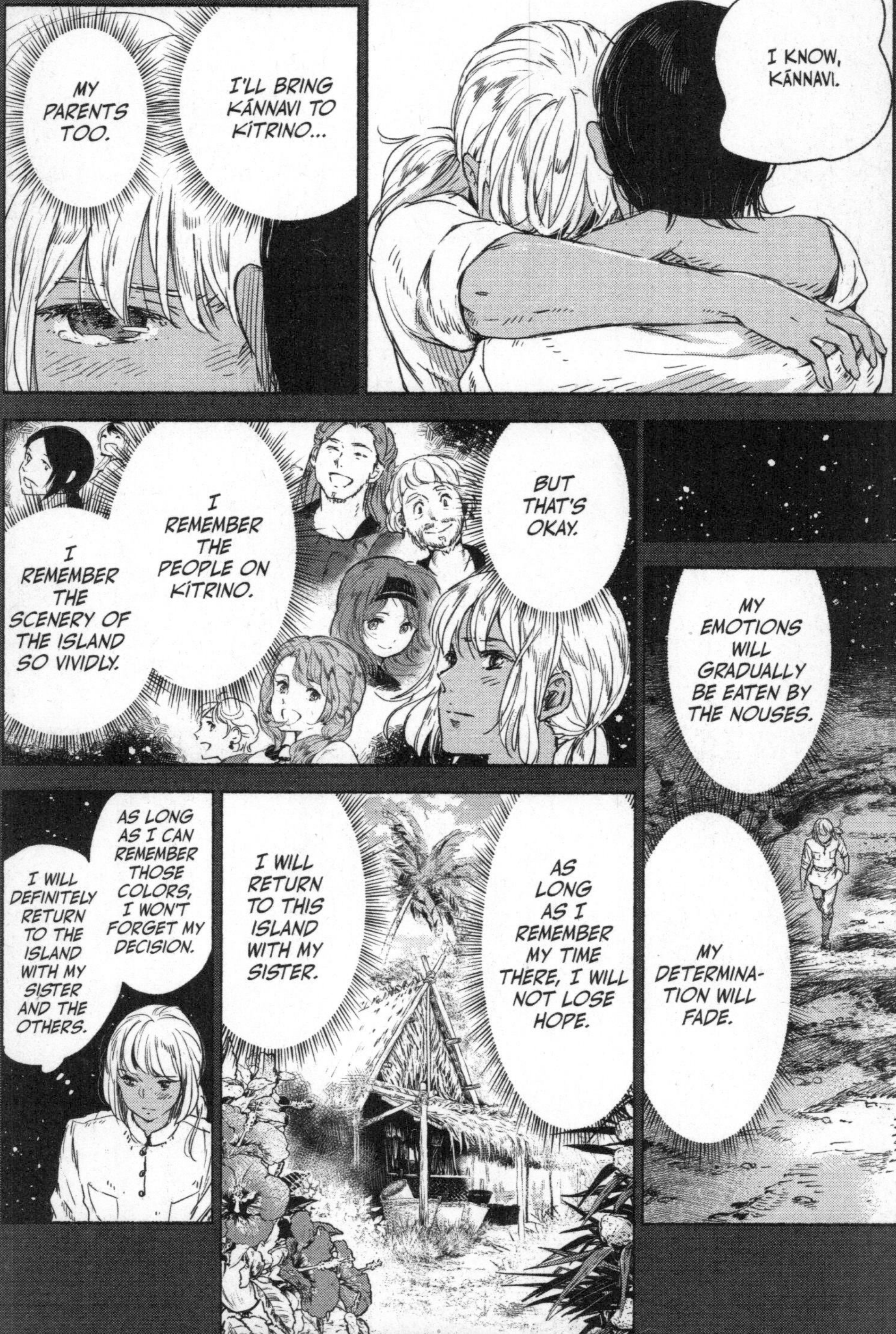
I KNOW, KĀNNAVI.
I'LL BRING KĀNNAVI TO KĪTRINO...
MY PARENTS TOO.
MY EMOTIONS WILL GRADUALLY BE EATEN BY THE NOUSES.
MY DETERMINATION WILL FADE.
BUT THAT'S OKAY.
I REMEMBER THE PEOPLE ON KĪTRINO.
I REMEMBER THE SCENERY OF THE ISLAND SO VIVIDLY.
AS LONG AS I REMEMBER MY TIME THERE, I WILL NOT LOSE HOPE.
I WILL RETURN TO THIS ISLAND WITH MY SISTER.
AS LONG AS I CAN REMEMBER THOSE COLORS, I WON'T FORGET MY DECISION.
I WILL DEFINITELY RETURN TO THE ISLAND WITH MY SISTER AND THE OTHERS.

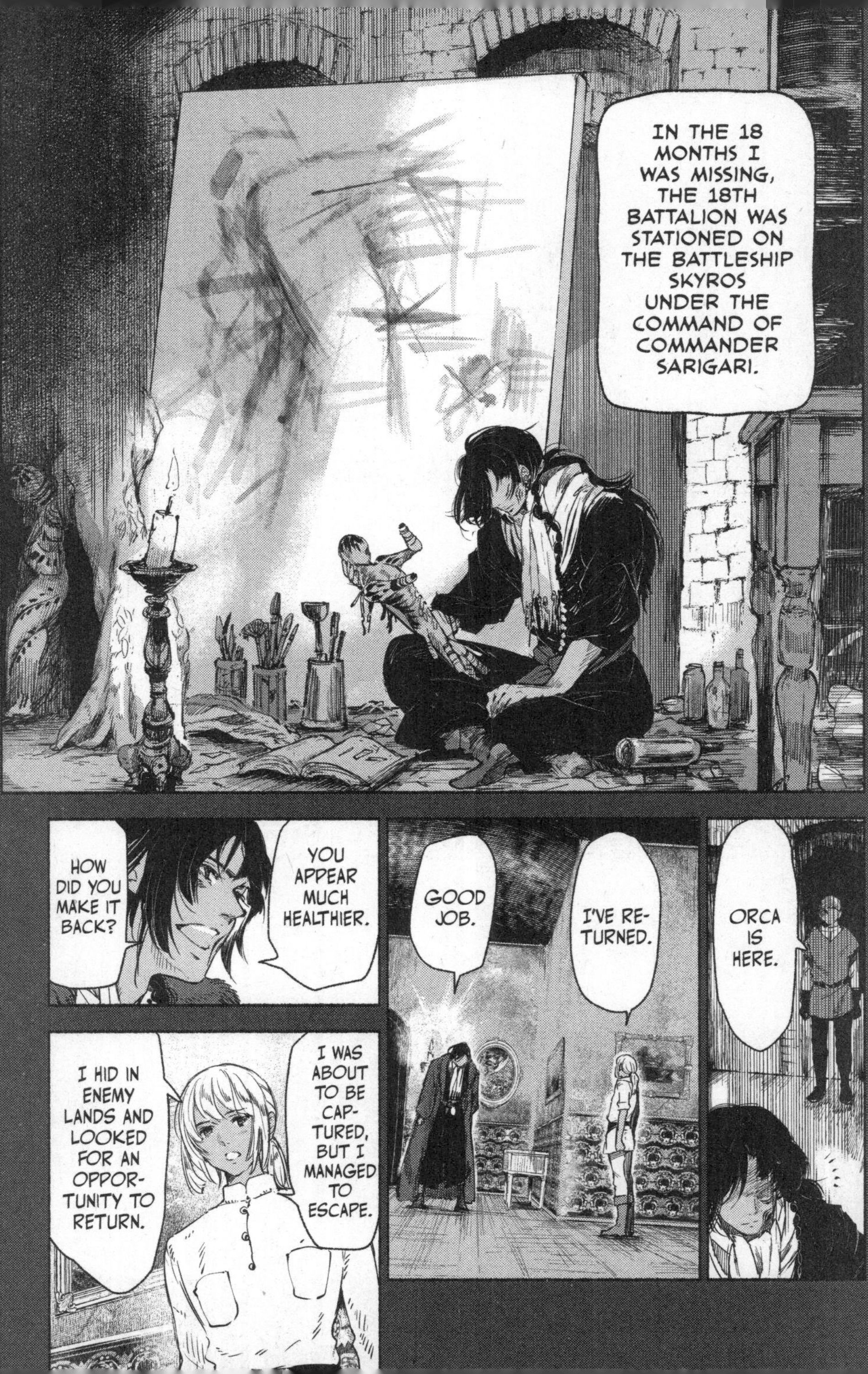
IN THE 18 MONTHS I WAS MISSING, THE 18TH BATTALION WAS STATIONED ON THE BATTLESHIP SKYROS UNDER THE COMMAND OF COMMANDER SARIGARI.
ORCA IS HERE.
I'VE RE-TURNED.
GOOD JOB.
YOU APPEAR MUCH HEALTHIER.
HOW DID YOU MAKE IT BACK?
I WAS ABOUT TO BE CAP-TURED, BUT I MANAGED TO ESCAPE.
I HID IN ENEMY LANDS AND LOOKED FOR AN OPPOR-TUNITY TO RETURN.

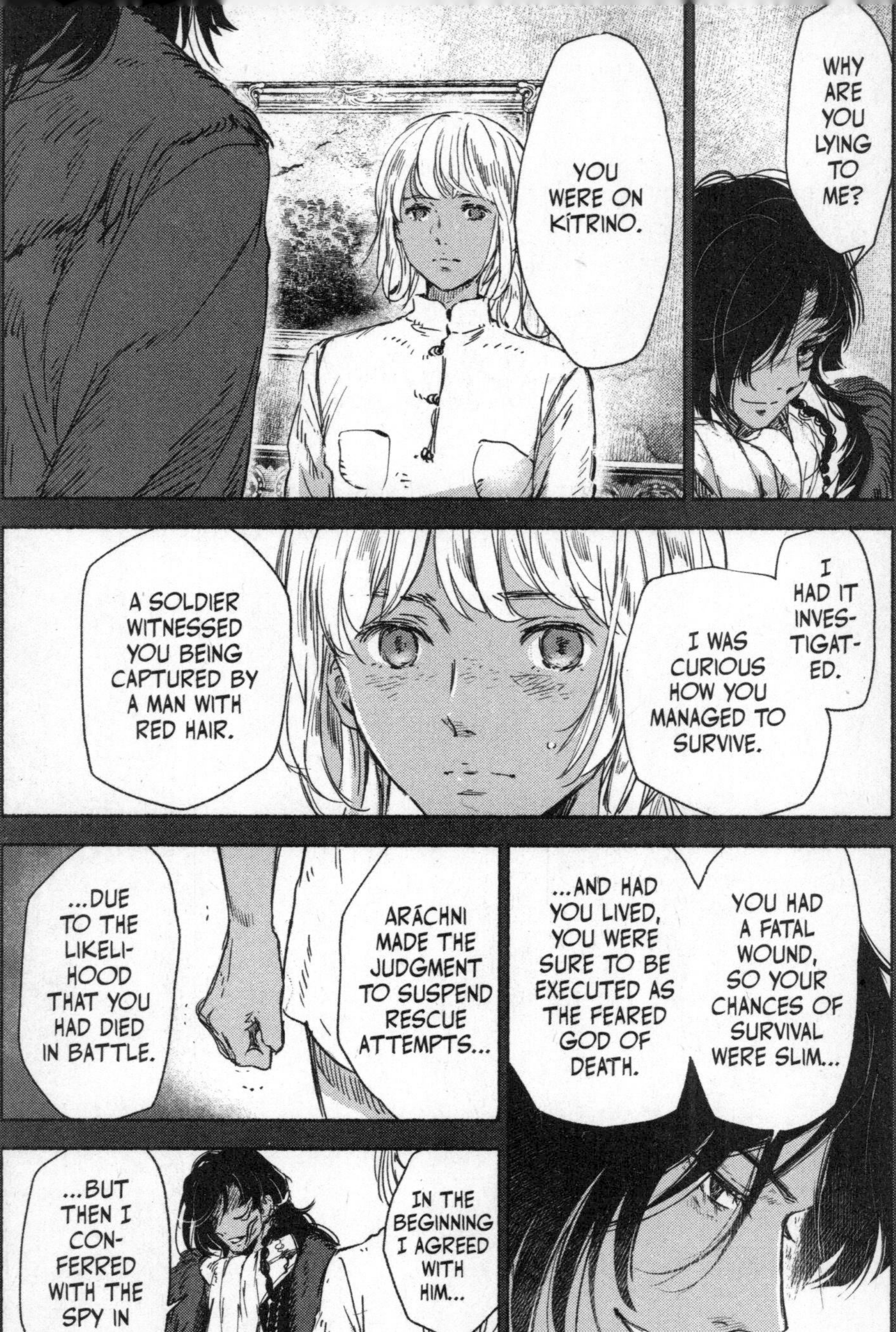
WHY ARE YOU LYING TO ME?
YOU WERE ON KÍTRINO.
I HAD IT INVES-TIGAT-ED.
I WAS CURIOUS HOW YOU MANAGED TO SURVIVE.
A SOLDIER WITNESSED YOU BEING CAPTURED BY A MAN WITH RED HAIR.
YOU HAD A FATAL WOUND, SO YOUR CHANCES OF SURVIVAL WERE SLIM...
...AND HAD YOU LIVED, YOU WERE SURE TO BE EXECUTED AS THE FEARED GOD OF DEATH.
ARÁCHNI MADE THE JUDGMENT TO SUSPEND RESCUE ATTEMPTS...
...DUE TO THE LIKELI-HOOD THAT YOU HAD DIED IN BATTLE.
IN THE BEGINNING I AGREED WITH HIM...
...BUT THEN I CON-FERRED WITH THE SPY IN VIOLA.

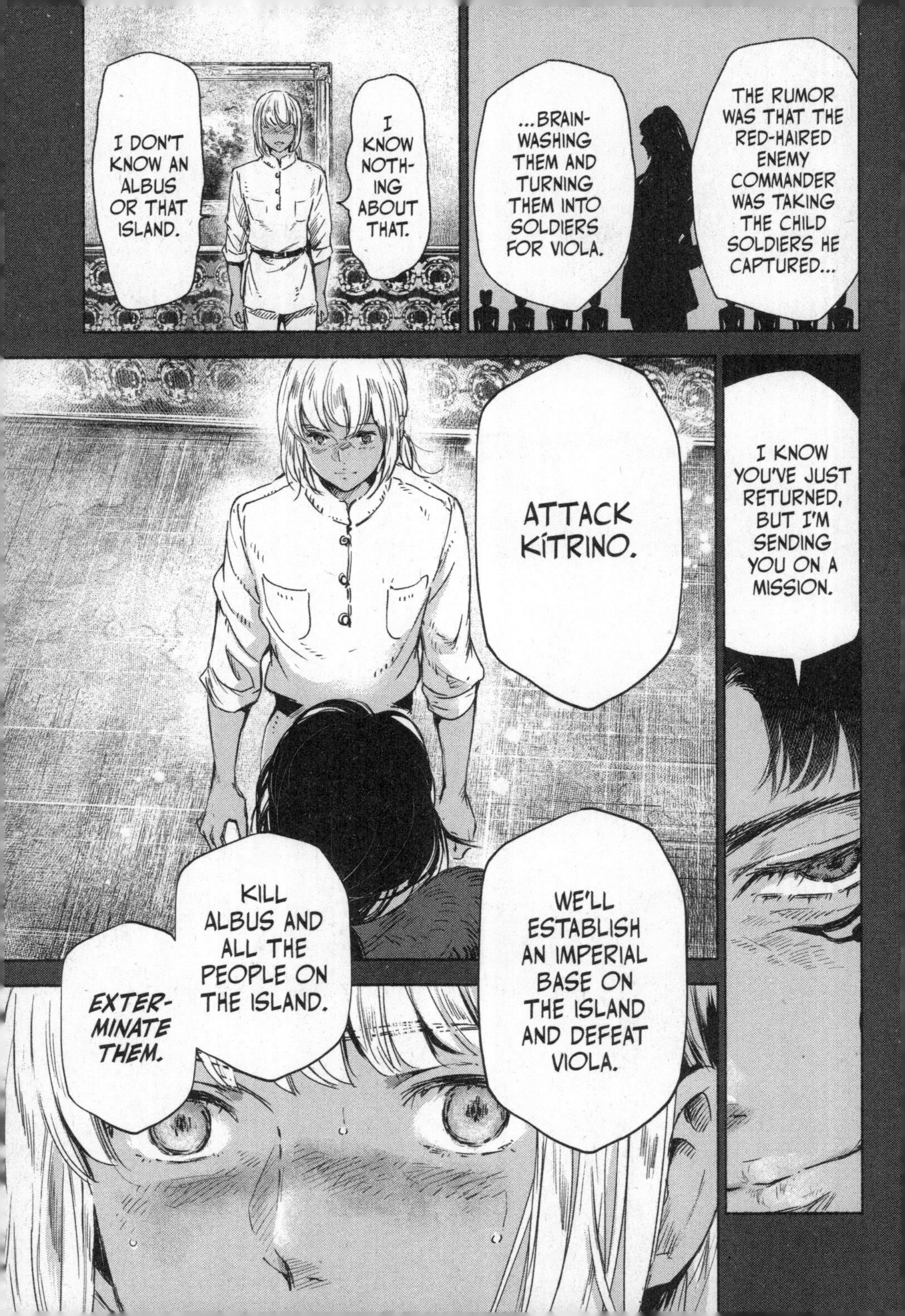
THE RUMOR WAS THAT THE RED-HAIRED ENEMY COMMANDER WAS TAKING THE CHILD SOLDIERS HE CAPTURED...
...BRAIN-WASHING THEM AND TURNING THEM INTO SOLDIERS FOR VIOLA.
I KNOW NOTHING ABOUT THAT.
I DON'T KNOW AN ALBUS OR THAT ISLAND.
I KNOW YOU'VE JUST RETURNED, BUT I'M SENDING YOU ON A MISSION.
ATTACK KÍTRINO.
WE'LL ESTABLISH AN IMPERIAL BASE ON THE ISLAND AND DEFEAT VIOLA.
KILL ALBUS AND ALL THE PEOPLE ON THE ISLAND.
EXTERMINATE THEM.

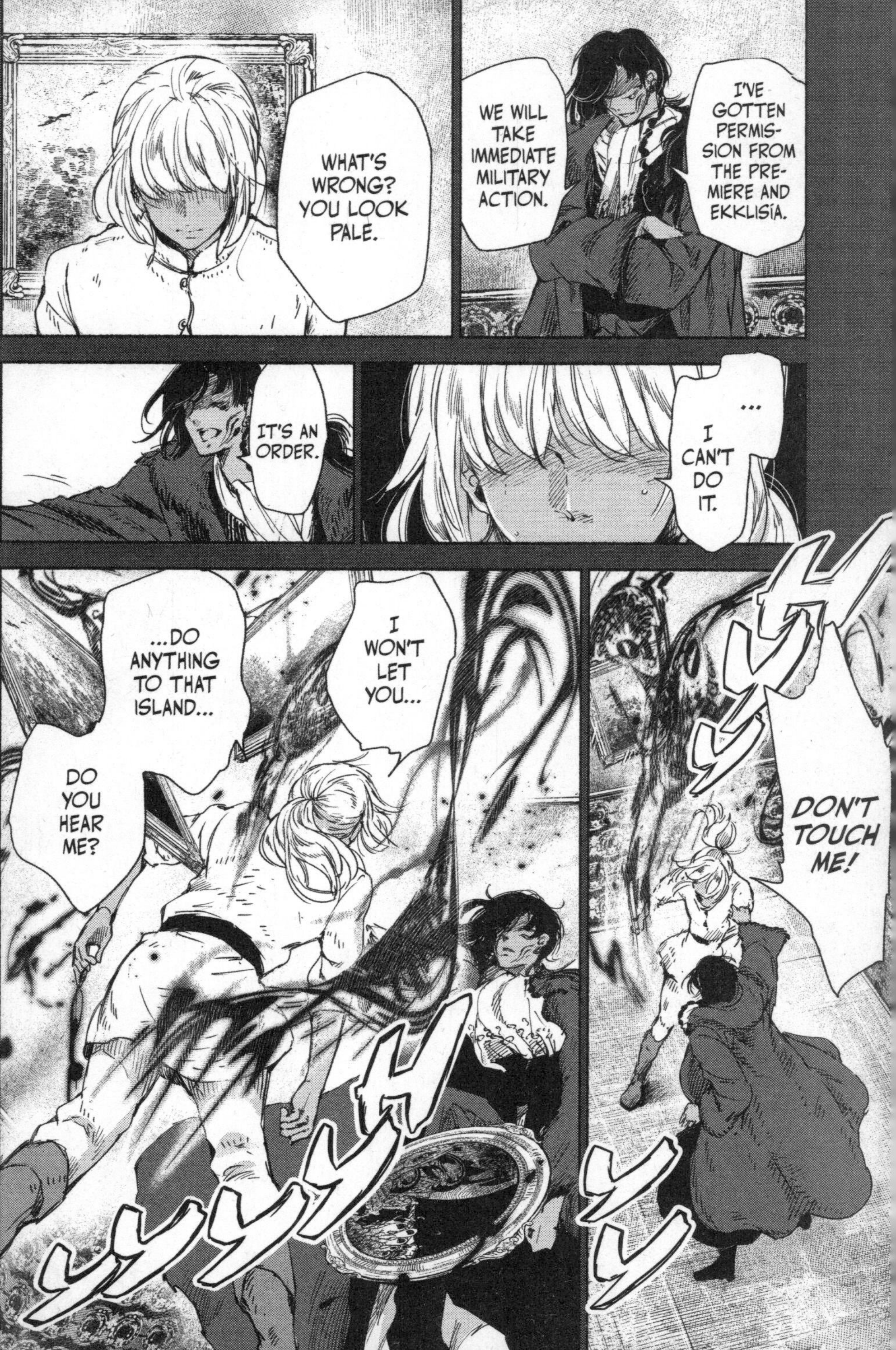
I'VE GOTTEN PERMISSION FROM THE PREMIERE AND EKKLISÍA.
WE WILL TAKE IMMEDIATE MILITARY ACTION.
WHAT'S WRONG? YOU LOOK PALE.
... I CAN'T DO IT.
IT'S AN ORDER.
DON'T TOUCH ME!
I WON'T LET YOU...
...DO ANYTHING TO THAT ISLAND...
DO YOU HEAR ME?

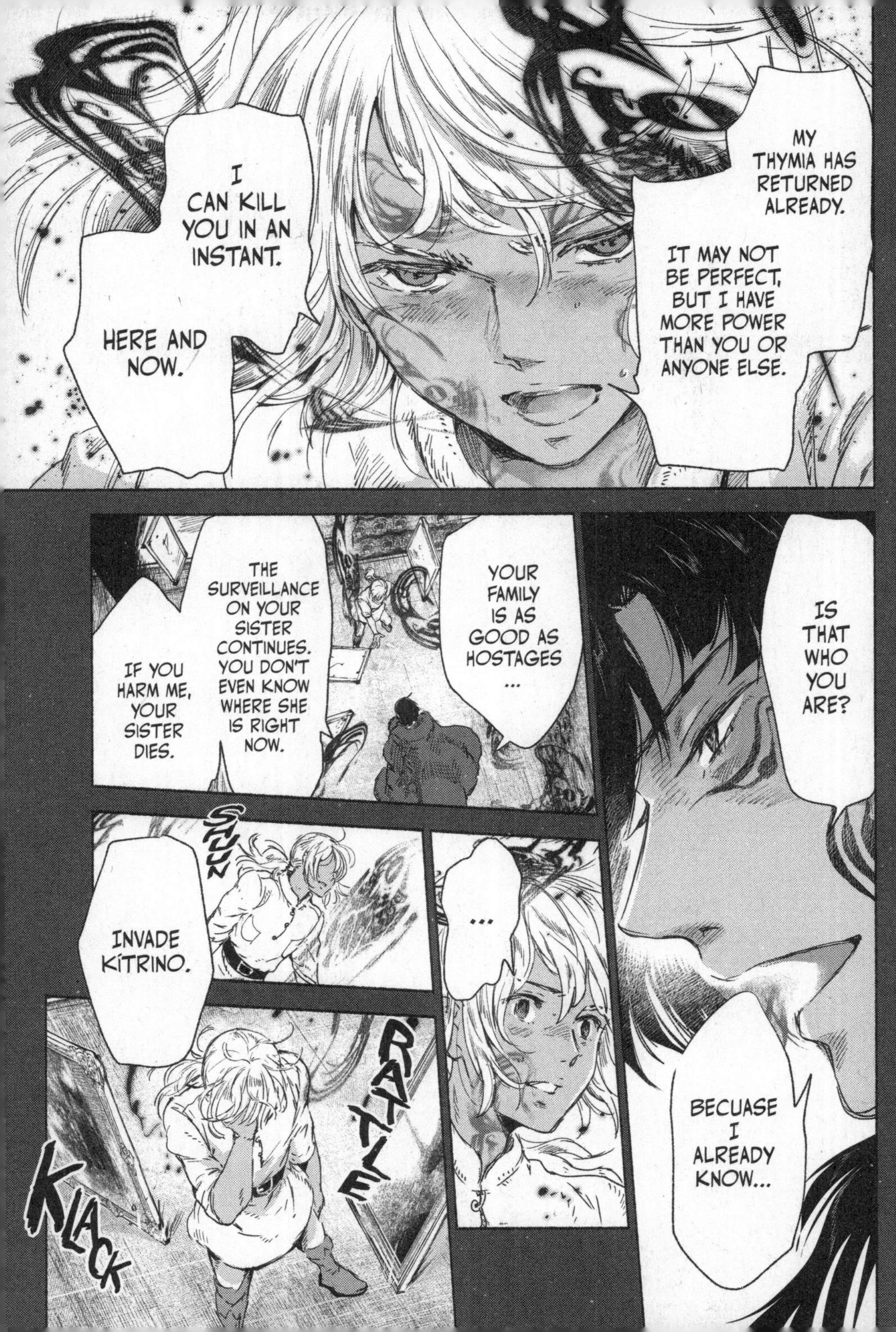
MY THYMIA HAS RETURNED ALREADY.
IT MAY NOT BE PERFECT, BUT I HAVE MORE POWER THAN YOU OR ANYONE ELSE.
I CAN KILL YOU IN AN INSTANT.
HERE AND NOW.
IS THAT WHO YOU ARE?
YOUR FAMILY IS AS GOOD AS HOSTAGES ...
THE SURVEILLANCE ON YOUR SISTER CONTINUES. YOU DON'T EVEN KNOW WHERE SHE IS RIGHT NOW.
IF YOU HARM ME, YOUR SISTER DIES.
...
SHUUN
INVADE KITRINO.
RATTLE
KLACK
BECUASE I ALREADY KNOW...

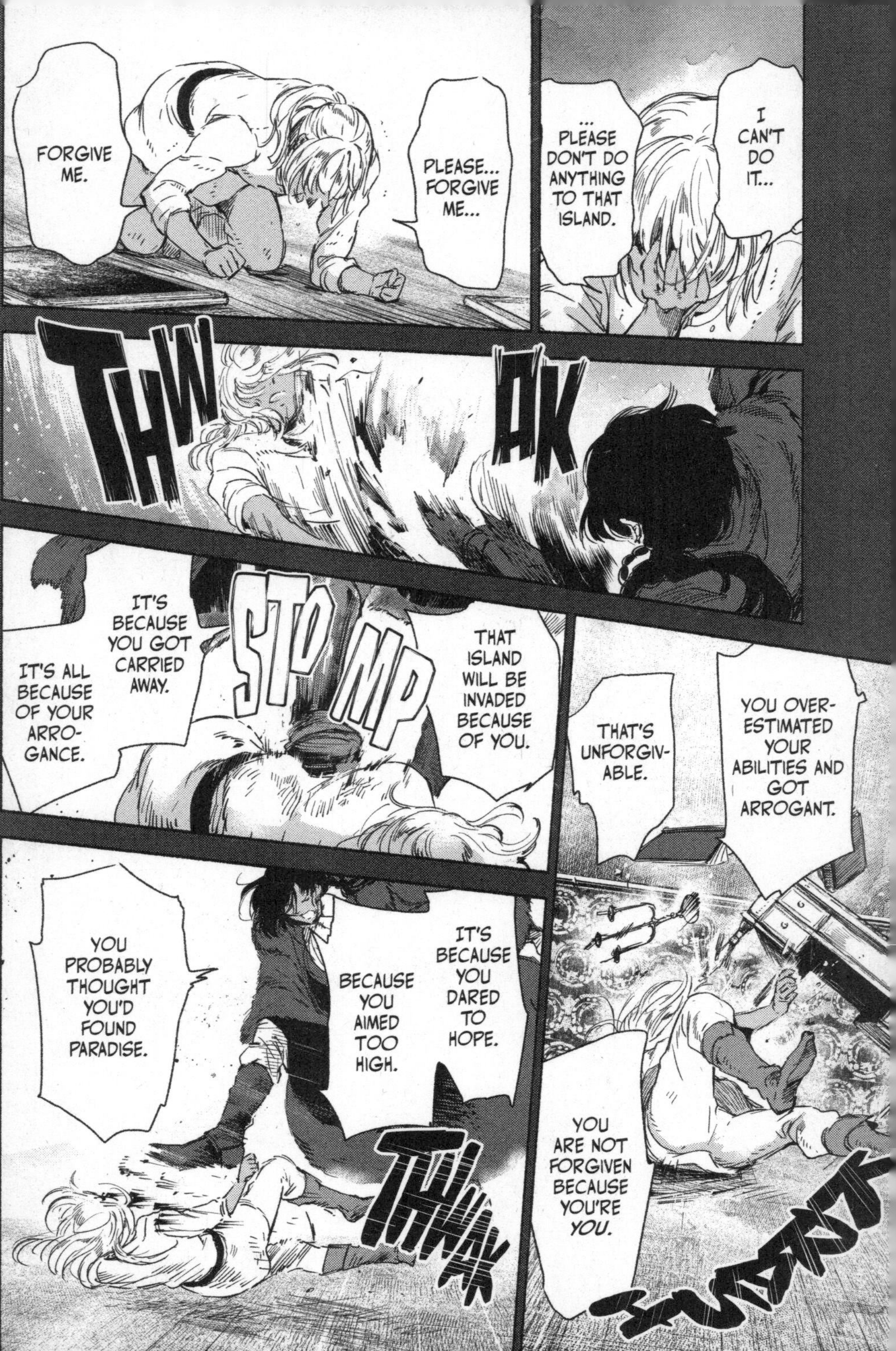
I CAN'T DO IT...
... PLEASE DON'T DO ANYTHING TO THAT ISLAND.
PLEASE... FORGIVE ME...
FORGIVE ME.
THWAK
YOU OVER-ESTIMATED YOUR ABILITIES AND GOT ARROGANT.
THAT'S UNFORGIV-ABLE.
THAT ISLAND WILL BE INVADED BECAUSE OF YOU.
STOMP
IT'S BECAUSE YOU GOT CARRIED AWAY.
IT'S ALL BECAUSE OF YOUR ARRO-GANCE.
YOU ARE NOT FORGIVEN BECAUSE YOU'RE *YOU*.
IT'S BECAUSE YOU DARED TO HOPE.
BECAUSE YOU AIMED TOO HIGH.
YOU PROBABLY THOUGHT YOU'D FOUND PARADISE.

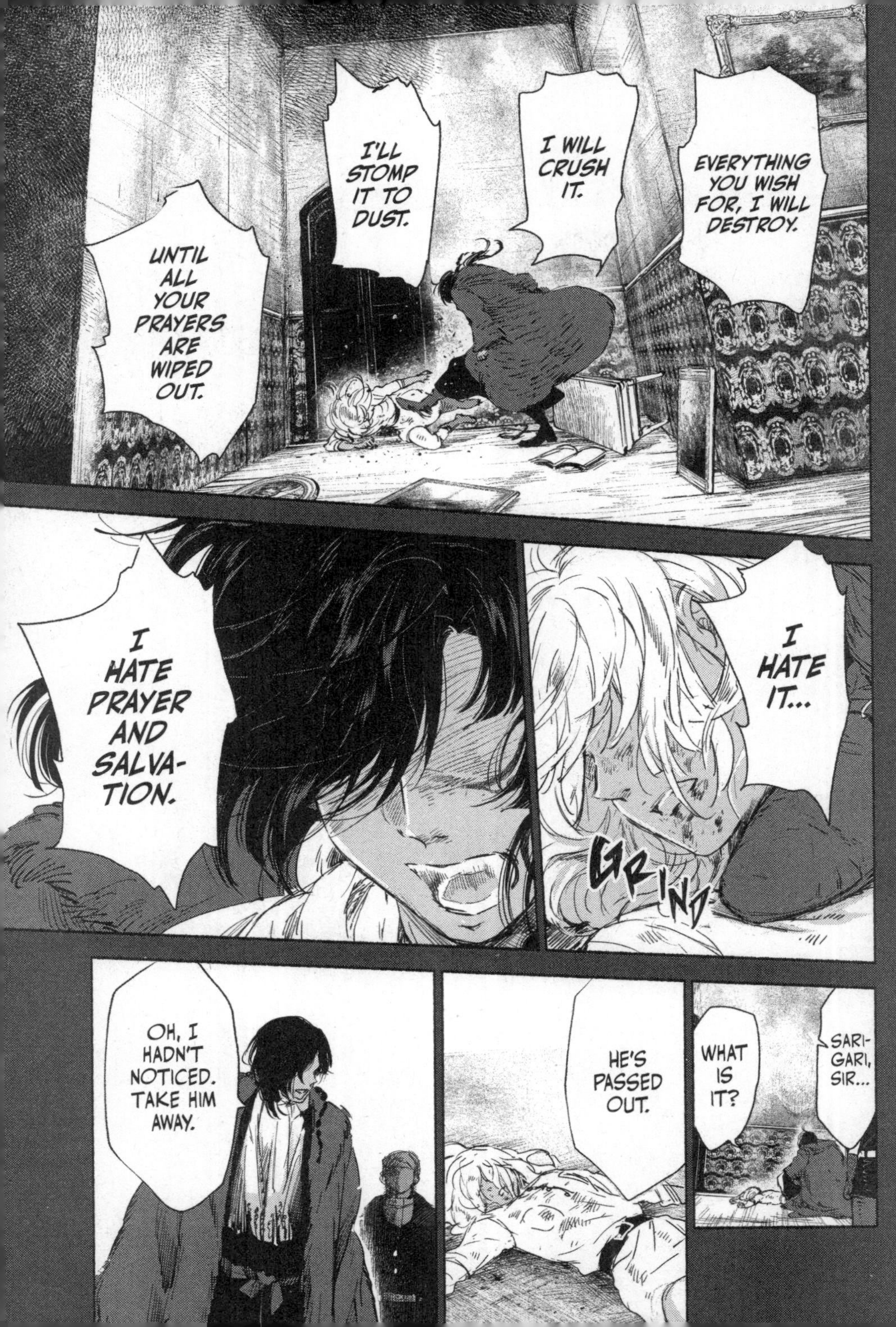
EVERYTHING YOU WISH FOR, I WILL DESTROY.
I WILL CRUSH IT.
I'LL STOMP IT TO DUST.
UNTIL ALL YOUR PRAYERS ARE WIPED OUT.
I HATE IT...
GRIND
I HATE PRAYER AND SALVATION.
SARI-GARI, SIR...
WHAT IS IT?
HE'S PASSED OUT.
OH, I HADN'T NOTICED. TAKE HIM AWAY.

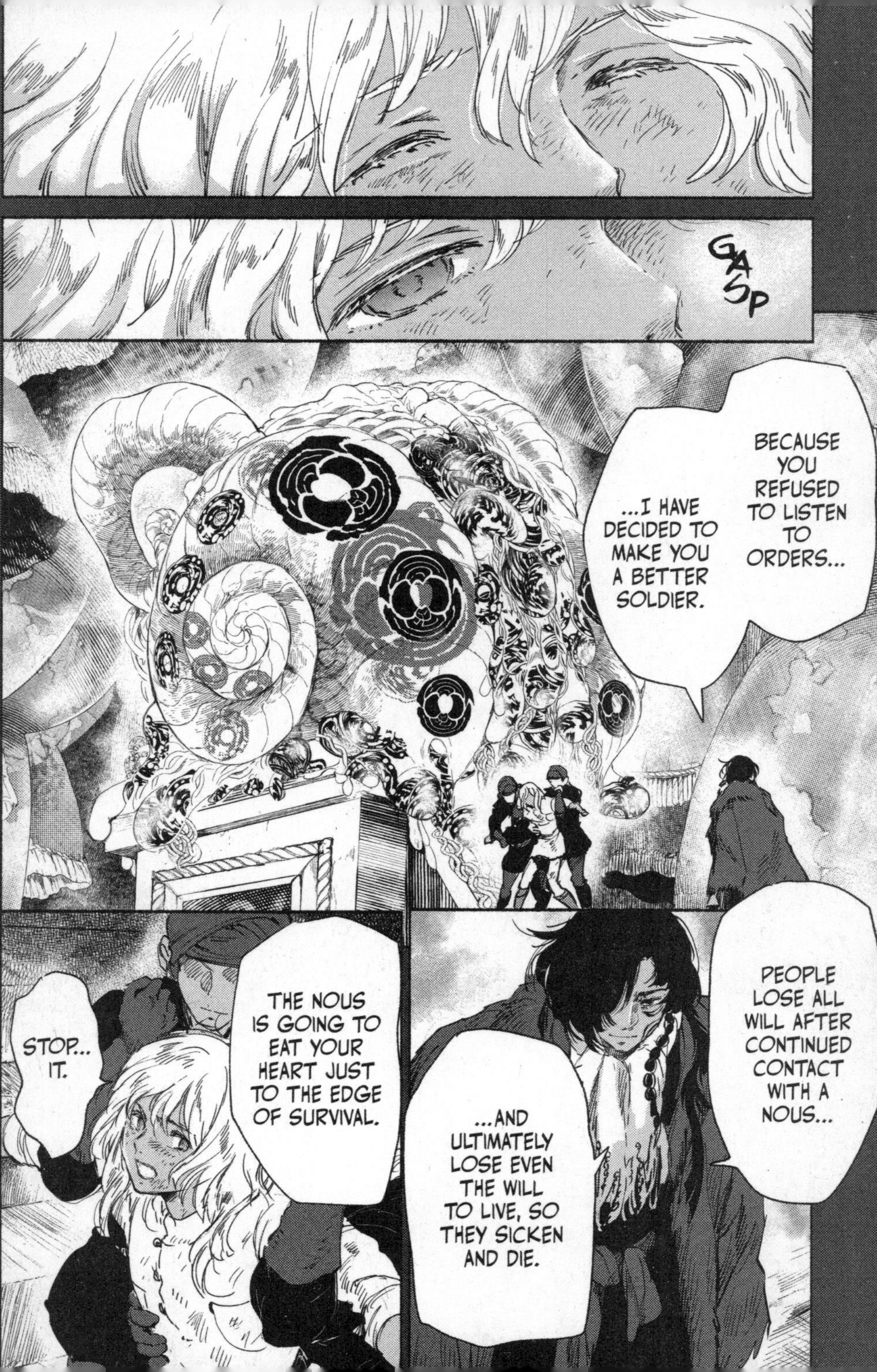
GASP
BECAUSE YOU REFUSED TO LISTEN TO ORDERS...
...I HAVE DECIDED TO MAKE YOU A BETTER SOLDIER.
PEOPLE LOSE ALL WILL AFTER CONTINUED CONTACT WITH A NOUS...
...AND ULTIMATELY LOSE EVEN THE WILL TO LIVE, SO THEY SICKEN AND DIE.
THE NOUS IS GOING TO EAT YOUR HEART JUST TO THE EDGE OF SURVIVAL.
STOP... IT.

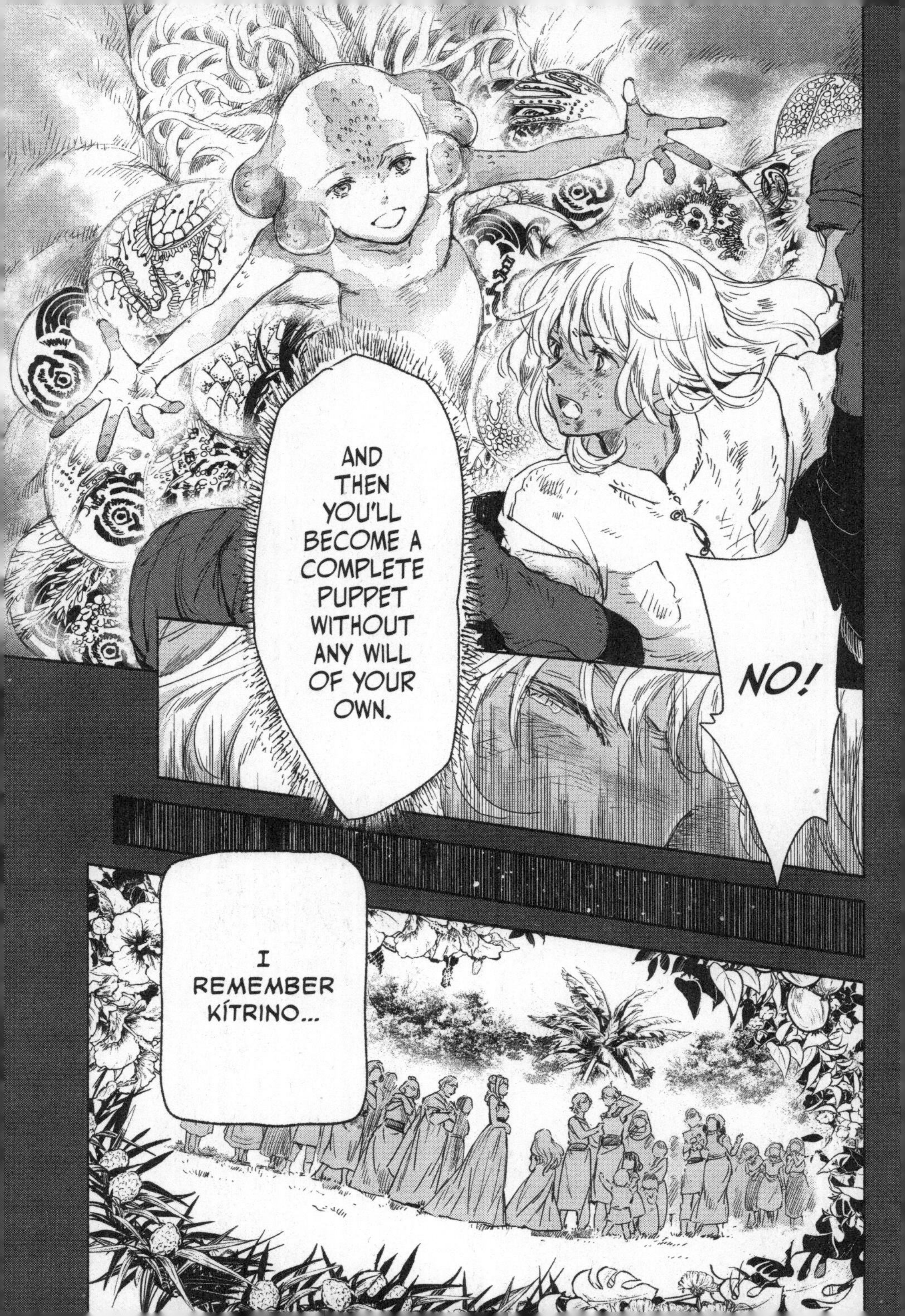
NO!
AND THEN YOU'LL BECOME A COMPLETE PUPPET WITHOUT ANY WILL OF YOUR OWN.
I REMEMBER KÍTRINO...

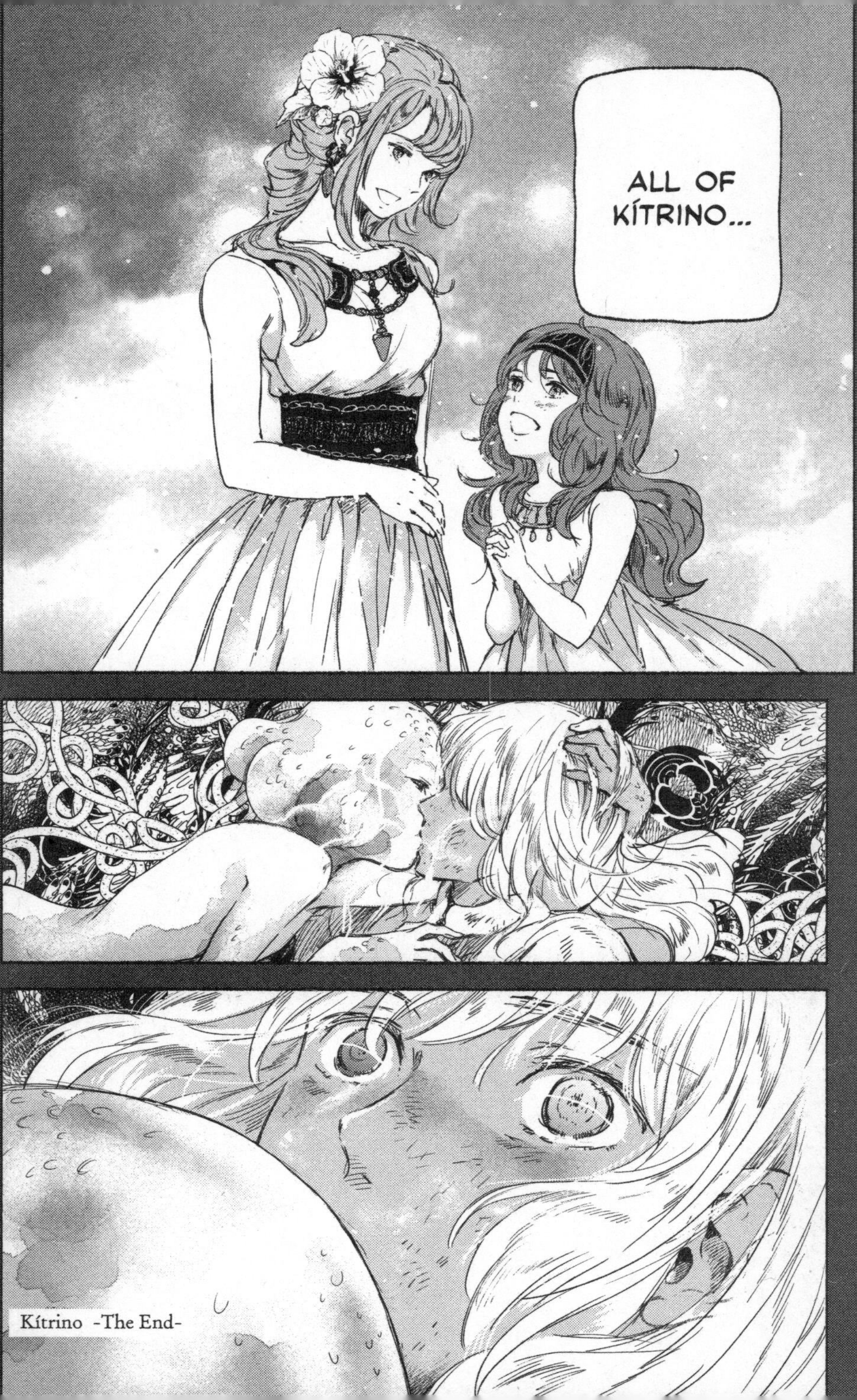
ALL OF KÍTRINO...
Kítrino -The End-

Chapter 64
The Island of Eternity

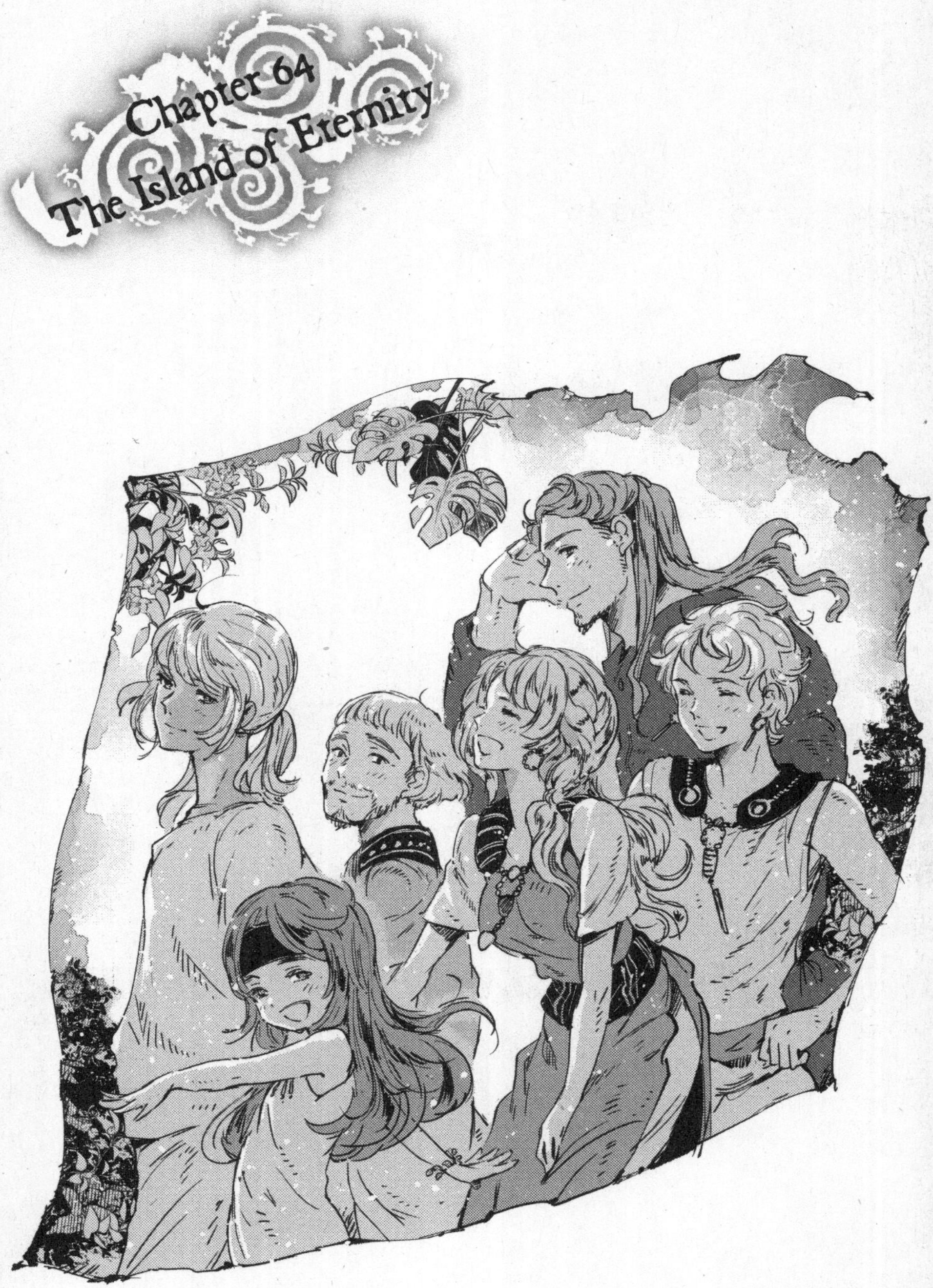

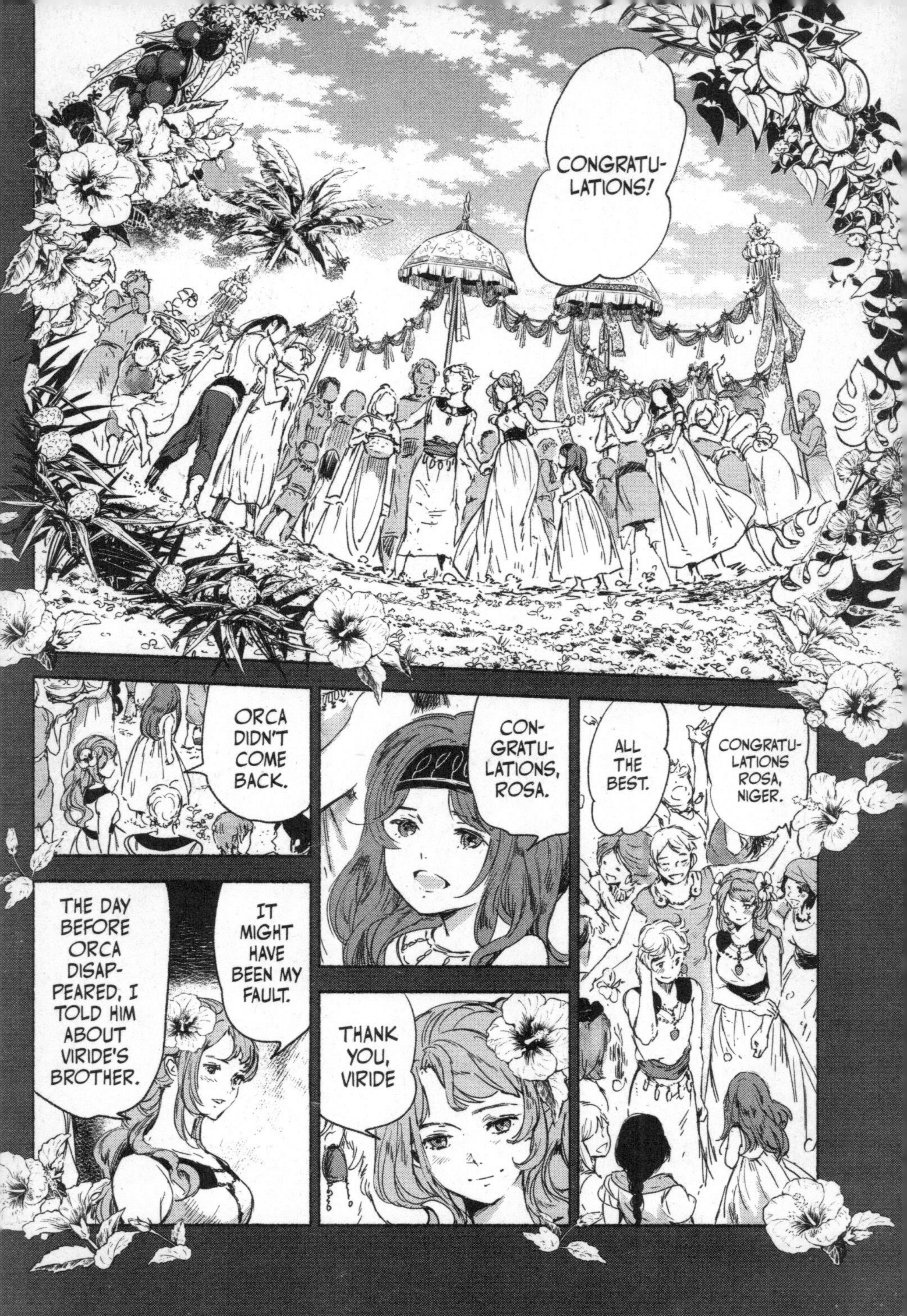
CONGRATU-LATIONS!
CONGRATU-LATIONS ROSA, NIGER.
ALL THE BEST.
CON-GRATU-LATIONS, ROSA.
THANK YOU, VIRIDE
ORCA DIDN'T COME BACK.
IT MIGHT HAVE BEEN MY FAULT.
THE DAY BEFORE ORCA DISAP-PEARED, I TOLD HIM ABOUT VIRIDE'S BROTHER.

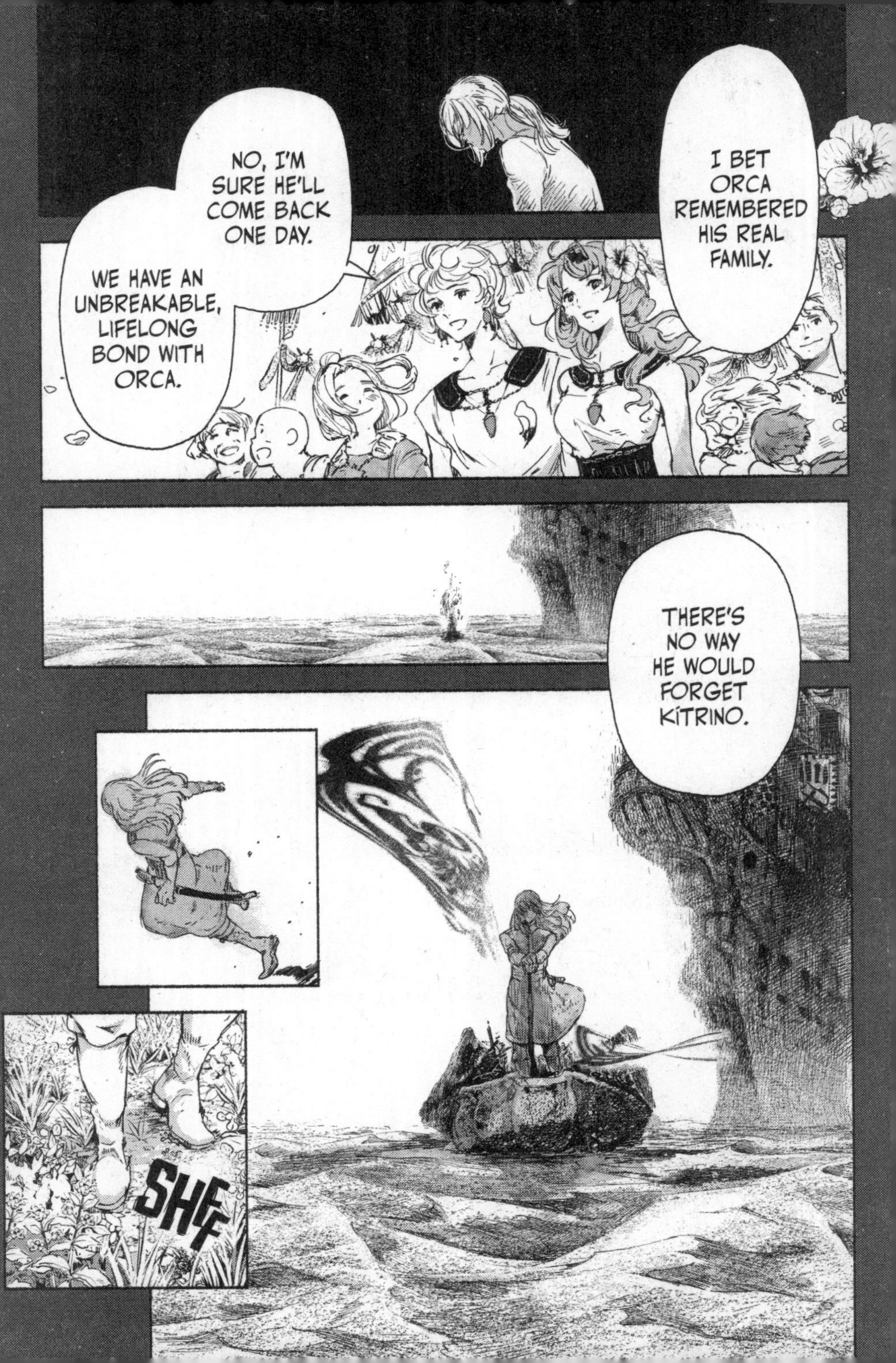
I BET ORCA REMEMBERED HIS REAL FAMILY.
NO, I'M SURE HE'LL COME BACK ONE DAY.
WE HAVE AN UNBREAKABLE, LIFELONG BOND WITH ORCA.
THERE'S NO WAY HE WOULD FORGET KITRINO.
SHFF

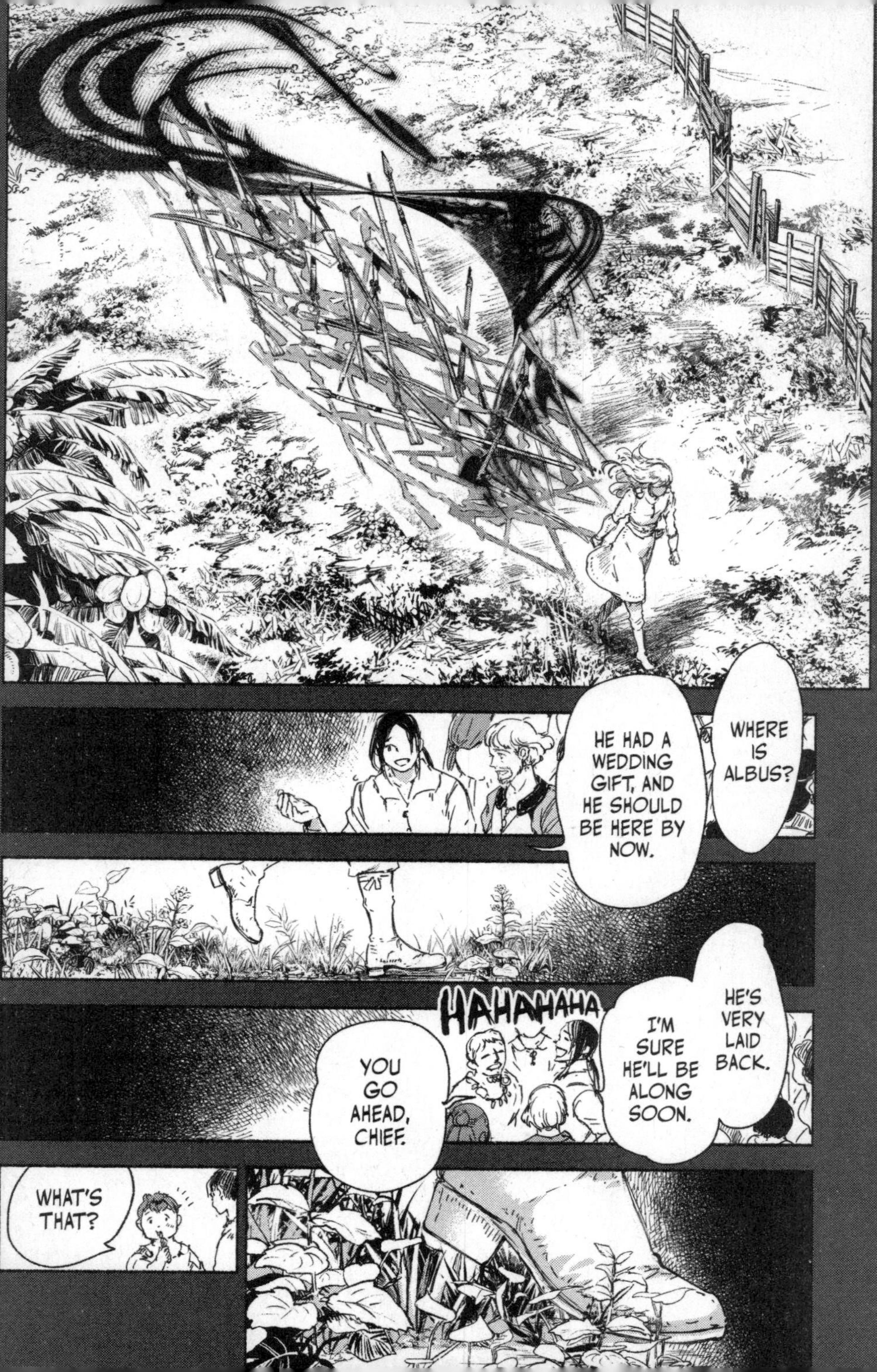
WHERE IS ALBUS?
HE HAD A WEDDING GIFT, AND HE SHOULD BE HERE BY NOW.
HE'S VERY LAID BACK.
I'M SURE HE'LL BE ALONG SOON.
HAHAHAHA
YOU GO AHEAD, CHIEF.
WHAT'S THAT?

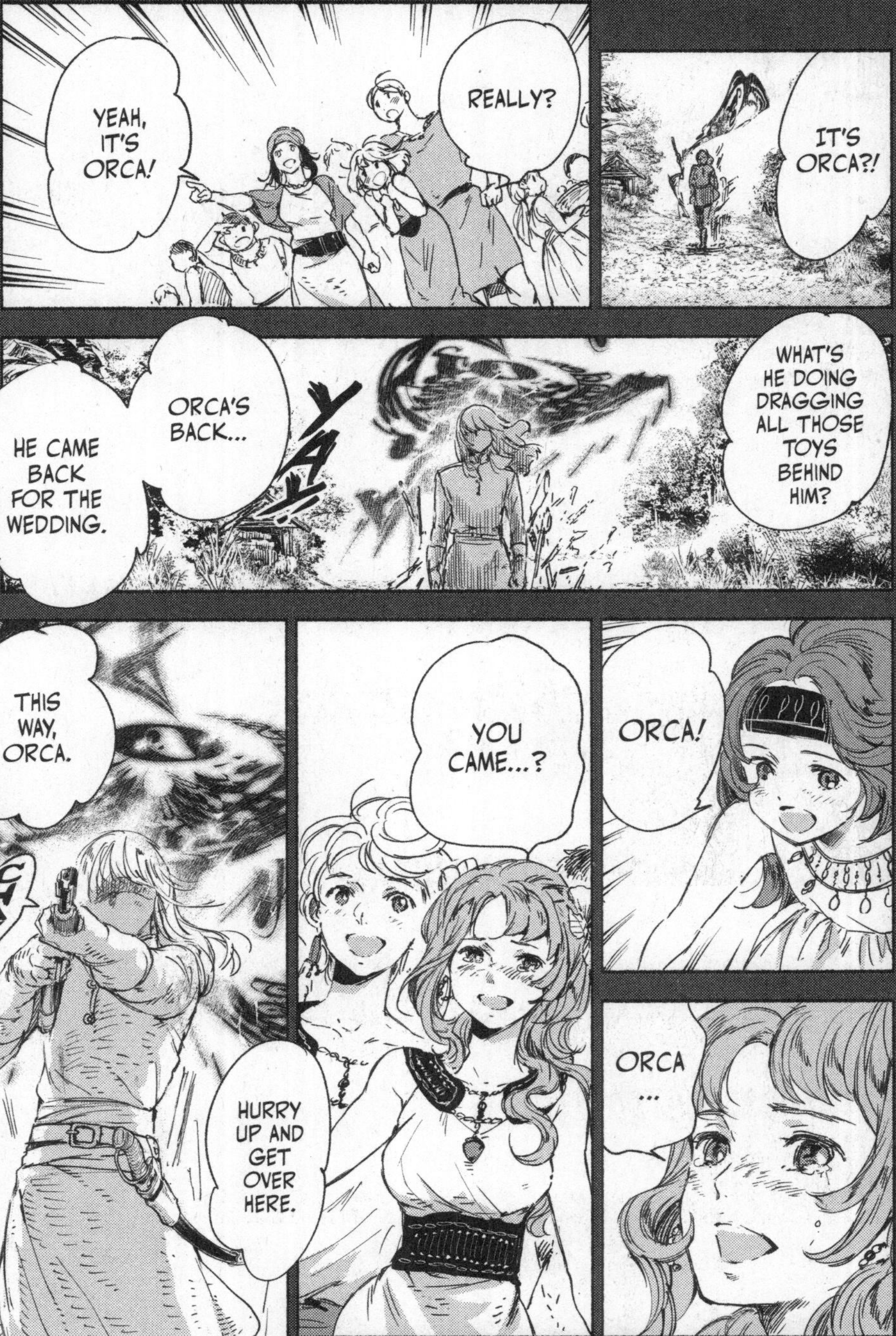
IT'S ORCA?!
REALLY?
YEAH, IT'S ORCA!
WHAT'S HE DOING DRAGGING ALL THOSE TOYS BEHIND HIM?
ORCA'S BACK...
YAY!
HE CAME BACK FOR THE WEDDING.
ORCA!
ORCA ...
YOU CAME...?
HURRY UP AND GET OVER HERE.
THIS WAY, ORCA.
CHAK

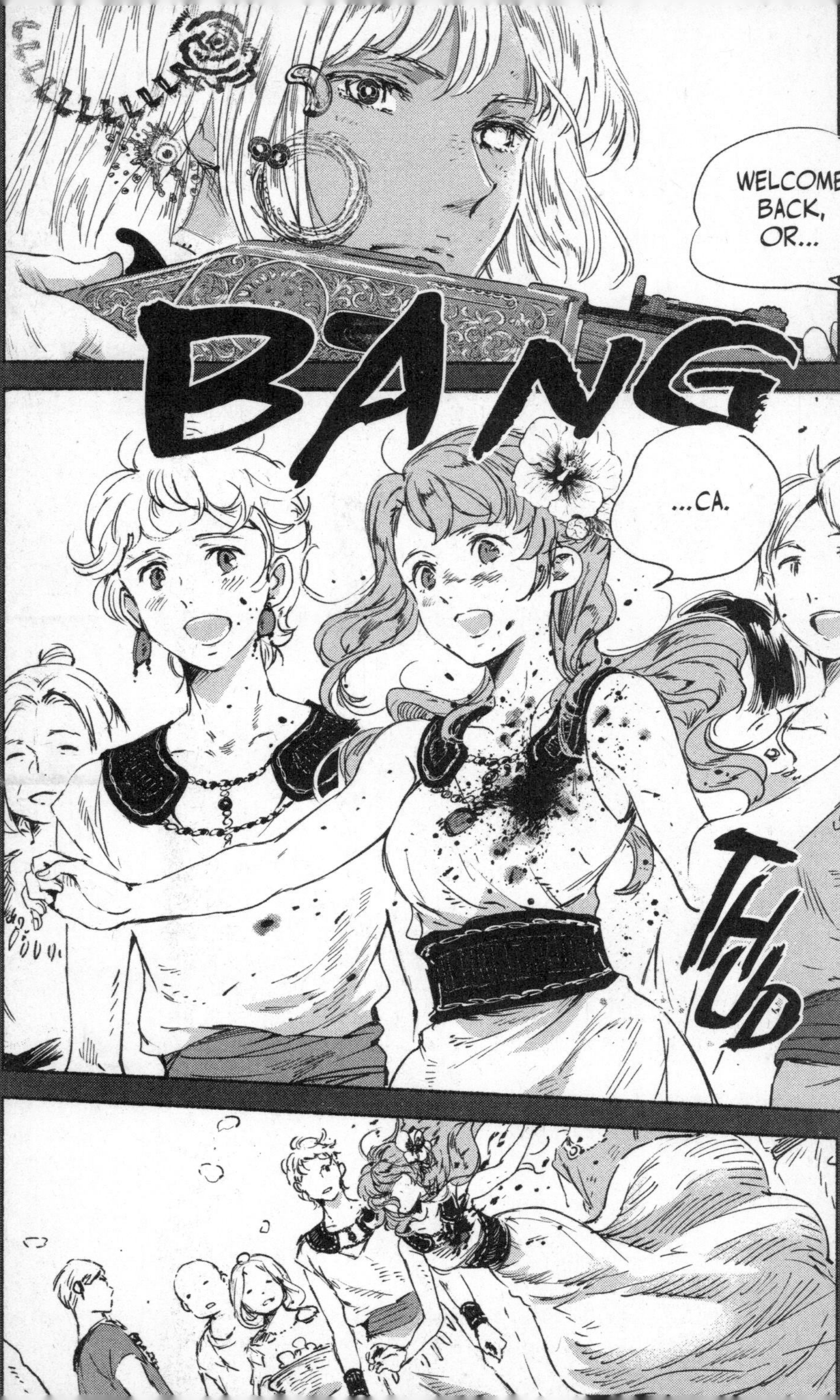
WELCOME BACK, OR...
BANG
...CA.
THUD

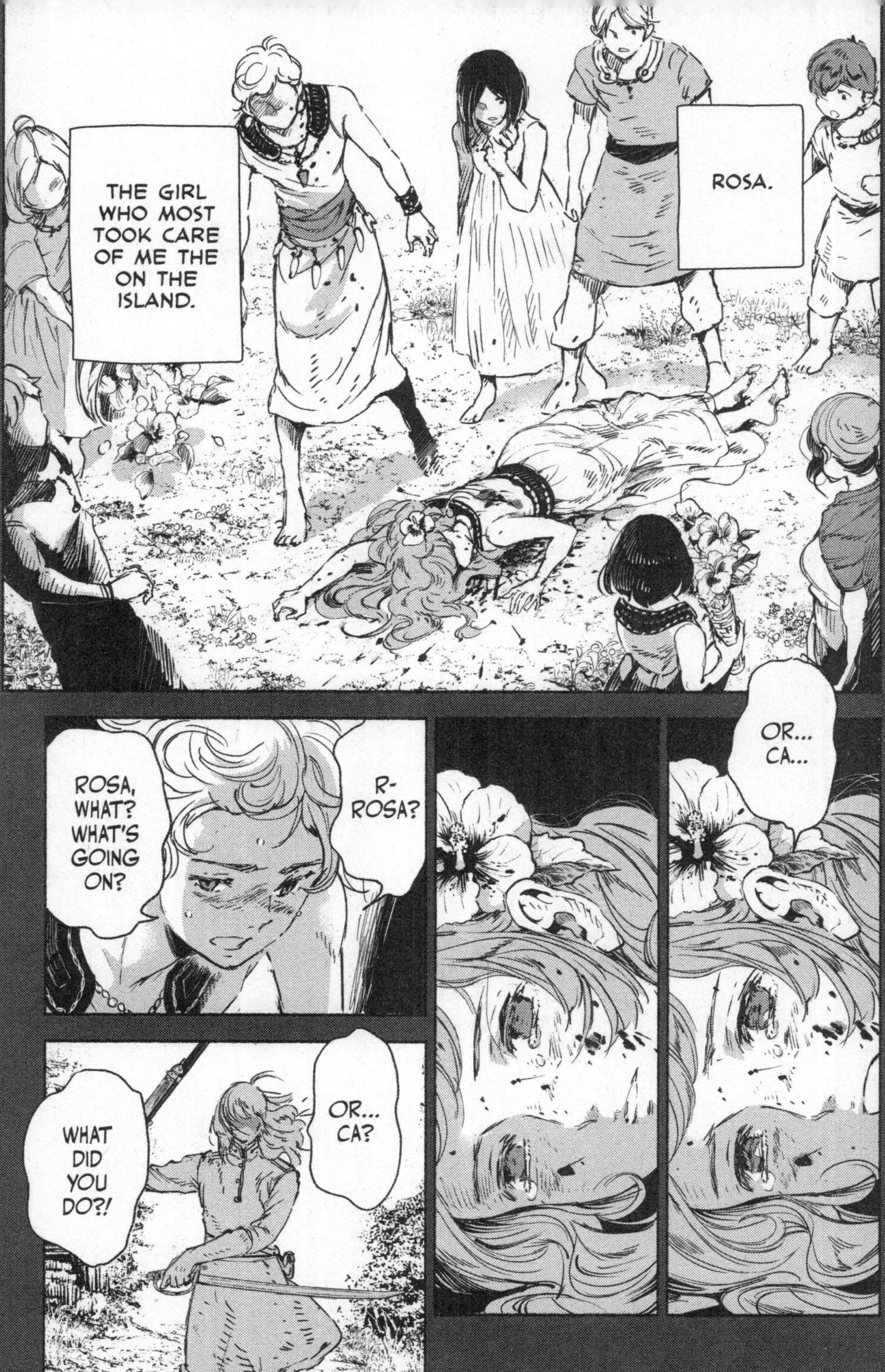
ROSA.
THE GIRL WHO MOST TOOK CARE OF ME THE ON THE ISLAND.
OR... CA...
R- ROSA?
ROSA, WHAT? WHAT'S GOING ON?
OR... CA?
WHAT DID YOU DO?!

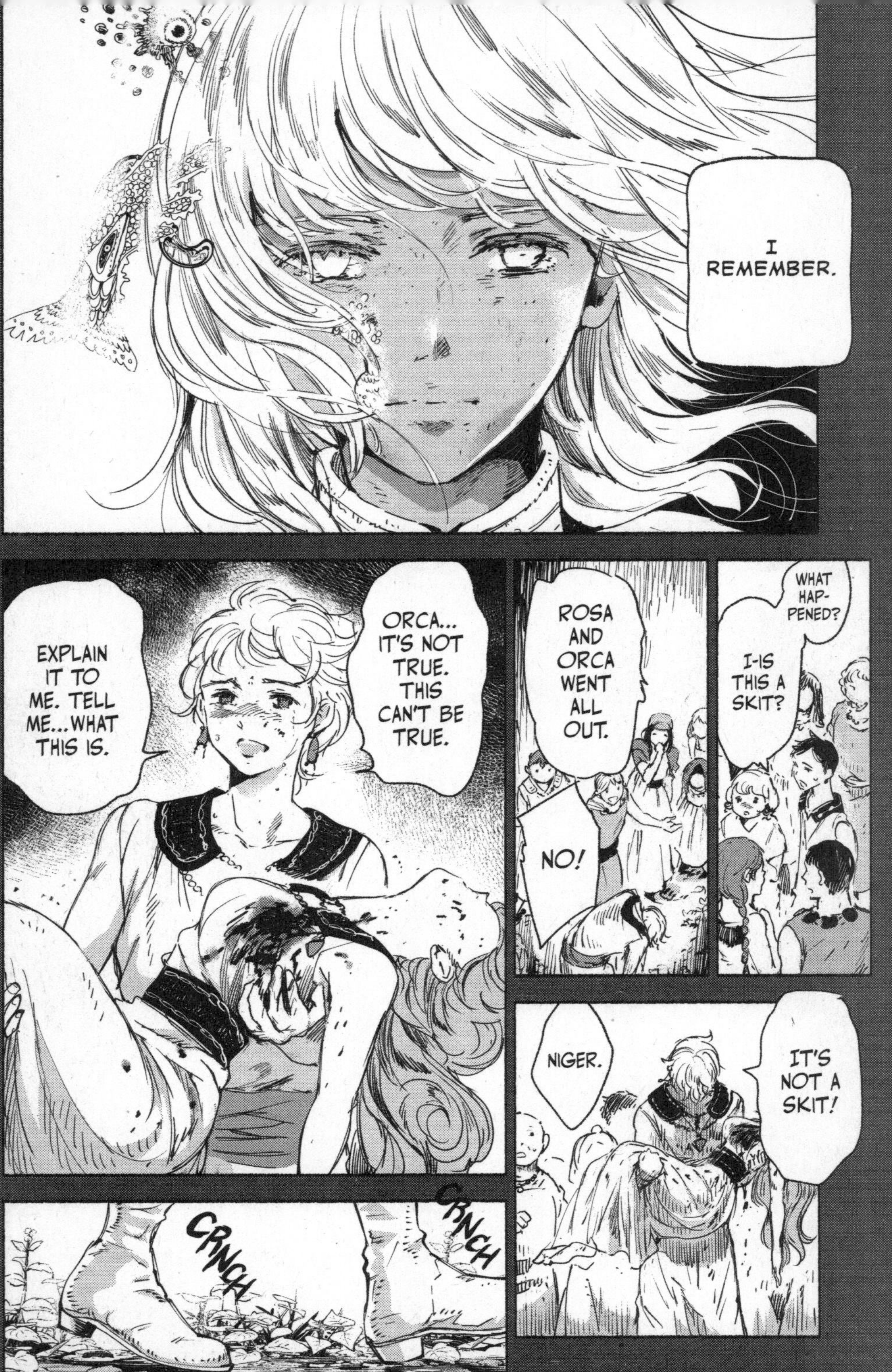
I REMEMBER.
WHAT HAPPENED?
I-IS THIS A SKIT?
ROSA AND ORCA WENT ALL OUT.
NO!
IT'S NOT A SKIT!
NIGER.
ORCA... IT'S NOT TRUE. THIS CAN'T BE TRUE.
EXPLAIN IT TO ME. TELL ME...WHAT THIS IS.
CRNCH
CRNCH

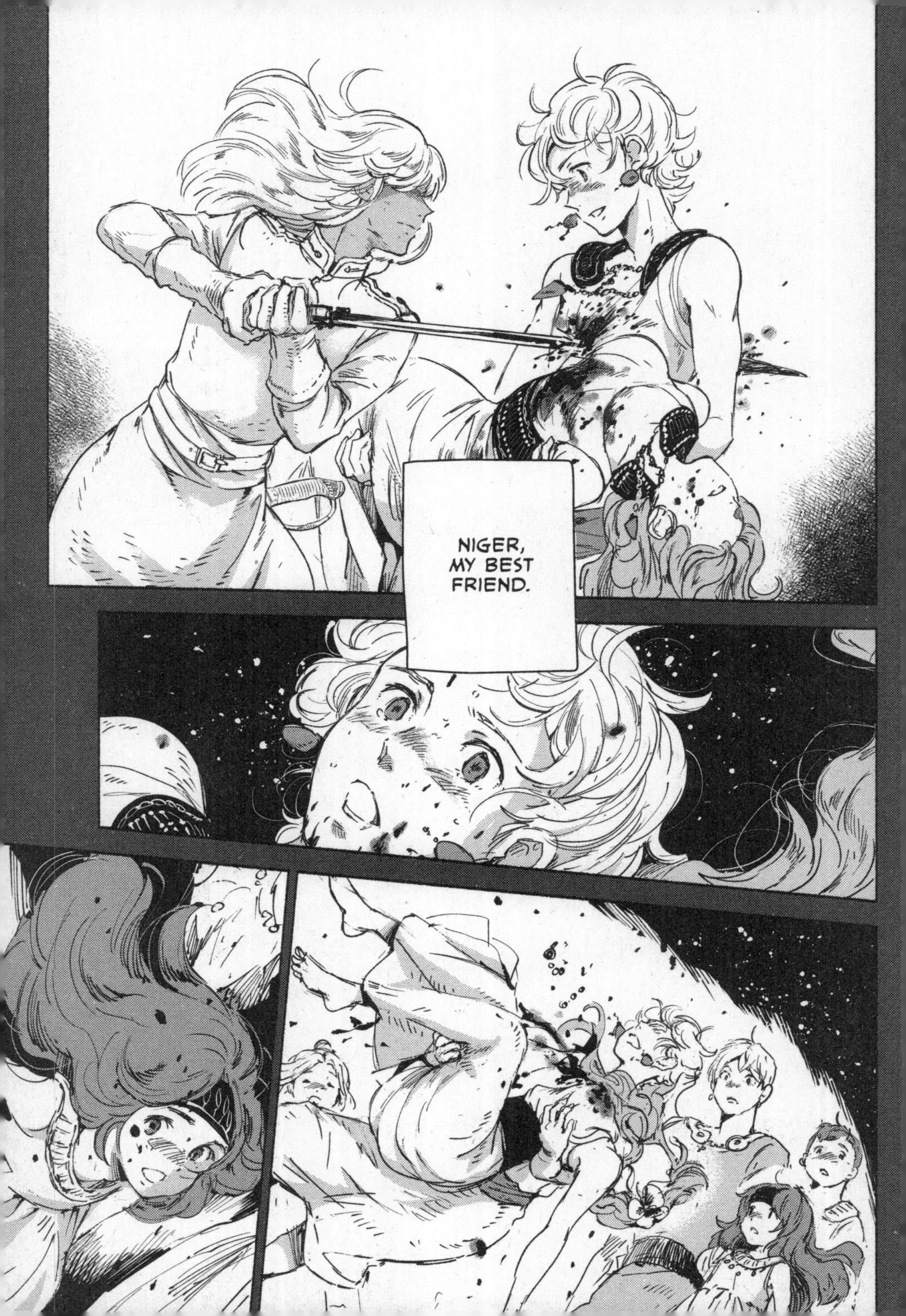
NIGER, MY BEST FRIEND.

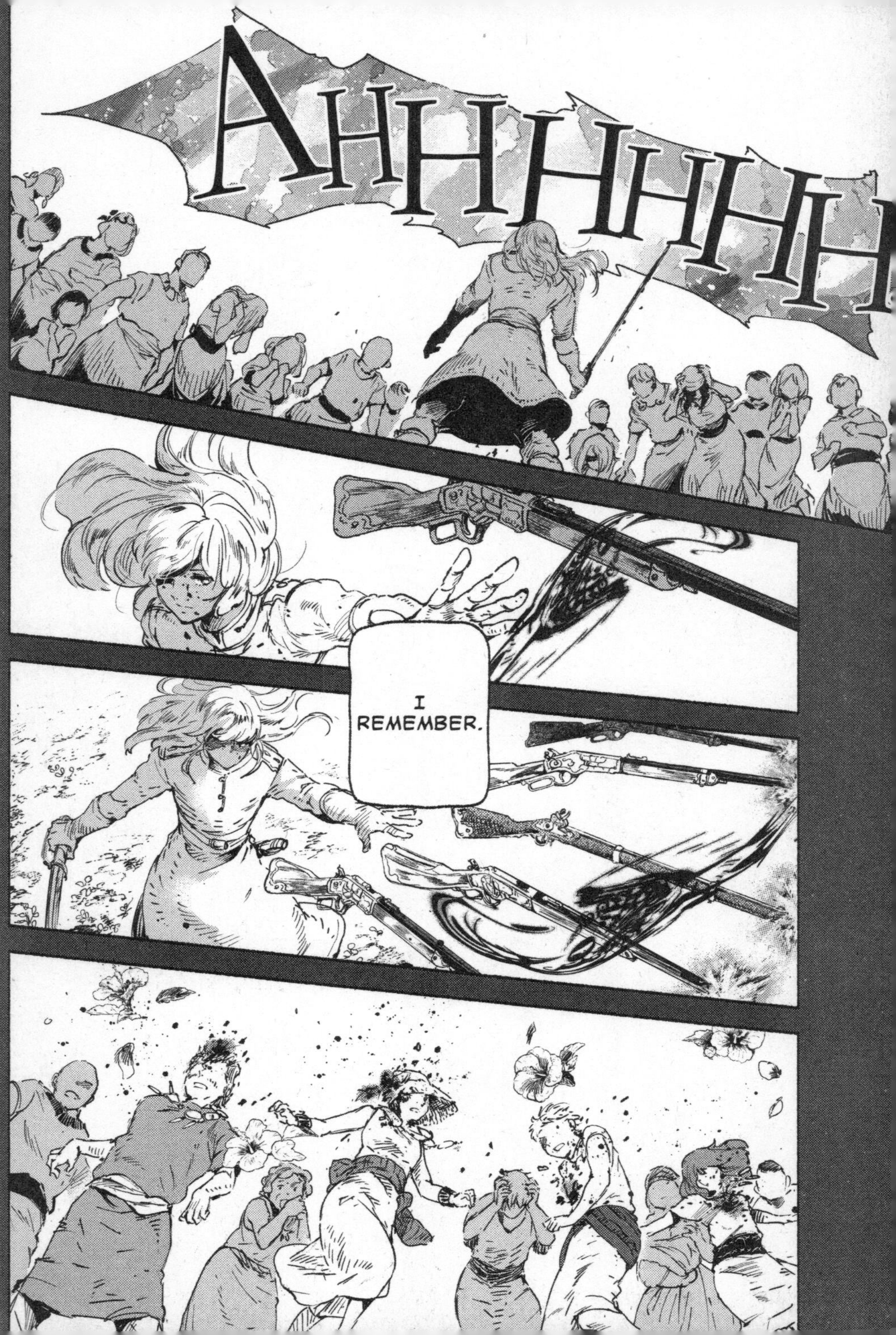
AHHHHHHH
I REMEMBER.

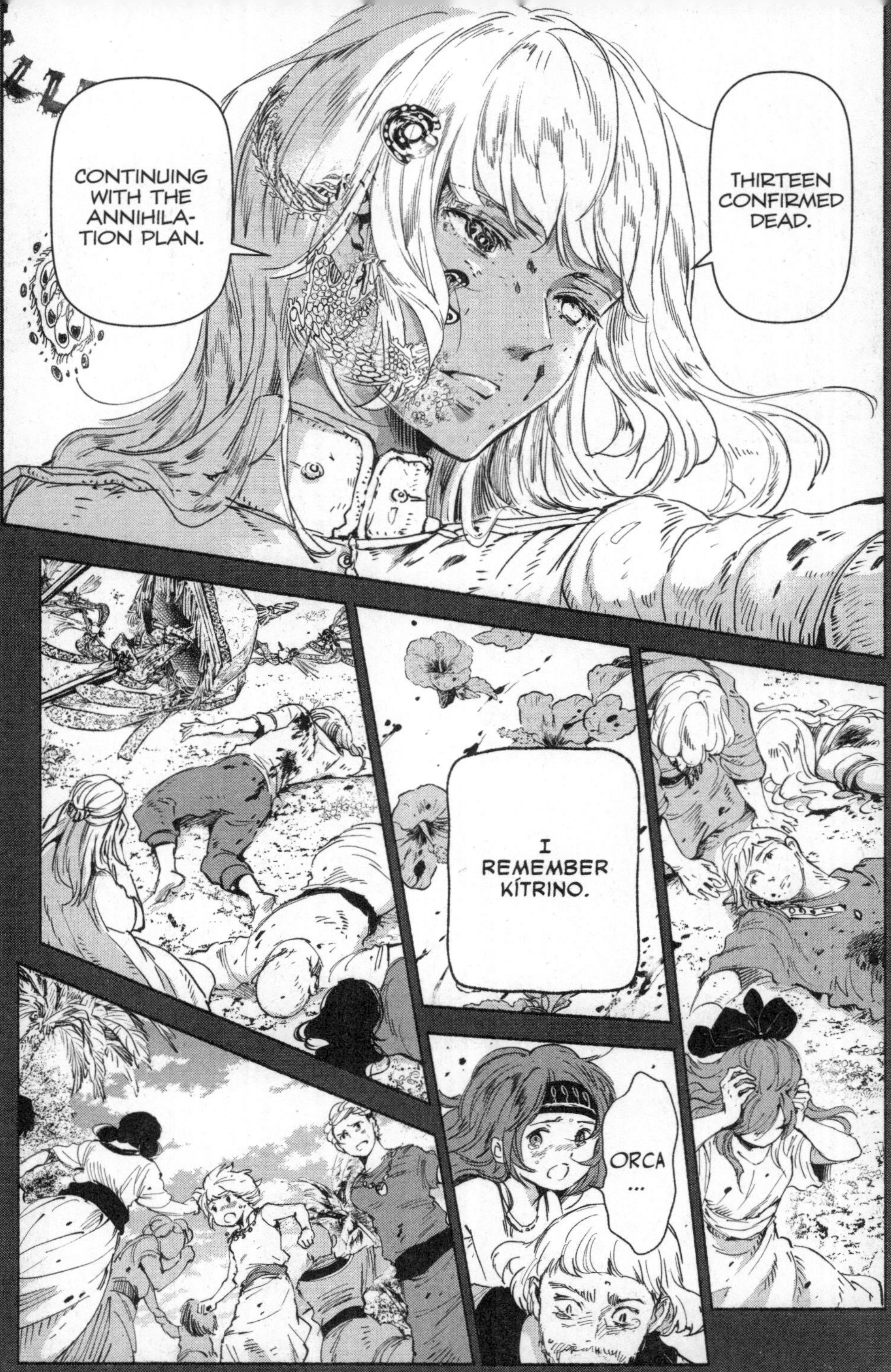
THIRTEEN CONFIRMED DEAD.
CONTINUING WITH THE ANNIHILATION PLAN.
I REMEMBER KÍTRINO.
ORCA ...

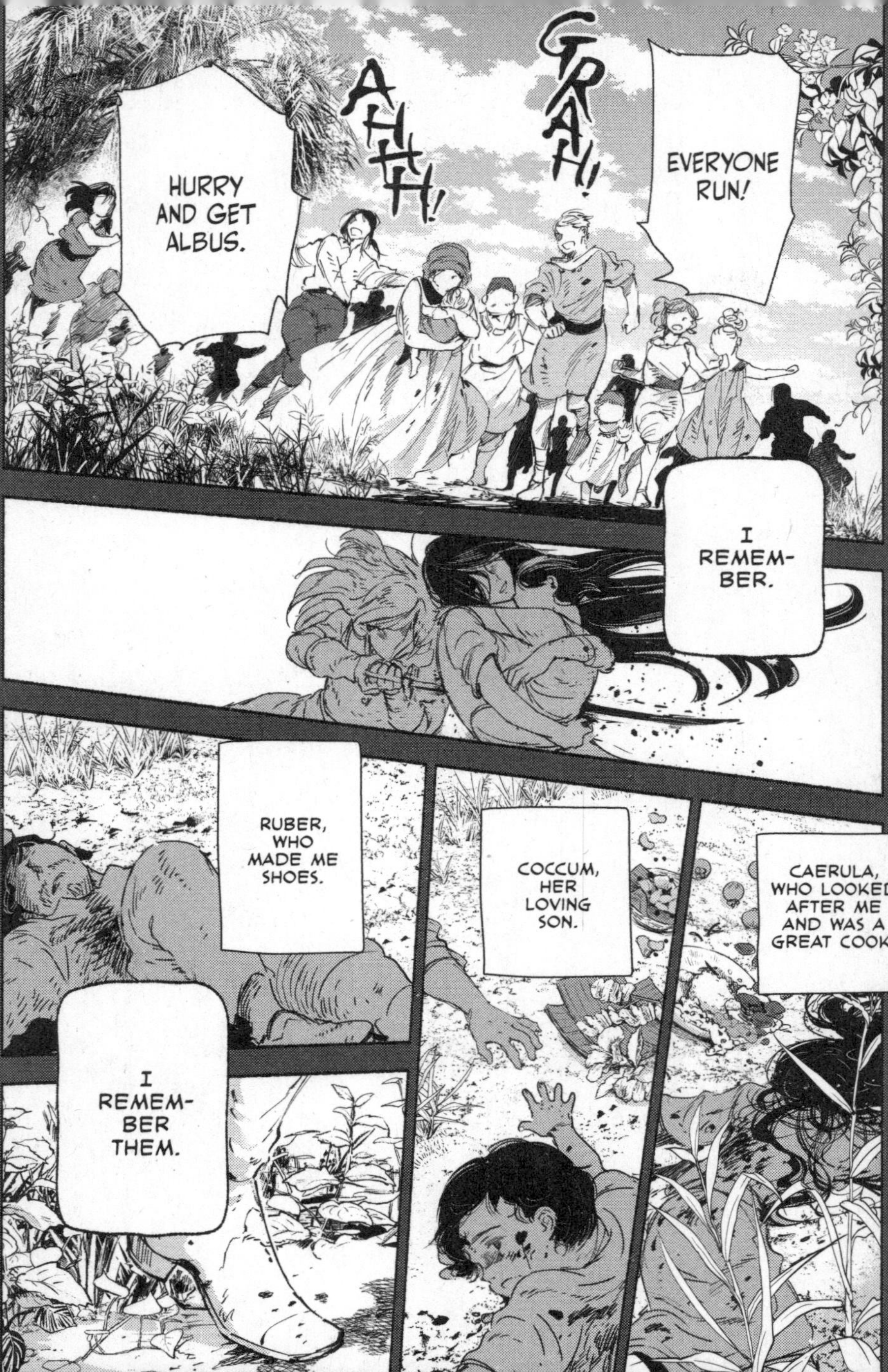
EVERYONE RUN!
GRAH!
AHHH!
HURRY AND GET ALBUS.
I REMEM-BER.
CAERULA, WHO LOOKED AFTER ME AND WAS A GREAT COOK.
COCCUM, HER LOVING SON.
RUBER, WHO MADE ME SHOES.
I REMEM-BER THEM.

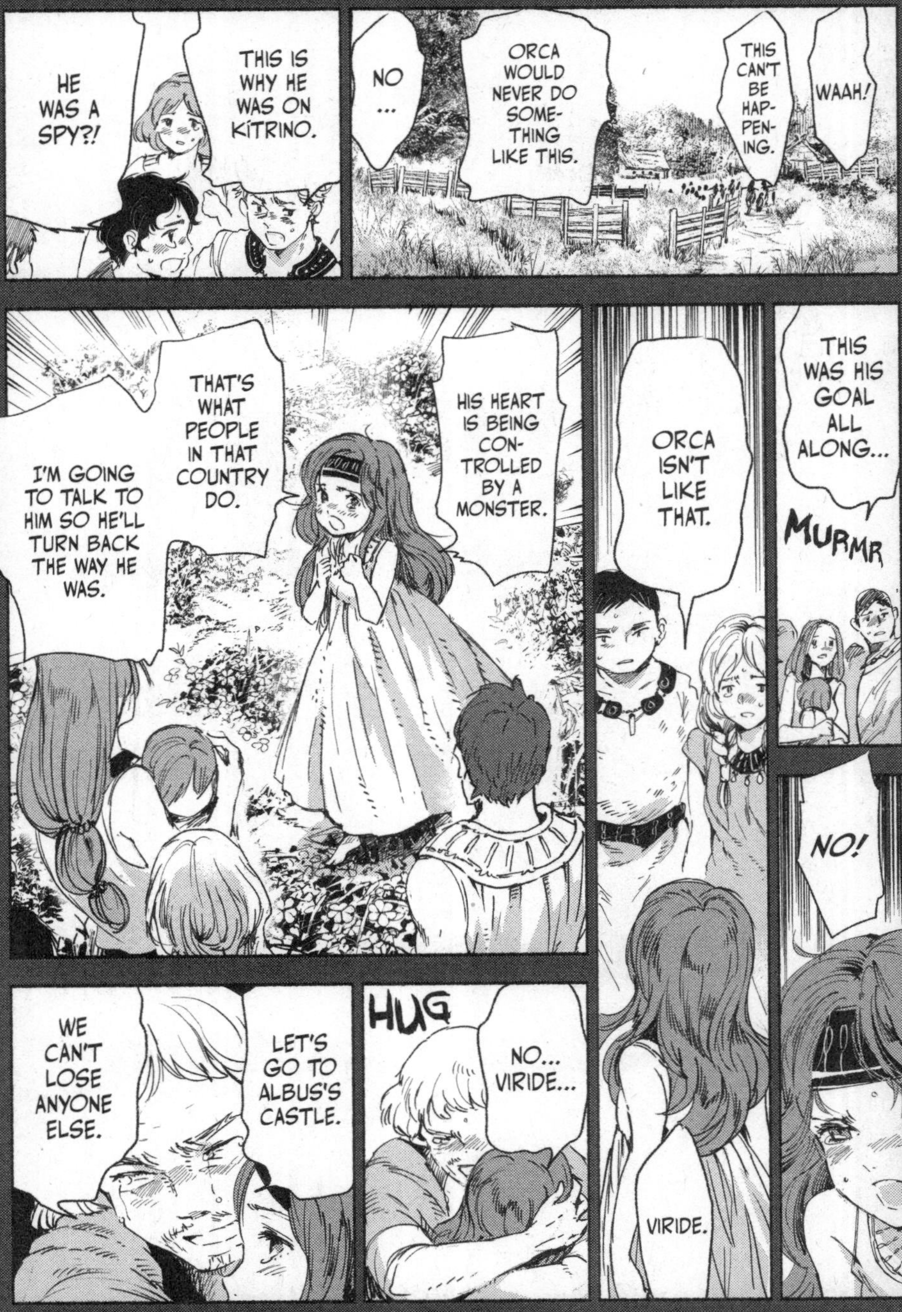
WAAH!
THIS CAN'T BE HAPPENING.
ORCA WOULD NEVER DO SOMETHING LIKE THIS.
NO ...
THIS IS WHY HE WAS ON KITRINO.
HE WAS A SPY?!
THIS WAS HIS GOAL ALL ALONG...
MURMR
NO!
ORCA ISN'T LIKE THAT.
VIRIDE.
HIS HEART IS BEING CONTROLLED BY A MONSTER.
THAT'S WHAT PEOPLE IN THAT COUNTRY DO.
I'M GOING TO TALK TO HIM SO HE'LL TURN BACK THE WAY HE WAS.
HUG
NO... VIRIDE...
LET'S GO TO ALBUS'S CASTLE.
WE CAN'T LOSE ANYONE ELSE.

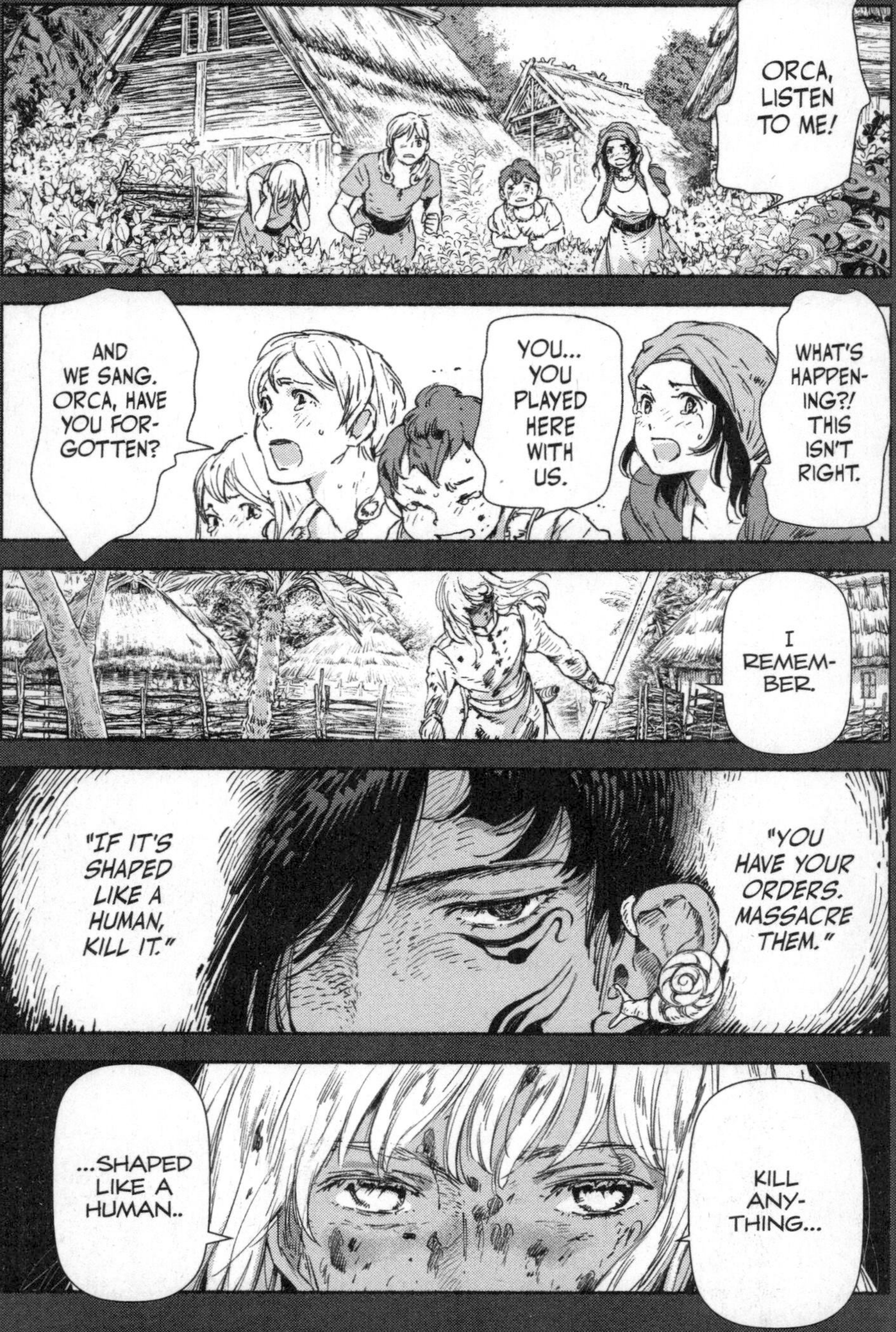
ORCA, LISTEN TO ME!
WHAT'S HAPPENING?! THIS ISN'T RIGHT.
YOU... YOU PLAYED HERE WITH US.
AND WE SANG. ORCA, HAVE YOU FORGOTTEN?
I REMEMBER.
"YOU HAVE YOUR ORDERS. MASSACRE THEM."
"IF IT'S SHAPED LIKE A HUMAN, KILL IT."
KILL ANYTHING...
...SHAPED LIKE A HUMAN..

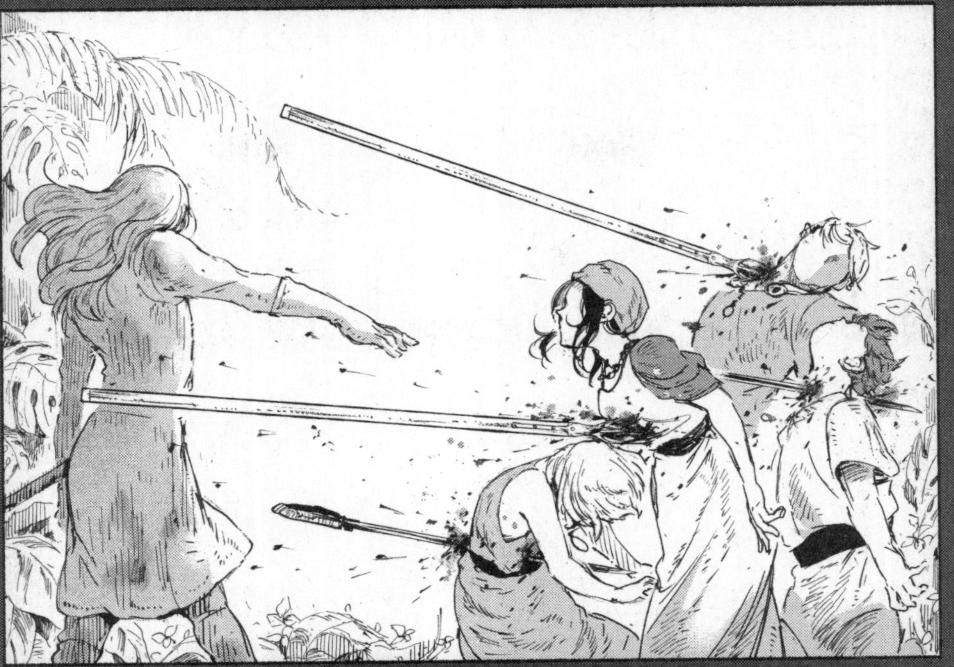

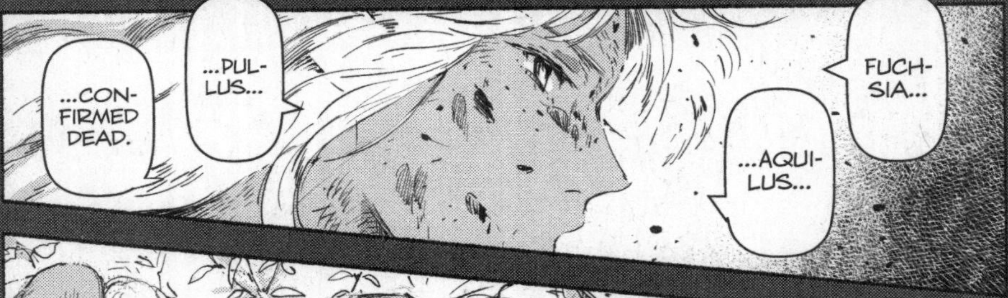
FUCHSIA...
...AQUILUS...
...PULLUS...
...CONFIRMED DEAD.

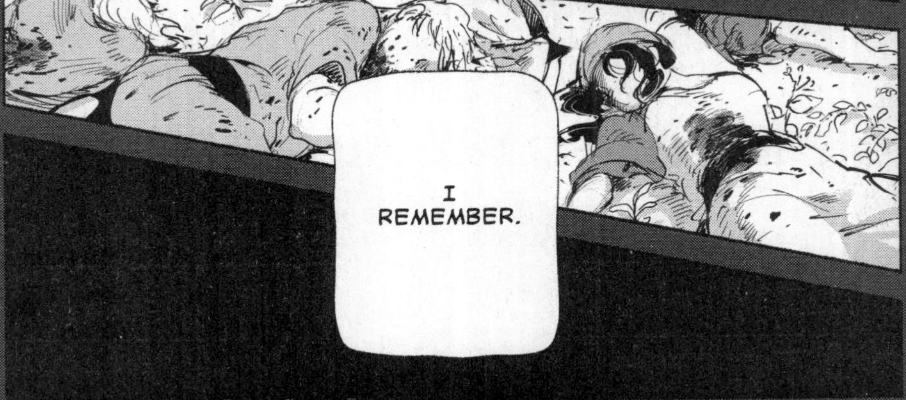
I REMEMBER.

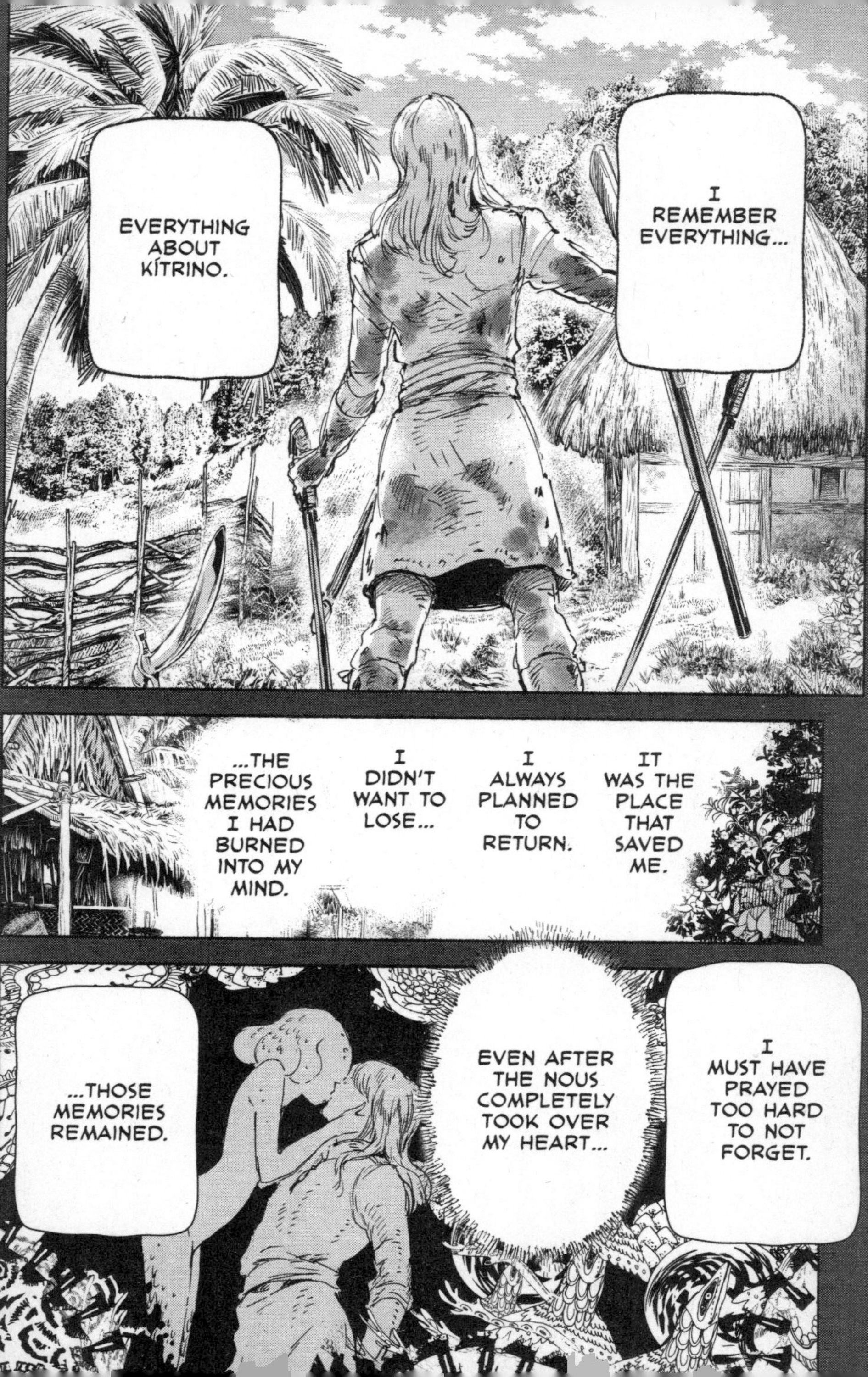
I REMEMBER EVERYTHING...
EVERYTHING ABOUT KÍTRINO.
IT WAS THE PLACE THAT SAVED ME.
I ALWAYS PLANNED TO RETURN.
I DIDN'T WANT TO LOSE...
...THE PRECIOUS MEMORIES I HAD BURNED INTO MY MIND.
I MUST HAVE PRAYED TOO HARD TO NOT FORGET.
EVEN AFTER THE NOUS COMPLETELY TOOK OVER MY HEART...
...THOSE MEMORIES REMAINED.

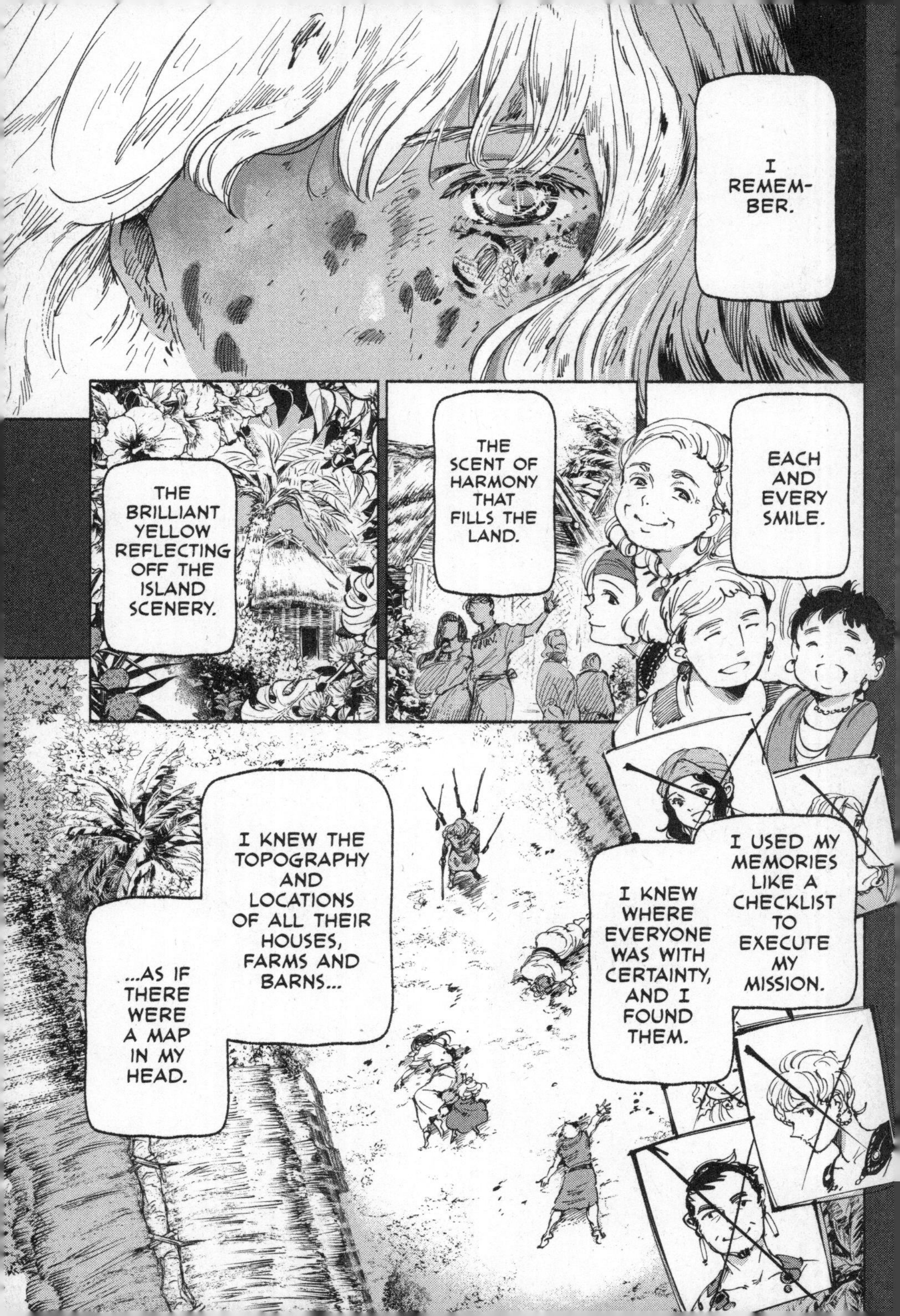
I REMEMBER.
EACH AND EVERY SMILE.
THE SCENT OF HARMONY THAT FILLS THE LAND.
THE BRILLIANT YELLOW REFLECTING OFF THE ISLAND SCENERY.
I USED MY MEMORIES LIKE A CHECKLIST TO EXECUTE MY MISSION.
I KNEW WHERE EVERYONE WAS WITH CERTAINTY, AND I FOUND THEM.
I KNEW THE TOPOGRAPHY AND LOCATIONS OF ALL THEIR HOUSES, FARMS AND BARNS...
...AS IF THERE WERE A MAP IN MY HEAD.

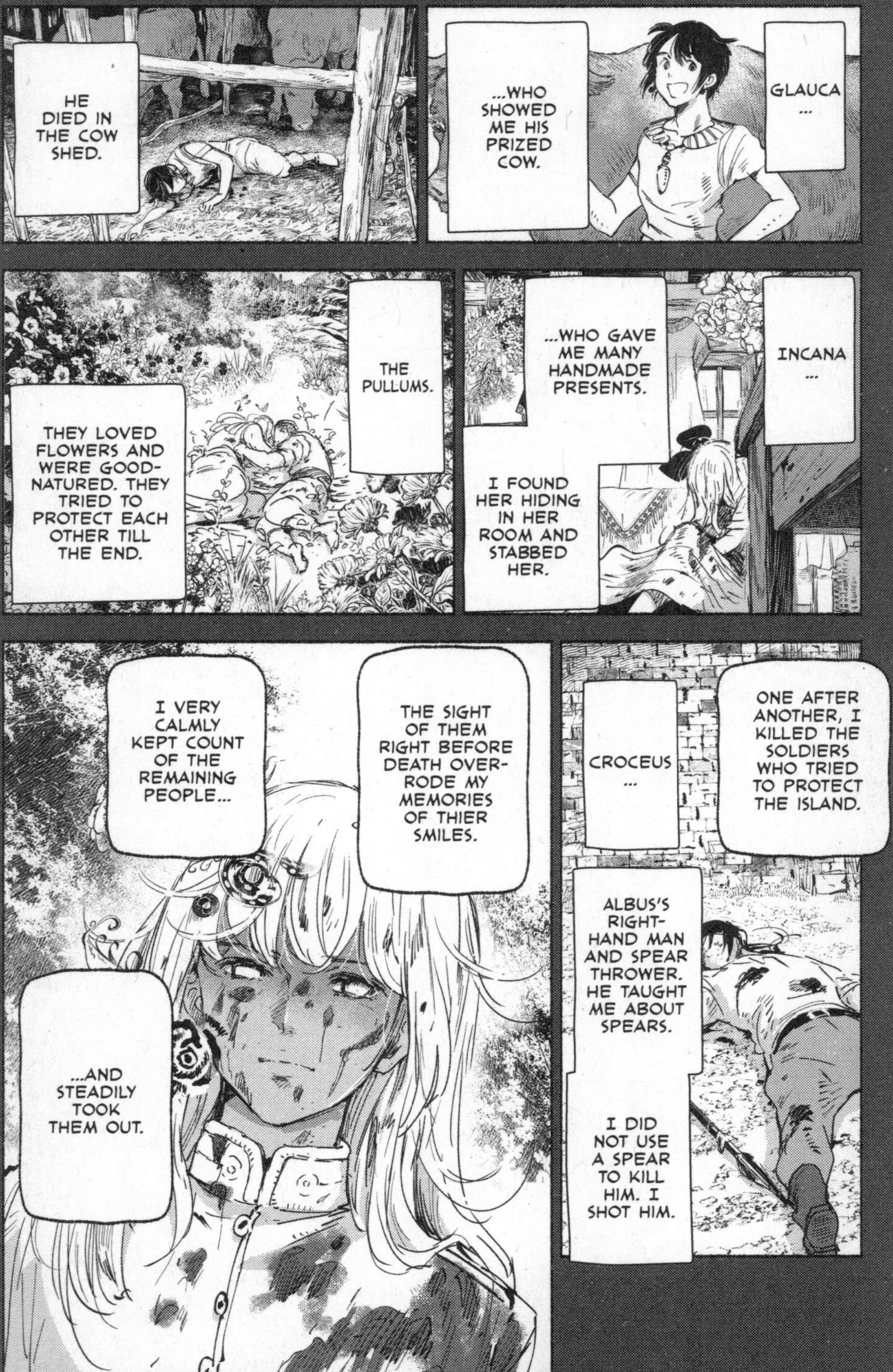
GLAUCA ...
...WHO SHOWED ME HIS PRIZED COW.
HE DIED IN THE COW SHED.
INCANA ...
...WHO GAVE ME MANY HANDMADE PRESENTS.
I FOUND HER HIDING IN HER ROOM AND STABBED HER.
THE PULLUMS.
THEY LOVED FLOWERS AND WERE GOOD-NATURED. THEY TRIED TO PROTECT EACH OTHER TILL THE END.
ONE AFTER ANOTHER, I KILLED THE SOLDIERS WHO TRIED TO PROTECT THE ISLAND.
CROCEUS ...
ALBUS'S RIGHT-HAND MAN AND SPEAR THROWER. HE TAUGHT ME ABOUT SPEARS.
I DID NOT USE A SPEAR TO KILL HIM. I SHOT HIM.
THE SIGHT OF THEM RIGHT BEFORE DEATH OVER-RODE MY MEMORIES OF THIER SMILES.
I VERY CALMLY KEPT COUNT OF THE REMAINING PEOPLE...
...AND STEADILY TOOK THEM OUT.

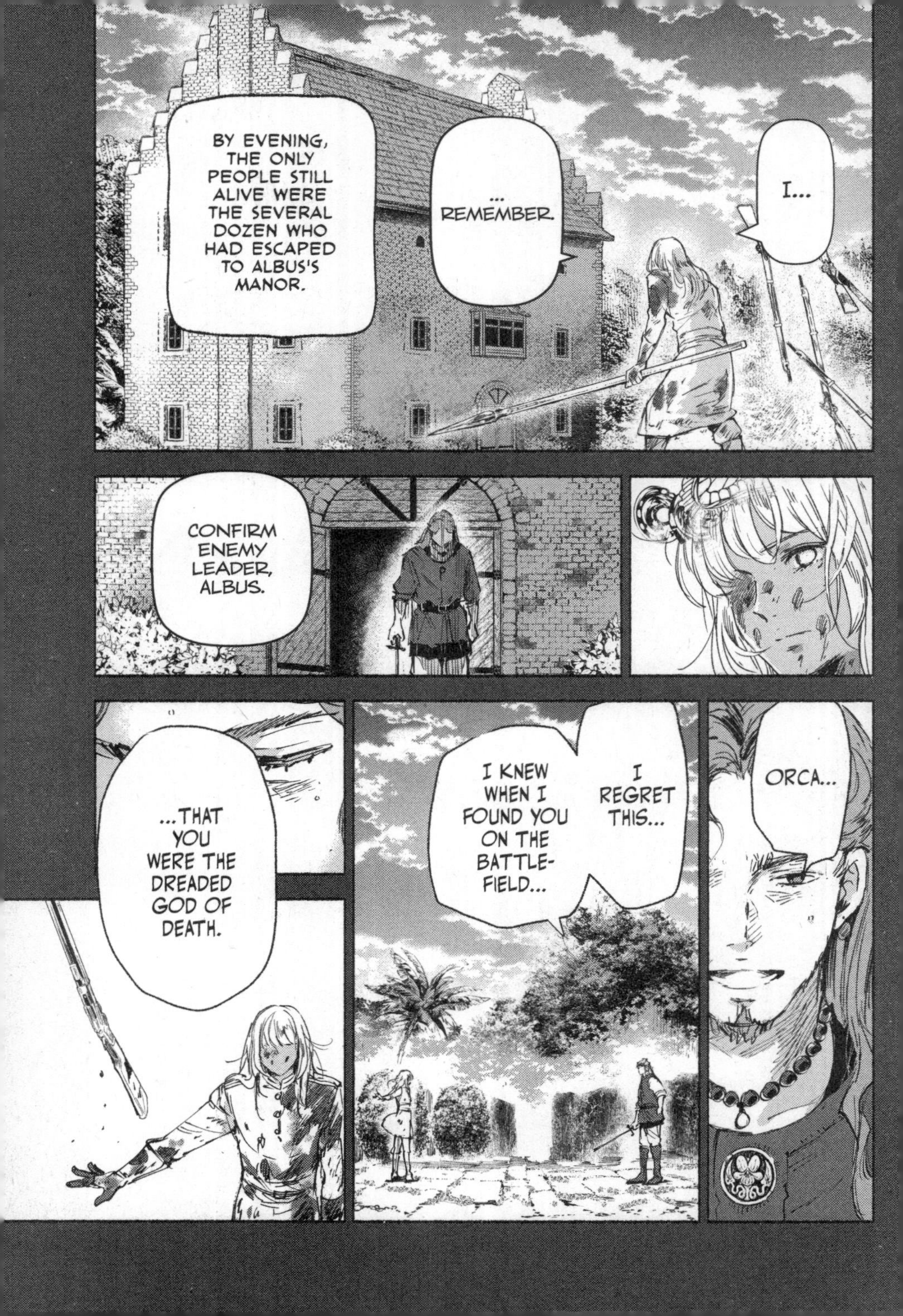
I...
...REMEMBER.
BY EVENING, THE ONLY PEOPLE STILL ALIVE WERE THE SEVERAL DOZEN WHO HAD ESCAPED TO ALBUS'S MANOR.
CONFIRM ENEMY LEADER, ALBUS.
ORCA...
I REGRET THIS...
I KNEW WHEN I FOUND YOU ON THE BATTLE-FIELD...
...THAT YOU WERE THE DREADED GOD OF DEATH.

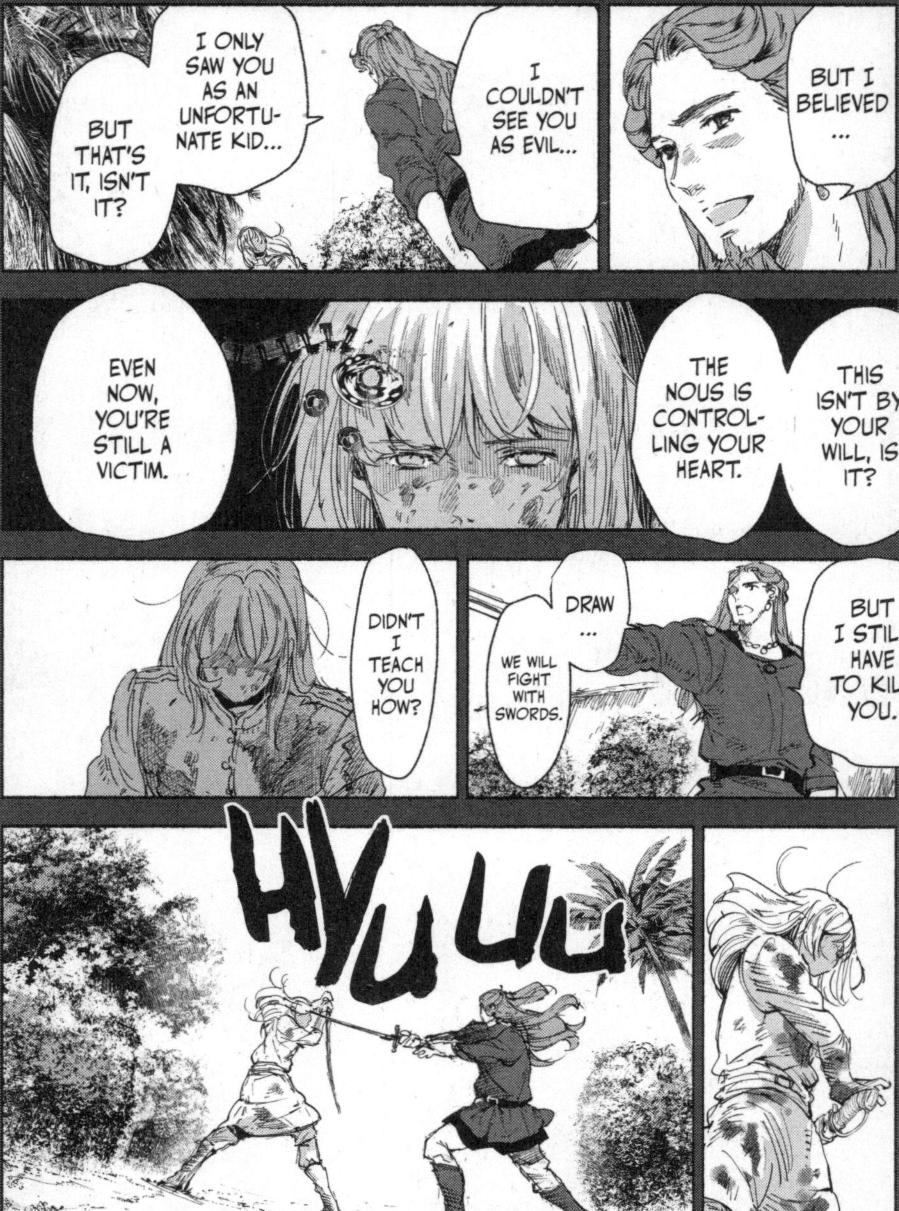
BUT I BELIEVED ...
I COULDN'T SEE YOU AS EVIL...
I ONLY SAW YOU AS AN UNFORTUNATE KID...
BUT THAT'S IT, ISN'T IT?
THIS ISN'T BY YOUR WILL, IS IT?
THE NOUS IS CONTROLLING YOUR HEART.
EVEN NOW, YOU'RE STILL A VICTIM.
BUT I STILL HAVE TO KILL YOU.
DRAW ...
WE WILL FIGHT WITH SWORDS.
DIDN'T I TEACH YOU HOW?
HYUUU

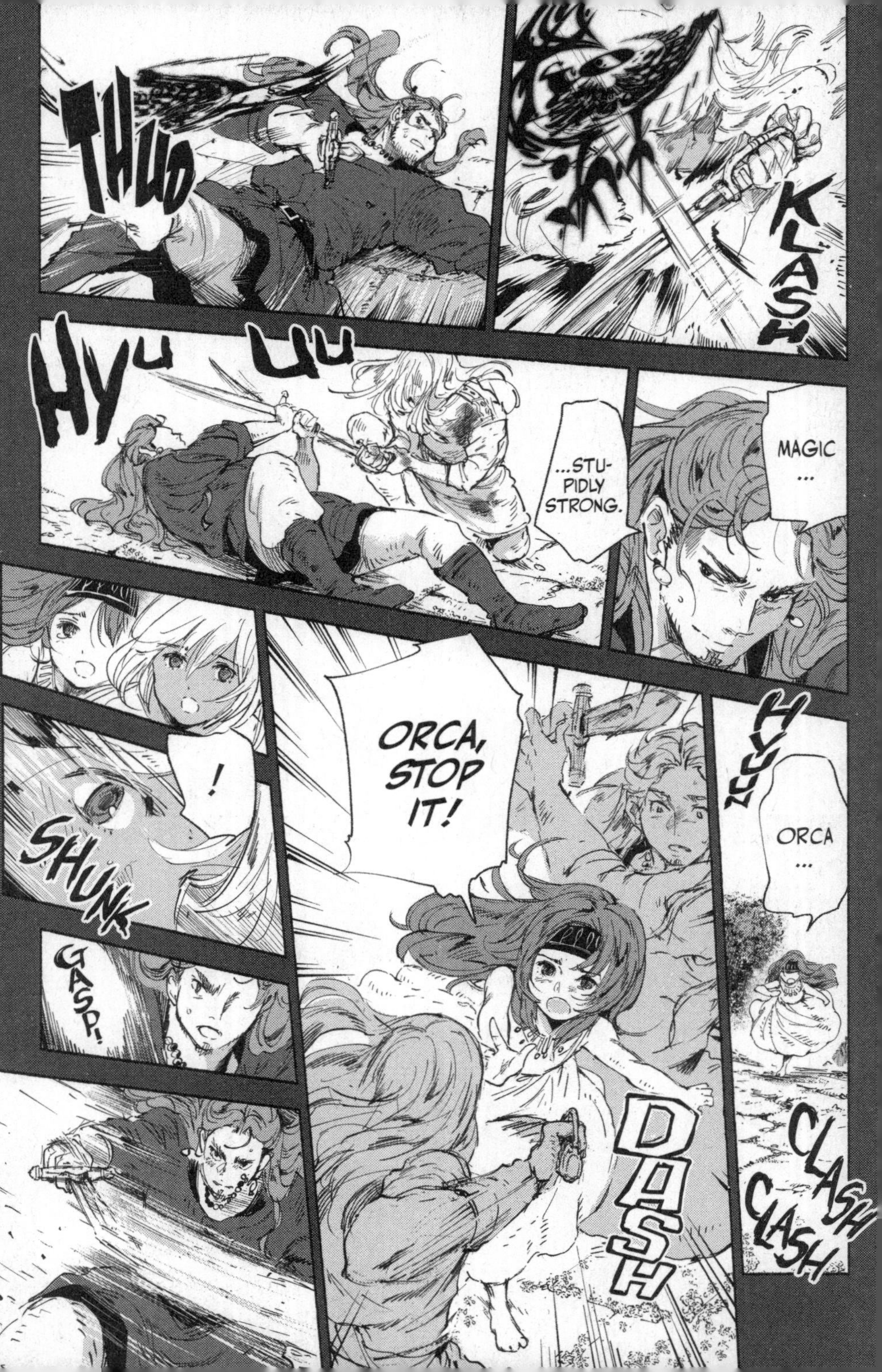
KLASH
THUD
MAGIC ...
...STU-PIDLY STRONG.
HYU UU
HYUUN
ORCA ...
CLASH
CLASH
ORCA, STOP IT!
DASH
!
SHUNK
GASP!

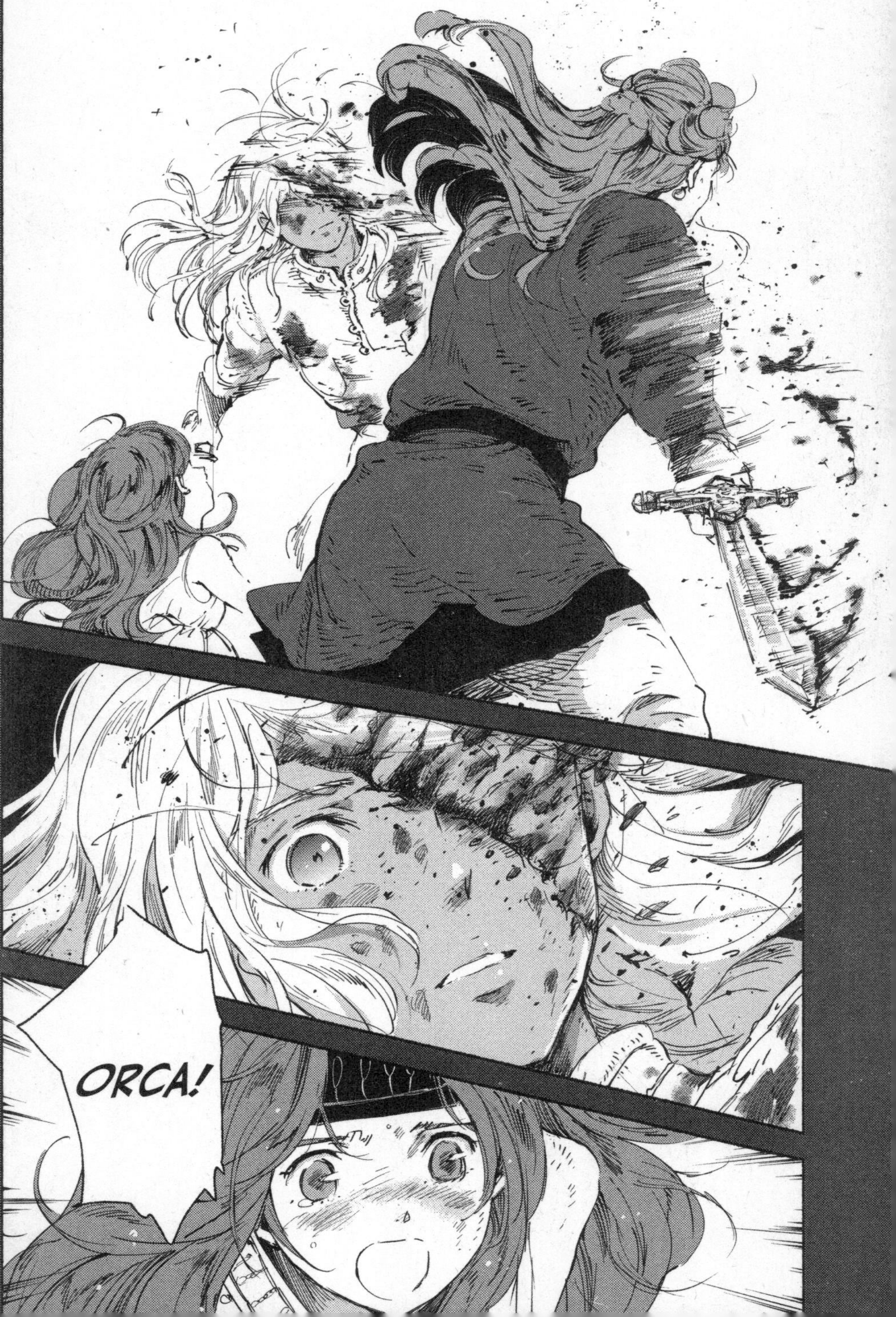
ORCA!

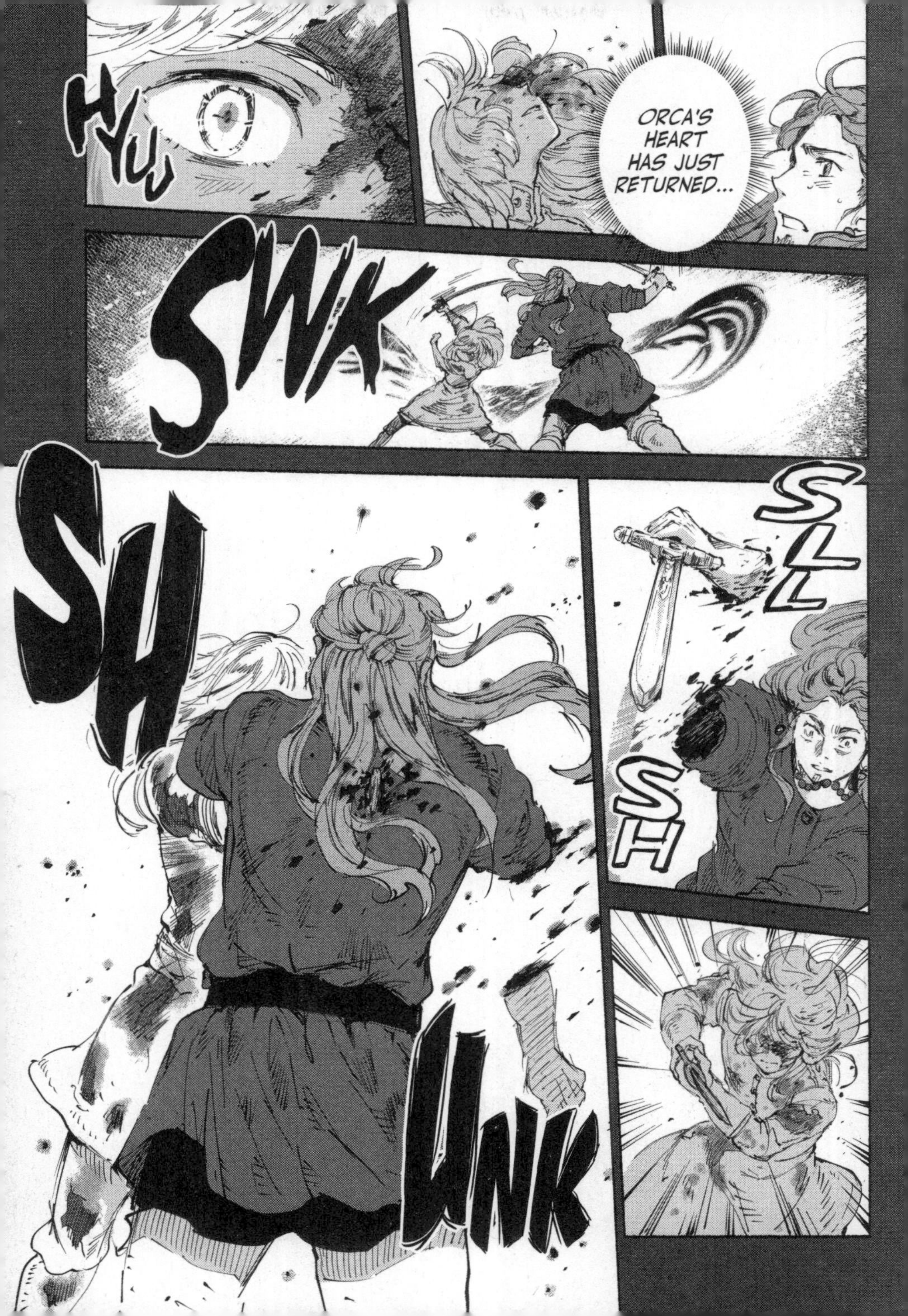
ORCA'S HEART HAS JUST RETURNED...
HYUU
SWK
SLL
SH
SHUNK

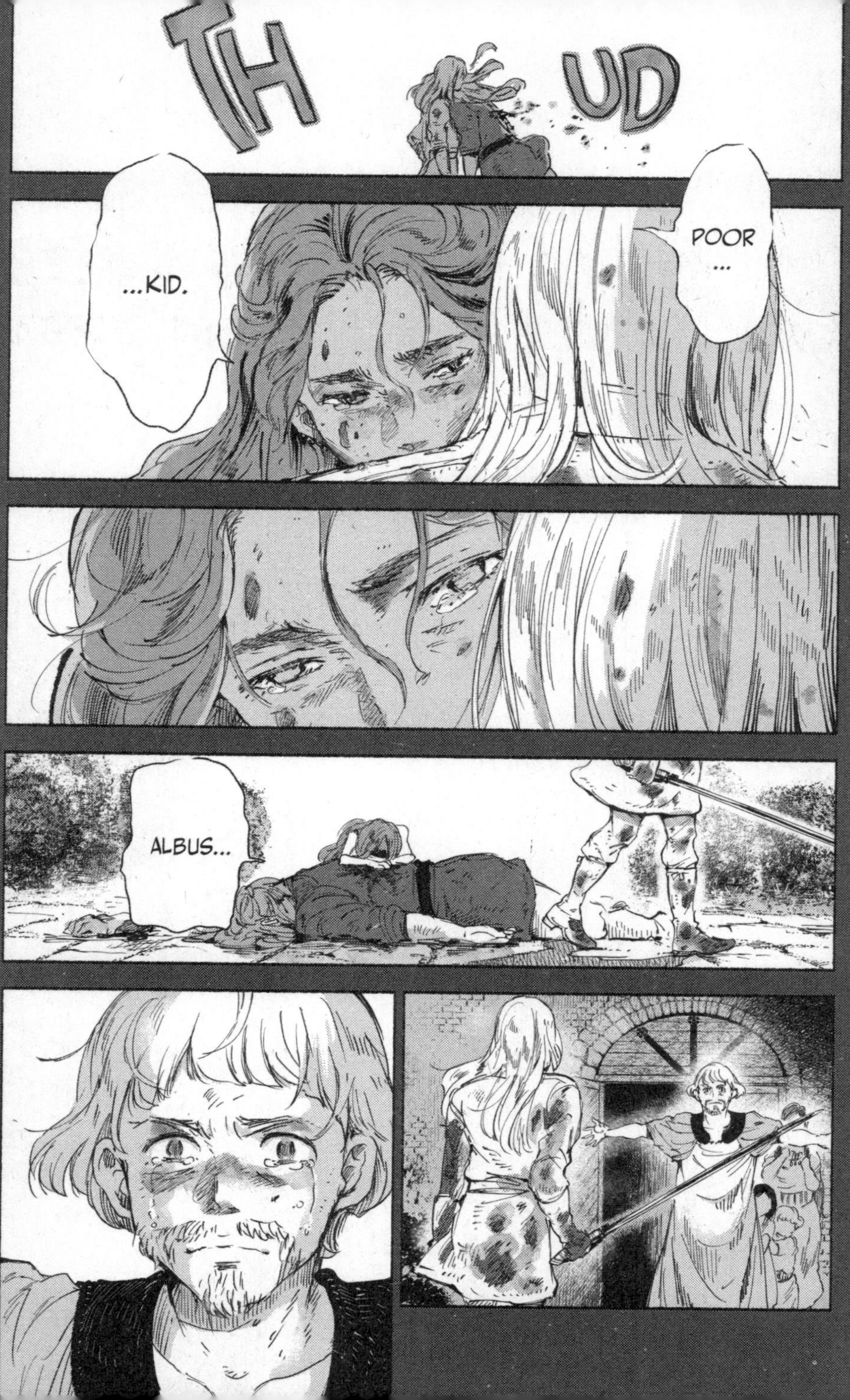
THUD
POOR...
...KID.
ALBUS...

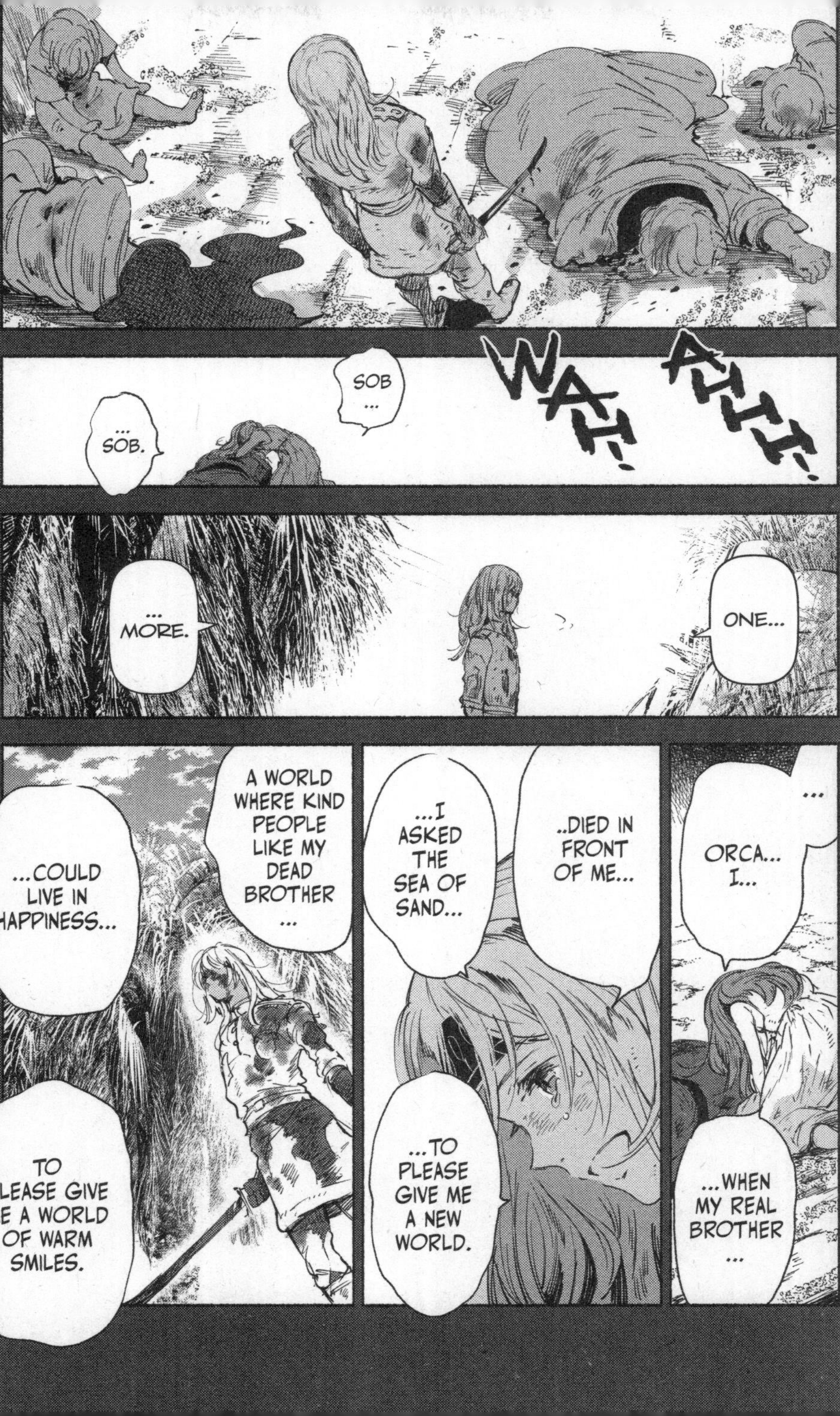
WAH! AHHH!
SOB ...
... SOB.
ONE...
... MORE.
...
ORCA... I...
...WHEN MY REAL BROTHER ...
..DIED IN FRONT OF ME...
...I ASKED THE SEA OF SAND...
...TO PLEASE GIVE ME A NEW WORLD.
A WORLD WHERE KIND PEOPLE LIKE MY DEAD BROTHER ...
...COULD LIVE IN HAPPINESS...
TO PLEASE GIVE ME A WORLD OF WARM SMILES.

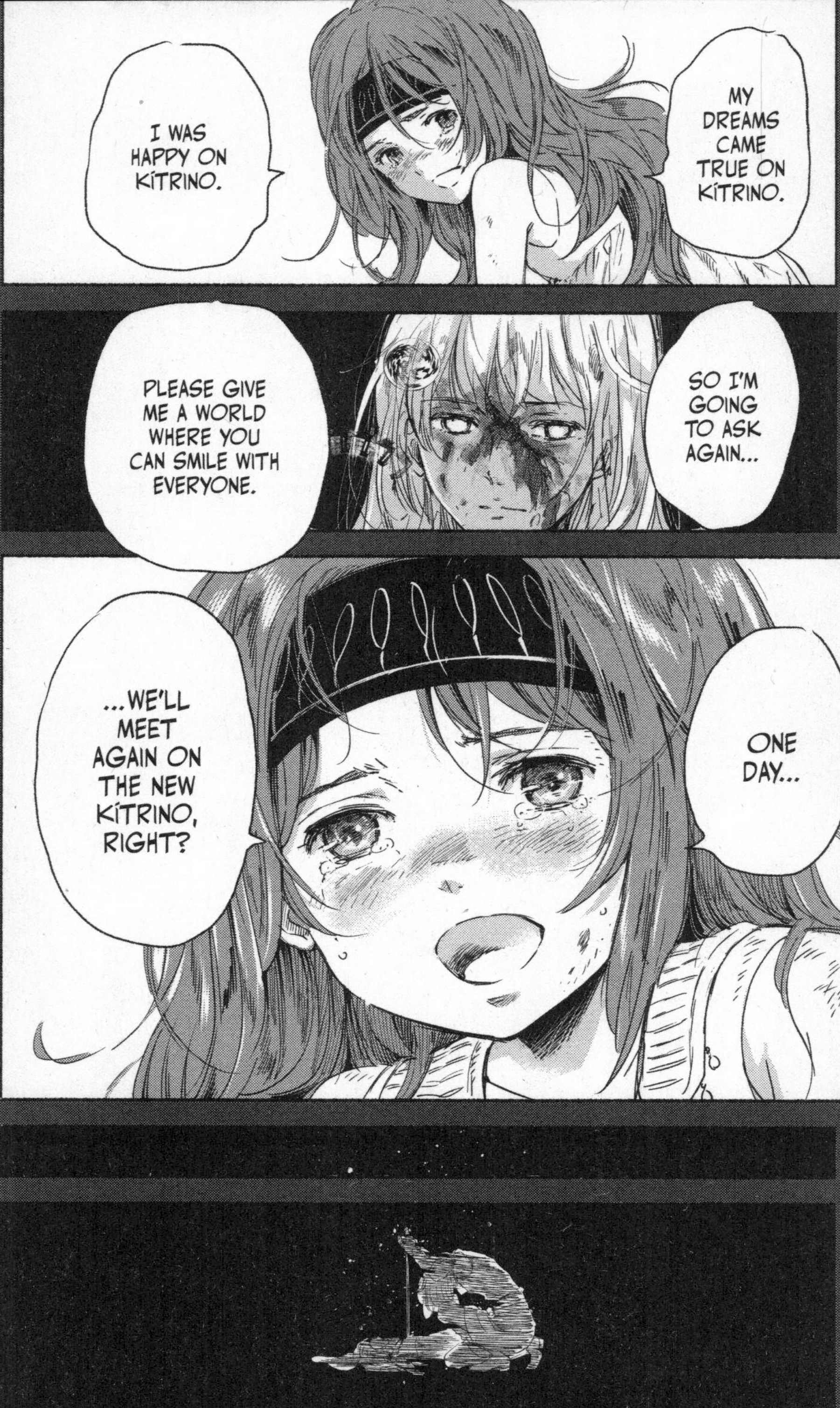
MY DREAMS CAME TRUE ON KíTRINO.
I WAS HAPPY ON KíTRINO.
SO I'M GOING TO ASK AGAIN...
PLEASE GIVE ME A WORLD WHERE YOU CAN SMILE WITH EVERYONE.
ONE DAY...
...WE'LL MEET AGAIN ON THE NEW KíTRINO, RIGHT?

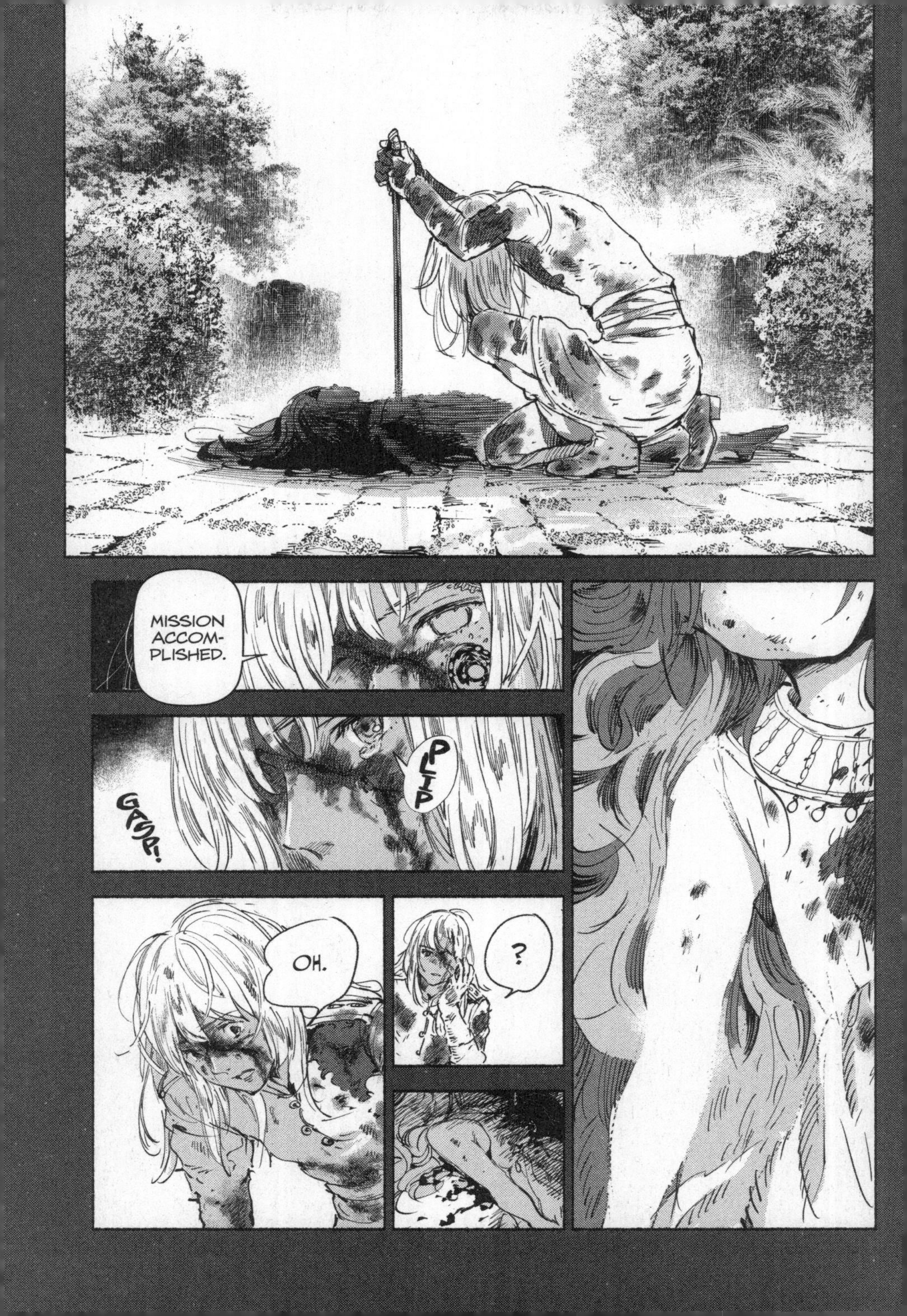
MISSION ACCOM-PLISHED.
PLIP
GASP!
?
OH.

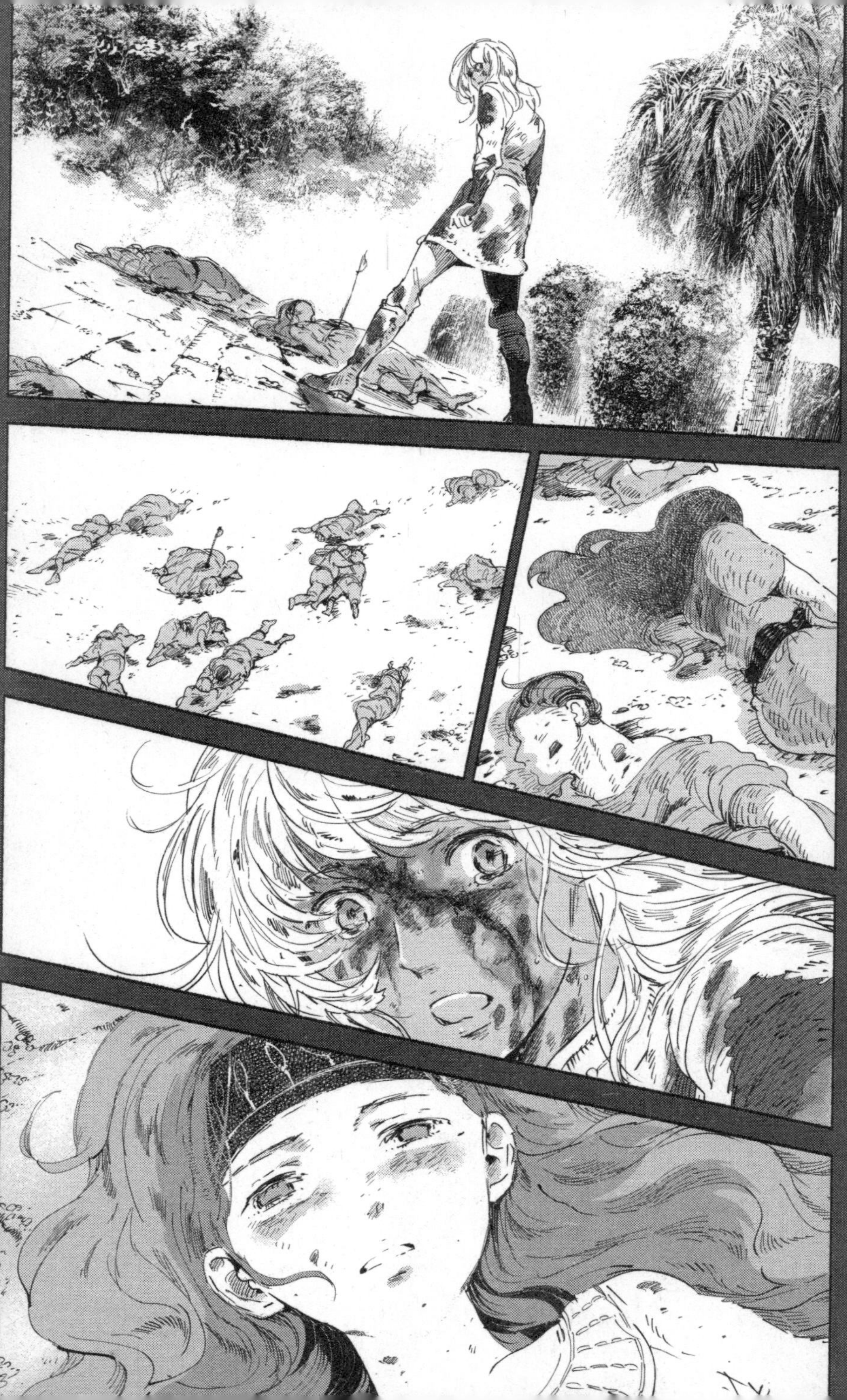

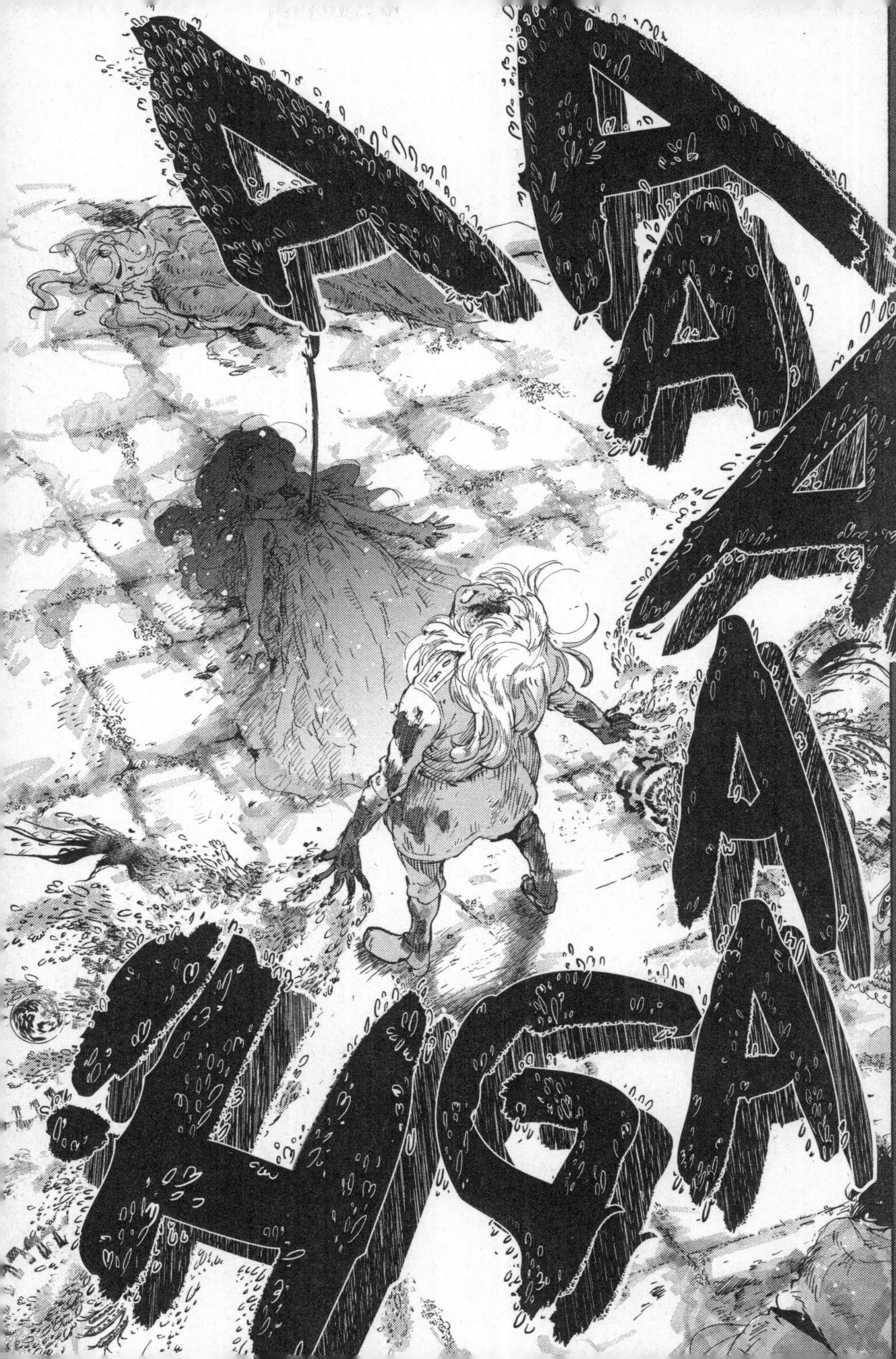
AAAAAAGH!

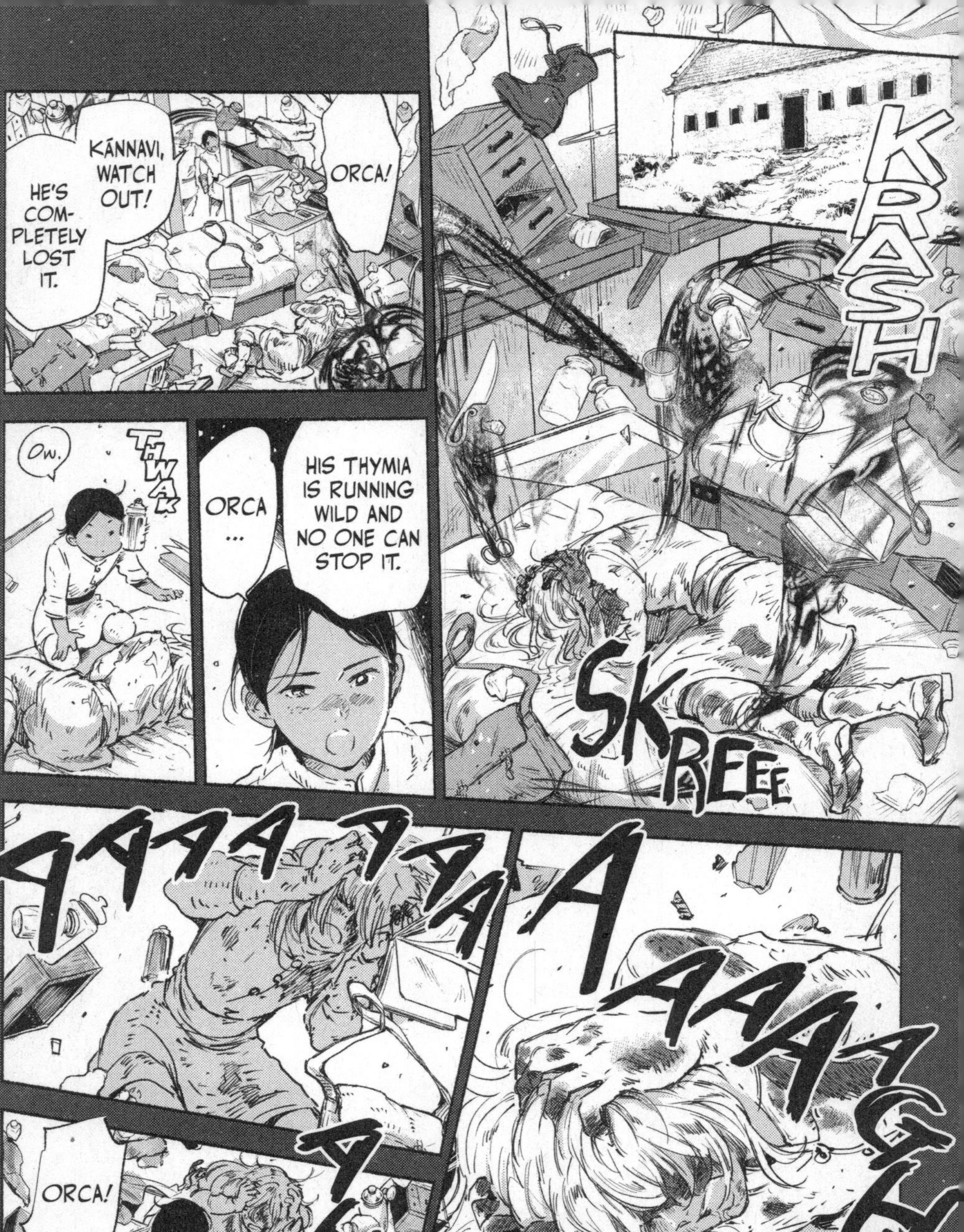
KRASH
SKREEE
ORCA!
KÁNNAVI, WATCH OUT!
HE'S COMPLETELY LOST IT.
HIS THYMIA IS RUNNING WILD AND NO ONE CAN STOP IT.
ORCA ...
THWAK
Ow.
AAAAAAAAAAAAAGH!
AAH!
ORCA!

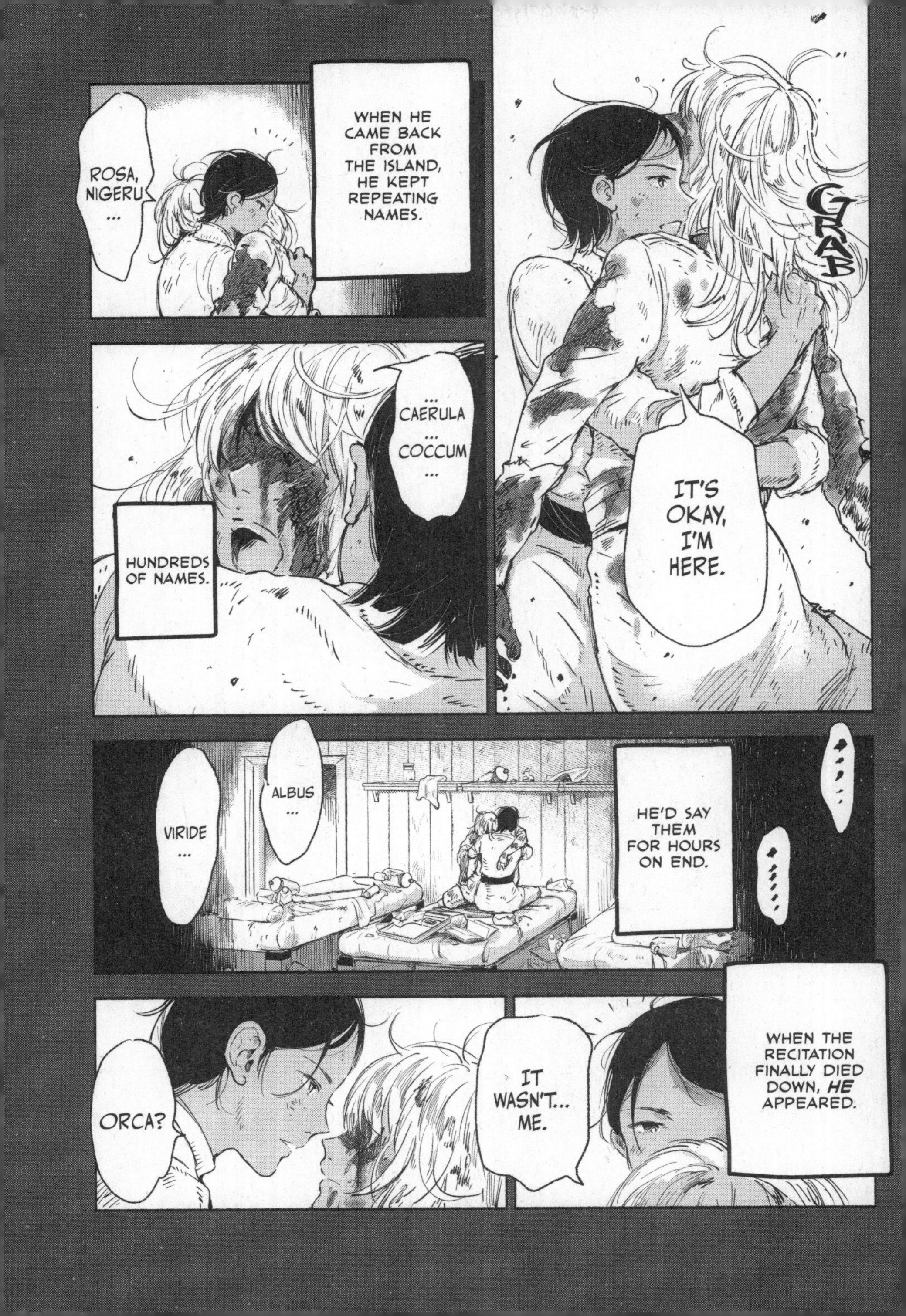
GRAB
IT'S OKAY, I'M HERE.
WHEN HE CAME BACK FROM THE ISLAND, HE KEPT REPEATING NAMES.
ROSA, NIGERU ...
... CAERULA ... COCCUM ...
HUNDREDS OF NAMES.
...
...
HE'D SAY THEM FOR HOURS ON END.
ALBUS ...
VIRIDE ...
WHEN THE RECITATION FINALLY DIED DOWN, HE APPEARED.
IT WASN'T... ME.
ORCA?

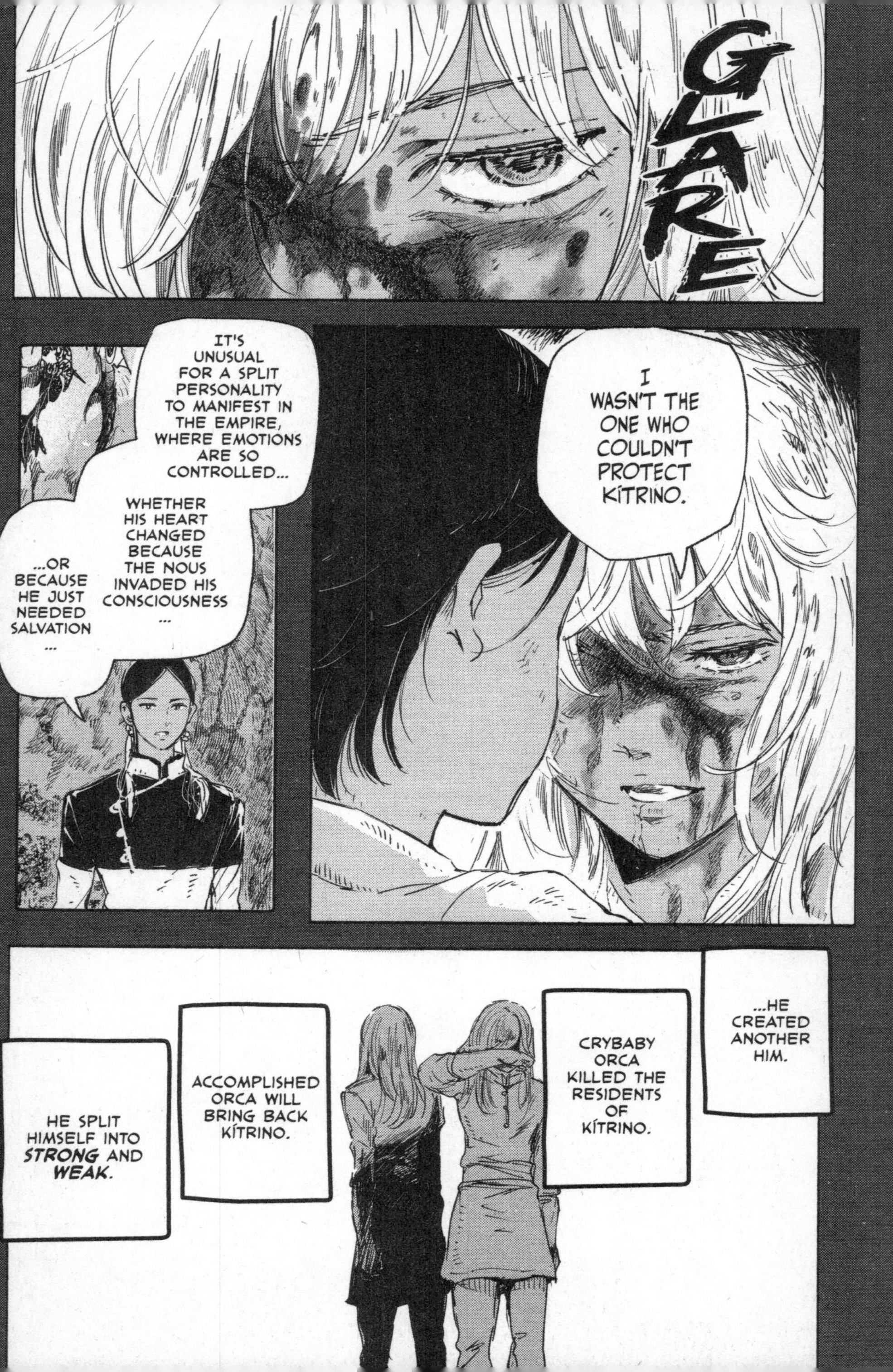
GLARE
I WASN'T THE ONE WHO COULDN'T PROTECT KÍTRINO.
IT'S UNUSUAL FOR A SPLIT PERSONALITY TO MANIFEST IN THE EMPIRE, WHERE EMOTIONS ARE SO CONTROLLED...
WHETHER HIS HEART CHANGED BECAUSE THE NOUS INVADED HIS CONSCIOUSNESS...
...OR BECAUSE HE JUST NEEDED SALVATION...
...HE CREATED ANOTHER HIM.
CRYBABY ORCA KILLED THE RESIDENTS OF KÍTRINO.
ACCOMPLISHED ORCA WILL BRING BACK KÍTRINO.
HE SPLIT HIMSELF INTO *STRONG* AND *WEAK*.

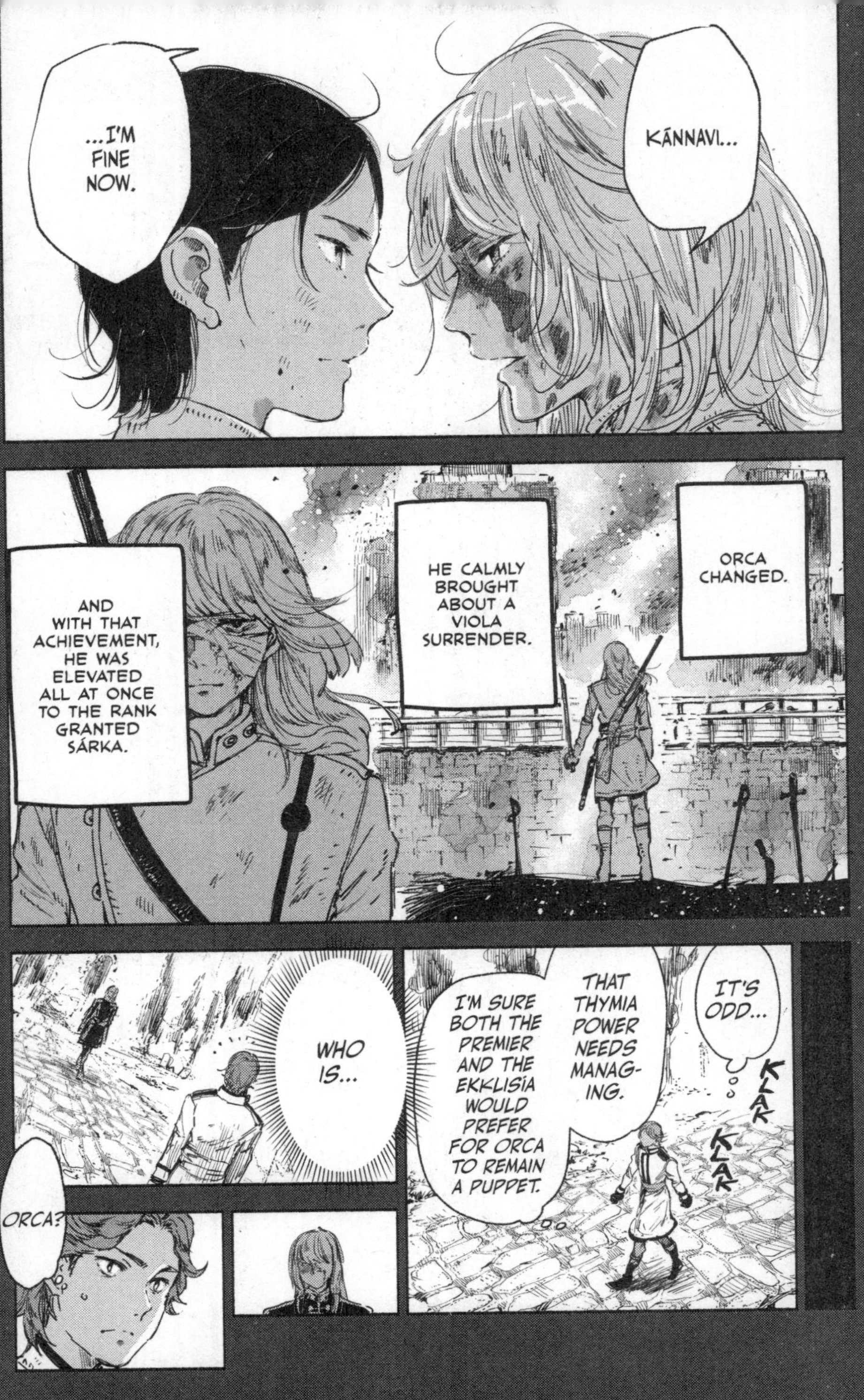
KĀNNAVI...
...I'M FINE NOW.
ORCA CHANGED.
HE CALMLY BROUGHT ABOUT A VIOLA SURRENDER.
AND WITH THAT ACHIEVEMENT, HE WAS ELEVATED ALL AT ONCE TO THE RANK GRANTED SÁRKA.
IT'S ODD...
KLAK
KLAK
THAT THYMIA POWER NEEDS MANAG-ING.
I'M SURE BOTH THE PREMIER AND THE EKKLISIA WOULD PREFER FOR ORCA TO REMAIN A PUPPET.
WHO IS...
ORCA?

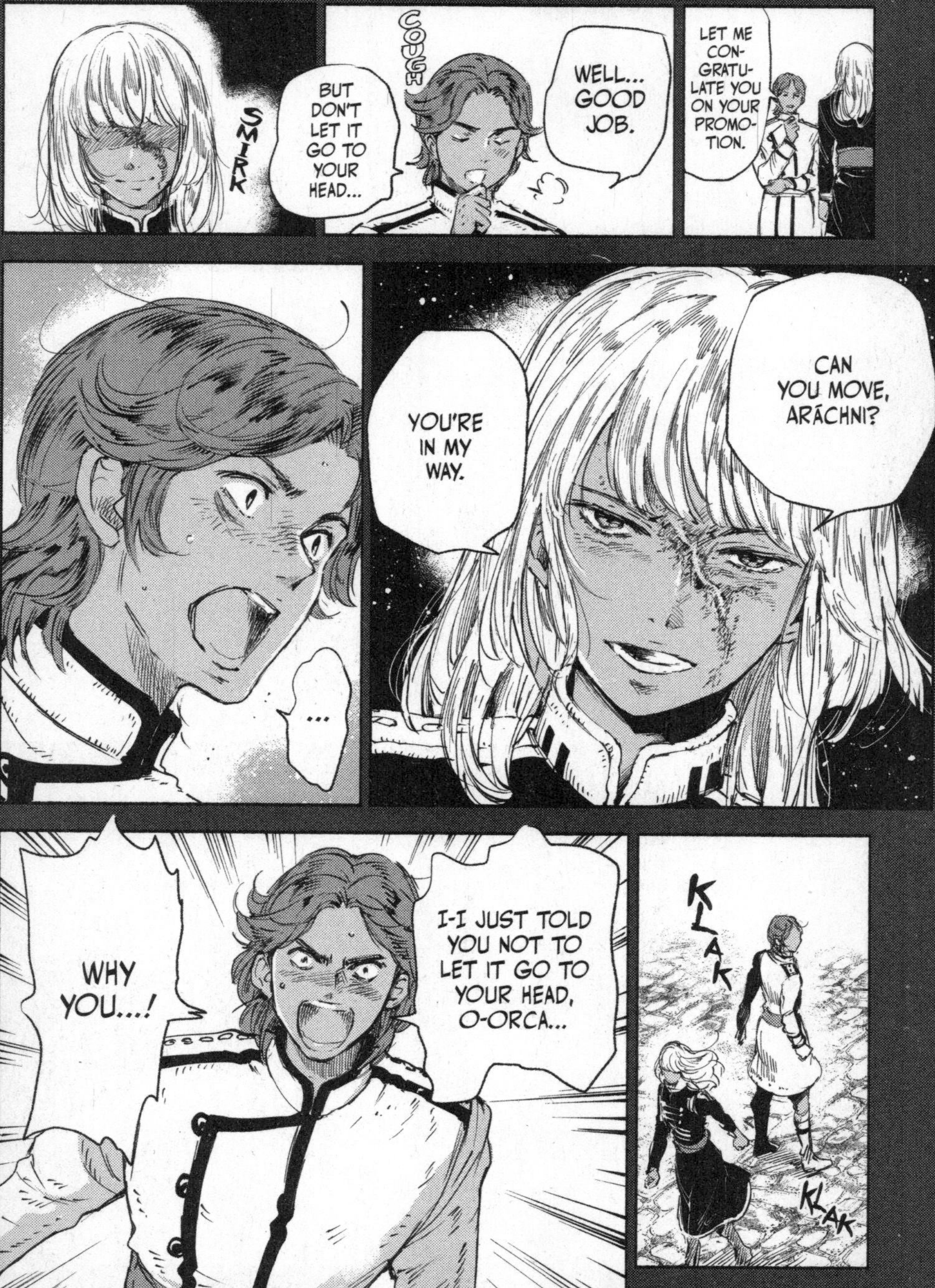
LET ME CON-GRATU-LATE YOU ON YOUR PROMO-TION.
WELL... GOOD JOB.
COUGH
BUT DON'T LET IT GO TO YOUR HEAD...
SMIRK
CAN YOU MOVE, ARÁCHNI?
YOU'RE IN MY WAY.
...
KLAK
KLAK
I-I JUST TOLD YOU NOT TO LET IT GO TO YOUR HEAD, O-ORCA...
WHY YOU...!

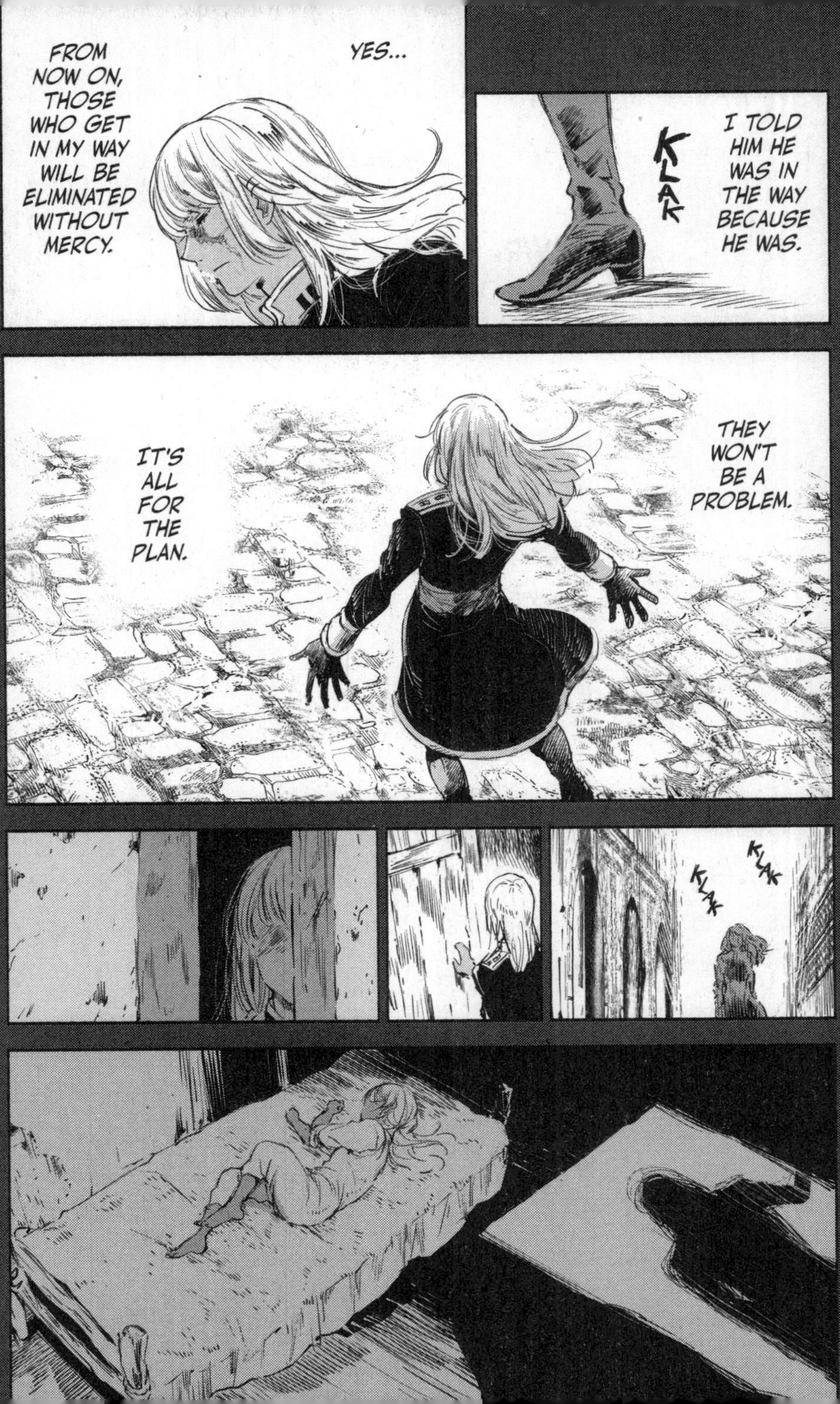
I TOLD HIM HE WAS IN THE WAY BECAUSE HE WAS.
KLAK
YES...
FROM NOW ON, THOSE WHO GET IN MY WAY WILL BE ELIMINATED WITHOUT MERCY.
THEY WON'T BE A PROBLEM.
IT'S ALL FOR THE PLAN.
KLAK
KLAK

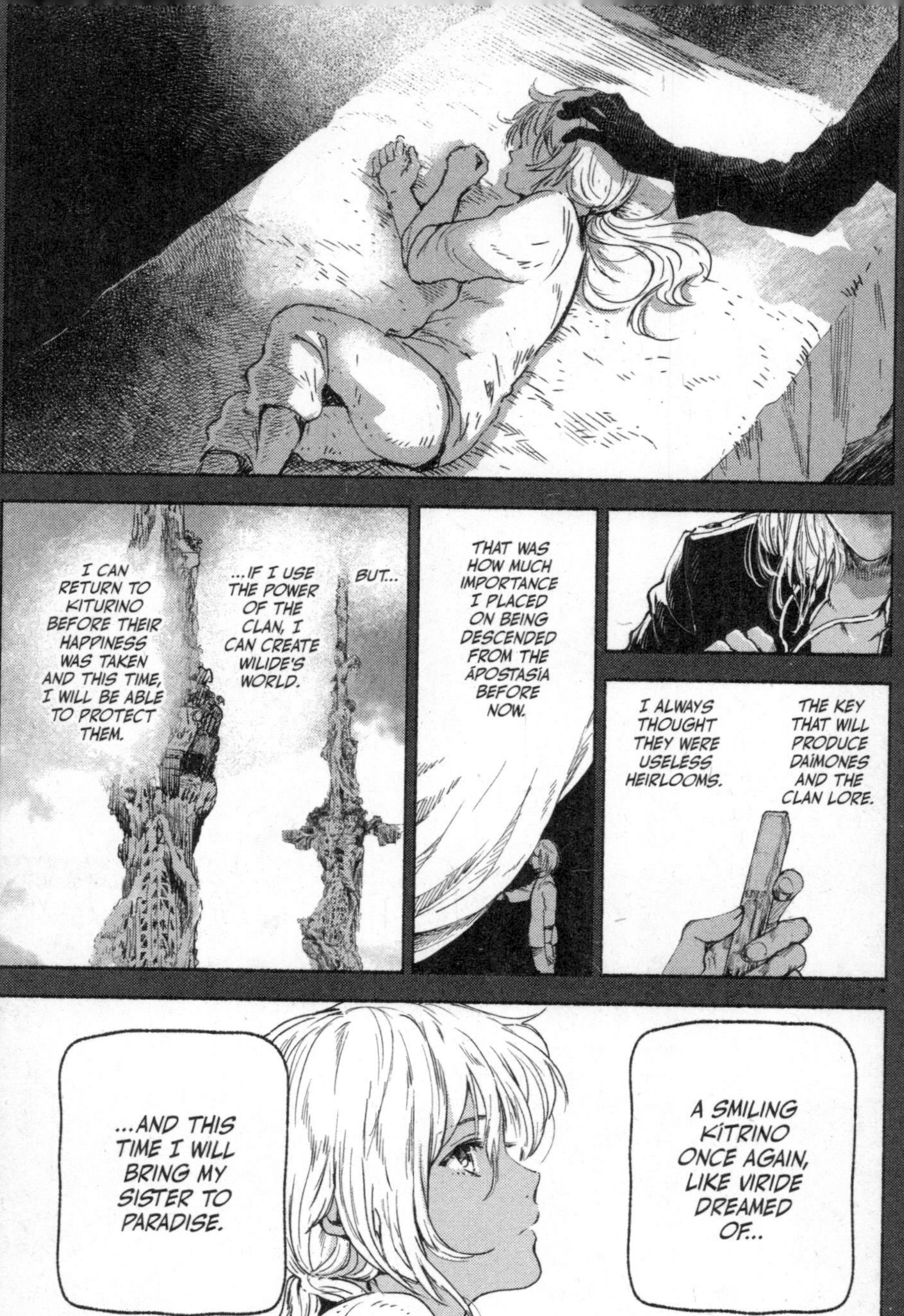
THE KEY THAT WILL PRODUCE DAÍMONES AND THE CLAN LORE.
I ALWAYS THOUGHT THEY WERE USELESS HEIRLOOMS.
THAT WAS HOW MUCH IMPORTANCE I PLACED ON BEING DESCENDED FROM THE ÁPOSTASÍA BEFORE NOW.
BUT...
...IF I USE THE POWER OF THE CLAN, I CAN CREATE WILIDE'S WORLD.
I CAN RETURN TO KITURINO BEFORE THEIR HAPPINESS WAS TAKEN AND THIS TIME, I WILL BE ABLE TO PROTECT THEM.
A SMILING KÍTRINO ONCE AGAIN, LIKE VIRIDE DREAMED OF...
...AND THIS TIME I WILL BRING MY SISTER TO PARADISE.

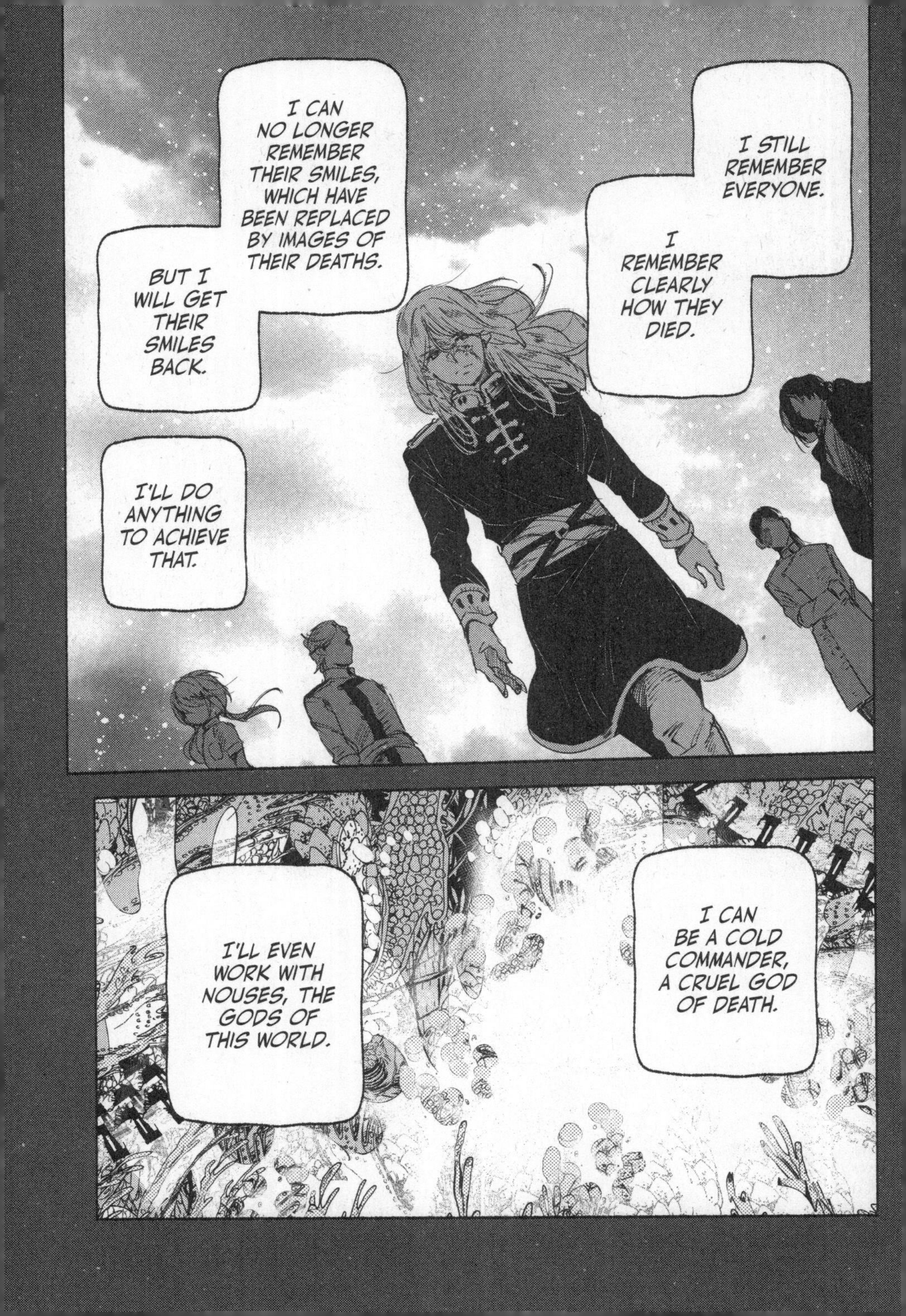
I STILL REMEMBER EVERYONE.
I REMEMBER CLEARLY HOW THEY DIED.
I CAN NO LONGER REMEMBER THEIR SMILES, WHICH HAVE BEEN REPLACED BY IMAGES OF THEIR DEATHS.
BUT I WILL GET THEIR SMILES BACK.
I'LL DO ANYTHING TO ACHIEVE THAT.
I CAN BE A COLD COMMANDER, A CRUEL GOD OF DEATH.
I'LL EVEN WORK WITH NOUSES, THE GODS OF THIS WORLD.

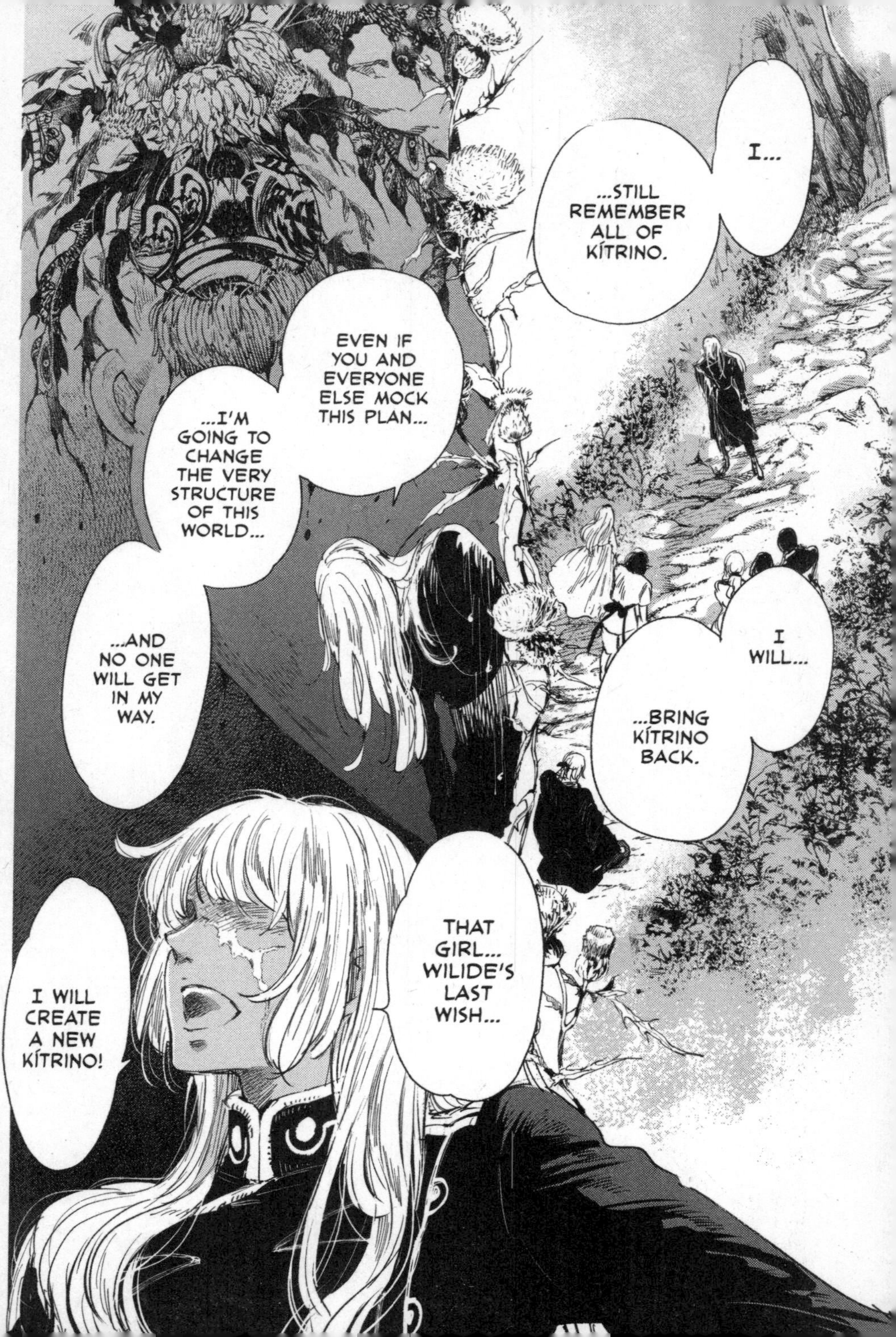
I...
...STILL REMEMBER ALL OF KÍTRINO.
EVEN IF YOU AND EVERYONE ELSE MOCK THIS PLAN...
...I'M GOING TO CHANGE THE VERY STRUCTURE OF THIS WORLD...
...AND NO ONE WILL GET IN MY WAY.
I WILL...
...BRING KÍTRINO BACK.
THAT GIRL... WILIDE'S LAST WISH...
I WILL CREATE A NEW KÍTRINO!

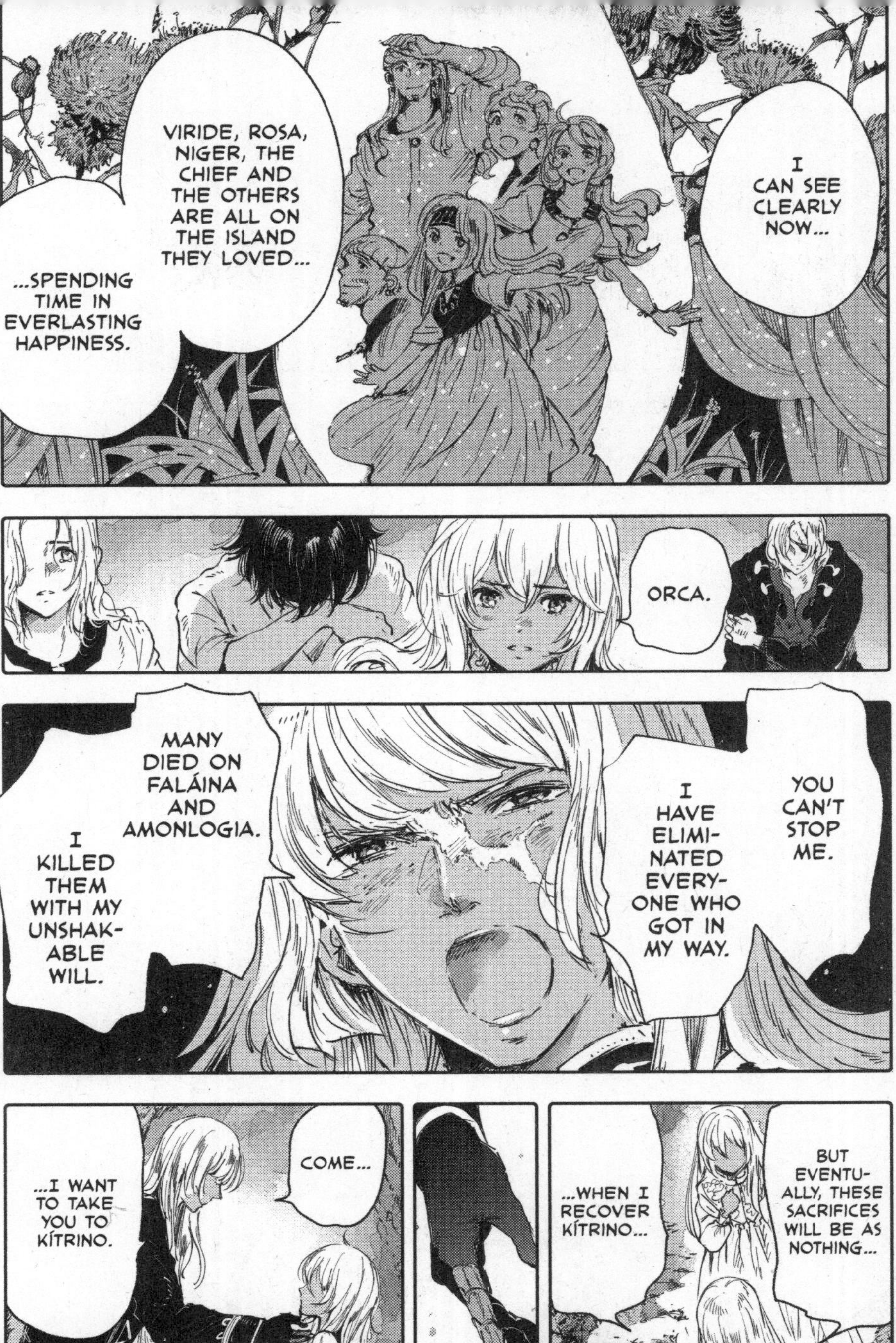
I CAN SEE CLEARLY NOW...
VIRIDE, ROSA, NIGER, THE CHIEF AND THE OTHERS ARE ALL ON THE ISLAND THEY LOVED...
...SPENDING TIME IN EVERLASTING HAPPINESS.
ORCA.
YOU CAN'T STOP ME.
I HAVE ELIMINATED EVERYONE WHO GOT IN MY WAY.
MANY DIED ON FALÁINA AND AMONLOGIA.
I KILLED THEM WITH MY UNSHAKABLE WILL.
BUT EVENTUALLY, THESE SACRIFICES WILL BE AS NOTHING...
...WHEN I RECOVER KÍTRINO...
COME...
...I WANT TO TAKE YOU TO KÍTRINO.

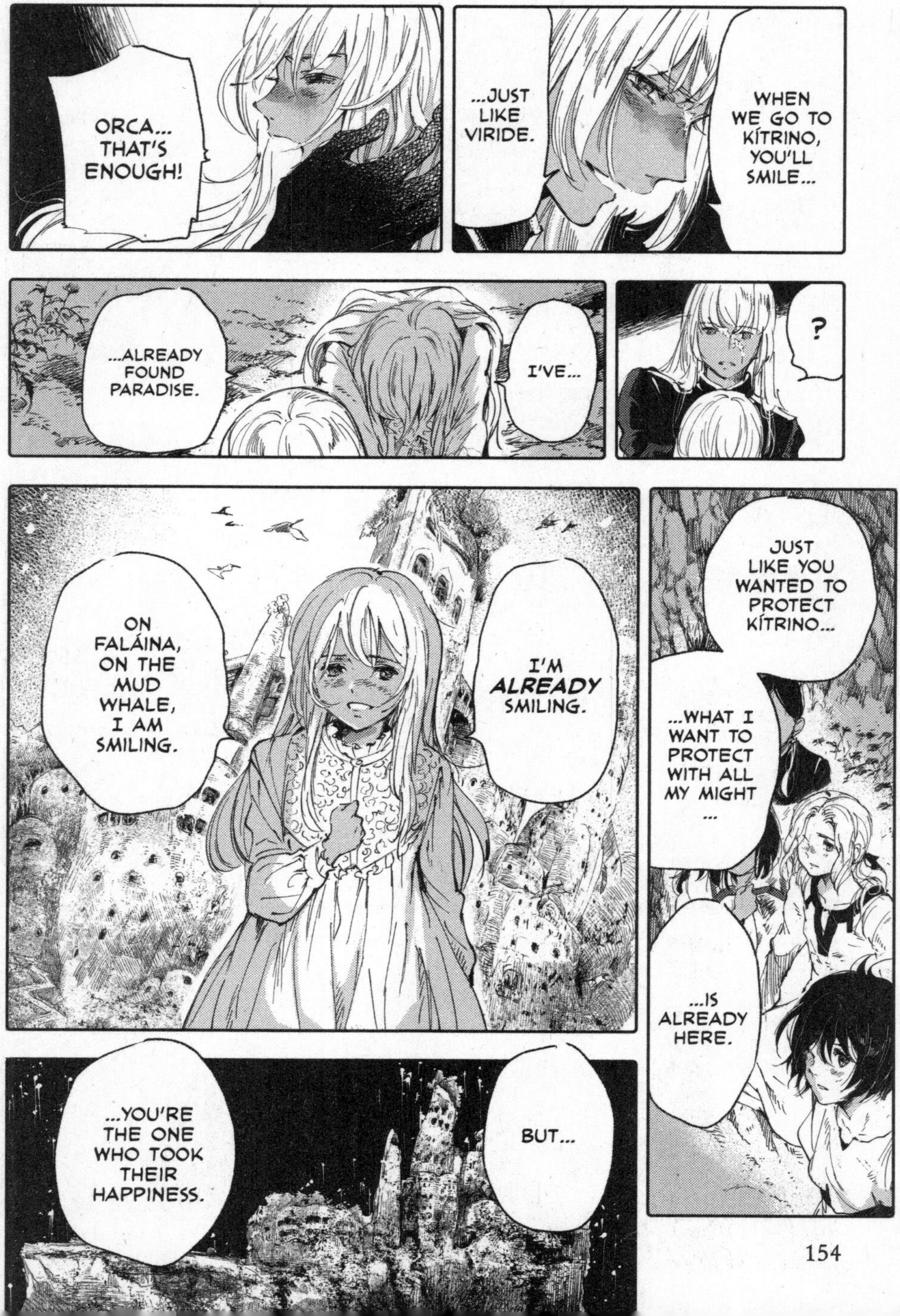
WHEN WE GO TO KÍTRINO, YOU'LL SMILE...
...JUST LIKE VIRIDE.
ORCA... THAT'S ENOUGH!
?
I'VE...
...ALREADY FOUND PARADISE.
JUST LIKE YOU WANTED TO PROTECT KÍTRINO...
...WHAT I WANT TO PROTECT WITH ALL MY MIGHT ...
...IS ALREADY HERE.
I'M *ALREADY* SMILING.
ON FALÁINA, ON THE MUD WHALE, I AM SMILING.
BUT...
...YOU'RE THE ONE WHO TOOK THEIR HAPPINESS.

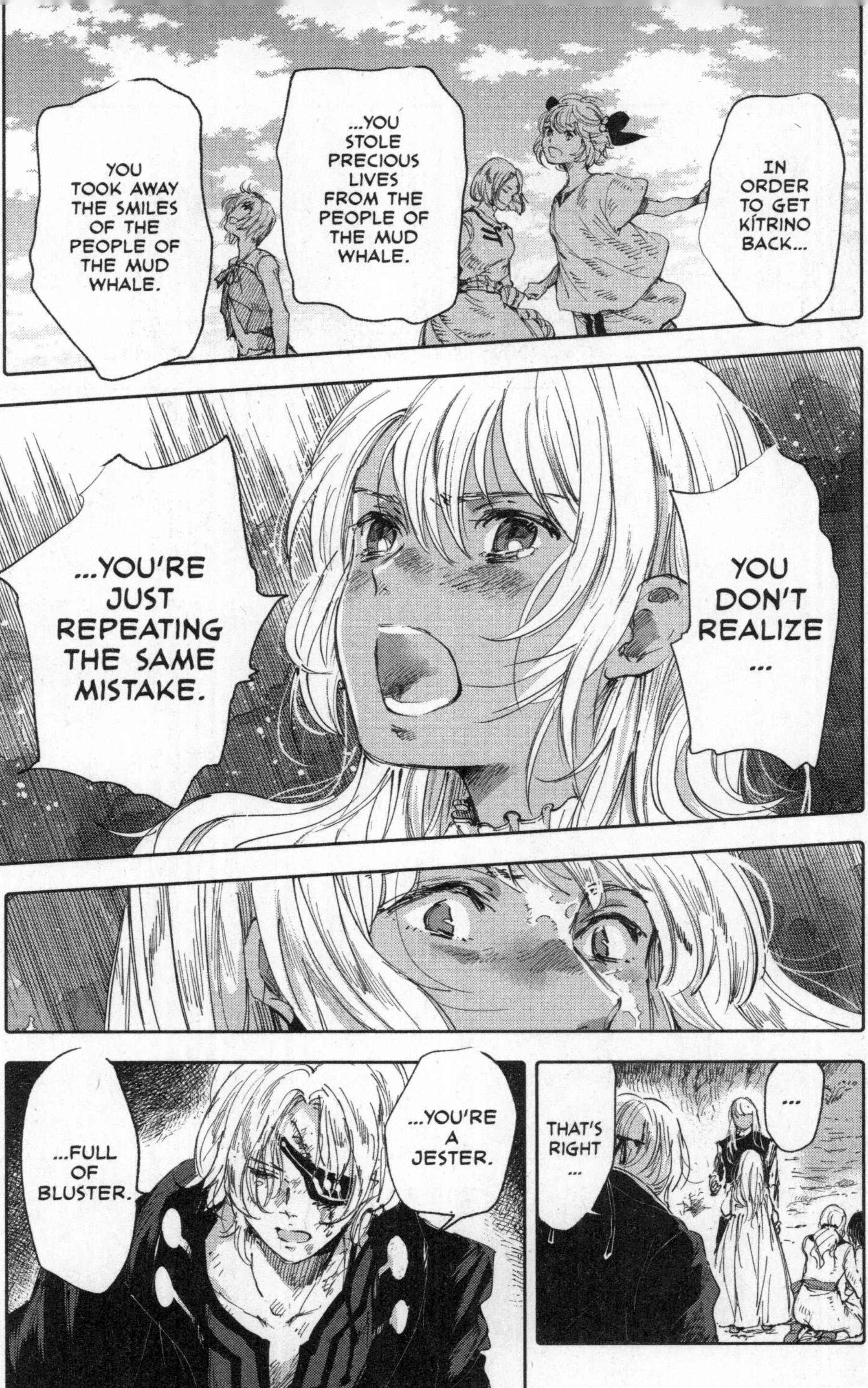
IN ORDER TO GET KÍTRINO BACK...
...YOU STOLE PRECIOUS LIVES FROM THE PEOPLE OF THE MUD WHALE.
YOU TOOK AWAY THE SMILES OF THE PEOPLE OF THE MUD WHALE.
YOU DON'T REALIZE ...
...YOU'RE JUST REPEATING THE SAME MISTAKE.
...
THAT'S RIGHT ...
...YOU'RE A JESTER.
...FULL OF BLUSTER.

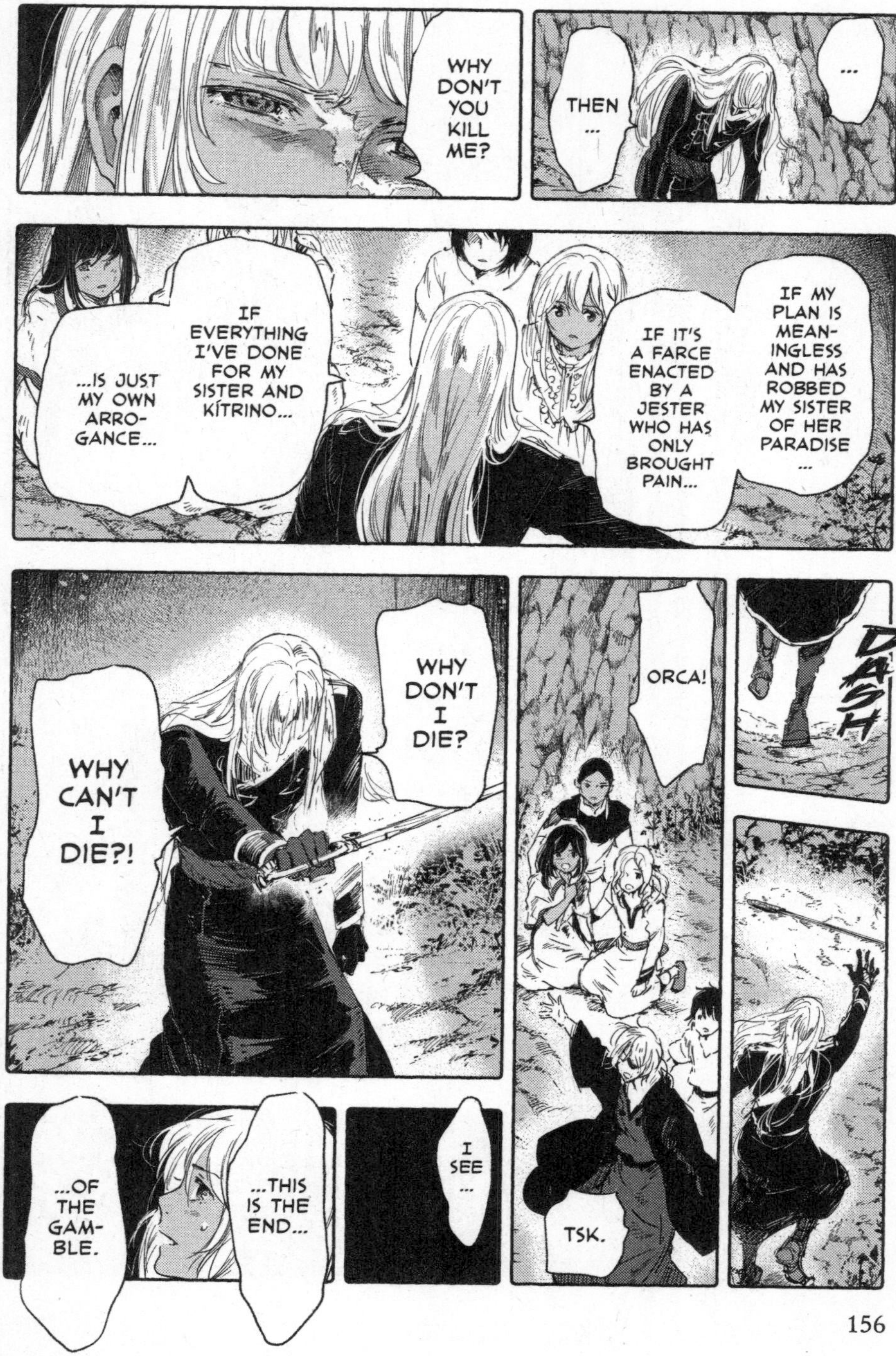
...
THEN ...
WHY DON'T YOU KILL ME?
IF MY PLAN IS MEANINGLESS AND HAS ROBBED MY SISTER OF HER PARADISE ...
IF IT'S A FARCE ENACTED BY A JESTER WHO HAS ONLY BROUGHT PAIN...
IF EVERYTHING I'VE DONE FOR MY SISTER AND KÍTRINO...
...IS JUST MY OWN ARROGANCE...
DASH
ORCA!
TSK.
WHY DON'T I DIE?
WHY CAN'T I DIE?!
I SEE ...
...THIS IS THE END...
...OF THE GAMBLE.

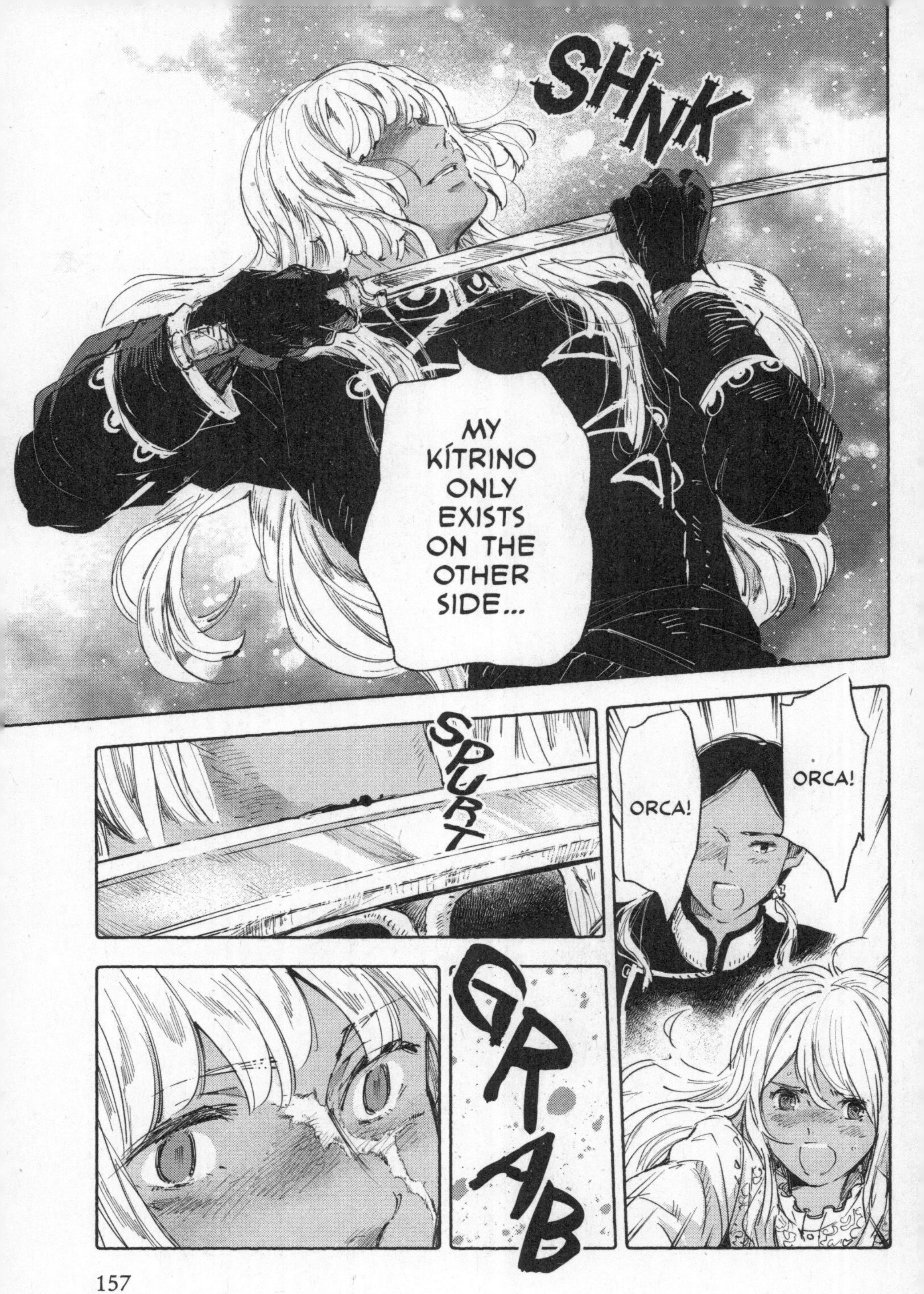
SHNK
MY KÍTRINO ONLY EXISTS ON THE OTHER SIDE...
ORCA!
ORCA!
SPURT
GRAB

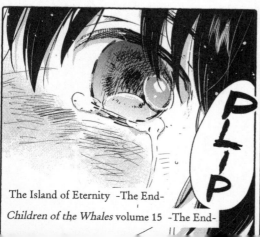

The Island of Eternity -The End-

Children of the Whales volume 15 -The End-

CHILDREN OF THE WHALES

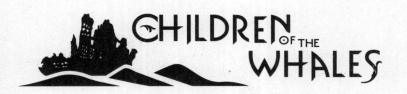

A Note on Names

Those who live on the Mud Whale are named after colors in a language unknown. Abi Umeda uses Japanese translations of the names, which we have maintained. Here is a list of the English equivalents for the curious.

Aijiro	pale blue
Benihi	scarlet
Buki	kerria flower (*yamabuki*)
Byakuroku	malachite mineral pigments, pale green tinged with white
Chakuro	blackish brown (*cha* = brown, *kuro* = black)
Furano	from "flannel," a soft-woven fabric traditionally made of wool
Ginshu	vermillion
Hakuji	porcelain white
Jiki	golden
Kicha	yellowish brown
Kikujin	koji mold, yellowish green
Kogare	burnt muskwood, dark reddish brown
Kuchiba	decayed-leaf brown
Masoh	cinnabar
Miru	seaweed green
Nashiji	a traditional Japanese crepe weave fabric
Neri	silk white
Nezu	mouse gray
Nibi	dark gray
Ouni	safflower red
Rasha	darkest blue, nearly black
Ro	lacquer black
Sami	light green (*asa* = light, *midori* = green)

Shikoku	purple-tinged black
Shikon	purple-tinged navy
Shinono	the color of dawn (*shinonome*)
Shuan	dark bloodred
Sienna	reddish brown
Sumi	ink black
Suou	raspberry red
Taisha	red ocher
Tobi	reddish brown like a kite's feather
Tokusa	scouring rush green
Tonoko	the color of powdered grindstone, a pale brown
Urumi	muddy gray

I did a meet-and-greet at an art gallery. I had such a lovely time chatting with all my readers. Thank you so much to everyone who came!

—Abi Umeda

ABI UMEDA debuted as a manga creator with the one-shot "Yukokugendan" in *Weekly Shonen Champion*. *Children of the Whales* is her eighth manga work.

CHILDREN OF THE WHALES

VOLUME 15
VIZ Signature Edition

Story and Art by Abi Umeda

Translation / JN Productions
Touch-Up Art & Lettering / Annaliese Christman
Design / Julian (JR) Robinson
Editor / Pancha Diaz

KUJIRANOKORAHA SAJOUNIUTAU Volume 15
© 2019 ABI UMEDA
First published in Japan in 2019 by AKITA PUBLISHING CO., LTD., Tokyo
English translation rights arranged with AKITA PUBLISHING CO., LTD. through
Tuttle-Mori Agency, Inc., Tokyo

Printed in Canada

Published by VIZ Media, LLC
P.O. Box 77010
San Francisco, CA 94107

10 9 8 7 6 5 4 3 2 1
First printing, July 2020

I'll tell you a story about the sea.

It's a story that no one knows yet.

The story of the sea that only I can tell...

Children of the Sea

BY DAISUKE IGARASHI

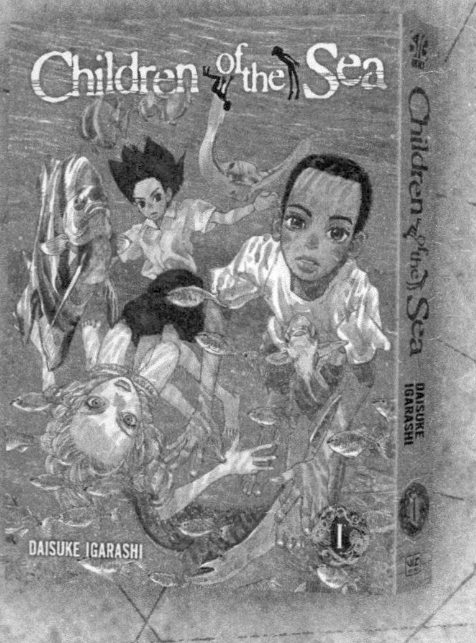

Uncover the mysterious tale with *Children of the Sea*—
BUY THE MANGA TODAY!

Available at your local bookstore and comic store.

Cats of the Louvre

by TAIYO MATSUMOTO

A surreal tale of the secret world of the cats of the Louvre, told by Eisner Award winner Taiyo Matsumoto.

The world-renowned Louvre museum in Paris contains more than just the most famous works of art in history. At night, within its darkened galleries, an unseen and surreal world comes alive— a world witnessed only by the small family of cats that lives in the attic. Until now...

Translated by *Tekkonkinkreet* film director Michael Arias.

My parents are clueless.

My boyfriend's a mooch.

My boss is a perv.

But who cares? I sure don't.
At least they know who they are.

Being young and dissatisfied
really makes it hard to care
about anything in this world...

solanin

STORY & ART BY INIO ASANO

THIS IS THE LAST PAGE!

Children of the Whales has been printed in the original Japanese format to preserve the orientation of the original artwork.